Digital Entrepreneurship in Africa

How a Continent Is Escaping Silicon Valley's Long Shadow

Nicolas Friederici, Michel Wahome, and Mark Graham

The MIT Press
Cambridge, Massachusetts
London, England

The open access edition of this book was made possible by generous funding from Knowledge Unlatched and Arcadia—a charitable fund of Lisbet Rausing and Peter Baldwin.

▌█▌ Knowledge Unlatched

This book was set in ITC Stone Serif Std and ITC Stone Sans Std by Toppan Best-set Premedia Limited. Printed and bound in the United States of America.

Library of Congress Cataloging-in-Publication Data

Names: Friederici, Nicolas, 1985- author. | Wahome, Michel, author. |
   Graham, Mark, 1980- author.
Title: Digital entrepreneurship in Africa : how a continent is escaping Silicon
   Valley's long shadow / Nicolas Friederici, Michel Wahome, and Mark Graham.
Description: Cambridge : The MIT Press, 2020. | Includes bibliographical
   references and index.
Identifiers: LCCN 2019034676 | ISBN 9780262538183 (paperback)
Subjects: LCSH: Electronic commerce--Africa, Sub-Saharan. | Entrepreneurship--
   Information technology--Africa, Sub-Saharan. | Information technology--
   Economic aspects--Africa, Sub-Saharan.
Classification: LCC HF5548.325.A357 F75 2020 | DDC 381.14206567--dc23
LC record available at https://lccn.loc.gov/2019034676

10 9 8 7 6 5 4 3 2 1

Digital Entrepreneurship in Africa

Contents

Acknowledgments

This book emerged from a five-year European Research Council (ERC) funded project called Geonet. The project (ERC-2013-StG335716-GeoNet) gave us the opportunity to fund both the salaries of the authors (Nicolas and Michel as full-time Postdoctoral Researchers on the project, and Mark as the Principal Investigator) and the extensive fieldwork that was required to undertake a research project of this size. Needless to say that our research in this area—and by extension, this book—would not have existed without the support of the ERC.

The Geonet project incorporated three core research areas, of which the work in the book represents one. Each area of the project has been shaped by the innovative research and hard work of our colleagues in the rest of the team. Therefore, we wish to thank our Geonet collaborators: Mohammed Amir Anwar, Fabian Braesemann, Chris Foster, Sanna Ojanperä, Stefano De Sabbata, and Ralph Straumann. We are especially thankful to Sanna and Fabian for providing data-scientific inputs to this book.

This book is an exercise in empirical grounding and, as such, it could not be written without the participation of the people "on the ground": Africa's digital entrepreneurs and their supporters. We conducted 202 in-depth research interviews including with 143 digital entrepreneurs, plus countless informal conversations with people we met during field visits. Many of these individuals are pioneers and leaders in their local communities, making them sought-after candidates for studies and media pieces. We found it fascinating and inspiring to be invited into their professional lives, and we are grateful for their hospitality and the time they dedicated to participate in our research. We especially want to thank the founders of AgroCenta for allowing us to profile their companies as a case study.

Our fieldwork spanned eleven African cities. To make such ambitious data collection effective, we relied on help from friends and colleagues who live in those cities or have experience working in them. They introduced us to participants, showed us around the most important spots of entrepreneurial ecosystems, and sometimes even helped us with travel essentials like visas and accommodation. We want to extend our thanks to Claude Migisha for Rwanda; Tessy Onaji, Abi Jagun, Tunde Akinnuwa, David Souter, and Tim Kelly for Nigeria; Gerawork Aynekulu, Enku Wendwosen, Seyram Avle, and Markos Lemma for Ethiopia; Bitange Ndemo, Tim Weiss, and Moses Kemibaro for Nairobi; Maxine Moffet and Arielle Kitio for Yaoundé; Parfait Ouattara for Abidjan; and Linda Swart for Johannesburg. We also thank all representatives of local organizations who reviewed and approved the research ethics of our project: Olufunbi Falayi, Akintunde Oyebode, Kayode Adegbola in Nigeria; Dr. Ernest Mwebaze and Dr. Grace Kamulegeya in Uganda; Adama Camara and Baidy Sy in Senegal; Thomas Herve Mboa Nkoudou and Horace Fonkwe in Cameroon; Jean-Jacques Bogui Maomra and Obin Guiako in Côte d'Ivoire; and Francisco Mabila and Ruben Manhica in Mozambique.

We presented the findings discussed in this book in talks and workshops with Humboldt University in June 2017; with the DIODE group in Oxford in October 2017; with the GIZ Make IT Alliance in Berlin in May 2018; and with audiences at Freie University Berlin, Humboldt Institute for Internet and Society, the World Bank, Michigan State University, Weizenbaum Institute, and University of Bayreuth audiences throughout 2019. We thank all participants for their feedback and encouragement. We also want to acknowledge the Higher Education Impact Fund at Oxford which was the source funding for the Geonet conference in South Africa, where a large majority of presenters and panelists were the digital workers and digital entrepreneurs who had informed the research. This was an invaluable opportunity to share and validate analyses, and to engage in constructive debate and discussion with participants.

Emily Taber and Laura Keeler of the MIT Press have been a wonderful source of support, seeing the value of our book from day one and guiding us through the editorial process. We very much appreciated Kathy Caruso's diligent and constructive editing, which made for a seamless journey from manuscript to final product. We also thank Melinda Rankin for copyediting our text and greatly improving its legibility. Several anonymous reviewers of sample chapters and the first full draft provided valuable guidance on how we could more effectively communicate our findings. We want to especially thank one reviewer who clearly dedicated a great deal of their time to a comprehensive review, making valid suggestions on how to restructure the manuscript. Their ideas contributed to the ultimate message of chapter 7 in particular.

The project found a supportive home at the Oxford Internet Institute, and we wish to thank Duncan Passey, Tim Davies, Emily Shipway, Adham Tamer, Arthur Bullard, and Clarence Singleton for their extensive administrative support over the life of the project. We thank David Sutcliffe for providing editorial support on the first full draft of the book. Anouchka Stephan and Elly Otieno transcribed a vast amount of audio-recorded interview material, and we thank them for their diligence and patience throughout this process.

The Humboldt Institute for Internet and Society supported Nicolas in disseminating the book's findings through workshops, presentations, and media outreach. We want to thank Florian Lüdtke at HIIG for supporting this effort. Laleah Fernandez and Dylan Curtis at Michigan State University and Wouter Bernhardt in Berlin produced audiovisual material to convey our insights to a wider audience. The Oxford Internet Institute also funded a dissemination trip in 2019.

Mark would additionally like to acknowledge the Leverhulme Prize (PLP-2016-155) and The Alan Turing Institute (EPSRC grant EP/N510129/1) for their support for some of his research time while working on this project, and the ESRC/DFID-funded project Development and Broadband Internet Access in East Africa that seeded the initial work for the research that is presented in this book. He also wishes to thank Ravi Palepu, Erik Hersman, and Jessica Colaço for giving him a home at the Nairobi iHub back in 2010 and introducing him to what felt like the entire Kenyan technology ecosystem. It is from that initial research, that many of the ideas for the Geonet project took shape. Finally, like any large project, the research that went into this book involved a lot of time away from home, and many long days and nights of work. Mark would therefore like to thank Kat for her support, guidance, and unwavering good spirit over the years that we conducted this project.

1 Hopes and Potentials

Africa, so the saying goes, is rising. From Mark Zuckerberg to Emmanuel Macron to Paul Kagame, presidents, prime ministers, technologists, and policymakers have proposed hopeful narratives, arguing that digital technologies are enabling Africa to leapfrog and experience groundbreaking economic progress. Entrepreneurs and innovators who exploit these opportunities are construed as the driving forces of the "African century." Accordingly, Africa has seen a digital entrepreneurship boom: in just a few years, hundreds of millions and maybe billions of dollars have been invested in tech cities, entrepreneurship trainings, coworking spaces, innovation prizes, and investment funds.

In this book, we unpack aspirations concerning "digital" and "entrepreneurship," contrasting them with empirical research about what is actually happening on the ground. The book grapples with the large gap between boundless ambition on the one side and sobering statistics on the other: in any imaginable measure for digital economies, Africa does far worse than any other continent, and global divides seem to be widening.

Our book draws on research conducted as part of a five-year research project, including fieldwork in eleven African cities. It contrasts rich and vast empirical data with popular discourses about digital entrepreneurship in Africa and with literature from management studies. Through this empirical grounding, the book seeks to go beneath and beyond the hype, and explore, document, and analyze the phenomenon of African digital entrepreneurship. It aims to understand both the opportunities and the limits that the rise of the internet has brought to ventures in Africa, painting a richer and more realistic picture than the digital innovation literature, media articles, and policy documents have done.

This book finds that most expectations raised in discourses and management theory do not consider on-the-ground realities and thus miss the essence of digital entrepreneurship in Africa. Our analysis shows that African digital entrepreneurship

- is highly unevenly distributed across the continent;
- is characterized by slow and mostly linear growth;
- creates digital products largely for customers in urban markets at local and regional scales;
- depends on entrepreneurial learning and ecosystem evolution, both processes that extend over long periods of time before producing palpable outcomes;
- consists of strategy innovations like the last-mile platform, which blend digital technologies with analog outreach structures;
- has led to the emergence of new entrepreneurial identities; and
- has triggered cultural and racial tensions as Silicon Valley's ideals have clashed with local realities and reproduced postcolonial dependencies.

Altogether, contrary to expectations conveyed in popular discourses and management scholarship, the average African digital enterprise does not grow exponentially, does not scale internationally, does not produce digital infrastructure, does not attract venture capital (VC), and does not disrupt traditional industries. Instead, we see entrepreneurs who are creatively and productively applying and adapting digital technologies to their local economic, social, and political contexts. This appears to have many of the wished-for positive socioeconomic effects, just not at the rate and scale that the widespread narratives suggest.

Our book thus builds a nuanced review of what the digital revolution means in and to Africa as the world's most marginalized continent. The space-transcending, distance-bridging, fast-scaling, and zero-marginal-cost properties of digital products are sometimes in evidence but can only be brought into being by select actors in certain places. This book shows that the global expansion of digital infrastructure enables local digital enterprises but also their international competitors—the latter often to a greater extent. It examines in detail how exactly the global digital revolution touches down in African cities and nations as it makes possible a host of new activities but does not untether local digital economies from the continent's structural legacies.

Africa in the Global Economy

Sub-Saharan Africa[1] is the world's poorest, most disadvantaged, and most disconnected region. Although it is a resource-rich continent, gross domestic product (GDP) per capita in Africa is about 6 percent of what it is in Europe and 5 percent of what it is in North America. This is despite Africa's GDP tripling since 2000 (African Union Commission and OECD 2018).

Of the 1.3 billion people in Africa, almost 400 million can be characterized as extremely poor (living on US$1.90 or less) (African Union Commission and OECD 2018). The average African lives for fifteen fewer years than the average North American. One in every three people in sub-Saharan Africa is illiterate, there are still twelve African countries with literacy rates of less than 50 percent, and seventeen out of the forty-six countries in sub-Saharan Africa have female literacy rates of less than 50 percent (UNESCO 2015). Less than half of school-aged children in this region are attending school, and only four percent of children are expected to enter in graduate institutions (Musua 2018).

Despite being extremely rich in energy resources, only 43 percent of sub-Saharan Africa's total population and 25 percent of its rural population have access to electricity (Blimpo and Cosgrove-Davies 2019). Although hundreds of millions of dollars have been spent building submarine fiber-optic cables (Graham, Andersen, and Mann 2015), sub-Saharan Africa remains the planet's least connected region. Only 22 percent of people in the region have internet access, meaning that there are more illiterate people than there are internet users in the region. Even the region's best performers—South Africa, Nigeria, and Kenya—have internet penetration rates of only about 50 percent (Graham 2019). The relatively high cost of internet access is part of the reason for these low rates. As Ojanperä (2018) notes: "A monthly broadband subscription costs around 50 USD in Niger and in Ireland. However, while the Irish internet user earns an average yearly gross income of 53,000 USD, the Nigerien will make 390 USD. So, whereas an Irish person would spend just over half of her weekly salary to cover the subscription for an entire year, the Nigerien would need to allocate over one and a half year's earnings to do the same."

These statistics are presented neither to paint a picture of despair nor to imply that Africa cannot change, but rather as a backdrop for what comes next. Sub-Saharan Africa, in other words, is not necessarily a place in which one might expect a digital revolution to be underway.

New Connectivities, New Beginnings

> What you are doing is the right thing. Get the undersea cable, lower the cost, and everything will flow to Kenya. You will have flattened the world to which you can do any work globally. (Thomas Friedman speaking to Bitange Ndemo, former permanent secretary of Kenya's ICT Ministry in 2006 [Bright and Hruby 2015a, 156])

Although just over 5 percent of humanity was connected to the internet at the dawn of the millennium, only twenty years later we are approaching a world in which a majority of the population has access (see figure 1.1; World Bank 2019). The majority of these new connections are in low- and middle-income countries: often places with high levels of un- and underemployment.

Not only are most people in the world now connected, the majority also live where access is physically possible. Ninety-five percent of the world's population live in a place serviced by a mobile-cellular network, and as many as 84 percent of people reside under the shadow of mobile broadband networks (ITU 2017).

The world's remaining gaps in connectivity have been the focus of a range of initiatives by governments, international organizations, and corporations (Friederici, Ojanperä, and Graham 2017). Internet.org (a partnership led by Facebook), for instance, explicitly defined its aim as connecting the planet. It exclaims that this "means the whole world, not just some of us." The partnership aims to achieve this with a combination of zero-rated apps (i.e., helping the poor get online in contexts where access is physically possible, but unaffordable) and unmanned aircraft (in contexts where internet access was previously a physical impossibility). The Alphabet Corporation (Google's parent company) has a similar initiative with its Project Loon. The project utilizes high-altitude balloons that promise to beam internet access down to rural areas. Governments and international organizations have also invested heavily in connectivity projects. The World Bank has allocated over a billion dollars to projects related to broadband infrastructure in Africa, and the African Development Bank claims that $55

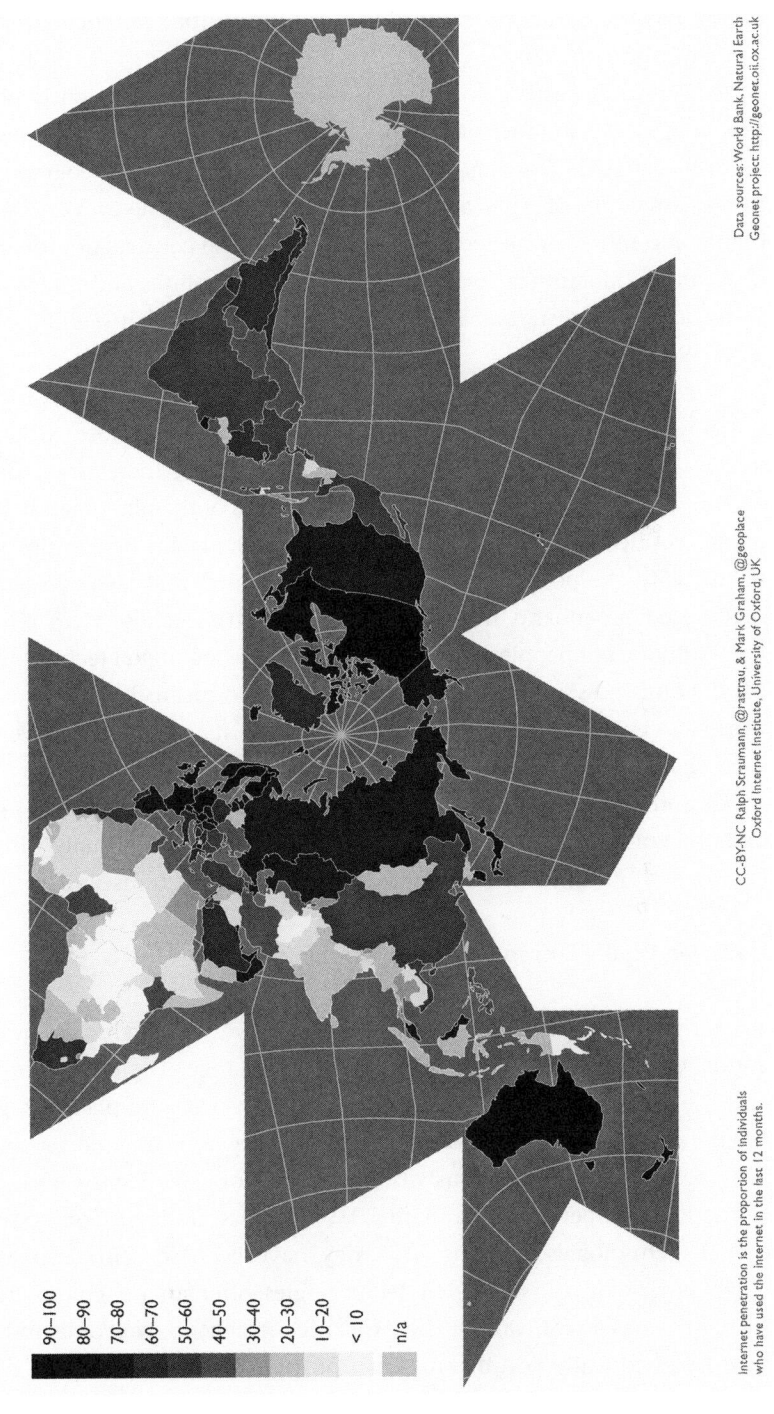

Access to the Internet

Internet penetration 2015, in percent

- 90–100
- 80–90
- 70–80
- 60–70
- 50–60
- 40–50
- 30–40
- 20–30
- 10–20
- < 10
- n/a

Internet penetration is the proportion of individuals
who have used the internet in the last 12 months.

Data sources: World Bank, Natural Earth
Geonet project: http://geonet.oii.ox.ac.uk

Figure 1.1

Internet penetration in 2015. *Data source:* World Bank, Natural Earth. http://geonet.oii.ox.ac.uk/blog/who-can-access-the-internet/.

billion has been pledged for its Connect Africa initiative (Friederici, Ojanperä, and Graham 2017).

As the world has become more connected, it has concurrently become more digital. All manner of products, services, and processes are now digital and digitized. This has profound implications for the geography and the organization of work and global supply chains. The move to a more digital and more connected world has enabled the construction of a range of virtual production networks that form complex links and interrelationships between consumers and workers around the planet (Lehdonvirta et al. 2019).

The "world is flat" narrative came and went with the hype of the dot-com boom two decades ago (Zook 2009). But now, almost two decades into the millennium, we have a human planet that is increasingly defined by connectivity. There are few inhabited corners of the planet left in which digital connectivity is impossible. Today, there are no large cities in the world (with the possible exception of Pyongyang) that lack access to the high-speed broadband needed to interface with such services (Graham 2019). Billions of people and organizations are using digital technologies to conduct business and seek prosperity. This by no means has given us a flat world—as evidenced by the fact that the majority of Africans have never used the internet. Yet the creation of planetary-scale markets for digital goods and services has left many people with the impression that a global digital revolution is underway (see box 1.1) and that now, finally, old barriers, constraints, and borders might truly be able to be transcended.

Is African Digital Entrepreneurship on the Rise?

To many, Africa's economic growth combined with these changes in global connectivity heralds a radical moment of change. Digital technologies and the internet have long been framed as footloose and placeless, giving them potential to level economic opportunity and include or upgrade geographies that had previously been deprived or excluded (Avgerou 2003; Friederici, Ojanperä, and Graham 2017). This aspirational component of digital technologies explains why they have been so central to African development discourse: digital technologies offer an imaginary[2] within which there is a pathway for the African continent to overcome and overturn its historically peripheral global position and its history of colonial

Box 1.1

The Global Digital Revolution

Over the last four decades, enormous scaling economies for several generations of technology corporations have driven the global diffusion of the internet and digital technologies. As microprocessors became more powerful, smaller, and cheaper, they began to be used in many more devices than just the personal computer, generating ever greater possibilities of connectivity and quantities of data. In the early 2000s, smartphones and laptops started to be manufactured and marketed at mass scale in high-income countries, and previously analog tools (such as medical devices, assembly lines, cars, or household items) were "digitized": they were equipped with chips that can process digital signals. In parallel, the internet diffused at a global scale, emerging as the primary technology to interconnect microprocessors and data storage units (e.g., servers and hard drives) at a distance. Increasing internet bandwidth and affordability allowed for near-instantaneous transmissions of larger and larger data volumes. Ultimately, it became possible to run software remotely, enabling browser-based applications, cloud computing, and software as a service (SaaS).

The availability of cheap and powerful data processing and storage facilities in combination with the rise of the internet has resulted in three global phenomena, which together can be referred to as the *digital revolution* (Brynjolfsson and McAfee 2011):

1. Global digital infrastructure consisting of hardware (fiber-optic cables, switching stations, mobile devices, etc.) and software (operating systems, cloud applications, web browsers, app stores, search engines, etc.), which are internationally interconnected and standardized, in principle enabling any internet user to access any digital artifact (software, data) that is physically stored on another internet-connected device (Steinbock 2003; Tilson, Lyytinen, and Sørensen 2010)

2. Pervasive digitization, in which digital technologies augment or transform previously analog processes of value creation, capture, and exchange (e.g., smart electric grids or tracking systems in freight management; Nambisan et al. 2017; Yoo, Henfridsson, and Lyytinen 2010)

3. Growth, convergence, and reconfiguration of information-based industries—that is, those industries that enable or depend on the codification, processing, or transmission of information, including computer and device manufacturing, software and content production, networking infrastructure (fiber cables, data centers, internet exchange points, transmission towers), telecommunications, and media (Malecki and Moriset 2007)

extraction, exploitation, and denigration (Graham, Andersen, and Mann 2015; Jasanoff and Kim 2016).

Now that connectivity has diffused and "democratized," a range of actors are betting that fundamental economic shifts will ensue (Deichmann and Mishra 2016; World Wide Web Foundation 2014). The analog, traditional economic world is deemed to be on the verge of "transformation" and "revolution" (Murphy and Carmody 2015; Ndemo and Weiss 2017a, 2017b). Paul Kagame, the president of Rwanda, perhaps best captures hopes for change with this famous quote: "In Africa, we have missed both the agricultural and industrial revolutions [but] in Rwanda, we are determined to take full advantage of the digital revolution. This revolution is summed up by the fact that it no longer is of utmost importance where you are but rather what you can do—this is of great benefit to traditionally marginalized regions and geographically isolated populations" (quoted in Graham, Andersen, and Mann 2015, 344).

Digital entrepreneurship is widely believed to be a key driver of these changes (Drouillard et al. 2014; Ndemo and Weiss 2017a).[3] According to Ndemo and Weiss (2017a), "The laying of the first fiber-optic cable . . . heralded a new chapter for cheaper telecommunication access. With it, opportunities to mainstream internet access were created, such as . . . startup hubs where entrepreneurs had access to high-speed internet." Policymakers, donors, investors, and media have bought into this narrative. For instance, former UN secretary general Ban Ki Moon told an audience at iHub, Africa's best-known digital entrepreneurship organization, that they "are the hope of Africa" (Wakoba 2014). Mark Zuckerberg, Facebook's founder and CEO, stated when visiting Nairobi that places like iHub are "where the future is going to be built" now that "things [in Africa] are moving from a resource-based economy . . . to [an] entrepreneurial, knowledge-based economy" (Shapshak 2016). Widely read media outlets like *National Geographic* proclaim that "Africa's tech generation is changing the continent" (Draper 2017), and Al Jazeera has produced an entire TV series showcasing how "lives are being changed across the continent by home-grown innovations" (Al Jazeera English 2014). Hundreds of other such stories proliferate in the media (see Nothias 2014).

Such far-reaching aspirations have paved the way for concrete actions and interventions: there has been an *African digital entrepreneurship boom*. The number of African incubators and innovation hubs[4] has risen to several hundred within just a few years (Bayen and Giuliani 2018; Firestone and Kelly 2016), notwithstanding the absence of evidence regarding their effectiveness (Friederici 2019). There are no good figures on the number of smaller-scale initiatives (e.g., innovation prizes, hackathons, and events) but it is safe to say that thousands per year happen in cities across Africa, sponsored by a mixture of philanthropists, development organizations, technology corporations, and (more rarely) local governments. To name just four recent and high-profile examples: the GSMA Innovation Fund[5] injected mentorship and between $1 and $2.3 million into African digital enterprises in just its first round (Mulligan 2017); the World Bank's XL Africa program created an elite community of twenty startups from across the continent and connected them to investors (Kapil, Andjelkovic, and Lu 2018); Google's Nigeria-based accelerator recently funded startups with $3 million, in addition to in-kind support (Jackson 2018a); and the Tony Elumelu Entrepreneurship Programme has committed $100 million in grants for African early-stage entrepreneurs.

Governments and development organizations have also contributed their share. The French Development Agency launched the Digital Africa initiative, committing around $76 million to a startup fund (Olupot 2018). In 2019, the World Bank started a moonshot initiative to boost Africa's digital economy that is said to cost hundreds of millions of dollars, with digital entrepreneurship forming a key pillar (Goldberg 2019). The large-scale technology park Konza City in Kenya will cost the government and investors an estimated $14.5 billion. Similarly ambitious—and similarly expensive—plans exist in Senegal, Nigeria, Rwanda, Ghana, and South Africa (Giles 2018). An illustrious group of celebrities and decision-makers—from Mark Zuckerberg to Christine Lagarde to Bono—has visited places like iHub in Nairobi, CcHub in Lagos, MEST in Accra, or kLab in Kigali, showering these organizations with praise and encouragement.

Digital Technology and Entrepreneurship: How Two Gospels Have Become One

Why do policymakers, investors, and entrepreneurs devote vast sums of money and attention to fostering digital entrepreneurship in a region characterized by so many structural and maybe more fundamental issues? It certainly is not because there is of a wealth of empirical evidence that suggests success. Rather, it is in large part because of two unverified discursive belief systems, or *gospels*, about what changing connectivity does to Africa's economic geographies. These are variably deployed, in sometimes overlapping, sometimes contradictory, but always powerful ways (see Avgerou 2003; Birtchnell 2011; Pansera and Owen 2018).

The Internet as a Global Leveler of Opportunity

According to the first gospel, thanks to digital technologies, African entrepreneurs are becoming part of a global landscape of opportunity (Autio et al. 2018; Mavhunga 2017; Nambisan 2017). As alluded to earlier, digital tools and technologies have properties that sometimes allow their users to transcend traditional constraints to economic activity. Here the world is essentially shrunk onto the head of a pin: being located in Africa is no longer of much consequence to an entrepreneur's ability to transact with people and firms anywhere else in world. "Tech-enabled startups . . . can operate on internet scale from day one; propelled by software that makes the fundamental aspects of reaching a broad user-base and going global a lot easier," claims an advisor to the Obama Foundation in an article titled "Why Africa's Youth Should Be Encouraged to Launch Tech Startups" (Jackson 2018b).

The key reason for this change is said to be access to the internet. Markets for software development are globalizing, which is argued to bring enormous potential for African coders and outsourcing businesses, who can offer competitively low labor prices. Digital entrepreneurship is understood as a global movement (Auerswald 2012; Honig 2017): ideas like the lean startup or the business accelerator have spread worldwide; organizations such as Seedstars, TechCrunch, and the Global Entrepreneurship Network have run events in most African countries; and online learning providers and elite universities such as Stanford are offering courses on technology entrepreneurship to anyone with a reliable internet connection. As the internet has made digital tools and infrastructures easily and cheaply available to startups (Aldrich 2014), entry barriers to digital entrepreneurship are deemed to be relatively low (Dy, Marlow, and Martin 2017; Greengard 2010).

The *Economist* coined a phrase for this development, picturing a *Cambrian moment* (Siegele 2014) at which the internet enables a plethora of new organizations that create value through technologies in any place on earth.

A key argument is that, though talent has always been distributed equally across the globe, now the internet gives everyone the same opportunity to be creative and make money. Paul Kagame, in the same spirit as his earlier mentioned quote, summed up that "digital innovation means ideas do not have borders and cannot be landlocked" (Tumwebaze 2014).

Entrepreneurs as the New Hope

The second gospel hails the African grassroots entrepreneur as a powerful agent of change. Entrepreneurship complements the aspirational component of digital technologies by offering a more local and bottom-up vision of who will bring about economic development (see Smith et al. 2017). Inside and outside of Africa, the actors who have tried to "develop" the continent in the past are rarely looked at favorably (see Escobar 2011). Multilateral development organizations like the World Bank and IMF have been mistrusted latest since the Washington Consensus (Easterly 2001; Moyo 2009). Multinational corporations have extracted Africa's resources without creating significant benefits for its peoples. Bilateral donors, foundations, and nongovernmental organizations (NGOs) are accused of waste and inefficiency, as well as "distorting markets" and creating "perverse incentives" (Ferguson 1990). Many African governments are blamed for supporting particular tribal groups, ethnic groups, or political and economic elites rather than the public good (Acemoglu and Robinson 2013).

In contrast, the African grassroots entrepreneur's image is wholly unblemished. Young, smart Africans, often with college degrees from elite universities in the United States and Europe, are easily construed as impatient, driven, and astute change makers (Avle 2014; Bright and Hruby 2015a; Olopade 2014). Digital entrepreneurship offers new hope because the actors who are creating and capturing value are inherently locally driven. This, in turn, makes grassroots participation in the economy much more likely than in older models of development dropped down from afar (see Smith et al. 2017). Entrepreneurship thus suggests that this particular group of Africans may be better positioned than any other actor before them. France's president, Emmanuel Macron, argues that digital innovation is therefore "the best way to provide the solution made by, and for African people" (Olupot 2018).

In addition, entrepreneurship is seen as a path toward alleviating youth underemployment (Dolan and Rajak 2016). Africa's demographic and employment numbers emphasize the discrepancy between job creation and the numbers of youth who will be seeking employment in upcoming years. Entrepreneurship is characterized as a remedy that enables individuals to create their own jobs and jobs for others (Chang 2015; Dolan and Rajak 2016; Farny et al. 2016). Startup "methodologies" (like the lean startup) promise that by following simple templates (like the business model canvas), everyone can be a successful entrepreneur and any city can become a thriving entrepreneurial ecosystem (Feld 2012; Ries 2011). The narrative of Silicon Valley has a proclivity toward highlighting youthfulness as a positive attribute, thus signaling that digital entrepreneurship is an ideal solution to the youth bulge. Actors are thus operating within an environment in which innovation and entrepreneurship are extolled and encouraged at global and national levels.

Leapfrogging: The Time Is Now
In the tradition of modernist development (Rostow 1960), Africa is thus seen to potentially be leapfrogging developmental stages that high-income countries have already gone through. Digital entrepreneurship is now framed as both an indicator of and pathway to modernity, and therefore prosperity. Digital enterprises promise to be transformational, scientific, and high-growth ventures, a departure from the subsistence-, necessity-, and microentrepreneurship that Africa is typically associated with. The narrative thus goes that Africa is catching up with, or even overtaking, richer countries (Bright and Hruby 2015a). Having missed the industrial revolution, so the argument goes, Africa will now be at the forefront of the ongoing digital revolution.

Digital entrepreneurs are cast as visionaries who will bring about leapfrogging with groundbreaking technological products. Young Africans are depicted as the "mobile-first" or "mobile-only" generation, and low-tech "inclusive" or "frugal" innovations (see Birtchnell 2011; Pansera and Martinez 2017), such as Kenya's M-Pesa or the Pan-African Esoko are cited as examples of this progress (Mbiti and Weil 2011; Morawczynski 2009; Omwansa and Sullivan 2012). Africa is deemed capable of developing its own innovations for home-grown problems (Avle and Lindtner 2016)—for instance, "rugged" technology like the Kenyan-made BRCK, a "backup generator for the internet" (Sotunde 2013) that works even in rural areas without cell phone coverage. Kenya's president, Uhuru Kenyatta, recently argued that "MPESA, M-Kopa, GroIntelligence, Andela and others, show that we can lead the world with innovations that drive financial inclusion, access to energy, better data to drive our agriculture, and the essential skills required to support the young innovators of the future" (Government of Kenya 2018).

Africa is argued to be better positioned than any other continent due to improving political stability, strong economic growth, and its "demographic dividend" (Ahmed et al. 2016). The continent is repositioned as the new frontier, as risk is reframed from the potential of losses to the potential of gains (Nyamnjoh 2013). Scarcities are reinterpreted as commercial opportunities (Srinivas and Sutz 2008), as bottom-of-the-pyramid customers (Prahalad 2009) are construed as an underserved market segment eagerly awaiting service provision, preferably through mobile phones. The continent is seen as a unique opportunity for financial investors, given that a number of African nations (including Ghana, Ethiopia, and Côte d'Ivoire) continue to be among the fastest-growing countries globally (Bright and Hruby 2015a; Signé 2018). As a result of these factors, the *Economist* (2011) coined another catchy slogan: "Africa rising." Meanwhile, politicians across the continent have proclaimed the "African century."

What Does Digital Entrepreneurship Theory Suggest?

Not just popular narratives but also management research tends to downplay the role of distance for digital entrepreneurship. In fact, Satish Nambisan, in his foundational and widely noted paper (Nambisan 2017), highlights less boundedness of entrepreneurial agency and entrepreneurial opportunity as the defining feature of digital entrepreneurship compared to traditional or analog entrepreneurship. A burgeoning management literature has become infatuated with the idea that digital entrepreneurship and digital business models hold particular potential for transcending analog geographical constraints (see Aldrich 2014; Autio et al. 2018; Sussan and Acs 2017). In the following sections, we briefly review foundational concepts from this literature to show why it comes to rather similar (albeit less explicit and sweeping) affirmations as those from the policy gospels we reviewed in the previous section.

Digital Infrastructure, Affordances, and Generativity

All entrepreneurship consists of economic actors (individuals, firms, or other organizations) pursuing an uncertain market opportunity, creating and capturing value in the process (Alvarez and Barney 2005; Alvarez, Barney, and Anderson 2012; Davidsson 2005). Technology entrepreneurship is distinct in that the affordances of a given technological innovation constrain and enable potential pathways for the pursuit of opportunity.[6] This is because particular technologies lend themselves to particular ways of creating and capturing value, which makes some entrepreneurial strategies viable and others less so. Consider telephony as an example. Telephony is an end-to-end individual communication technology. Users derive value by being able to hear an audio signal (voice) in real time, emitted by a person located in a distant place. Strong network and critical mass effects apply (Katz and Shapiro 1985; Markus 1987): the more users there are, the higher the value of having a phone line for any given user. Telephone operators can make money by charging users fees for the phone line or for its usage. For operators, typical strategies are thus investing in telephony infrastructure, owning customer relationships, partnering with value-added service providers (e.g., telephone marketing or hotlines), standardizing technology through associations and regulators, reaching interconnection agreements with large competitors, and crowding out smaller competitors. All of these strategies allow for maximizing value creation while creating opportunities for value capture. On the market level, without regulation, oligopolies or monopolies will ensue, because small, localized phone providers cannot achieve the necessary minimum efficient scale. Ultimately, telephony's technological affordances shape (but do not wholly predetermine) both business strategies and market structures.

By extension, digital entrepreneurship is about economic actors pursuing market opportunities that exist by virtue of *digital* technologies' affordances (Nambisan 2017). Most people intuitively understand contemporary technologies like the internet, mobile applications, social media, cloud computing, or artificial intelligence (AI) as digital. Yet to comprehend why digital technologies are often celebrated as offering the fastest and widest scaling opportunities, we will briefly clarify what distinguishes digital from analog.

In *digital technologies*, information is represented and transmitted by means of binary signals (e.g., high vs. low voltage), whereas *analog technologies* use continuous signals (e.g., continuous amounts of voltage). Binary signals are easier to transfer and interpret compared to signals on a continuum because they are less susceptible to noise and disturbances (Null and Lobur 2006). The first commercial technology to exploit digital signaling as a more efficient way of information processing and transmission was the personal computer—or more specifically, the microprocessors that computers run on (Campbell-Kelly et al. 2013). Hardware (computers using microprocessors) can interpret and process software and data. Data and software are digital artifacts: they adhere to standardized information structures (e.g., programming languages or operating systems), which can be represented as binary electronic transmission signals that microprocessors can interpret.

By virtue of adhering to standardized information structures, digital artifacts become *reprogrammable, editable, interactive,* and *open* (Kallinikos, Aaltonen, and Marton 2010; Yoo, Henfridsson, and Lyytinen 2010). Furthermore, any computer can efficiently process any information once it has been "digitized" (i.e., it has been brought into a format that can be represented as zeros and ones). This enables what Bruno Latour (1986) refers to as the *immutable mobile,* the *separation of form and function,* and the ability to transport information without significantly altering its characteristics of meaning (Yoo et al. 2012; Yoo, Henfridsson, and Lyytinen 2010). For instance, though a physical book can only ever represent the text and images that were initially printed in it, a smartphone can process any digital information, and the same phone can be reprogrammed for different uses at different points in time.

Together, separation of form and function and the attributes of digital artifacts enable *combinatorial innovation*: new generations of digital technologies can integrate with and build on previous generations (Benkler 2006; Gao and Iyer 2006; Yoo et al. 2012). The ease of combinatorial innovation is a key affordance of digital technologies. As a result of this affordance, digital innovation (i.e., the creation of new digital technologies) has advanced through a *generative* process: many digital technologies have enabled further innovations to build on them, without the need for the creators of the original technologies to stay involved (Zittrain 2009).

Ultimately, the separation of form and function together with the stacking of technological layers upon layers has brought about a rich *digital infrastructure* (Henfridsson and Bygstad 2013; Tilson, Lyytinen, and Sørensen

2010), consisting of a broad set of interoperable and modular digital tools, platforms, and standards. Digital infrastructure represents an external enabler of opportunity for entrepreneurs (Briel, Davidsson, and Recker 2018; Nambisan 2017).

Unconstrained generativity and combinatorial innovation are thus the key affordances of digital versus other technologies. Yet this does not mean that they are entirely technology driven. In fact, a number of organizations and other social and institutional arrangements (standards, programming languages, open-source communities, internet commissions, regulations, protocols, programming interfaces, etc.) are safeguarding and maintaining the integrative and combinatorial potential of digital technologies.

Exploiting Digital Technology for Value Creation and Capture

To survive and grow, digital enterprises engage in value creation and value capture (Amit and Zott 2001; Zott, Amit, and Massa 2011). Economic value creation using digital technologies (which we will refer to as *digital value creation*) can be categorized into four types (see table 1.1). The most pervasive and basic type is *digital production*: the creation of a digital artifact such as code, online content, a website, a mobile application, or software (Ojanperä et al. 2017; Schradie 2011). Digital production typically differs from analog production (e.g., traditional manufacturing) because marginal costs are reduced for production and distribution. Software, applications, and content can be replicated at almost no cost; where broadband is available, it is cheap and fast to distribute to faraway users; and customers can search easily even for niche items (Brynjolfsson, Hu, and Simester 2011; Shapiro and Varian 1998). The cost-benefit ratio of production and innovation is particularly low in software development, as existing layers of software can be stacked on top of each other to create new products (Gao and Iyer 2006).

Table 1.1
Four types of value creation using digital technologies

Type	Summary
Digital production	Creation of a digital artifact
Information processing	Editing, integrating, and analyzing existing information
User interconnection	Allowing users to share and collaborate
Market intermediation	Connecting buyers and suppliers

All digital entrepreneurship involves digital production. In contrast, most digital production itself is not entrepreneurial (i.e., market-opportunity oriented). Types of nonentrepreneurial digital production that we will discuss in this chapter and elsewhere in the book include some types of digital labor, commits to GitHub (the world's largest collaborative software development platform), and posts on Stack Overflow (a global software developer knowledge platform).

A second and similarly common type is *information processing.* In a digital world, meaningful (new) information can be created at low cost by editing, transferring, integrating, and analyzing existing information (Amit and Zott 2001; Shapiro and Varian 1998; Yoo, Henfridsson, and Lyytinen 2010; Zook and Grote 2017). Activities such as big data analytics, data science, machine learning, automation, algorithmic computing, and artificial intelligence are all facets of information processing.

The third type is *user interconnection,* which lets users interact or develop content collaboratively, thereby leveraging network effects. The internet and mass-produced consumer devices, such as laptops and smartphones, have allowed users to interact with each other in ever more diverse and elaborate ways (e.g., sharing images and videos), thus increasing the potential value of interconnection compared to telephony. Social networks and crowdsourcing platforms are key examples of such user-driven, collective value creation.

Fourth, *market intermediation* exploits digital technologies to alleviate information asymmetries and reduce transaction costs in two-sided markets (Amit and Zott 2001; Eisenmann, Parker, and Van Alstyne 2006). More than just connecting buyers and suppliers, intermediaries also create market institutions—typically by guaranteeing transactions and safeguarding norms, thereby generating trust (Lehdonvirta et al. 2019). As with user interconnection, the value for a given user increases with others' adoption; however, for market intermediation, it is adoption on the other side of the market that benefits them (Amit and Zott 2001; Shapiro and Varian 1998). Digital platforms (Gawer 2011; Parker, Van Alstyne, and Choudary 2016; Srnicek 2016) are sophisticated forms of market intermediaries.

Whereas information processing, user interconnection, and market intermediation all depend on regular internet-enabled interactions between enterprises and customers (Amit and Han 2017; Arakji and Lang 2007), for digital production, customers can obtain a copy of the digital artifact and derive value from usage even when disconnected from the supplier.

Accordingly, digital production predates the rise of the internet by several decades. Moreover, the four types of digital value creation are not mutually exclusive. For instance, a software-as-a-service (SaaS) provider may leverage cloud servers and allow users to develop and share customizations through APIs, thus combining digital production, user interconnection, and information processing.

Most digital enterprises (with the exception of some not-for-profits like open-source software providers) seek not only to create but also to capture economic value. Value capture consists of transforming a share of overall created economic value into monetary value that is owned or controlled by the enterprise and can be traded with others, such as cash, assets, current and projected revenues, or a company's valuation.

Again, the affordances of digital technologies partially predetermine possible value-capture strategies, often leading to vastly different approaches compared to, say, manufacturers of physical goods. For example, to make money, digital enterprises may artificially reduce the quality and quantity of software, making it exclusive to paying users (e.g., through license keys or freemium models). For value creation based on user interconnection, enterprises may avoid charging users directly and instead monetize their attention from third parties like online advertisers. For market intermediation, enterprises may charge one side of a dual-sided market for access to the other or analyze data about one side and sell it to the other (Eisenmann, Parker, and Van Alstyne 2006; Wu 2016).

Ultimately, the "many-to-many" nature of internet-enabled technologies means that the lion's share of value-creating activity (e.g., content production and data generation) is done by users and not by the enterprise itself (Amit and Han 2017; Enders et al. 2008; Teece 2018). In a digital world, many users move from being consumers to indispensable coproducers of value (Baldwin and von Hippel 2011; Ramírez 1999). Instead of creating a finished product and selling it to a passive recipient, digital enterprises become facilitators or orchestrators of users' collective and often unintentional value creation (Amit and Han 2017; Amit and Zott 2015; Eisenmann, Parker, and Van Alstyne 2006).

Spatial Decoupling of Value Creation and Capture

The distance-bridging potential of the internet and the global diffusion of digital infrastructure results in far wider geographical decoupling of value creation and capture compared to analog entrepreneurship. For physical goods (cars, furniture, food, etc.), users consume value after making a one-off purchase, and the infrastructure for disseminating or producing and using the products (power grids, roads, airports, ports, mass transport, etc.) tends to be nationally or locally owned, controlled or regulated by public agencies. In analog economies, producers assemble resources and assets in a particular location, creating value embodied in a physical output, the value of which is then split into use value and monetary value when sold. For illustration, a German car manufacturer may create value embodied in cars produced in a plant in, say, China to service the Chinese market. The German headquarters may skim off most of the value that is captured when the car is sold, but the Chinese plant, Chinese distributors, and other supply chain partners in China are bound to capture some of the value simply by virtue of the fact that the car is a physical object that has to be distributed to a customer.

In the digital economy, on the other hand, a transnational producer provides a virtual setting for user-driven value cocreation while continuously skimming off a share of the value created by users around the world. The value of a digital platform can be continuously created by billions of users around the world (by uploading content, providing personal information, creating usage data patterns, etc.), while value capture happens almost exclusively in the digital platform's headquarters (e.g., in San Francisco) as this company's main physical site of operation (Teece 2018; Zuboff 2019). In fact, users and user innovators develop locally relevant content, introducing economics of scale and scope for the platform without it needing to invest in local product knowledge. Through the global harmonization of digital infrastructure, market-leading digital products can thus spread to any place where the internet and all other necessary infrastructures are in place (e.g., logistics and transport infrastructure for Amazon). Especially for digital products that depend on limited analog infrastructures, value creation can thus happen in any interconnected place, while value capture happens only in the select locations of company headquarters or subsidiaries (Friederici and Graham 2018; UNCTAD 2019).

It is this potential to harness value that has been cocreated across a vast geographical expanse that has led management scholarship into arguing that market opportunities are generally less bounded for digital compared to analog enterprises. Leading business model theorists Raphael Amit and

Christoph Zott (2001, 495) believe that "virtual markets have unprecedented reach because they are characterized by a near lack of geographical boundaries." They say that preexisting analog barriers (like cultural or language differences) "appear to be vastly reduced relative to the traditional 'bricks-and-mortar' world." Entrepreneurship researcher Erkko Autio and his colleagues (2018) argue that digital affordances "do not operate spatially" (77) because digital infrastructure is a "location nonspecific element" (81), such that the "Internet's architectural trust mechanisms can potentially offer a near full substitute for social and relational trust that is non-localized and does not depend on geographical proximity" (76). Satish Nambisan (2017), in his earlier-mentioned foundational paper on digital entrepreneurship, suggests that it is an intriguing research puzzle that "the same" digital infrastructure leads to different entrepreneurial outcomes in different places (1046).

These arguments assume that digital infrastructure and digital technologies are globally homogeneous, ubiquitous, openly accessible, and inclusive (Aldrich 2014; Greengard 2010; Sussan and Acs 2017; Tilson, Lyytinen, and Sørensen 2010). Any enterprise with an internet connection should thus have equal access to the same vast global market opportunities.

Global Digital Platforms as Idols of Exponential Growth

Beyond the abstract potential of vast global market opportunities, the management literature has also been inspired by a very concrete set of enterprises: the "big five" global technology corporations (Google, Apple, Facebook, Amazon, and Microsoft) and other fast-scaling US digital companies (Airbnb, Uber, Salesforce, etc.). Many academic papers mention these organizations to illustrate their ideas (e.g., Amit and Han 2017; Amit and Zott 2001; Huang et al. 2017; Sussan and Acs 2017; Yoo, Henfridsson, and Lyytinen 2010). The fact that these companies have achieved the world's highest market valuations over a very short period of time, making their founders among the richest and most influential people on the planet, has triggered thousands of pages of academic writing, which we will attempt to condense in the next few pages (see table 1.2 for a summary of key concepts).

In a nutshell, management scholarship has explained the rise of these companies by highlighting that they have pursued *digital platform business models* (Gawer 2011; Parker, Van Alstyne, and Choudary 2016; Teece 2018). Digital platform companies exploit the opportunity to capture value that

Table 1.2
Key terms for the scaling of digital platforms

Concept	Description
Digital platform business models	Business models that rely on extracting rent from creating virtual environments for mediated or hosted interactions.
Transaction platforms	Platforms that enable direct exchange between users.
Innovation platforms	Platforms that establish environments for software developers or other digital innovators to create applications and software.
Integrated platforms	Providers that offer both innovation and transaction platform products.
Cost-related scaling economies	Scaling economies through near-zero cost to copy digital artifacts.
Demand-side scaling economies	Network effects accelerate growth once a critical mass of users has been surpassed.
Big data analysis (as scaling economy)	Disproportionately better and more information can be derived from analyzing large quantities of user data than for smaller ones.
User base scaling	A platform's user base becomes its key asset, letting investors attribute value to these platforms based not on immediate revenue potential, but on user numbers.
Generativity scaling	Digital platforms become digital infrastructure in their own right, ultimately scaling together with the diffusion of the internet and increasing digitization.

is cocreated, enabling others around the world to build onto and enhance the digital environments they are offering while setting up minimal to no physical operations in the vicinity of their customers (Evans and Gawer 2016; Parker, Van Alstyne, and Choudary 2016).

An important distinction can be drawn between transaction and innovation platforms. *Transaction platforms* enable direct exchange between users (e.g., Facebook), often intermediating between two sides of a market (e.g., Airbnb). Innovation platforms, on the other hand, establish environments for software developers or other digital innovators to create applications and software, which are then offered to end users through the platform. They do this by setting up application programming interfaces (APIs), thereby setting standards and frameworks for what developers do. *Integrated platforms* are providers that offer both innovation and transaction platform products. For instance, Google has several transaction platform products (Gmail, Google Hangouts, Google Play, YouTube) but also innovation platforms (Android, Google APIs). Integrated platform companies tend to be the largest by market capitalization (e.g., Google, Apple, Alibaba, Facebook, and Amazon; Evans and Gawer 2016).

Importantly, transaction and innovation platforms scale differently. As mentioned earlier, the creation and distribution of digital software and applications is subject to substantial *cost-related* scaling economies (e.g., near-zero cost of the second copy). Yet, for transaction platforms, *demand-side* scaling economies are most important: network effects accelerate growth once a critical mass has been surpassed. Network effects are common for many-to-many communication technologies like telephony, but they can be enhanced for internet-based digital products due to richer interactivity and the importance of user-generated content, ultimately allowing end users to cocreate a significant share of the overall product value (Amit and Han 2017; Arakji and Lang 2007; Aral, Dellarocas, and Godes 2013). *Big data analysis* can represent a third scaling economy for these platforms: disproportionately better and more information can be derived from analyzing large quantities of user data than for smaller ones (Brynjolfsson, Hitt, and Kim 2011; Huang et al. 2017; Zuboff 2019). Machine learning and algorithmic computing allows this data processing to be automated (thus decreasing cost) while yielding more relevant results.

For many transaction platforms, all three scaling economies apply at the same time. This leads them to employ a *user base scaling* approach. Investors may attribute enormous economic value to these platforms, based not on financial but on user numbers (consider Facebook's acquisition of WhatsApp for $19 billion). Ultimately, the user base of such a digital enterprise becomes its key asset and sets in motion a self-sustaining growth process. Transaction platforms attempt to reap benefits from a first-mover advantage, which turns into monetization potential once they attain a monopolistic position, ideally at global scale. Using and enrolling into these platforms is usually extremely cheap (or free), simple, and convenient. Through this strategy, Google Search became the market leader for online search, Amazon for e-commerce, Airbnb for room sharing, Uber for hailing taxis, Facebook for social networking, WhatsApp for instant messaging, and so on.

The pattern that applies to innovation platforms is *generativity scaling*: some digital products become digital infrastructure in their own right, ultimately scaling together with the diffusion of the internet and increasing digitization (Henfridsson and Bygstad 2013; Teece 2018). Such products are sometimes visible to end users (e.g., operating systems, online payment providers, browsers, app stores), whereas others may be taken for granted or run in the background (e.g., content management systems, encryption services, APIs, plug-ins, servers, cloud storage). Consumers do not typically choose these products; rather, they are built into or underlie the brands they are actively choosing. For instance, customers may pick a hardware-software bundle (e.g., a Samsung smartphone running on Android, or a Dell laptop running Windows, Internet Explorer, Adobe Flash, Oracle's Java), in effect purchasing an integrated piece of digital infrastructure that gives them access to the services they seek to actively use. Accordingly, not all generatively scaling products are known brands. Generativity scaling applies to nonplatform digital infrastructure products (Intel processors, Akamai, Amazon Web Services, Qualcomm, Ericsson, Oracle, Adobe, etc.), but innovation platforms are at its core because they represent the very enablers of combinatorial digital innovation (Gawer and Cusumano 2014; Teece 2018). For maximum scaling, innovation platforms thus aim to achieve a standard character and selectively and strategically seek interoperability with other products through (application programming) interfaces.

True to its disciplinary frame, the rather extensive strategy and information systems literature sees the few globally leading transaction and innovation digital platforms as *astute role model strategists*. It implies that exponential business growth and "disruption" of old business models is a desirable outcome, thus seeking to identify strategy patterns that others can imitate. Specific incumbent platforms are used to illustrate platform business models (e.g., Gawer 2014), but platform strategies are ultimately presented as models and thus as action templates (see, e.g., chapters 3 and 5 in Parker, Van Alstyne, and Choudary 2016). Particular historical and geographical positionalities (who, when, where) of existing platforms are downplayed or completely ignored in this literature (see Srnicek 2016).

The Why and How of This Book: A Grounded Empirical Inquiry

Ultimately, both popular understandings and management theory suggest an optimistic and aspirational vision of digital enterprises' growth potential and thus for any location's potential for economic development in the internet age. If digital technologies are globally leveling the economic playing field, if anyone with an internet connection can be a digital entrepreneur, if larger and larger markets are becoming available, if enterprise scaling is quicker and easier through digital technologies, and if generativity affords endless potential for innovation, then why would the twenty-first century not be the time when Africa is finally reaping growth and catching up with the rest of the world?

Our book probes into this ambition, offering insights into what is actually happening on the ground. A legitimate worry is that such enthusiasm is based on overhyped expectations (Rodrigues et al. 2018). Channeling resources into supporting entrepreneurs is a trade-off that shifts the burden of development away from building public institutions and tackling structural issues (Birtchnell 2011; Honig 2017): what Ory Okolloh, a pioneer in the Kenyan digital technology scene, describes as the "fetishization of entrepreneurship" (Kuo 2015). Proponents of digital entrepreneurship can appear to proselytize a gospel of prosperity in which the subjects of development are encouraged to keep the faith in the face of failure and difficulty. Viewed critically, digital entrepreneurship may at best be a fad that will run the course of its hype cycle before disappearing from debates and at worst deceive us and make structural issues like inequality worse rather than better.

Discourses have always not just reflected the world, but also helped to produce it. However, because of the paucity of available evidence on this topic, we would argue that framings of and visions about African digital entrepreneurship have, thus far, been especially impactful on a range of related policy and practice. Our book thus seeks to discern if digital entrepreneurship is more than a current buzzword in international development, media, and policy circles. We will explore whether any of the related high-flying ambitions are translating into palpable growth and expansion among digital enterprises (and thus to local economic development), or if they simply risk distracting from real potentials and opportunities.

To probe into expectations, this book seeks to document and analyze the phenomenon of African digital entrepreneurship as it has become observable in recent years. It aims to understand both the opportunities and the limits that the rise of the internet has brought to ventures in Africa, painting a richer and more realistic picture than media articles and policy documents have done. Our mission is therefore to empirically ground the conversation that scholars, practitioners, and policymakers have begun, without getting lost in the descriptive detail of any particular success story or aspect.

No book could perfectly capture the diversity of African cities while also discussing the continent as a whole (Cheeseman and de Gramont 2017; Noorloos and Kloosterboer 2018; Phillips 2014; Watson 2015). We attempt to do justice to local contexts without losing sight of continent-wide themes that have emerged from our analysis. Namely, we mostly highlight generalizable patterns, but go into contextual detail whenever locally specific findings defied these patterns or gave them a particular shape. For instance, we explicitly discuss variations in dimensions of digital entrepreneurship that vary starkly across the continent, such as the size of domestic and urban digital markets (chapter 2) and the strength of the local digital entrepreneurship ecosystem (chapter 5). We also include factsheets for brief outlines of local digital entrepreneurship scenes and data points on local digital markets for each of our case studies in appendix B. North African nations are excluded from the analysis for two reasons: first, sub-Saharan Africa has traditionally been only poorly integrated in global digital production networks (Carmody 2013; Ojanperä et al. 2017), and second, most sub-Saharan nations (with South Africa as the primary exception) have a shared internet connectivity history, as submarine and overland fiber-optic cables arrived in these countries later than almost anywhere else in the world (Graham, Andersen, and Mann 2015).[7] We thereby extend and augment emerging work on technology entrepreneurship in Africa that has been limited to illustrative maps and case studies of sectors and companies (Rodrigues et al. 2018).

Our book provides readers with a broad-strokes summative overview of African digital entrepreneurship, while also offering analytical depth and highlighting previously undiscovered effect chains and patterns. Ultimately, our book is a departure from the few other books in this domain that have made sweeping statements that falsely generalize from exceptional success stories (see Bright and Hruby 2015a; Ndemo and Weiss 2017a; and to a lesser extent, Taura, Bolat, and Madichie 2019). Given our ambition to provide grounding and nuance, we also feel strongly that we should not "dumb down" and simplify the content of this book, as we steer clear of hyperbolic talk both of revolution and of failure (Gillwald 2019).

This may sound like a dry academic exercise, but from hundreds of interactions in recent years, we feel that there is a real hunger for well-reasoned, detailed, and rigorous analysis among policymakers, development organizations, investors, and also entrepreneurs themselves. This is because—as has been the case for so many technology and development fads—thorny issues can be ignored for some time, but disillusionment with overblown hype from the people on the ground is bound to set in sooner or later. We therefore hope that these audiences will find the evidence in this book useful and timely, and we have done our best to make our insights accessible to them.

As we also challenge and contextualize strategy literature on digital entrepreneurship, management scholars are another audience for whom this book should be useful. We want to add geographical sensitivity to the firm-level perspective espoused in this literature. We also want to move this discipline away from their focus on unique and nonrepresentative Silicon Valley success stories like Google or Amazon, and instead point to more inquiry into digital innovations that happen outside of the United States and China. Economic geography, economic history, science and technology studies, information and communication technologies for development (ICT4D), and evolutionary economics will hopefully find the nuance we provide to be useful. This book offers rich and multilayered empirical detail about how economic agency intersects with digital technologies and Africa's socioeconomic legacy in the early twenty-first century.

Our arguments can only ever be as strong as the evidence we have to support them, and so we have sought to gather a compelling and comprehensive assembly of datasets and observations on African digital entrepreneurship. To this end, we draw predominantly from the five-year Geonet research project at the Oxford Internet Institute, which all three authors were involved in. Our guiding research questions throughout the project were these: (1) Who are Africa's digital entrepreneurs (i.e., their backgrounds, motivations and mindsets)? (2) How are they and their enterprises pursuing market opportunities through digital technologies? (3) What markets (nature, size, scope) are they able to address? (4) How do their ecosystems and social environments support them (or not)?

We wanted to study digital entrepreneurship, a new phenomenon, across "Africa" as a whole, while also capturing local differences and diversity. Balancing ambitions of breadth and depth, and of generalizability and truthfulness to local differences, we opted for a multisited case study approach, with semistructured interviews as the primary means of data collection (see appendix A for details on methodology). We used a "least-similar" rationale to select city case studies: if we could detect patterns across all or most of a set of highly diverse cases, we would be more confident that those patterns also apply to cities that we did not examine empirically (i.e., other major African cities). We thus identified cases across Anglophone, Francophone, and Lusophone Africa, with varied sociopolitical, cultural, and economic environments. We ultimately conducted theory development based on case studies in Nairobi, Lagos, and Kigali, and later tested and extended preliminary theories through case studies of Abidjan, Accra, Addis Ababa, Dakar, Johannesburg/Pretoria, Kampala, Maputo, and Yaoundé. Between January 2017 and March 2018, we conducted 202 in-depth research interviews in these cities, including interviews with 143 digital entrepreneurs. In almost three hundred pages of field diary notes, we captured firsthand impressions gathered from meeting participants at startup offices and coffee shops, visiting dozens of innovations hubs, and attending policy events (see appendix B for summaries of our impressions for each case study).

Further, we draw from access to Geonet's quantitative mapping and digital outsourcing work (Braesemann, Stoehr, and Graham 2019; Ojanperä et al. 2017), as well as a previous project on the business process outsourcing sector in Kenya and Rwanda (Mann, Graham, and Friederici 2014), providing us with a wide-lens view of Africa's emerging digital economies. Two of the authors (Friederici and Wahome) completed doctoral theses on digital entrepreneurship in Africa. They investigated digital entrepreneurship organizations in Nairobi, Kigali, Accra, and Harare, conducting strategic ethnographies and sociologies of digital spaces, including 166 interviews.

Together, we have conducted many months of fieldwork across the continent, and this book captures the essence of what we have learned during this process. It attempts to codify what we find to be an accurate, realistic, and insightful account of African digital entrepreneurship in the early twenty-first century.

Analytical Framework

We use the domains of discourse outlined in this chapter to construct an analytical framework that our book can probe into and nuance (see table 1.3). We identify two bodies of discourses. *Popular discourses* are prevalent in media, documents and statements by policymakers, and reports and other

Table 1.3
Analytical framework based on popular and academic discourses

Expectation	Popular discourses	Academic discourses
Greater inclusiveness and acceleration of entrepreneurial activity	Cambrian moment; Silicon Savannah; youthful continent; lean startup; "mobile-first" generation	Democratization of entrepreneurship; less bounded entrepreneurial agency; "same" digital infrastructure as ubiquitous enabler
Fast-paced and transformative growth	Leapfrogging; Africa rising; digital entrepreneurship revolution; startup nation; M-Pesa and Andela	Growth on steroids; generativity; digital transformation; network effects and user-based growth; digital platform business models
Africa catching up due to global leveling of opportunities	Flat world; digital innovation knows no borders; leapfrogging	Democratization of entrepreneurship; less bounded entrepreneurial outcomes; reduced role of clusters; value capture at distance

contributions by international development organizations. *Academic discourses* derive from various strands of management scholarship, especially information systems, strategy, and entrepreneurship journals and books.

We do not employ a single overarching theory, for two reasons. First, we are in large part interested in verifying and challenging common beliefs among practitioners and policymakers. Second, it is hard to think of one established body of theory that captures digital entrepreneurship in Africa in a satisfying way. Digital entrepreneurship is an interdisciplinary construct, and academic debate on it is only just beginning—if by rather famous entrepreneurship scholars like Aldrich, Davidsson, Autio, and Acs. Theory building has begun in this new scholarly domain, but empirical studies have been confined to the United States, Europe, and Asia (Amit and Zott 2001; Briel, Davidsson, and Recker 2018; Huang et al. 2017).

Accordingly, neither popular nor academic discourses propose clear predictions or prescriptions. Still, both express and define expectations for observers and stakeholders of digital entrepreneurship in Africa (policymakers, scholars, investors, development organizations, etc.). The headline expectation set by popular discourses is this: "Following the arrival of broadband internet, digital entrepreneurship can become Africa's driver of rapid and inclusive socioeconomic development, and help the continent to catch up with the rest of the world." The headline expectation set by academic discourses is this: "Digital infrastructure has enabled relatively unbounded entrepreneurial opportunity and reduced the role of enterprise location and geography." Academic discourses do not speak about Africa directly, but imply that African digital enterprises should be able to pursue strategies and attain successes that are similar to their high-income country counterparts.

By proposing a condensed analytical framework, we are necessarily making simplifications and omissions as to what has been said about the phenomenon we are interested in. For instance, several media articles and reports deviate from the aforementioned popular discourses (Asemota 2018; Essien 2015; Ndiomewese 2017; Rodrigues et al. 2018). However, the discourses we seek to challenge and nuance represent dominant meso- and macro-level discourses, mostly put forward by powerful entities, thus shaping other actors' behavior (Alvesson and Kärreman 2000; Rose 2012). Actors and entities we encounter time and again as proponents of these discourses include policymakers (Kagame, Kenyatta, Macron), global media (BBC, CNN, Al Jazeera, CNBC, *National Geographic*), international technology media (TechCrunch, *Wired*, *MIT Technology Review*), African technology media (Disrupt Africa, Quartz Africa), local media (*Daily Nation* in Kenya, *New Times* in Rwanda), some international foundations (Rockefeller and Tony Elumelu Foundation), technology corporations and their surrogates (GSMA, Internet.org), development organizations (World Bank, UN organizations), and consultancies (McKinsey Global Institute, Accenture Development Partners).[8] It is an important scholarly exercise to put the claims and expectations that these powerful actors determine to the (empirical) test.

Likewise, emerging digital entrepreneurship theory does not explicitly claim to explain digital entrepreneurship in all its instantiations, everywhere in the world. Yet it seeks to advance theory that is generalizable to organizations of a certain kind (digital enterprises), irrespective of their location. Here, it is an important scholarly exercise to examine whether and how such theory indeed applies in a context that is radically different from the contexts that the theory developers had in mind, and to develop new contextualized theories to address any oversights (Barnard, Cuervo-Cazurra, and Manning 2017; Nkomo 2017; Walsh 2015).

Of course, this does not mean that other literatures have nothing to say about digital entrepreneurship in Africa, and indeed several related contributions are emerging (e.g., Avle and Lindtner 2016; Friederici 2018;

Jiménez and Zheng 2018; Marchant 2018; Ndemo and Weiss 2017b; Pijnaker and Spronk 2017; Wentrup, Ström, and Nakamura 2016). Management is only just "discovering" Africa (George et al. 2016; Nkomo 2017; Zoogah and Peng 2019), and other disciplines have established much deeper bodies of knowledge on the continent. Still, our analytical framework engages with management scholarship because this discipline has discussed digital entrepreneurship most explicitly and actively, thus staking a claim on interpreting and defining it. It is therefore here that we believe our work can lead to the greatest productive tension. For other academic disciplines, our book still makes valuable contributions, even if it does not challenge their theories head-on. Namely, we provide rich empirical detail on an economic process and practice that represents a new and unique constellation of long-standing areas of interest like economic development, technology, power, social structures, and African studies.

In sum, this book will verify and extend an analytical framework that condenses common expectations about digital entrepreneurship in Africa. The framework consists of two pillars: popular discourses about digital entrepreneurship in Africa and scholarly discourses on digital entrepreneurship in general. The book will test in what ways popular aspirations are accurate or only amount to hope and hype, and it will test the applicability of digital entrepreneurship theory to Africa as a context that differs from the implied contexts of this theory.

Book Outline

Following this introductory chapter, the book is divided into seven chapters. The red thread throughout the book is an empirical grounding and testing of the analytical framework outlined in the previous section. To this end, chapter 2 describes what we observed about digital entrepreneurship in Africa, while chapters 3–7 explain and dig deeper into our observations, especially those that challenge the analytical framework. Those chapters focus on answering "why" and "how" questions. The following is a brief outline of the key points made by each chapter:

- Chapter 2 provides a descriptive, broad-strokes overview, drawing on available indicators and first-level analysis of interview data. It shows that digital entrepreneurship is unevenly spread across Africa and that

African digital enterprises mostly focus on revenue generation in small, fragmented local markets.

- Chapter 3 analyzes why African digital enterprises have so far stayed local. Our findings suggest that African enterprises iteratively learn from local customers, creatively adapting to local conditions, for as long as their resources allow it. Mostly, product-market fit means a sustainable but not an expansive business. More scalable digital product categories (e.g., social network sites) are occupied by Silicon Valley competition.

- Chapter 4 analyzes how African digital enterprises can still succeed and grow. It outlines four strategies that often have led to sustainability: (1) scaling based on customer and partner relationships, (2) local information platforms, (3) investing in local assets with value for customers in high-income countries, and (4) blending digital platforms with an analog outreach structure (what we call *last-mile platforms*).

- Chapter 5 uses the entrepreneurial ecosystem as a conceptual lens to discuss African enterprises' access to resources. Based on analysis of resource shortages and bottlenecks, it distinguishes three tiers of African ecosystems: learning, incipient, and maturing. The chapter highlights that, due to vicious cycles in ecosystem development, lower-tier systems can be stuck at nascent levels. In such cases, supports like hubs and innovation competitions are not advancing ecosystems as much as many hope because they themselves depend on other resources.

- Chapter 6 discusses what it means to be an African digital entrepreneur. It shows that Africans are reconciling decontextualized ideals of digital entrepreneurship with the social world around them. They are breaking new ground and have begun to form a new professional class. However, they are for the most part a relatively exclusive cultural and economic urban avant-garde. This implies that preexisting social positionalities in African nations have changed in style but mostly been reproduced.

- Chapter 7 engages with the (dis)continuities of Africa's place in the world that digital entrepreneurship has brought about. It shows that developmentalist ideas of Silicon Valley as a gold standard of digital entrepreneurship are ubiquitous in Africa, forcing actors to wield its mythologies and expectations. Thereby, global asymmetries of privilege, capital, and capability are replicated in local microcosms, leading to significant tensions. Despite indignation, local entrepreneurs find pragmatic answers, like "white fronting" (i.e., partnering with white Westerners to attract investment capital).

- Chapter 8 explicitly contrasts the findings of chapters 2–7 with the expectations expressed in popular and management discourses. It highlights broader implications and summarizes what policymakers and others may do differently and better.

The consequence of our findings is *not* that digital entrepreneurship in Africa is economically futile. Entrepreneurs, investors, policymakers, and development organizations should not give up on digital entrepreneurship as a path toward local development. However, our book is a cautionary tale suggesting that effects will not be fast-paced and revolutionary. Rather, we see evolutions in the factors underlying sustainable digital entrepreneurship (entrepreneurial knowledge, networks, product and business model innovations, support interventions, etc.). And we also see waste of resources, time, and attention, spent on pipe dreams, ineffective action, and ephemeral successes with no lasting relevance for development (vanity enterprises, tech cities, investments based on racial stereotypes, hackathons as photo ops for development organizations, etc.). To maximize the positive work that digital entrepreneurship can do for Africa's development, all involved will have to play a long-term game that focuses on locally sticky assets and strategies while cutting out as much of the waste and misguided actionism as possible. If this is achieved, digital entrepreneurship will play not the most important, but a significant role for Africa's twenty-first-century economic history.

2 Taking Stock

Digital entrepreneurship in Africa is a recent, dynamic, and emergent phenomenon. This has made it challenging for practitioners, academics, and policymakers to understand and define it. As outlined in the previous chapter, a wide set of actors forcefully advance elaborate ideas about it. Development organizations, governments, policymakers, tech corporations, and innovation hubs all have had significant roles in framing African digital entrepreneurship as a revolutionary transformation (Ndemo and Weiss 2017a). Many of these organizations, especially those removed from on-the-ground realities or those with an interest to promote the agenda, end up overstating and overestimating the development impacts of digital technologies (Friederici 2019; Friederici, Ojanperä, and Graham 2017; Graham 2015).

Meanwhile, grounded, concrete, and reliable information and evidence from across the continent is in short supply. In every city we visited for this research, interviewees bemoaned widespread misconceptions about how easy or transformational the practice of digital entrepreneurship tends to be (see Friederici 2017b). Many entrepreneurs and investors also complained about the absence of reliable data on African digital entrepreneurship, which, they argued, greatly limited the quality and speed of their decision-making compared to their peers in high-income countries.[1]

In response, we use this chapter to take stock of the broad contours and characteristics of African digital entrepreneurship. To do so, this chapter mostly generalizes patterns across city cases; we refer readers to appendix B for short profiles and contextual information. In a single chapter, we seek to give an overview of what is happening on the ground and what the scope and extent of activity has been. This descriptive exercise provides readers with information that is valuable in its own right, but it also establishes contextual knowledge and grounding for the analysis in the remainder of the book. This chapter highlights *what* we observed, while the following chapters analyze *how* and *why* things came to be the way we found them.

This chapter first reflects on how we can observe digital entrepreneurship, given its fuzzy nature. To speak to discourses about leapfrogging and catch-up, it then puts African activity in a global context by using digital production as a proxy measure for digital entrepreneurship that allows us comparisons of Africa to other world regions. We then show differences on a Pan-African scale, illustrating that even though digital entrepreneurship has emerged in most large African cities, the extent and depth of activity varies immensely. Next, we depict the opportunity landscape for entrepreneurs, describing market and infrastructure conditions in African nations. Once all this contextual information has been established, this chapter depicts how digital enterprises in our sample create and capture value, highlighting patterns that emerged across all or most of the eleven city case studies.

We find that digital entrepreneurship activity is extremely unevenly spread across space, both at a global scale and within the continent. The same is true for digital markets and infrastructure, with large divides between nations and between cities and rural areas. The absence of integrated digital payment systems is an important contributor to fragmentation. African digital enterprises are mostly unable to reach beyond small and local markets and instead focus on short-term revenue from business customers and on digitizing previously analog local value chains. At the same time, innovations abound. They mostly consist of creative adaptations of digital technologies or of hardware-software-service bundles, adjusting to local conditions and market needs.

How Can We Take Stock of Digital Entrepreneurship in Africa?

The previous chapter introduced key ideas from digital entrepreneurship theory, including the role of digital technologies' affordances, digital infrastructure as an external enabler of entrepreneurial opportunity, the possibilities of generativity and combinatorial innovation, digital value creation and capture strategies, and the potential for digital platforms to scale fast, across a wide geography and without making revenue. However, this does not yet tell us much about on-the-ground realities of digital entrepreneurship in Africa. Abstract theory and concepts may or may not explain well what is happening in African contexts. As a phenomenon, digital entrepreneurship in Africa possesses five qualities that make it hard to grasp:

1. *Aspirational.* Many have proposed hopeful visions about what African digital entrepreneurship could or should be (see chapter 1), which has blurred the line between ambitions and on-the-ground realities.

2. *New.* So far, we lack agreed-upon understandings and measurements. Directly applying terminology from global entrepreneurship discourse (e.g., *startup, venture capital,* or *accelerator*) can obfuscate the fact that realities in Africa differ fundamentally from those in Silicon Valley, or indeed elsewhere in low- and middle-income countries.

3. *Local and global at the same time.* Every digital entrepreneur in every place on Earth by definition relies and builds on the outcomes of the global digital revolution. In doing so, they become part of an immensely complex and far-flung sociotechnological system (Bratton 2015; Davidson and Vaast 2010). Technologically, digital entrepreneurship in Africa—just as in Asia, Europe, or Latin America—relies on the leading providers of infrastructure, which are mostly private entities (Google, Microsoft, Oracle, Facebook, Huawei, Ericsson, etc.). Culturally, digital entrepreneurs the world over compare themselves to those from Silicon Valley, which means that local identities, myths, and narratives are never autarkic and can only be understood in relation to Silicon Valley as the global reference point (Avle and Lindtner 2016; Weiss and Weber 2016).

4. *Shaped by distant actors.* Many (if not most) supporters of African digital entrepreneurs (such as donors, policymakers, and investors) are located in Europe and North America, and thus cognitively and geographically removed from entrepreneurs' on-the-ground realities. Unavoidably, these groups' perceptions of—and misunderstandings about—Africa affect their understanding of African digital entrepreneurship.[2] Corporations based in the United States, Europe, and Asia produce and reshape the digital infrastructures and technologies that African enterprises build their own activities upon.

5. *Not clearly bounded.* Digital entrepreneurship does not form a coherent, standalone sector or industry, instead intersecting with traditional

economies in complex and unforeseen ways. This is because digitization variously affects sectors and geographies (Malecki and Moriset 2007) and because entrepreneurship is a social phenomenon that involves a number of diverse actors (Davidsson 2005).

How could we possibly measure such a phenomenon? For one, digital entrepreneurs' dual embeddedness in a global sociotechnological system and in local contexts means that this book has to discuss both global and local contexts, considering how both intersect for a given empirical case (nation, city, enterprise, etc.; see Quinones, Heeks, and Nicholson 2017).

Dual embeddedness by no means nullifies the importance of local context. In fact, as we will discuss in more depth in chapters 3 and 4, the opposite may be true. What we observe empirically is that "the 'same' digital infrastructure . . . has [vastly] different entrepreneurial outcomes in different contexts" (Nambisan 2017, 1046). Although improving internet access has made the use of digital technologies geographically more level, clearly, the production of digital technologies has remained highly spatially clustered both within and across nations. Today, the largest digital companies with immense market capitalizations are located in only a handful of specialized centers in the United States, Europe, and South and East Asia (Malecki and Moriset 2007; Steinbock 2003). Leading the charge are five companies based in Silicon Valley and Seattle (Google, Facebook, Apple, Microsoft, and Amazon), shaping the digital economy at a global scale.

This suggests that digital entrepreneurship may be subject to *stronger* economic agglomeration than analog entrepreneurship. This is in large part because it depends on immobile specialized capital and labor and because entrepreneurs and employees benefit from trust- and expertise-based face-to-face learning and networking (Benner 2008; Saxenian 1994; Zook 2002, 2005).

Ultimately, the low cost and high benefits of enrolling ever-more users (see chapter 1), in combination with strong agglomeration effects, has resulted in a *stark geographical divergence of digital production and usage* (Leamer and Storper 2001; Malecki and Moriset 2007). This means that access to the internet and to digital infrastructure may be a necessary enabling condition for digital entrepreneurship to emerge in a given locale (Briel, Davidsson, and Recker 2018), but it is not sufficient for digital enterprises to be successful and scale widely.

Altogether, this chapter (and indeed the book as a whole) has to treat the availability of broadband internet as not more and not less than a starting point of possibilities. "What happened next" in African cities will be the subject of our empirical analysis. We seek to identify how African contexts affect the local physical embodiments of digital enterprises (founders, staff, social networks, etc.), while also considering their embeddedness in an interconnected global digital economy (consisting of markets, products, regulations, infrastructures, etc.) that continues to be dominated by actors in Silicon Valley and other high-income countries. We also need to distinguish digital production, as highly clustered in space, from digital usage, as potentially geographically dispersed.

Comparing Digital Production in Africa versus High-Income Countries

To understand spatial disparities in digital entrepreneurship at a global scale, we would need a globally standardized and quantifiable measure for it. However, we are not aware of any single rigorously collected international dataset that captures digital entrepreneurship as such. Indices like the Doing Business index, the Global Entrepreneurship Index, the Global Accelerator Learning Initiative database, or the Global Entrepreneurship Monitor either suffer from poor or incomplete data for African nations, or they capture "entrepreneurship" too broadly, including rural and micro entrepreneurship. Data available in grey literature, such as popular and policy books (Adesida and Karuri-Sebina 2016; Bright and Hruby 2015a) or reports by organizations like the McKinsey Global Institute, the World Economic Forum, and the GSMA (GSMA 2017; Kanza 2016; Manyika et al. 2013), tends to use unverified assumptions, convenience samples, and questionable statistical methodologies (see Friederici, Ojanperä, and Graham 2017).

Accordingly, we limit our analysis to two kinds of proxy data. First, we use two datasets that capture geographies of digital production—namely, geocoded GitHub and Online Labour Index data (Kässi and Lehdonvirta 2018; Ojanperä et al. 2017). These sources have major advantages: they capture observed and complete data from dominant online platforms at a truly global scale. Analyzing them allows us to investigate how Africa's digital entrepreneurship compares to other world regions, assuming that the spatial distribution of digital entrepreneurship is roughly similar to that

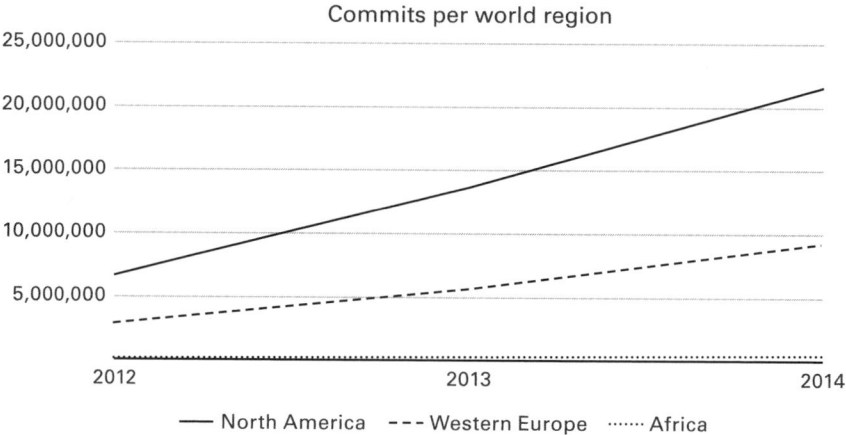

Figure 2.1
Number of GitHub commits for select world regions from 2012 to 2014.

of digital production. Second, we use World Bank data on information and communications technology (ICT) service exports to show the long-term trend of increasing global divides.

These datasets show that while Africa as a whole is characterized by impressive growth rates, the continent is playing catch-up from a starting place that is incredibly far behind the current positions of other dominant world regions. Figure 2.1 illustrates the sheer scale of some of these differences. Coding as a practice is certainly growing in Africa, but it remains an almost insignificant activity when compared to the volume of activity happening in other regions of the planet.

With the rapid spread of the internet around the world and over a third of Africans now online, one would expect there to be fewer barriers to participation in a platform via which developers share their code, as compared to more specialized forms of knowledge production (such as, for instance, the production of academic journal articles). Yet in reality, the opposite is true. Some of our previous research has compared the production of three forms of digital knowledge production (Ojanperä et al. 2017): examining the distribution of academic articles (as an example of traditional or predigital knowledge production) as compared to the registration of domain names and GitHub commits (as two leading indicators of how much digital activity is occurring in a country). The findings in figure 2.2 illustrate not only

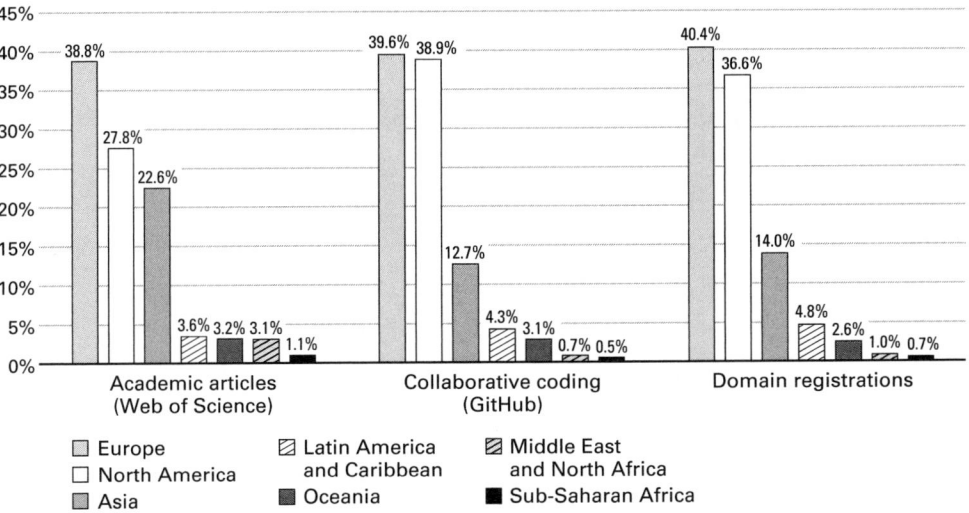

Figure 2.2
Content creation across continents, based on Ojanperä et al. 2017.

Africa's poor showing on all three metrics, but also that the region performs even worse on digital metrics as compared to traditional ones. Sub-Saharan Africa has about 13 percent of the world's population and about 8 percent of the world's internet users, and yet only 0.5 percent of GitHub commits and 0.7 percent of domain registrations come from this region.

Another key way in which Africa is missing from the global network of code development is evident in figure 2.3. A lot of software development is based on the remixing and reworking of existing repositories of code. Users on GitHub thus tend to follow each other for updates about the work these others are doing. As such, it is instructive to see how users follow each other from different parts of the world. Figure 2.3 shows that Africa again barely registers on a graph of the world's activity. There are only 1,767 users from sub-Saharan Africa who are followed by people from outside of the region. This means that only an insignificant fraction of software developers worldwide takes note of coders in the region. Conversely, 5,292 users based in sub-Saharan Africa follow others outside the region, illustrating that coders in sub-Saharan Africa are three times more likely to follow someone from outside of the region than to be followed.

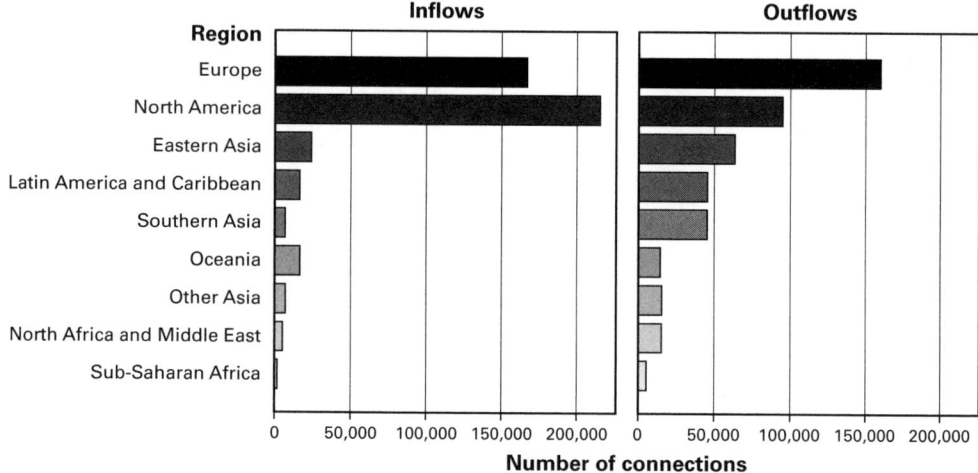

Figure 2.3
Number of connections in the GitHub follower network. *Source:* Graphic and analysis by Fabian Braesemann.

A very similar pattern emerges when we look at a more traditional measure of international exchange: ICT service exports. This statistic, published by the World Bank (2018) using International Monetary Fund data (IMF 2018), adds up transactions between residents and nonresidents of a country, where ICT service exports include "computer and communications services (telecommunications and postal and courier services) and information services (computer data and news-related service transactions)." This data source is thus much more inclusive than the GitHub data we used for figures 2.2 and 2.3, and it includes nondigital technology services as well. Figure 2.4 shows that, just like for the GitHub and domain registration data, Africa shows marginally low figures compared to other world regions and actually a minor decrease in exports in the most recent years for which the statistic is available. The data further indicates the rise of South and East Asia as ICT exporters and the vast size of intra-European trade.

The data presented thus far all offers illustrations of the amount of digital production and international exchange happening per world region. With data from the Online Labour Index (Kässi and Lehdonvirta 2018), we are also able to examine the workforce employed in digital entrepreneurship-related activities in each region. For instance, in February 2019, Africa's shares of total global digital labor were 3.5 percent in the software development and

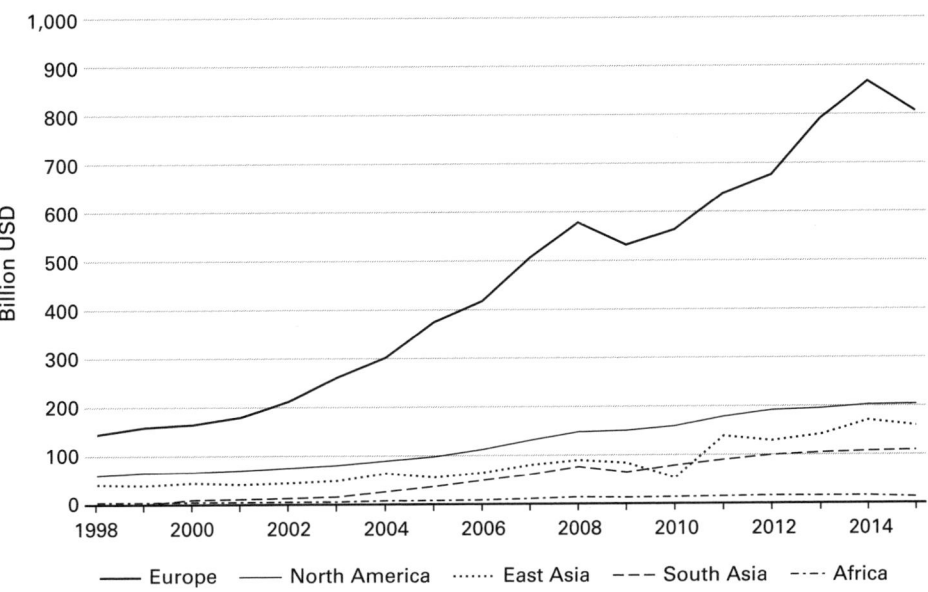

Figure 2.4
ICT service exports for selected world regions, using World Bank 2018 data.

technology category and 4.6 percent in creative and multimedia. This is in contrast to more significant shares for activities in which content is digitized but its creation does not require involved use of digital technology, such as writing and translation (14.2 percent).

Altogether, in digital production, Africa does far worse than any other continent. Smartphone penetration has been growing, but growth has recently stagnated (IDC 2017, 2018), and Africa is still far behind the rest of the world. The gaps are even wider for bandwidth and affordability (Chen, Feamster, and Calandro 2017; Deichmann and Mishra 2016). While apps like YouTube, WhatsApp, and Facebook have achieved continent-wide reach (Chen, Feamster, and Calandro 2017; Stork, Esselaar, and Chair 2017; Wentrup, Ström, and Nakamura 2016), there are no African-made, African-owned, or Africa-based smartphone apps that are widely used within or outside of the continent, and even leading African nations only represent a fraction of the global app economy (Caribou Digital 2016). Few software developers outside of the continent take note of those within it. For measures of digital production available at a global scale, Africa barely shows up in the statistics.

Africa Is Not a Country: Continent-Wide Variation of Activity

Similar to the divergence of digital entrepreneurship activity at a global scale, there are also major differences within Africa. For instance, when we tried to sample diverse sets of enterprises in a given city, it was much easier to find older, sustainable, midsize or large digital enterprises in Johannesburg, Nairobi, Lagos, and Accra than it was in Abidjan, Kigali, or Addis Ababa. Enterprises in the former four cities also appeared to attempt a more diverse set of business models and technologies, and their employees tended to be more experienced and professional than elsewhere. Typical salaries and investment sizes were also clearly higher in Lagos and Nairobi compared to other cities, and they showed higher numbers of events, innovation competitions, hubs, and incubators.

In sum, a lot more was going on in the digital entrepreneurship scenes of some cities compared to those of others. The various dimensions of "more" (number/size/diversity of enterprises, number/size/diversity of incubators and innovation hubs, investment capital, salaries, technologies, knowledge, etc.) seemed to be highly correlated: whenever there was "more" of one dimension in a given city, there was likely to be to "more" of the others as well.

Before we analyze mechanisms and reasons explicitly in later chapters (in particular chapter 4 on startup scalability and chapter 5 on entrepreneurial ecosystems), here we will only try to get a sense of the magnitude of differences in digital enterprise activity across African contexts. The interviews we conducted clearly confirm that differences exist and give some indication of what constitutes them, but this data cannot tell us exactly how unevenly digital entrepreneurship is distributed across the continent.

In the absence of reliable digital entrepreneurship databases (like business registers; see Jerven 2016), our analysis is confined to nontraditional data sources. Numerous mapping efforts are underway for individual cases of ecosystems and sectors ("Entrepreneural Ecosystem Snapshots," 2019; "Innovation Maps," 2019), but we are aware of only three variables (startups, angel investors, and innovation hubs) measured in six quantitative indicators for digital entrepreneurship activity that are available for all fifty-four African nations:

- Startups:
  - As indicated on Crunchbase.com
  - As indicated on F6S.com

- Angel investors with a location in Africa, registered with AngelList
- Innovation hubs, as defined by the following:
  - A crowdsourcing exercise by Bongo Hive (BongoHive 2017)
  - A stocktaking effort organized by the World Bank (Firestone and Kelly 2016)
  - A stocktaking by GSMA (Boucher 2016)

Each of these six quantitative indicators has limitations, and there are questions about the completeness and representativeness of each. Similarly, no dataset is a direct measure of "digital entrepreneurship." Yet these indicators are nonetheless helpful to measure relative differences in the quantity of digital entrepreneurship activity across Africa because sampling biases should be roughly similar across African nations for each of the six datasets. Moreover, aggregating and thus triangulating across six sources helps to neutralize idiosyncrasies in any given source. Even if the specific numbers are not reliable, an aggregate of the six datasets should thus give us a rough estimate of the distribution of digital entrepreneurship across African nations.

To derive a distribution, first we calculated the share (percentage) of organizations that a given country had of the African total. We then calculated the simple mean of the two startup values and the mean of the three hubs values to arrive at three percentage values for each country in each of the three variables. Finally, we took the simple mean across the percentage values for the three variables, thus giving equal weight to startups, angels, and hubs.

The results (see figure 2.5) indicate that just four countries (South Africa, Nigeria, Egypt, and Kenya) account for about 60 percent of the continent's total activity. The next eight countries (Ghana, Morocco, Uganda, Tunisia, Tanzania, Côte d'Ivoire, Senegal, and Rwanda) together account for another 25 percent of activity. The remaining forty-two countries together make up only 15 percent.

These findings are in line with the limited available data on investment amounts. Reports and online publications by VC4Africa, Disrupt Africa, and Partech from 2014 to 2018 (Collon 2017, 2018; Disrupt Africa 2016, 2017b, 2018; VC4Africa 2014, 2016, 2017, 2018) published only incomplete data, usually focusing on the top-ranked African countries. Yet all show similar patterns: investments are heavily skewed toward a few

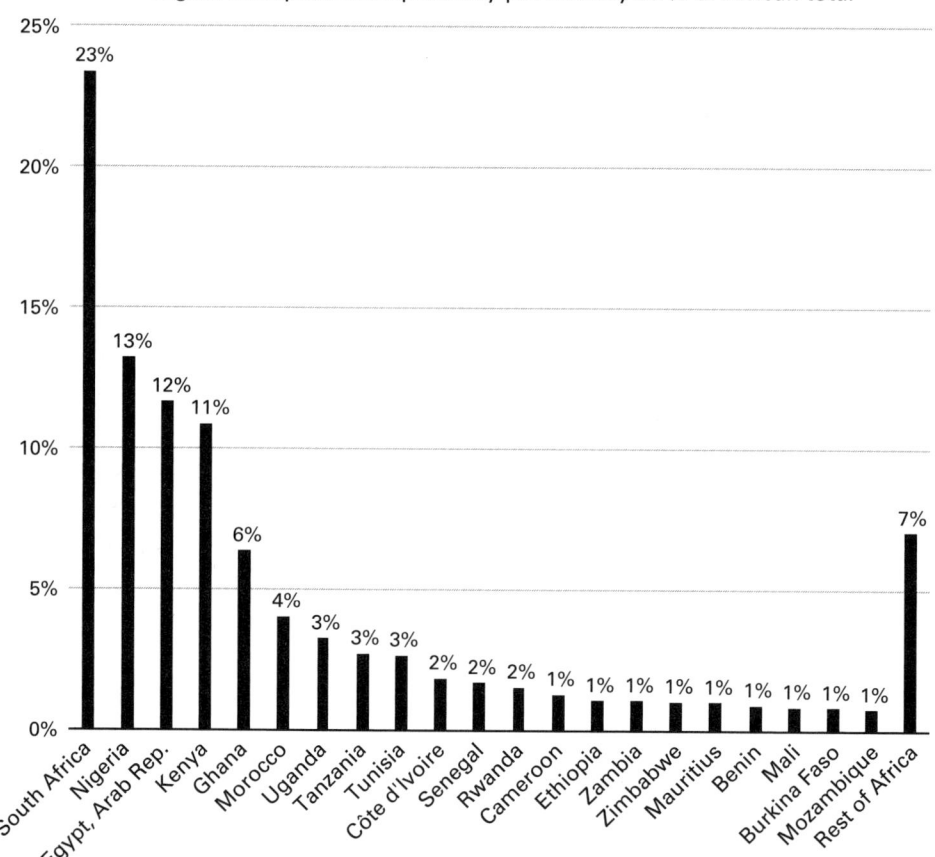

Figure 2.5

Distribution of digital entrepreneurship activity across Africa. *Note:* Data sources used are Crunchbase.com, F6S.com, BongoHive (2017), Firestone and Kelly (2016), and Boucher (2016). The bars indicate averages of three percentage values—namely, the share of startups, angel investors, and hubs that a given country has of the African total. Data for fifty-four African countries was analyzed. "Rest of Africa" includes, in the order of average values from highest to lowest: Seychelles, Botswana, Togo, Malawi, Guinea, Namibia, Angola, Democratic Republic of the Congo, Liberia, Algeria, The Gambia, Madagascar, Sierra Leone, Republic of Congo, Sudan, Burundi, Somalia, Niger, Mauritania, Gabon, Lesotho, Libya, Central African Republic, Swaziland, Djibouti, Sao Tome and Principe, South Sudan, Guinea-Bissau, Comoros, Chad, Cabo Verde, Equatorial Guinea, and Eritrea.

nations. For instance, Partech's most recent data on the thirteen countries with the highest investments (Collon 2018) indicates that startups in South Africa, Kenya, Nigeria, and Egypt secured $167.9, $147, $114.6, and $36.9 million respectively, while startups in the next nine countries only raised a combined $93.5 million. Partech's distribution is strikingly similar to the one we derived: twelve out of the top thirteen countries in the investment data reported by Partech are also in the top thirteen in the distribution we derived, even though they were calculated based on rather different data sources. These recent data sources convey a clear message: digital entrepreneurship is unevenly distributed across the fifty-four countries on the African continent.

Proponents of the aspiration that digital entrepreneurship may level economic opportunity (see chapter 1) may argue that this is a temporary divide, which will close as high-speed internet diffuses. Unfortunately, reliable trend data suitable for statistical methods like time series analysis is unavailable.

To still get a sense of how divides are developing over time, we present descriptive statistics of trend data for a measure of digital production: commits on the world's largest collaborative software development platform, GitHub (Ojanperä et al. 2017). Many digital enterprises innovate, in part, through the development and deployment of tools and products built through software. As such, it is instructive to explore where on the continent software developers are creating their code.

We obtained datasets of all commits (i.e., recorded or published activity on the platform, such as uploading code) made by GitHub users indicating their location on the platform between 2012 and 2014. The data shows that the number of commits increased drastically across the continent, rising from 114,000 in 2012 to almost 400,000 in 2014 (see figure 2.6).

Although the growth in commits from the remaining fifty African countries is 458 percent between 2012 and 2014, as compared to 352 percent for South Africa, Egypt, Kenya, and Nigeria, this growth differential is not enough to even begin to overcome the significant head start of the top four. In 2012, coders in South Africa, Egypt, Kenya, and Nigeria published ninety-three thousand commits, versus only twenty thousand for all other African countries combined. In 2014, GitHub users in the top four African countries thus still made more than three times as many commits as the other fifty countries together. South Africa alone accounted for

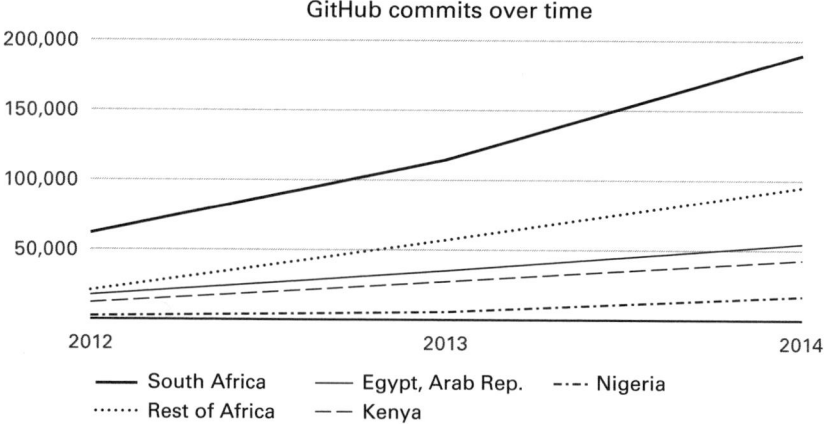

Figure 2.6
GitHub commits in select African countries and the rest of Africa.

twice as many commits as the bottom fifty (see figure 2.6). These trends are again roughly in line with the incomplete investment data published by VC4Africa, Disrupt Africa, and Partech: growth rates can be higher for nations with currently lower investment sums (e.g., Collon 2018), but they are nowhere near large enough for the investment amounts to be leveling in the foreseeable future.

In sum, despite the paucity of reliable data, we can say with confidence that stark divides exist within Africa's digital entrepreneurship landscape. Four countries (South Africa, Kenya, Nigeria, and Egypt) account for the vast majority of digital entrepreneurship activity. Ghana, Morocco, Uganda, Tanzania, Tunisia, Senegal, Côte d'Ivoire, Rwanda, and Cameroon are home to a noteworthy, but much lower level, of activity. The rest of Africa—forty-one countries—has a similar total population compared to the top thirteen nations (567 vs. 613 million in 2015) but makes up only a fifth of the continent's total activity. It appears that these divides are only growing each year.

African Digital Markets and Infrastructures

To capture on-the-ground realities in richer detail, we now move on to findings derived from interviews conducted in eleven African cities. We represent the immediate insights of digital enterprise founders, startup employees, freelancers, and entrepreneurship supporters like incubator managers and investors (see appendix A for details). The remainder of this chapter condenses our interview data into descriptions and uses extensive direct quotes from participants.

This section begins by outlining African digital markets and infrastructures. Given the major differences in digital usage across Africa (see appendix B), it was unsurprising that interview participants reported a number of local idiosyncrasies—for example, regarding the dominance of particular market actors (e.g., Safaricom in Kenya) or the extent of government support (e.g., major infrastructure subsidies in Rwanda). Still, digital markets and infrastructures emerged in roughly similar patterns across all cases.

Across all cities, participants consistently spoke of digital entrepreneurship as a new economic practice, with the oldest local firms typically established in the 1990s or early 2000s, starting with customized software development for local corporate clients. With the increasing availability of mobile phones throughout the 2000s, value-added mobile service providers then started to emerge, targeting a mass consumer audience. These companies offered simple products like ringtones or bulk text message delivery. A few fixed-broadband internet service providers usually served a narrow client base in cities (e.g., banks or multinationals).

From around 2010, mobile broadband became more widely available, enabled by the arrival of fiber-optic submarine cables on the shores of West and East Africa (Graham, Andersen, and Mann 2015). In parallel, mobile money services were introduced by mobile network operators, with M-Pesa in Kenya as a technological frontrunner. Such applications are usually USSD (Unstructured Supplementary Service Data)- and SMS-based, allowing users to have a digital wallet and transfer money. While the overall success of mobile money is undeniable, a mostly unresolved issue is a lack interoperability between operators. Another complaint from entrepreneurs concerned malfunctioning or lacking interfaces, as well as poor reliability:

> We have the easiest possible way for making a payment [through M-Pesa] and still, it is pretty arduous. If you look at the payment conversion rates, they are between 15–20 percent, meaning that 80 percent of people drop out during the payment cycle. (Entrepreneur in Nairobi)

With increasing mobile broadband coverage, cheap smartphones became more common, especially among wealthy and middle-class populations in cities and peri-urban areas. However, interviewees complained that local users have typically been extremely price-sensitive and were rarely exposed to digital technology:

> Customers don't want to have smartphones and . . . if you're above average price, nobody will ever take you. . . . There's just so many unknowns here. The phones are worse. The internet speeds are not effective. People don't have a history of using apps. Many people don't have email. . . . People have extremely low disposable income. (Entrepreneur in Kigali)

Accordingly, local clients typically demand cheap and simple digital services (e.g., modifying WordPress templates), and only very few applications have reached wider audiences. Common features appear to be zero or transaction-based pricing, low data consumption, sufficient functionality for feature phones or low-level smartphones (e.g., through offline usability and SMS/USSD integration), and the fulfilment of a basic, widespread need (such as interpersonal communication). Accordingly, aside from applications offered by mobile operators, only WhatsApp and Facebook (often in its low-bandwidth Facebook Zero and Facebook Basic versions) have reached significant user populations outside of major cities (Chen, Feamster, and Calandro 2017; Stork, Esselaar, and Chair 2017).

Although the African digital enterprises in our sample have not typically reached national audiences via the web, they use various elements of global digital infrastructure beyond physical internet infrastructure. Many entrepreneurs reported that they primarily used Facebook for digital marketing and WhatsApp and SMS to communicate with existing customers (e.g., sending confirmations and updates):

> So we decided, let's just take a few pictures and post them on Facebook and see if anyone buys. . . . There was such an interest! . . . Facebook has always helped us actually . . . because a lot of young people, that's what they use, and then you direct them to [our own] site. (Entrepreneur in Nairobi)

We also saw digital enterprises in our sample employing digital infrastructure for managing internal processes, using cloud and SaaS platforms originating mostly in Silicon Valley. Most enterprises relied on services like Windows, iOS, Google products, WhatsApp, Microsoft Office, Amazon Web Services (AWS), PayPal, WordPress, GitHub, Slack, and Dropbox.

Interestingly, we found a number of digital enterprises (mainly in Nigeria and Kenya, but also in Rwanda and Cameroon) that outsourced software development to India and Europe—to Poland in particular. This typically became necessary due to a missing local supply of software developer labor:

> [The prototype] was developed in Poland [through a] freelancer website. . . . I found the designer . . . the engineer, [and] the second engineer on Elance [a major online labor platform, now called Upwork]. I don't have any engineer here. . . . That type of knowledge [is not available] in Rwanda. (Entrepreneur in Kigali)

Overall, increasing availability of high-bandwidth internet in Africa has mainly fueled the uptake of digital products that form part of the global digital infrastructure: consumers adopted Facebook and WhatsApp, enterprises started using cloud-enabled solutions, and both groups relied on mobile broadband hardware (including wireless network technology, mostly from Europe, and cheap devices from East Asia).

Limited Technology Adoption

> In Africa, you take the market for what it is. If you try to want to correct or change the culture of people, you better have like 200 million dollars to do that. (Seasoned Nigerian founder)

The broadest possible measurement for the size of digital markets is the number of mobile phone and internet users, representing the maximally reachable group of users for any digital product. In the early 2010s, development organizations, technology corporations, and researchers became infatuated with the so-called mobile revolution that was said to sweep the African continent (Deloitte and GSMA 2012; Etzo and Collender 2010; World Bank 2012). The belief that practically every African has access to a phone ultimately became important for digital entrepreneurs because it turned into a taken-for-granted assumption promising the existence of vast and growing digital market opportunities in Africa (see chapter 1). For instance, one study found that mobile technology has become so essential in Africa that the poorest users would forego food to buy mobile credit (infoDev 2013). Many digital entrepreneurs we interviewed echoed the idea that "everyone has a phone everywhere, thank God" (entrepreneur in Nairobi).

Yet when probing more deeply, those same entrepreneurs also told us that supply-side technology adoption statistics like mobile or internet penetration rates can be misleading, and that the actual potential user base for their digital products is much smaller (see Graham 2015):

> All these numbers around these thirty million people being connected, or according to Google, twenty-three million Kenyans—it's bullshit, it's just ridiculous. . . . If you look at the Nigerian markets, you have a lot of guys who saw it as an opportunity and now they're pulling out because the promise of the market is not there. (Entrepreneur in Nairobi)

> [The farmers] don't even have phones . . . [not] even feature phones. Smartphones? Forget about it. A lot of them are not educated. So even how to read the phone is a problem. So a lot of the time, to recharge their credit, maybe your son has to do it on your behalf. . . . We know the farmer is not going to use that technology. (Entrepreneur in Ghana)

> Rwanda is peculiar but Rwanda allows a window into many of the challenges you'd face in other places. . . . The level of tech literacy for Rwandans is very low. They're using super cheap thirty-dollar Android smartphones with no internal storage and bad-capacity touch screen on shoddy internet networks that are extremely overpriced. (Entrepreneur in Kigali)

In fact, this reality is reflected in statistics that are more meaningful than penetration rates. For instance, the GSMA has begun to clean penetration data for multiple SIM card ownership, leading it to estimate that still only about half of all Africans have at least one active mobile subscription (GSMA 2017). Similarly persistent digital divides are revealed by demand-side survey data about digital usage (e.g., Chair 2018; RIA 2017a, 2017b). Moreover, the percentage of internet users varies drastically across nations, posing market challenges especially for entrepreneurs located in small and poor nations with low penetration rates and small capital cities, such as Kampala, Addis Ababa, Maputo, or Kigali (see appendix B). We will revisit this point in more detail when discussing market bottlenecks in chapter 5.

Rural-Urban Market Fragmentation and Infrastructure Divides

It is important to consider cities rather than nations as typical target geographies for African digital enterprises. As outlined further ahead, the customers of most types of digital products can be found almost exclusively in the cities in which the enterprises themselves are located. In cases of large cities like Nairobi and Lagos, these urban markets were sometimes more sizeable than national or regional markets would be elsewhere in Africa:

So majority of our staff are in the field. . . . We have a risk and compliance team; we have customer service; we have second-level support . . . sales, [those who] are managing the agents. . . . So it's sometimes hard to understand how big Nigeria is. . . . [When I suggested expanding to Abuja to my mentor, he answered,] "Why are you even thinking of leaving Lagos right now? You're telling me about Abuja. . . . You should stay here." There are only four countries in Africa that have a GDP bigger than Lagos. Twenty million people, it's bigger than Ghana. I mean, just think about that economic opportunity here. (Financial technology entrepreneur in Lagos)

Similarly, this entrepreneur in Senegal explains that the lack of a large urban market in geographical proximity is a key issue for his competitiveness (see McCann and Acs 2011):

We have many cities, but they are not big cities. Chinese cities are bigger than the entire population of Senegal. We don't have cities that are big enough to support these opportunities. In a city of twenty million, you will find someone to buy your thing, whatever it is, and the logistics will be easier. Colonization separated us into small countries, with one capital of about two million people. . . . We need to make intercontinental trade easier. If no one likes your thing in Dakar, maybe someone in Bamako will like it.

We found that entrepreneurs are not usually able to reach outside of their urban contexts because of insurmountable market fragmentation. The major differences that entrepreneurs highlighted mostly focused on different levels of user capacities and technology adoption. Typical barriers to technology usage applied to urban markets as well, but to rural ones to a much greater extent. Frequently mentioned barriers included

- many users' low levels of technology experience,
- intermittent and unreliable rather than always-on internet connectivity,
- limited bandwidth,
- limited capacity of devices (e.g., leading to overheating or low usability),
- prohibitive cost of data in mobile phone contracts and lack of availability of Wi-Fi spots where unlimited data usage would be possible, and
- variety in digital technology standards (e.g., myriad kinds of low-cost smartphones and feature phones running various dated versions of Android or Nokia's Symbian).

An additional key difference between urban and rural areas was the limitations in *physical infrastructures* that are needed to enable digital infrastructures. Rural areas were mostly lacking reliable electricity, but low availability of support and service staff and difficult physical transportation were also mentioned. An entrepreneur in Nairobi insists that poor rural areas are barely viable as digital markets:

> Yeah, you go to rural: there is no power, there is no staff so you can sell, . . . The cost structure is very different.

Ultimately, only those sectors that focused on small businesses (as a customer group that is more homogenous across rural-urban divides than consumers), that did not depend on analog infrastructures, or that made bridging rural-urban divides their business model focused on nation-spanning markets. The latter scenario existed for supply chain logistics and some e-commerce enterprises.

Low Willingness to Pay and User Capacity

Even the most rigorous internet subscriber and smartphone data still give an inflated idea of the size of realizable user numbers for digital products. Participants in all cities flagged that the average African user's willingness to pay for, and their capacity to use, digital products is extremely low. One entrepreneur in Ghana described to us in detail why even smartphone users are rarely a viable target market for digital products:

> **Interviewer:** You mentioned the smartphone statistics . . . usually people say, "there's so much opportunity in Africa, smartphones are growing so quickly, [there is a] young population, it's just going to go up, up, up." Do you think that's not the case?
>
> **Respondent:** It is not. You see, in Ghana the majority of people use dumb phones, and the majority of the percentage that uses smartphones are not that smart to use the smartphones. . . . The only reason why people get smartphones is because they want to use WhatsApp. . . . My dad has a smartphone but he probably doesn't even have a payment system on it because, even though there are a lot of payment systems in Ghana, but he doesn't even see it as a tool for that. The only payment system that he probably will use is MTN Mobile Money or any of these mobile money platforms because they use USSD services. . . . You just type *124 and then you're able to send money. They understand that language—not your regular app on the Play Store [Google Play]. They don't even update their phones, for that matter. There's a huge smartphone influx, but there's a gap between the phone and the people.

This is a well-known issue in the digital inequality literature: beyond access, second-level digital divides can exist where users are unable to make productive uses of digital technology or where other socioeconomic barriers are in the way (Donner 2015; Gillwald 2017; Hargittai 2002). Market information systems in particular have had mixed success because they assume certain levels of digital literacy among users and a certain homogeneity in the market conditions that users are facing (Burrell and Oreglia 2015; Wyche and Steinfield 2016). Africa's socioeconomic problems are often construed as opportunities for entrepreneurs to solve, yet our findings clearly show that these issues are themselves barriers to the development of markets (Srinivas and Sutz 2008). It has become ever more apparent that mobile phone adoption has not translated into widespread uptake of more sophisticated technologies and innovations (Carmody 2013; Danquah and Amankwah-Amoah 2017). Instead, internet users have mostly limited themselves to using basic communication apps like WhatsApp and Facebook (Chen, Feamster, and Calandro 2017; Stork, Esselaar, and Chair 2017; Wentrup, Ström, and Nakamura 2016).

Our interview data also confirmed that low user capacity is a systemic and embedded issue (Drouillard 2017; Onsongo 2017). For instance, in several cities we visited, Uber drivers struggle to read maps and do not like to be paid through credit cards, and restaurant workers have trouble processing orders submitted via Jumia (an e-commerce and delivery platform). A Rwandan entrepreneur ran us through a litany of such challenges for his system to be used:

> Now the biggest challenge that we're facing is to have a merchant accepting payment through mobile money. They are the ones who are resisting now. Some of the point-of-sale devices, we have given [them] for free to some of the supermarkets here, but sometimes I surprise them. Let's say I just bought a chocolate bar and I want to pay with mobile money, and they say, "We don't receive such payment." [To which I say] "Look, I created the system with you. You look in the drawer. I mean, there is a point-of-sale device. Bring it." And it's not turned on. When they turn it on, they forgot the PIN.

In these examples, it was not usually the end user who struggled using an app but the people who needed to make the technology work at different points of the value chain. While technology is often seen as an enabler, technology itself needs to be enabled by social factors like norms and trust. A Ghanaian entrepreneur highlights the symbolic importance of the rollback of Tonaton.com, an electronics e-commerce company with Swedish investor backing:

It was shocking to me that Tonaton, which is now one of Ghana's biggest, also is shutting down . . . In Ghana, technology, you need to be on the spot with security, with fraud, with all of that, because that is what has brought Tonaton down. [Say] I have a phone to sell. Because delivery was a problem at a time . . . you go meet them, then they beat you up, take your money because they knew you had the money to pay that. That was happening a lot on Tonaton so now people don't even trust these systems anymore. . . . The Ghanaian market or even the African market is so different from what we see from here in Amazon—it's so different!

The troubles of e-commerce providers especially revealed that the hopes that Africa's growing middle class would soon become a digital market opportunity may have been premature. Jumia, the Pan-African e-commerce brand of African Internet Holding, has been making losses for years, and French-German Rocket Internet is reportedly withdrawing as its main investor (Akinloye 2018; Ekekwe 2015; Mutegi 2017). It appears that margins for African e-commerce businesses are extremely low—maybe too low for profitability in the foreseeable future, especially because they depend on expensive analog operations such as call centers, warehouses, and distribution infrastructure.

The combination of low levels of trust and capacity and low disposable incomes leads to generally low willingness to pay among users in African markets. This is an immediate issue for subscription-based and transaction-fee-based digital products, but it is also relevant for free applications because users are not ready to afford the bandwidth necessary to use them. The founder of an Ivorian taxi-hailing application discusses how purchasing power affects the use of digital applications:

The second challenge that we faced was the data. You know, in this part of the world, data is so expensive. It's very, very expensive for most of the people here, so they do not use it like in [the] other part of the world.

Contrary to the narrative that Africa's young population could represent a particularly large market opportunity, some participants pointed out that youth often had especially low disposable incomes. A youthful populace is likely to view digital services as essential, but it may not be likely to afford to spend too much on them. Over time, this benefits providers that offer low-bandwidth products for free to users through mobile operators' vast retail networks, but this may only be a viable option for large transnational competitors, as this Ugandan interviewee points out:

You can't expect to hit massive penetration when you only have 30 percent internet penetration and your country is 50 percent under fifteen . . . 78 percent [of Uganda's population is] under thirty. So we're like babies without money. . . . What kind of product can we throw at them where they can pay one or two cents and we can work on volume? . . . The other thing [about] smartphone penetration: that's great but those guys don't have a single cent to buy data. They don't have the disposable income to buy data. That's why they're buying bundles where WhatsApp is free or Facebook is included, but there's not much outside of that ecosystem that has been provided. That's why I look down on those sponsor social media packages for periods. They are very dangerous in terms of training a very young demographic to understanding what the power of the internet is. If you limit them to thinking it's only Facebook, WhatsApp—and that's only one company. What about the rest of the internet? Good and great for Facebook but terrible for the entire ecosystem.

Yet other "killer apps" were seen to popularize digital technology use more generally, making things easier for African digital entrepreneurs. The clearest example was Kenya's M-Pesa. Several participants explained how M-Pesa had created trust in technology among the general population, making any new digital product easier to sell. In Accra and Abidjan, entrepreneurs related that wide usage of e-commerce and ride-sharing solutions had a similar effect. In one case, an e-commerce entrepreneur actually welcomed Jumia as a direct competitor in his market because he felt that Jumia's aggressive—and expensive—marketing campaign had raised awareness for the benefits of technology more generally.

Ultimately, many entrepreneurs believe that the time has not yet come for business-to-consumer (B2C) digital products to thrive in most African countries. The rationale is that there are simply not enough users for a self-sustaining user base growth pattern, and it is impossible to charge users directly because they are not willing to pay and because digital payment systems are fragmented. An entrepreneur with a ride-hailing business in Kenya reveals that this dynamic applies even in a large city like Nairobi:

No, there was never a time when we thought we would be a Nairobi business. The economics don't work. . . . You need huge scale to become profitable, and so I always said: "There's no version of our story where we end up as a barber shop." We're either going to scale very big or we'll die a glorious death.

As a result, we found that a large share of the stable and sustainable digital enterprises in our sample were those that had business customers, especially in less advanced ecosystems (see also chapter 5).

The clear advantage of targeting businesses is they can be charged directly, generating revenue immediately:

> So a lot of the B2C business ideas are failing to gain a lot of traction. . . . Success [lies in] B2B solutions that allow quick monetization, high volume, growth structure (Hub manager in Uganda)

The downside of targeting and charging businesses is that each individual customer requires significant attention, making scaling slower (chapter 4 will discuss this in more detail). Entrepreneurs who target large corporations almost always use one-off contracts, which leads to difficult trade-offs between needing to customize products for a given corporation and standardizing products for quicker and cheaper scalability. Entrepreneurs highlighted that in many local corporations, managers do not trust small startups and responsibilities for technology procurement are not clearly defined, making it hard to find the appropriate counterpart. Sales cycles are thus typically very long and require frequent face-to-face meetings. Corporate customers were often described as lacking payment discipline, with no recourse for entrepreneurs. Finally, entrepreneurs complained that corporate managers lack an appreciation for the value of technology and are unable to distinguish between high- and low-quality digital products:

> It's been fantastically rewarding to see how good our product is and then to go in when we get called in. They're like: "Hey, you guys seem to be driving our sales very quickly, what are you doing? . . . Oh, we have a mobile app, can you look at it?" You're like, "My, did you guys pay for this?" . . . They're like: "We paid $15,000 for it." My God, I should be in the business of ripping people off because we go in for a week, we've fixed everything. . . . We're now doing a lot of technology advisory. . . . We're like: "Yeah, we can help you guys, but we're going to be expensive because we've spent the last four years figuring out how to build these things." . . . We've just closed a retainer contract now, $5,000 every month. [However] you end up spending, selling your time so much that you never get to be good. (Kenyan digital entrepreneur)

Software-as-a-service approaches were more prevalent for small business customers. For this segment, challenges included the need to set up extensive customer support structures (e.g., call centers) and to acquire large numbers of customers given low willingness to pay:

> The market is pulling us; it's looking promising . . . we have found something that people want and probably at a price that they can afford but in our business you need thousands [of customers]—no one can pay you much money, right?

And handling thousands of businesses is extremely difficult because, only because they are small and maybe not as rich, it doesn't make them less demanding. . . . If I'm small or big, and I buy something for any significant portion of my income or my business budget, I request [a high level of quality], and rightfully so. (Entrepreneur in Uganda)

Telecoms Legacies and Fragmented Digital Infrastructures

In Africa, mobile phone companies are the backbone upon which a large number of entrepreneurs have built their firms (Allen 1988; Chavula 2013; Joseph 2017). Although Africa's increasing reliance on mobile internet has mostly usurped digital enterprises like internet service providers (ISPs) and Voice over Internet Protocol (VoIP) companies, it has slowly expanded the market size for digital services. Many firms were established to take advantage of this new space, and founders tailored them so that they could be accommodated within it.

Mobile operators are an important avenue through which other digital firms can access a large customer base (see box 2.1 for the example of Safaricom). Inking a deal with a mobile phone operator to become a value-added

---

Box 2.1

Safaricom: Friend or Foe?

Safaricom is a case of an almost monopolistic private-sector power player providing market and infrastructural support for technology innovators. Aside from preferring horizontal integration and revenue-share agreements to delivering all services itself, Safaricom's decision to release the M-Pesa API had a great impact on the proliferation of firms in Nairobi. It enabled companies to integrate a payment infrastructure into their applications. Payments are a significant pain point for firms in Africa, and this approach eliminated much of the issue. Naturally, the benevolence of Safaricom is strategic: once actors have developed a reliance on its infrastructures, it becomes possible to increase prices or suddenly vertically integrate by creating an in-house facility that can compete with other digital enterprises. Nevertheless, these acts of competition, should companies survive them, tend to make them stronger. The firm Cellulant formerly sold ringtones but had to develop a gateway to bypass Safaricom when the revenue-share agreement became too unfavorable. That gateway is banking software that Cellulant was later able to sell to banks across Africa.

service (VAS) all but guarantees business success. When telcos are willing to partner with smaller companies, this can have a significant positive effect on the number and diversity of local enterprises. Safaricom Kenya's decision to outsource bulk messaging services and premium-rate service provisions (PRSPs; e.g., SMS short codes or premium-rate phone numbers) meant that these were among the first revenue-generating digital enterprises in many African nations (and thus are the oldest companies in our sample). Others include mobile service aggregators (MSAs) that allow for the delivery of SMSs across multiple mobile operators through a single point of contact, so that users do not all have to be with the same mobile carrier.

Mobile money services, in particular, significantly altered the landscape in some locales by providing a mechanism for collecting payments. Safaricom's M-Pesa is the most prominent example. In effect, Safaricom formalized the process of airtime remittances (Joseph 2017; Suri and Jack 2016). M-Pesa allows customers to convert and "store" money on their phones and later collect and/or deposit it with a (physical) Safaricom agent. Ultimately, Safaricom benefited from its intermediary role by collecting transaction fees from those using the add-on services, and M-Pesa became digital infrastructure for payments (Karanja 2010; Park and Donovan 2016). Operators across Africa pursued similar approaches with various levels of success, often suffering from a lack of integration between the regimes of individual operators. In exceptional cases, like Senegal's Wari, mobile payment providers are autonomous, not tied to any mobile operators.

Yet mobile money has been far from a silver bullet for Africa's digital payment issues. Even when operators make mobile money APIs available, they can be clunky and unreliable. An entrepreneur in Kenya relates how difficult it is for anyone trying to pay for his app through Safaricom:

> Unfortunately, the dominant players in these markets haven't really yet made mobile payments as easy as they should be. We have the easiest possible way for making a payment and still it is pretty arduous. If you look at the payment conversion rates, they are between 15 and 20 percent, meaning that 80 percent of people drop out during the payment cycle. . . . The operators want to keep these channels to themselves and to dominate the space. Of course, there are some measured security-related issues there as well, so that could be misused; I think that's one of the reasons why it hasn't been opened. . . . In our case, you need to choose a product, choose how you're going to pay, which operator you're going to use, and then you get instructions over estimates, then you go to your SIM Toolkits [an Android application], you go to M-Pesa, click the code, the value of

the money and especially if you are using a simple handset, [then] you basically have to kill your browser session . . . [*crosstalk*] . . . exactly. It's not good. . . . So monetization still is the biggest thing.

Digital payment structures beyond mobile money are only just emerging, and it seems to be taking longer than many expected to integrate various cashless formats. Across Africa, the myriad common local and international payment channels (cash, mobile money, airtime vouchers, debit cards, credit cards, PayPal, cryptocurrencies, remittance services like Western Union) make integration difficult, especially when a digital payment solution is meant to operate across diverse technology standards (web, mobile-optimized web, Android, USSD, SMS). Payments and banking are usually regulated by arcane and opaque national laws and licensing regimes.

Digital infrastructure for payments thus remains a significant pain point for African firms. In the long run, the challenge offers an arena in which many financial technology (fintech) digital enterprises, as well as incumbent banks, aim to develop solutions (Taura, Bolat, and Madichie 2019). In the short run, it makes monetization for digital products (i.e., charging users directly) technically difficult and costly for all other digital enterprises. In countries like Ethiopia, where local businesses and entrepreneurs are unable to obtain foreign credit cards or set up accounts with international payment providers, entrepreneurs have to be particularly resourceful:

> Eventually we tried to monetize it with a commission-based model. . . . That model was not scalable in a country where online payment is not available. People actually had to come to the office to give us money and that didn't work. We needed to iterate the idea. It became a business model of selling coupons. . . . You buy a coupon in [our] headquarters . . . but also on Hello Cash [a novel local digital payment platform]. After you bought it, you fill in the promo code in your profile account on [our app] and whenever you [make a transaction] it will deduct three birr [about eleven US cents]. There are coupons of 50 birr, 100 birr, and 200 birr [the latter about seven US dollars]. (Entrepreneur in Addis Ababa)

Even beyond payment systems, technical integration is a challenge for African digital entrepreneurs. Participants told us about a number of issues depending on the type of digital product and the local context. A Nigerian incubator manager highlights entrepreneurs' neglect of feature phone applications:

> All across the supply chains. We say, "It's software-enabled," right? I use the term 'software' very loosely. It depends on the market. . . . I know that there's a huge

market in people who don't have smartphones, but they still need technology to enable their lives and their businesses. For me, the challenge is not, "How do I build applications that will sit on the smartphone?" That's easy. There are all sorts of tools and free stuff and code repositories. . . . My challenge for a lot of our startups is, "How do you build applications that can sit on a device that is not a smartphone and can actually enable these people to do better, even if you have other technology running somewhere in that chain?"

And even developing smartphone apps may not always be straight-forward. An Ethiopian developer mentioned to us that most users have cheap used phones, often running outdated or obscure versions of Android, which leads to glitches like battery overuse when apps are not specifically debugged across the various standards. A Ghanaian entrepreneur offering an ERP system for small businesses feels that his company is behind the hardware integration standards that European providers are setting:

> This is our new innovation. . . . It's a hardware/software conversation . . . so we're going to have to commit a lot more resources into that front. We're not doing it as aggressively as we should, because we are now really focused on the software part of the business. . . . We have to assimilate our research into what could be the ideal storefront device for what side of business and become more active in that space. You see in Europe, there are a lot of companies that are customizing the storefront; there's a lot of research going into what that storefront could look like. We need to be part of that conversation.

Although 4G mobile broadband was available in central areas of all the cities we visited, we also heard about and experienced hardware issues that are rarer in high-income countries, such as outages, low availability of Wi-Fi hotspots with unlimited data usage, overheating smartphones, or erroneous maps. It is easy to take the functionalities of Google Maps for granted until you realize that they affect the quality of service that digital products are able to offer. A taxi-hailing app founder lamented the inaccuracy of Google Maps in Abidjan:

> We use Google Maps for the moment. It's not as [accurate] as we want, but it's still working in some part, in some ways. We are working [with] GDG, Google Developer Groups. They are the ones that are able to fix some points. So we used to tell them this place is not inside, please can you add it.

Hardware and access technologies are extremely fragmented across Africa, but internet-enabled software created in Silicon Valley is consistently available and used across the entire continent. Various Google applications and systems (Gmail, YouTube, Google Maps, Google App Engine, Android, Google Play, Google Wallet, etc.), Facebook, WhatsApp, Microsoft products and services, Dropbox, Stack Overflow, GitHub, and Slack were used by digital entrepreneurs in every city we visited. These solutions have made a strong imprint, not only as inspiration for startups, but also as infrastructures on which local entrepreneurs depend when building their digital services:

> **Respondent:** Actually, it's like a prototype . . . and if we get customers, let's say, we can put it out there, and then people will start using it.
>
> **Interviewer:** And did you put anything out there?
>
> **Respondent:** Actually, I work on a project but I got some problem to put it out there because the backend needs to rely on the Google App Engine, and there is some free storage that Google gave you. You can send your codes there, but there is some limitation on what you can do. If you want, let's say, to use it for a scalable purpose so everyone can use it, you need at least to start paying Google . . . but for me, at least, I need to have customers before yeah. You can't just go there and then I start paying Google without anyone who would be using the project. It doesn't really make sense. (Burundian freelancer in Kigali)

A number of firms use social media apps—for instance, to manage customer relationships. WhatsApp and Twitter are similarly utilized to target customer audiences for service and advertising. Facebook is particularly popular to host business webpages and virtual storefronts. Broadly defined, maybe the most ubiquitous digital enterprise in Africa is the e-commerce site that presents wares on Facebook for cash on delivery.

Because integration of local and international digital infrastructures can be impossible, cash has remained the predominant means of payment for many providers:

> I also then point my finger at guys like Google and so forth because . . . I still think, it is the situation today that we don't really have proper prepaid payment integrations with Google Play either, and that's something we had with Nokia five or six years ago, so that we had negotiated with operators to be able to integrate payments to your own mobile account . . . I think still you need to be going to your USSD kit and so forth to make that payment, even though Google could have easily done it. They've had years and years to do that. (Entrepreneur in Uganda)

A Nigerian entrepreneur is philosophical about the long-term impacts of foreign domination of the digital infrastructure that is used in Africa, and sees digital payment platforms as the key technological frontier for the continent:

> It is really about pathways to scale. So what a lot of people don't really understand about how the web came to be what it was. . . . You had Yahoo! first, then you had Google. So these are pathways to the web. [In Africa] we still don't have platforms that are that big. . . . Google and Facebook basically filled the void. . . . The next thing we have to think about is essentially what are the primary functions people would do on the internet? I think what it would boil down to is entertainment, porn, commerce. You have YouTube, you're fine. You have your IROKO, you're fine. Porn, you don't need guidance in that. Music, you have your streaming services, you're good. But underlying all of this is, you need some method of electronic payment . . . It wouldn't make sense for you to hand in cash somewhere to download the movie, which is what we do today, or to hand in cash for pay on delivery, which is what we do today. . . . Without the likes of your Authorize.Net, your PayPal, your Stripe, we would have no internet. [*laughter*] Right? . . . Even then, it's still pretty shady. Like, I sent money to somebody on PayPal, they couldn't get out the money for twenty-one days, and that's ridiculous. . . . Now unfortunately, what happens is the core infrastructure, because there are brave people who came and built that infrastructure, is owned by entities or vested interest. I guess the challenge for [new African platforms] over the next twenty years is really, "How do we either compete as an open alternative to these closed platforms [by mobile operators and banks] and by so doing build up the ecosystem?" or, "How do we co-opt [*laughs*] these closed platforms and plug them into our ecosystem?"

What African Digital Enterprises Do

Interviews with founders also allowed us to code information about 135 digital enterprises. Although our sample is not representative in a strict sense, we interviewed a large and diverse set of founders, thus increasing our confidence that the patterns we captured are accurate representations of what digital enterprises do in Africa's major cities.

Despite lasting issues and the slower than expected evolution of digital markets and infrastructures described in the previous section, the number and diversity of African digital enterprises notably increased around 2010, once improved broadband became available in large cities. Only a few enterprises in our sample were founded earlier: for instance, a corporate software development firm, a job search portal, and a bulk SMS provider.

Value Creation: Digitizing Information Flows

First, we examined which types of digital value creation (see chapter 1) the 135 sampled enterprises engage in. Four out of five conducted either market intermediation (58) or digital production (43), making these the dominant types of value creation. Information processing was also common (29), while user interconnection was rare (5).

Market intermediation typically consisted of connecting small businesses with individual users. It was therefore prevalent in sectors like e-commerce, ride sharing, agricultural supply chains, and job search (see table 2.1). Digital production consisted of customized software development for businesses (e.g., banks, insurances, traders) or of enterprise resource planning (ERP) systems. Typically, ERP system providers saw that local businesses in a particular sector were unable to effectively use or afford sophisticated solutions by providers (like SAP) from high-income countries, leading these digital enterprises to develop cheaper solutions adapted to local businesses' needs (e.g., local tax reporting requirements).

Information processing was prevalent where digitization, collection, or aggregation of private, proprietary, sensitive, or complex information could be used to derive new insights, such as in logistics or the financial sector. For example, a Ghanaian identity verification provider collated analog and digital repositories of financial data about individuals and informal businesses to allow them to access to financial services. Information processing also often consisted of integrating existing but fragmented data sources and systems:

> Nigeria is an informational data desert. . . . Being able to get that data, mak[ing] it somewhat real-time, is really valuable for [our customers]. . . . The lesson we've learned is, we make it modular . . . There's the reporting module and the visualization module. . . . [That's] how we get entrenched in their system. (Founder of a logistics digital enterprise)

User interconnection enterprises included three crowdsourcing applications, one interactive smartphone app, and one ride-sharing application (focusing only on riders, not drivers). Two of the crowdsourcing applications focused on users in large urban cities (Accra and Nairobi), asking them to report traffic data and public service issues. One crowdsourcing application focused explicitly on rural users, making micropayments to content contributors. Finally, the smartphone app attempted to assemble

Table 2.1
Types of digital value creation by sector

	Intermediation	Digital production	Information processing	User interconnection	#
Job search	100%				12
E-commerce	100%				9
Agricultural supply chain	100%				6
Music streaming	100%				1
Ride sharing	80%			20%	5
Education	75%	25%			4
Technology consulting	60%	40%			5
Financial technology	58%	5%	37%		19
Logistics and supply chain (excluding agriculture)	57%		43%		7
Health	50%	33%	17%		6
Digital marketing	25%	25%	50%		4
Custom software development	8%	92%			25
Gaming		100%			2
Artificial intelligence		100%			1
ERP systems		92%	8%		13
Last-mile online access		50%	50%		2
News, content, and public information		33%	17%	50%	6
Internet of Things (IoT), tracking			100%		3
Bulk SMS			100%		2
Financial services			100%		2
Data and analytics			86%	14%	7

an international lifestyle community, but it struggled to generate content contributions from users and achieve critical mass.

Because different types of digital value creation are not mutually exclusive (see chapter 1), we also coded secondary value creation. Information processing was the most widespread secondary type of value creation (47), thus often complementing the three other types. More than half of the sampled enterprises (76) used information processing either as a primary or a secondary type of value creation, confirming our expectation that it would be prevalent. Information processing was used in particular to complement market intermediation (see table 2.2). This would also be unsurprising for digital enterprises outside of Africa: when users interact with each other through a digital product, it is a logical next step to process the information that is generated as a by-product. In particular, in two-sided markets, it can be beneficial to process information about one side for market actors on the other.

However, in our sample of African digital enterprises, information processing by market intermediators consisted less of analytics and automation, and more of basic digitization: enterprises were making available previously analog information about end users and informal service providers, complementing this with only lightweight automation and analytics, if any. This often depended on initial manual work to digitize information:

> Initially you go to customers, understand what they want, and computerize the manual operation . . . So it was nothing new, just automating what they already had. (Entrepreneur in Nairobi)

For instance, an entrepreneur running a market platform for mechanical parts in Ghana felt uncomfortable with the term *e-commerce*, arguing that while he wished for his company to become an e-commerce business, the local digital infrastructure and markets still limited him to modest transaction cost savings:

> It's not really e-commerce . . . our market had not really matured to the point where people can confidently get out their [credit] cards, or go to a website and then buy something from there and have it delivered. . . . We've not gotten to that full or high-level automation. (Entrepreneur in Accra)

In sum, information processing was the most common way that we saw African digital enterprises creating value, but this relied more on the digitization of information than on complex and scalable analytical

Table 2.2
Primary and secondary modes of value creation

		Secondary type of value creation			
		Digital production	Information processing	Intermediation	User interconnection	Total
Primary type of value creation	**Intermediation**	3	33			58
	Digital production		10	1		43
	Information processing	2		5	1	29
	User interconnection		4			5
	Total	5	47	6	1	135

technologies and techniques (such as machine learning, algorithms, automation, and artificial intelligence). Customized technology production and specialized intermediation was also common. Digital value creation that depends on a large customer base (such as SaaS-based software development and user-generated content models) was very rare. In each case, digital enterprises adapted to locally specific market dynamics, infrastructure constraints, and user requirements.

Value Capture: Going for Short-Term Revenue Opportunities

We will analyze entrepreneurial strategies in more depth in chapter 4, but a clear pattern across all regions was that digital enterprises strongly emphasized revenue generation, beginning in the very initial stages. Already this indicates a clear departure from the user base scaling approach of major digital platforms from Silicon Valley (see chapter 1). Locally and internationally, business customers were usually the only ones showing significant willingness to pay, leading digital enterprises to focus strongly on sectors such as customized and ERP software development (32), financial technology and services (21), or logistics and supply chain systems (7).

Private consumers were reached mostly by market intermediation enterprises, which connected them to service providers in two-sided markets. Digital enterprises typically charged one side (either consumers or businesses) a fee for accessing or transacting with the other side, especially in sectors like e-commerce (9), ride sharing (5), and job search (12). Across all types of value creation, only seven digital enterprises in the sample (5 percent) effectively addressed a large-scale market of private users: two ride-sharing platforms, a job platform, a microloan provider, a mobile payment provider, a bulk SMS provider, and a traffic data crowdsourcing application. Revenue from web- or app-based advertisements was insignificant in most other cases.

Scale and Scope: Local and Piecemeal Markets

One of the most unambiguous findings in our research is that instead of harnessing some of the most-touted potentials of the internet to reach international markets, African digital enterprises mostly target markets within their home nation (117 out of 135, or 87 percent). All types of digital value creation were thus overwhelmingly focused on domestic rather than international markets (see table 2.3).

Table 2.3
Types of value creation compared to geographical market scope

	International	Local	Total
Intermediation	6	52	58
Digital production	7	36	43
Information processing	4	25	29
User interconnection	1	4	5
Total	18	117	135

Barriers often existed already at the subnational level, with most locally oriented enterprises serving only proximate urban contexts (see table 2.4). A majority of domestically oriented enterprises (61 out of 117) addressed customers mainly in their own city. Geographical limitations for enterprise scaling resulted from enterprises identifying problems in their vicinity, but also because digital value creation depended on a minimum degree of technology readiness among users, which typically existed only in cities (see chapter 4 for details).

Out of eighteen enterprises (13 percent) targeting customers abroad, six focused on customers in other African nations and seven interviews were inconclusive about where the enterprises' customers were located. This leaves only five confirmed cases out of a total of 135 that focused on markets in high-income countries. Digital production enterprises were more likely than others to target high-income countries, which is unsurprising given the potential for outsourcing digital products (for which some traditional geographic barriers to trade are seemingly less pronounced). This category also included one globally operating SaaS provider.

Cross-border scaling was envisioned but proved elusive for many enterprises. The most common reason given was that enterprises needed to first perfect their products in local markets to be able to raise investments, generate significant revenue, and rely on customer referrals. Indeed, this was the experience of the few sampled digital enterprises that had Pan-African market reach (we will discuss this in more depth in chapter 4).

So far, we have specified the location of enterprises' primary customers—that is, those customers that enterprises explicitly targeted with most of their efforts. We also examined whether enterprises were targeting customers abroad as secondary customers—that is, as an additional

Table 2.4
Dominance of geographically proximate markets for African digital enterprises

		Digital production	Information processing	Intermediation	User interconnection	Total
International		7	4	6	1	18
	High-income countries	3	1	1		5
	Other African countries	1	3	1	1	6
	n/a	3		4		7
Domestic		36	25	52	4	117
	National	3	8	5		16
	Rural	2	2	2	1	7
	Urban	21	11	26	3	61
	n/a	10	4	19		33
Total		43	29	58	5	135

Note: The n/a rows denote cases in which interviews were inconclusive on enterprises' market scope.

business track. We found a higher number of incidences of foreign customers than for the primary customer analysis, but these cases were rather idiosyncratic, and admittedly our data is incomplete for this category because we could not reliably code this information from all interviews. For illustration, we mention a few case examples. For instance, development organizations were sometimes targeted by enterprises with a local primary market scope because they were a welcome if ad hoc alternative revenue source. One Nigerian digital enterprise used its unique local understanding to make sense of available datasets, delivering analytical reports to development organizations. In another case, a digital media enterprise in Kigali accepted contracts from development organizations whenever it could get them. A few enterprises were able to use preexisting relationships with contacts abroad to strike ad hoc deals. Two money transfer services and one investment broker targeted the diaspora, but adoption numbers remained low. In one case, a smartphone app was offered through the Google Play app store, without this amounting to a lasting uptake abroad or to revenue generation. In another outlier case, a French entrepreneur found that his initial focus on the local market in Ghana (where he was based) was misguided once he realized that an expansion to French-speaking West African countries would be more feasible due to easier customer relationship management:

> [In] Côte d'Ivoire . . . it was in French, so it was a thousand times easier. . . . As a matter of fact, we closed more deals in Ivory Coast in six months than we did in three years in Ghana. We have two clients there and we are not even there full-time. (French digital entrepreneur in Ghana)

Excluding outsourcing businesses, in only two cases did an African digital enterprise compete in a global digital market with enterprises from high-income countries. One enterprise offered a specialized integrative e-commerce platform for online shops, with customers mainly in the United States, the United Kingdom, Australia, and several European countries. The founder reported that growth had been satisfying at first, but it soon stagnated. He felt that even in a market that is ostensibly entirely digital, geographical distance to customers and the enterprise's location mattered greatly:

> Can we compete with some of the companies that we started out with back in the day? The answer is no. The technology probably didn't scale the way we wanted

it to be, customers didn't go the way we wanted; revenue also. [Our competitors were more successful because of their] proximity to the market, proximity to investors, proximity to networks within maybe [the] US, or the Valley, or wherever they are—all those things count. Also, sometimes, just even common simple time zone difference affected the business. . . . We didn't have the resources to plan customer management, sales.

The second enterprise was an artificial intelligence (AI) provider. In this case, the enterprise founder was embedded in a global network of AI specialists and evangelists, including Ben Goertzel, founder of SingularityNET and creator of the Sophia robot. The enterprise develops AI components based on contracts, mostly obtained through the founder's network. Other enterprises that identified themselves as global were primarily market intermediation companies that mediated between local markets and global suppliers, and vice versa. They were primarily logistics companies: their value was in getting wares from one area to another.

In sum, African digital enterprises were not able to surpass local markets based on the distance-bridging potential of digital technologies alone. Instead, they required various combinations of time, resources, trust-based relationships, unique local knowledge, and cost advantages. This was true even when outputs were digital in nature—and thus in theory could have been disseminated easily to anywhere in the world—as in the case of software outsourcing. These findings are directly in line with recent evidence on the global smartphone app market (Caribou Digital 2016).

Technological Innovation and Adaptation

The African digital enterprises we analyzed were mostly small and local, but this does not mean that they were not innovative. Founders creatively grappled with local market conditions, finding work-arounds for infrastructure and capacity issues. Across the continent, we were able to identify interesting digital innovations that adapted to particular local constraints. Such innovations typically consisted of assembling existing digital building blocks in new ways:

The first thing I tell [new software developer hires] is: 'There is nothing that you will do that is new—that's for sure.' . . . When you break it apart into its components, none of it is new. It's maybe the result which is new. (Entrepreneur in Kenya)

The most widespread technological adaptation we found is the integration of non-internet-based connectivity technologies, such as SMS, USSD, and interactive voice response (IVR), with web and smartphone applications. African mobile money and agricultural information service providers are known to adopt this approach, but we also found it in many other sectors, especially for e-commerce platforms, ERP providers, and job search platforms. In every city that we traveled to, with the exception of Addis Ababa (Ethiopia),[3] WhatsApp is increasingly complementing USSD and SMS as a low-bandwidth and easy-to-use tool to interact with customers (even if it is rarely technologically integrated). In one example, an education app allowed users to download course material when they had bandwidth at school, and data could be submitted when students were at their homes, where most of them did not have internet access. The app translated user inputs and tracking data into piecemeal cleartext passages, which could then be submitted to a server via a string of SMS.

Like Odumosu (2009, 2017), we find constitutive appropriation of imported technologies, where user groups develop locally specific use cultures around digital technologies—in particular, the mobile phone. For instance, both in Nairobi and Kampala, startups developed plugins that connected businesses to customers through WhatsApp. Another example is an enterprise that developed a plug-in allowing customers to pay for products on Facebook pages. Many retailers across Africa located their business websites on the Facebook platform. Integrating the plug-in allowed customers to purchase goods directly instead of only browsing and obtaining information about how to contact the seller.

The second most widespread technological adaptation was the creation of lean applications with simple user interfaces, needing limited device memory and processing power while offering enhanced offline functionalities:

> So, if you download the Uber app, it's sixty megabytes. You download our app, it's six megabytes. Why? People have small hard drives on their phones, they don't want to download a heavy app. Lots of small things like this that we understand about our users here to make it more relevant on the technology side. (Entrepreneur in Nairobi)

This approach was particularly prominent for consumer-facing applications, like in e-commerce, and for digital products used in supply chains, where different types of users along the chain had to engage with technology. For instance, a patient management software that has clients in the United States and Senegal developed a cleaner, simpler design for the Senegal version. One of the lessons that the designers learned early on was that they should not overload the screen. They "needed to keep it simple to prevent users from feeling intimidated" (entrepreneur in Dakar).

As another example, an Ethiopian ERP provider describes how his company deployed servers on-site at clients, letting them operate offline and only synchronizing them when connectivity is available:

> Every time I travel, I always start to copy what I can get, but to be honest, we cannot copy because most of the things are different here. . . . [A] cloud ERP system, even now it's difficult, if not impossible. We've managed to create many alternatives. . . . The thing is, each branch has its own server. . . . It has no dependency on the internet, okay? It's like an offline disconnected database. We synchronize it, so our product has this [function] of sending encrypted files when it has a connection. . . . The central server grabs this file and saves it to the database.

The third most widespread adaptation consisted of entrepreneurs taking the matter of low usage capacities into their own hands. Digital enterprises conducted physical outreach, employing extension agents, running trainings, and selling devices

> No, [the farmers] don't even have feature phones. Smartphones? Forget about it. A lot of them are not educated. . . . That is one thing we learned from the beginning: that we're going to use technology, yes, but we know the farmer is not going to use that technology. . . . So we have agents who live in the communities with these farmers. They are empowered with tablets with the app, and then they go to the farmers, register them, take their stock levels . . . and just upload it into the platform. (Entrepreneur in Ghana)

Some digital enterprises turned the constraints into market opportunities. For instance, a Rwandan enterprise developed a solar-powered mobile internet kiosk and charging station for deployment in rural areas of the country. Similarly, an Ivorian company combined Li-Fi, Wi-Fi, and solar technology to provide internet in rural areas. Li-Fi technology downloads information through a solar-powered light source provided by the company. Uploads occurred whenever the user's device had access to mobile phone network.

In several cases in the financial sector, innovations involved the development of new digital infrastructure. Several digital enterprises developed payment integration systems, usually trying to interconnect mobile money services of local telecom operators, to integrate local and international means of payment, or to ensure interoperability between various modes of payment and locally available point of sale (POS) devices. In one exceptional case, a digital enterprise was in the process of building a Pan-African financial technology infrastructure to interconnect African banks with highly fragmented information systems and regulatory constraints.

In sum, African digital entrepreneurs have pursued diverse and innovative approaches, creating value for a range of people and organizations. They usually digitize local information flows and develop digital products that are suitable for local contexts, often adapting to capacity constraints. Yet examples of fast-scaling African enterprises that are able to appropriate significant value in the form of revenues or investments are rare. Few are able to reach international customers, stimulate significant user-based value creation, address large domestic markets, automate information processing, or develop digital infrastructure that becomes the foundation for generative innovation. Digital technologies that have so far reached mass markets tend either to be technologically simple and low value (e.g., bulk SMS or job boards) or to originate from digital technology corporations in the United States, Europe, and parts of Asia.

Summary: An Uneven and Uncertain Landscape

Three core findings emerge from this chapter. First, we find clear evidence that Africa is far behind the rest of the world in digital production. In fact, it is further behind in digital production than in traditional knowledge production. The limited trend data that is available appears to indicate that the divides are growing further and further, even if growth is happening in Africa.

Second, stark divides exist within Africa: a few countries (South Africa, Kenya, Nigeria, and Egypt) account for most of the digital entrepreneurship activity on the continent, while countries such as Ghana, Tanzania, Uganda, Tunisia, Morocco, Mauritius, and Rwanda account for a noteworthy but much lower level. All other nations show activity levels that appear negligible in international comparison. In turn, activity levels are clearly growing fast almost everywhere in Africa, and in some measures, growth figures are stronger in countries with currently lower levels. This brings up several open and challenging questions. For one, it will be important for policymakers and development organizations to understand how sizeable the contribution of digital entrepreneurship to national and urban economic development can become. It will also be important to track how divides and inequalities in Africa's digital economy evolve, and what kinds of risks for African economies and societies this could bring. We will revisit these problems in chapters 5, 6, and 8.

Third, we showed that the rise of digital entrepreneurship in Africa has been enabled by the global digital revolution, but market opportunities and operational realities remain shaped—and often constrained—by local economic legacies and structures. Local digital markets and infrastructure are fragmented, and large divides persist across nations and between cities and rural areas. Enterprises typically digitize limited portions of existing value creation processes in close geographical proximity, generating revenue mostly from business customers. Innovative solutions are abundant: they typically consist of inventive work-arounds to local constraints and technological adaptations. Yet the absence of harmonized digital payment systems makes scaling hard. More generally, African enterprises rarely build new digital infrastructure that others across Africa and elsewhere in low- and middle-income countries could build on.

These findings immediately challenge aspirations that Africa could leapfrog or catch up through digital entrepreneurship (see chapter 1). Ultimately, we find that vibrant digital entrepreneurship landscapes are indeed emerging across Africa, but this is an uneven development that cannot live up to the far-reaching ambitions that many actors have put forth.

3   Bounded Opportunities

The findings of the previous chapter showed that international scaling is the absolute exception among African digital enterprises. In fact, most enterprises do not reach customers beyond city limits. Founders often have to realize that they either cannot access potential customers at all, or that the existing demand does not translate into a substantial and sustained source of revenue. Even the few enterprises in our sample that did scale abroad were mostly able to address only small and piecemeal markets.

The fact of the matter is that few African-born technology enterprises have scaled widely. Today, the typical internet user in Africa uses WhatsApp, Facebook, and Google on a cheap smartphone produced in East Asia but does not use any locally produced software or hardware, with the possible exception of a mobile money service (Chen, Feamster, and Calandro 2017; Stork, Esselaar, and Chair 2017). Although the diffusion of the smartphone has been hailed as an enormous market opportunity for African developers, mobile apps produced in Africa have been able to reach neither domestic nor international market leadership (Caribou Digital 2016).

In this chapter, we analyze why African digital enterprises have so far stayed local. Like the last section of the previous chapter, this chapter maintains a focus on the African digital enterprise as the unit of analysis, but we move from descriptive results to "why" and "how" questions. The chapter first will outline the typical process of how enterprises become entrenched in local contexts. The two remaining sections highlight the role of global competitors in constraining African digital enterprises and how the few examples of internally operating African digital enterprises were able to market their products abroad. This chapter as well as chapters 4–7 use extensive direct quotes from participants to represent their voice more immediately.

Our analysis suggests that the exponential growth that has inspired scholars and commentators of digital entrepreneurship (Evans and Gawer 2016; Huang et al. 2017; Parker, Van Alstyne, and Choudary 2016; Ries 2011) seems to be possible only for enterprises located in a region where a number of conditions are in place that are not given in African cities. Like their Silicon Valley counterparts, African enterprises learn from local customers and tinker with their products until they reach product-market fit. Yet African enterprises do not usually find large addressable markets close by, and both infrastructures and demand for digital products are fragmented and sparse. So long as their resources allowed, the digital enterprises we studied iteratively tested and learned about such conditions and constraints and creatively adapted to them. The theoretical contribution of the chapter is that it enriches general theory on entrepreneurial opportunity recognition and contexts (Alvarez, Barney, and Anderson 2012; Autio et al. 2014) with a sociomaterial practice view of digital entrepreneurship (Avle and Lindtner 2016; Davidson and Vaast 2010; Katila, Laine, and Parkkari 2019), refining this perspective using the empirical context of African digital markets and infrastructures outlined in the previous chapter.

Close to Home: How Most African Enterprises Become Specialists for Localization

Ultimately, African digital entrepreneurship is always both local and global. African digital enterprises are never entirely virtual. They are physically embodied in African cities, for instance, through offices, employees, computer hardware, and the like. African digital entrepreneurs and their staff engage in sociomaterial practices, such as investor search, managing the design and development of digital products, or operations and customer acquisition (Avle and Lindtner 2016; Brusoni, Prencipe, and Pavitt 2001; Hersman 2012; Hill and Mudambi 2010; Katila, Laine, and Parkkari 2019).

These may sound like trivial statements, yet they are easily dismissed or glanced over in depictions of digital market opportunities. As chapter 1 indicates, digital markets are often construed as scale-free and unbounded, and thus independent of space and the enterprise's location. We will show in this section why this is a problematic and unrealistic understanding of how markets for digital products are geographically structured, leading to misconceptions and false expectations about possible strategies and scaling potential for African digital enterprises.

Validating Assumptions Requires Rich Market Signals

Most digital enterprises in our sample pursued market opportunities through an iterative, context-dependent process (Alvarez, Barney, and Anderson 2012; Autio et al. 2014). Founders set up a venture because they felt they had discovered a market need, which they believed could now be addressed through digital technology that had recently become available in their local contexts. All founders we interviewed perceived an opportunity brought about by the diffusion of the internet in Africa, assembled a digital product, and then probed into the opportunity by executing a business model. Most discovered specifically a local need that could be addressed by digital technologies. Early on, execution consisted of trial-and-error testing of what worked. Entrepreneurs who had the resources and ability to do so made adjustments whenever they perceived that a signal from customers suggested they should change course.

Such market testing, however, was difficult or impossible to do at a distance. Almost all digital companies in our sample started by focusing on customers in their vicinity (e.g., home city or country). Only a narrow geographical scope allowed them to understand the complexities of what customers needed and to make strategic adjustments in a quick and cost-effective manner:

> We validated our assumptions. When we said "loan," we said "How is this going to work? Are we going to approach banks and say we can do this platform for you, we need to be lending money?" That might not work. We went out there and validated. . . . We started from downstairs, right downstairs, here. We went to the security officers [of our building], I asked them how much they earn, how they go about borrowing money, when they're in need, and a lot of them spoke about associations and a lot of them spoke about . . . need[ing] little amounts before pay day. (CEO of a microloan enterprise in Lagos)

Interpreting market signals and designing a suitable product is difficult for any entrepreneur anywhere. But for many African digital enterprises, this process was particularly challenging because relevant market data was not easily sourced or generated (see Athreye 2005; Li et al. 2012). Even basic exercises like estimating addressable market sizes for a given digital product can be impossible in African contexts because simple statistics on the usage of digital technologies are unreliable or unavailable (Gillwald 2017).

African digital enterprises thus often started with digital product designs and business models inspired by role models from the United States and Europe. Templates for product and business model design were available to them from university courses, massive open online courses, books, and online media, but all this codified learning material was based on Silicon Valley and other role models from high-income countries.

As a result, the digital enterprises in our sample realized that foreign templates needed significant modifications to become applicable in African contexts (Rodrigues et al. 2018; Weiss and Weber 2016; Williams and Woodson 2012). They mostly had no other choice but to try something that looked workable at face value, then develop locally relevant knowledge from experience. But to be able to learn from experience, enterprises literally needed to "be there," gathering and interpreting market signals that would be unforeseeable from a distance:

> Thank God Nairobi has traffic, because in the traffic, that's when we get more orders, because someone has nothing to do except flip through your phone [*laughter*]. . . . At 4:00 p.m. until 7:00 p.m., you can tell [from our user data], there is something happening. (E-commerce entrepreneur in Nairobi)

Adopt, Adapt, and Improve

> We seem to have copied the same Silicon Valley theatre in Africa, but the difference in Africa is, each event I attend is typically filled with the same set of people or the same ideas recycled once again. Startups I meet are almost always into payments, e-commerce, education or agriculture with little iteration. This charade cannot continue. Building the future involves "building and growing." (Asemota 2018)

African enterprises learned that several complementary enabling resources, systems, and infrastructures were needed to make foreign digital enterprise strategy templates work (see Williams and Woodson 2012). They realized that the business models suggested in popular business and technology literature take for granted things like addresses and dense logistics infrastructures, workers' experience with using smartphones, or the availability of digital payment channels—all foundational requirements for most e-commerce and gig economy products in high-income countries (Uber, Deliveroo, Amazon Marketplace, etc.). Locally specific formal and informal

---

Box 3.1

Crossing the Border Begins Online

We visit an enterprise in Yaoundé, which is built on the requirements for Cameroonians' travel to France. The manager indicates that each transaction on their platform costs between $500 and $1,000, revealing not only the cost of legal travel but also customers' willingness to pay. The connections between former colonies and colonizing nations are evident in directions of travel. Many Cameroonians in French-speaking Cameroon look to France as the ideal place to relocate for education and to improve their life prospects. The firm's web-based platform and software application enable customers to submit and receive certifications that legitimate their visa applications. The company has been so successful that it has expanded into Burkina Faso and Mali, despite variations in banking regulatory environments. It does not operate in English-speaking Cameroon because residents of that part of the country tend to travel to Germany, the United Kingdom, and the United States, further illustrating the persistence of postcolonial ties. To serve customers in Western Cameroon, the firm would have to develop networks with banks, political actors, and individual embassies of the Western countries. In the absence of shared language and long-standing connections within Françafrique, making new ties to Anglophone Africa make no business sense.

---

institutions (e.g., laws, social norms, trust in technology) constrain market boundaries and require further adaptations (see box 3.1). For instance, an online learning provider in the Ivory Coast realized that companies were not prepared to create and upload digital courses, but instead needed someone else to create the content for them. Digital enterprises across all sampled cities highlighted that customers were missing easy-to-use and seamlessly integrated technology bundles rather than just apps or software:

> When we started, we said, "Oh, this market needs this software." . . . But also we realized that there was a huge need for devices. So we were going to people; they say, "You're proposing a software but we need also some computers. We need also some website." We kind of sensed that the market wasn't—for them, an IT should do anything that is related to IT. We, as young entrepreneurs, lost focus in the meantime. . . . We were finding ourselves stopping the software part . . . looking [more] like [an] emergency team. (Entrepreneur in Rwanda)

Once entrepreneurs were clear about the market need, they realized a functional digital product and tested the market's response. A few enterprises we interviewed were able to define a digital product that fit a market need rather swiftly and easily. This seemed to be the case wherever there was pent-up but unmet local consumer demand for cheap, easy-to-use digital services fulfilling a basic need. Entrepreneurs who were keen observers of their environments could develop tools that automated or facilitated a preexisting practice. Examples included a job board, a digitally enabled payday microloan provider, an app to hail motorcycle couriers, and an e-commerce site aggregating and digitizing secondhand clothes supplies (using Facebook and WhatsApp for customer interactions and offering a central warehouse for self-pick-up and cash on delivery):

> You can feel people and you can understand, when I design products, those people will use [them], not because they have money or not. They will use [them] because they will get connected to this product. . . . Our challenge every day is to be this kind of agency who understands people, more than tools. So, I understand my city, I understand where I live. (Entrepreneur in Maputo)

In most cases, however, unexpected preferences and challenges transpired from initial customer responses, requiring entrepreneurs to iteratively adjust their understanding of what exactly the market need was and how they could address it. The CEO of a local news portal describes a resource-intensive process of stepwise testing:

> I feel like I'm wearing my little white coat every day and tweaking things. So we assume certain things . . . then how can we test those hypotheses in the least costly way possible. . . . The readers are not in love with what we're producing. We're doing okay . . . but we definitely have not stumbled upon the format and topic and delivery that just takes off. We can read it in the data, immediately. . . . We were bleeding a lot of cash, printing—imagine the logistics! Our sales guy was here and he cost a lot of money as well, so we stopped it. It cost us quite a lot of money to do that but by then we had a bit of a breakthrough with our content, we used to do quite traditional content, like normal local news, and then we decided to do much lighter stuff . . . and that's when our traffic really took off . . . so that now we were able to actually provide online advertisement to big brands at the national level.

Within their local contexts, entrepreneurs thus became experts for digital market niches. These were often defined by preexisting socioeconomic conditions and boundaries, like those of sectors and industries (see Drouillard 2017). An information portal founder discovered a rather opposite market reality in the financial sector compared to the previously cited entrepreneur:

So [the original portal] was really going to be more of news, community, essentially like discussion forums and a lot of news components. [My investors] felt it scaled a lot. . . . At some point I stopped following what they were proposing and I started doing a lot more longer form factual content—and our traffic skyrocketed. . . . [Our users] trust us for our research, for our writing, for our content.

Improving products usually also was impossible at a distance, based on digitally mediated customer interactions alone, even when the ultimate product was meant to be a piece of software or an app:

Why not make a digital platform available and that's it? Funny enough, it doesn't work that way and I think it's because it's transport, I really don't know. First, someone has to know the routes [here in Lagos], but if I'm not knowledgeable about Abuja, I can't tell the customer that "Oh, we don't have this route, but I think you can pass this route." . . . That's why we need at least two people set up there [in Abuja] and make the platform . . . The technology is not hard, it's just the knowledge of the area that is important, that's where we need people. (Ride-sharing entrepreneur in Nigeria)

Over time, entrepreneurs thus developed more complete but also more locally specific definitions of the market need and how they could go about meeting it. Put simply, digital businesses did not come out of nowhere, and digital technologies could not be plugged into local markets. Instead, digital enterprises developed experience and insight over time, refining their strategies and product designs, localizing initially foreign technologies and business models.

Market Segmentation According to Founders' Social Networks

For digital technologies to be useful and commercially viable at the sites of adoption, they need to be appropriate (Wyche and Murphy 2012; Wyche and Steinfield 2016) and *appropriable*, which refers to a process of synchronization with local environments (Odumosu 2009, 2017).[1] Environments that select for particular entrepreneurs effectively also are selecting for particular customers. Proximity to users facilitates developing understandings of how best to cater to them and design products that they can appropriate. Distance, be it spatial or cultural, only makes it harder for this knowledge gap to be filled.

Accordingly, entrepreneurs often converted their social networks into customers, especially for business-to-business models. This was usually via a combination of social contacts wanting to support them and those contacts' financial wherewithal. For instance, an entrepreneur who developed a product within urban elite circles was more successful at attracting those groups to become customers of his grocery e-commerce delivery business than nonelites (box 3.2).

Driving Adoption and Focusing on the Revenue at Hand

Such iterative entrepreneurial learning requires time and resources. African digital enterprises employed the financial capital, infrastructures, and

---

Box 3.2
Word of Mouth

Many entrepreneurs mentioned word of mouth as an essential channel for getting clients. The importance of word of mouth indicates that the insertion of digital tools within markets does not replace the importance of social capital.

An e-commerce entrepreneur in Kampala provides a good example. His service delivers groceries to customers' doors. He developed the idea after growing a list of customers for whom he had run shopping errands. He began by doing the Saturday morning shopping for his sister. His sister's neighbors, willing to support him and also interested in avoiding the traffic and bustle of shopping in the city, also began handing him shopping lists and paying him to run their errands. As word of mouth grew, he was able to hire staff who collected shopping lists from customers around town, in person, and eventually over the phone. Shopping lists read out over the phone, however, increased the number of errors in the process, which led him to automate the process of ordering through an e-commerce site.

The expectation that this would lead to more customers, however, was not met. He was able to get customers in his immediate social networks to support his enterprise, but beyond those networks, this proved more challenging. In fact, even many of his existing customers failed to transition to the platform, probably shying away from the cost of data and unwilling to form new habits. The entrepreneur also speculated that people did not trust unknown quantities. Perhaps by eliminating the human element he had increased the distance between himself and the customer and thus increased the need for proxies of trust. He also spoke to us of the damaging perception that the service is for elite urbanites and expatriates. The founder's original background is a social environment in which this service would be considered an unseemly luxury. Digitization had transformed what seemed to be a simple grocery errand business into something that was culturally inaccessible to his social group.

support networks (partners, mentors, investors, applicable regulations, offices, etc.) at their disposal to improve digital products and their potential to turn a profit. Given user and technology capacity challenges (see chapter 2), many enterprises complemented software rollouts with painstaking analog work to drive adoption:

> Within the next three months, we want to acquire some more users than ever, and the way we want to achieve that is, first, by making info sessions, at the universities. The other one is online marketing. (Task platform founder in Ethiopia)

Crucially, most of the digital enterprises we studied were unable to raise significant financial investments, and they were thus constrained to business models that would predictably generate revenue in the short term. Customer trust was an oft-mentioned prerequisite for revenue generation: African consumers and businesses were described as skeptical about making payments based on digital interactions alone. To build up a baseline of trust, African digital enterprises engaged in brand building and direct customer engagement—for instance, through face-to-face interactions, phone calls, or establishing a physical office that customers can visit. Especially providers of specialized digital products for large businesses required consistent and direct customer engagement:

> The people we target are enterprise [customers]. . . . [It's a] gradual scaling process . . . the sales cycle has [now] been reduced. Why is that? One is we're more proven. . . . Number two is, we understand even better what they need to hear because . . . we know the KPIs and we know the budgets. . . . It becomes a lot more seamless. (Logistics provider in Lagos)

These enterprises were thus further locked into local markets because only within their geographical proximity were they able to cost-effectively establish the analog outreach that (paying) customers asked for.

Global Competition, at Home and Abroad

Most African digital enterprises thus engage in extensive localization: through cheap trial-and-error exercises, they perfect strategies that adapt digital technologies to local market needs. One may argue that this was in no way different for a company like Facebook or Airbnb: their founders discovered a market opportunity in their immediate local social context, developed a digital product, and scaled it "organically" in domestic markets until eventually hitting hockey-stick growth and benefitting from network effects.

However, precisely because those companies pursued these strategies for many years, successfully conquering winner-take-all markets, exponential scaling at international scale becomes impossible for African digital enterprises. Our sample included two ventures in Accra that strategized that they could offer products equivalent to the solutions of market leaders in high-income countries, but more cheaply given lower labor costs in Ghana. These enterprises soon realized that they could not entirely avoid postsale customer interaction at distance and that it was difficult to outcompete better-resourced enterprises from high-income countries in terms of achieving network effects and other scaling economies:

> You would have a case where a customer is awake in the US; it's midnight [here]. They send a ticket and they expect a speedy resolution to the issue. When you don't do that, they get angry or give a negative review or they uninstall the app, and even if you want to do sales, it was a big problem. . . . If you look in terms of customers, in terms of raising money . . . our platform, is it much more robust? Can we compete with some of the . . . companies that we started out with back in the day? The answer is no. The technology probably didn't scale the way we wanted it to; customers didn't go the way we wanted; revenue also. . . . If we had investments, we could make a difference because, at a point, we're constrained by the talent and engineering. Getting the required kind of engineer to scale the platform as we wanted back in Ghana was a big problem. (Online marketing tool provider in Ghana)

An entrepreneur in Ethiopia describes a similar problem for the software market: that it is impossible to compete with global providers without being able to hire world-class local software engineering talent—and a lot of it. He outlines that he contemplated competing for cutting-edge programming projects at global scale, but thought better of it:

> We have enough projects on hand . . . and also you'll have [the problem of] scalability. When you take one project, a big project, you instantly should hire, train staff. You can't compete with those people. I mean, they can bid projects with two people, when they got that project, instantly they hire. If you are in Silicon Valley, it's easy to hire anyone.

Another example was a Nigerian-founded community-based lifestyle app targeting smartphone users on Google Play. The app struggled to attract a critical mass of users to achieve self-sustained user base growth (see Caribou Digital 2016).

Catering to customers abroad produces further difficulties, particularly related to financial flows, standardization, and interoperability (Akpan 2011; Avle and Lindtner 2016; Hill and Mudambi 2010). For instance, international provider rules make it difficult for local companies to process international credit card payments. A men's fashion enterprise in the Ivory Coast thus had to use Shopify to sell to its US-based customers—but credit card processing companies like Square or Shopify often do not accept African vendors. Because one of the company's partners was US-based, it could act as an American e-commerce company with an Ivorian supply chain. Ivorian customers, on the other hand, have had difficulty using their credit cards on the platform.

Ultimately, those enterprises that addressed markets in high-income countries either occupied niches or used ad hoc relationships, or they ended up facing intensified competition. African digital enterprises had to create new localized digital products (i.e., they created new local markets) or differentiate from international competition or both. In any case, enterprises *exploited their location in an African city as an asset*. African digital enterprises typically remain local even after product-market fit because whenever they address a digital product category that can scale internationally, there is likely to be better-resourced, more experienced, and technologically more advanced competition from elsewhere that has already occupied the market or is in the process of doing so.

In fact, African digital enterprises increasingly face international competition at home. Digital multinational corporations scale across geographies, have authority, and mobilize transnational capital. This is an existential challenge for digital enterprises in Africa that happen to operate in the same product market. An entrepreneur in Nairobi who has previously been successful in the enterprise banking software market speaks about the difficulty of launching a mass-market taxi-hailing app and competing with Uber:

> I think, the only problem I think we have with Uber is more and more it's becoming the battle of capital and not battle of innovation. Because these guys have a lot of capital, sometimes we really suffer. (Digital entrepreneur in Nairobi)

Another entrepreneur we interviewed in Abidjan faces new competition from Uber, which has just set up shop there. Aside from the fact that the company is well-financed, the fact that local policymakers view Uber's attraction to the locale as a policy success (box 3.3) means that incentives

Box 3.3

When Postcolonialism and Silicon Valley Competition Conspire

The Ivory Coast has made concerted efforts to ease relocation—that is, if one qualifies as an investor. Entrepreneurs who relocate and enterprises that receive foreign investments benefit from tax credits that allow them to operate without paying taxes for seven to fifteen years, depending on the applicable legislation.

Ivorian digital entrepreneurs can benefit from these laws if they are able to show that they have received foreign investment. The rules, however, are not extended to digital enterprises that had been founded on the investments of Ivorians alone.

The colonial history of the Ivory Coast is a factor: France has been involved in the development of these regulations, and because French companies are the prevalent foreign investors in the Ivory Coast, they are the primary beneficiaries of the benefits.

Toward the end of our Abidjan visit, Uber opens an office in Plateau, the city's business district. The owner of a local taxi-hailing company notes that the government's favoring of foreigners is not only reflected in policies. He has never had the same access to government officials as Uber did when it arrived. Whereas he had to build and nurture relationships over time, Uber's clout gives it a vast competitive advantage.

like tax breaks are put in place to attract foreign companies, but not to support his company's advancement:

> You know, when Uber came to Abidjan they went to meet the director of CEPICI [Ivory Coast Investment Promotion Centre]. I've never met him. The time they went to the ministry; I've never met the ministry. They have access to all our government, but for us to have access to them it is not easy, it is very difficult. Very, very difficult.

Companies like Uber have been able to enter into markets around the world without ever showing a profit. Investors continue to finance its expansion, trusting in projections that these firms will produce the desired results in several years. Things are different for their African competitors:

> I mean maybe in Europe, yes, you look at all the Instagrams of this world and whatnot, the WhatsApps of this world, but in the African market where ideas, successful ideas are the basic ones, the ability for these ideas to make money is very, very critical and there is no how you're going to show that other than actually making the real money and paying the bills" (Entrepreneur in Lagos)

For entrepreneurs not bolstered by cash injections from investors, international expansion is thus reliant on revenues. Blindly acquiring users in the hope of future returns seems like a vain and futile exercise to them:

> Okay, so there is something about Africa also. In Africa, you take the market for what it is. If you try to want to correct or change the culture of people, you better have like $200 million to do that. (Entrepreneur in Lagos)

> So you find yourself spending a lot of energy trying to change the mindset to have people use the platform online which is not [a task] for startuppers. That's for bigger companies like MTN, Orange who have all the billions, they can invest in Yu Mobile Money through that and invest to have people change cultures yeah. (Entrepreneur in Yaoundé)

On the contrary, careful localization of digital products functions as protection from better-funded international competition:

> What's the deeper lessons learned? It took me like three years . . . where I think, [now] it would be hard for [other] companies to move faster, because [our] business model is maybe a unique hybrid or an iteration of existing business models, but something that probably hasn't worked successfully in another place yet. It takes a long time to get those lessons learned. I think . . . everybody's maybe in too much of a rush here. (Founder of ride-sharing enterprise in East Africa)

Given their geographical starting point and everything that goes with it (especially limited resources and challenging nearby markets), our analysis suggests that it is therefore a rational and maybe optimal strategy for most African digital enterprises to become *specialists of localization.* The digital markets of African cities and nations (and of other economic peripheries) are riddled with infrastructural and institutional challenges, generating small but more immediate and protected niches for digital products that represent local adaptations of digital technologies. The diffusion of the internet and digital infrastructure thus creates fertile ground for the emergence of successful and innovative ventures, but the market boundaries for their newly created digital products are inherently more bounded than those of Silicon Valley role models.

Pan-African Expansion: Resources and Relationships

So far, we have shown that very few African digital enterprises target markets abroad (chapter 2) and that successful strategies often involve becoming localization experts (previous section). The question that we have not yet examined is what happens when African digital enterprises actively try to reach customers abroad. Are digital enterprises trying and failing to expand, or are there indeed easy market opportunities that they are simply not aware of?

Many digital enterprises in our sample had the ambition to address foreign markets, but most of them saw this as something to think about in the future. In our sample, 18 out of 135 digital enterprises addressed customers abroad. Six of them targeted other African countries and five high-income countries (see chapter 2).

Pan-African scaling meant adapting an initially homegrown digital product abroad. The six Pan-African scalers in our sample fell into three categories:

1. Companies having received large amounts of risk investment, allowing them to establish operations and networks in several African countries in parallel, addressing a widespread issue or creating a Pan-African structure (e.g., Jumia/Africa Internet Group, Andela, Flutterwave)

2. Older companies that had become leaders in large domestic markets and used previous revenue, reputational advantages, and customer relationships for iterative expansion (e.g., Jobberman in Nigeria, Hubtel in Ghana, Craft Silicon in Kenya)

3. Midsize companies establishing small offices or stationing a representative abroad, following ad hoc demand that arose from relationships (e.g., BudgIT in Nigeria, WeFly Agri in the Ivory Coast)

Notably, this list only includes digital enterprises that have some combination of financial resources, persistence, and trusted networks at their disposal. Our analysis suggests that this is due to two reasons. First, foreign markets bring new, unexpected pitfalls that require digital entrepreneurs to make adaptations to the original digital product. Second, setting up some sort of permanent physical presence abroad is usually necessary to effectively address a new market, and this is a costly endeavor that small and young digital enterprises can rarely afford.

Market Fragmentation Requires Product Innovations

I'll do it. I'll scale my company to what I want it to scale, but I can't scale it to look at Africa [as a whole]. It's naïve that Africa is one country. (Founder in Addis Ababa)

Given extreme digital market fragmentation across Africa, it may be unsurprising that simply duplicating a digital product from one African country
to another is not among the strategies we have found to work. Achieving
product-market fit sometimes led to fast growth, but a first threshold was
reached where a homogeneous home market (neighborhood, city, farming
region, nation, etc.) was exhausted:

> We have an office with Sierra Leone, we don't have [one] for Ghana, yet. We're try-
> ing to get Ghana but scaling is something that I'm really, really conservative about
> because I know the culture. The contexts are always different. [Just] because it
> works in Nigeria, it won't work with Sierra Leone. (Digital entrepreneur in Nigeria)

Some entrepreneurs attempt franchise models, in which technology
stacks stay similar across sites and franchisees conduct localization (see box
3.4). Others argue that focusing on local perfection is necessary even when
the technological components of the product remain the same:

> I think [the] technology would stay quite similar if you're going to Uganda or
> Kenya. . . . But say, for an example, the concept of how long people would wait
> for [the taxi], or the pricing mechanisms, or the incentive structures [for the driv-
> ers], would be quite different. . . . The consumer product you'd be building—we'd
> need to have a different field and marketing and business model for Kenya. . . .
> This is a slower approach, [not] rushing into other markets as quickly as pos-
> sible . . . in line with what the realities of these markets are—which is, every
> country does have its own unique lessons to learn. There's a lot of risk involved,
> specifically when you consider how much markets are based off of human net
> worth, corruption, nonopen markets, friction points. I think, rather than trying
> to do a numbers game but like, trying to get ten million customers, [it's bet-
> ter] focusing on what's the highest profit per customer and trying to increase
> profitability at every point, rather than increasing growth with low profitability
> point. . . . I actually think that the concept of these startups that work across
> Africa without having modifications is not really realistic. (Mobility entrepreneur
> in Kigali)

There is usually no way for entrepreneurs to know ahead of time
whether digital products work abroad. Interviewees spoke of the difficulty
of expanding even as far as the neighboring country. They were aware that
expanding may mean needing to go through another painstaking localization process—and this time at distance. Many concluded that acting slowly
and carefully, learning cheap lessons step by step, was the best way to go:

> I was in Tanzania a while back, and they really have bad fabrics in their clothes
> and it's such a sunny place, and then they don't have a secondhand clothes

---

Box 3.4

Taxi!

The founder of one of the many taxi-hailing applications that we came across in our fieldwork talked about the team's initial expectation that the company would have the same trajectory as Uber: "Open an office, hire a team, launch the product, but it's super capital-intensive." They found that African capital markets are not structured to support firms the way Silicon Valley capital markets do. The team also discovered that markets were much smaller, which made them far riskier to enter. "Everything pointed to derisking our expansion and again, looking at the capital markets saying all right, if they're not going to support it, how can we actually turn expansion from a cost center into a revenue center and be able to do it so much faster." They pivoted to establish a continent-wide network of interoperable taxi applications but were willing to outsource the operations and marketing to local franchisees who understood their local markets better. They felt that a difference between Africa and other places "is that the taxi market from city to city to city is quite different; comparing the taxi market from Chicago to New York to San Francisco to LA, they're pretty similar." The founder predicted that a big monolith like Uber would be unable to localize well. The learnings that he and his team had developed from Nairobi required them to embed trust as a feature of their product. He indicated that "there's no other place that the trust concept I think could have been born. Again, if we think about why Uber is built the way it is and why Lyft is built the way it is and why Easy Taxi is built, they're a product of their environments."

[market]. I feel that is a market we'd want to test out. We just need to know how things work, which is why I'm going to Rwanda, but then [my partner] will go to Tanzania to take a look, and then we can now decide from that if we want to move forward or not. . . . We would want to find . . . to get us going, a local person . . . living in your own country is easier. [*laughter*] (Last-mile platform entrepreneur in East Africa)

There's a huge opportunity in Ethiopia and that's exciting [but] one of the partners [of our fund] had made an investment in Ethiopia, personal funds, and they saw it grow like this [*points up*], but it was shut down by the government. It was a bit of a learning that, if we're going to be able to figure Ethiopia out, we have to do it properly. And yes, it can be expensive right now. (Investor in Nairobi)

Entrepreneurs in Francophone Africa also aspired to Pan-African expansion, but not usually into Anglophone or Lusophone nations. For instance, an online learning provider in Côte d'Ivoire reported that translating course material into English would be too costly. Other accounts showed that, for digital just as for traditional enterprises, postcolonial and language geographies determine patterns of trade more than physical distance. For example, a French-speaking entrepreneur we interviewed in Yaoundé had customers in Cameroon, Mali, and Burkina Faso, with plans for imminent expansion to Gabon, Ivory Coast, Morocco, Algeria, and Tunisia—all countries where French is a major language. We also found cases of enterprises with Moroccan customers in Dakar and Abidjan.

Setting Up Local Operations at a Distance Is Necessary but Costly

Once a digital enterprise decided to address a foreign African market, it was generally confronted with the necessity of setting up a local representation abroad:

> Largely, it's a function of cost on us. Where do customers want to see our presence? In Nigeria, we have nine clients that are financial institutions—and financial institutions are very big on physical presence. (Entrepreneur in Lagos)

As in this case, the purpose of a presence abroad was almost always to establish customer and partner networks, which were required for revenue generation and to learn about market needs. A Nigerian founder of a platform that became a domestic market leader before expanding abroad points to the need for building up financial resources:

> Africa is very fragmented and it comes with its own bottlenecks. In the early stages, you don't want to keep all the complexities of the African market. I remember when we wanted to set up in Ghana: it was hell. Just Ghana—it was hell . . . regulations, registrations, regulations. It was—I won't say mess, but it was very tough. . . . If it's purely online, virtual, good! Awesome! just create a page and create some payment platform, and you're good. . . . But in something where you have to do some real operations . . . win your market, make a lot of cash; then you can go to other markets and use that cash to go fight, but if you're still bleeding in your local market, I'd advise, "Stay in your market!" [*laughter*]

A few enterprises in our sample also managed to expand without setting up foreign offices, namely by doing referral-based work for clients abroad. The founder of a Pan-African enterprise describes this process:

> [The expansion beyond Kenya] happened in the same way [as the domestic expansion]. We got one customer [who] was well-connected . . . so he liked what I used to do, and he was a good promoter for us. . . . So from there I got exposure to five [African] countries.

However, interviews with founders of younger enterprises reveal that the scope of such expansions is typically piecemeal, slow, and ad hoc, at least initially:

> Ghana, it was just an opportunity. . . . Someone recommended us. . . . No [we didn't set up an office]. We just service one client. We didn't want to go into many clients. We were specific. Just one client and it's a continuous project. (ERP provider in Rwanda)

In the end, digital enterprises had to weigh the distant market potential against the cost of foreign operations and the likelihood of effectively penetrating the market. Given problems of market fragmentation and low technological capacity, user-base-scaling approaches were particularly difficult to effect across African nations. Addressable market sizes for many digital products have to be calculated conservatively, often leaving only large African cities as target markets:

> So our [Pan-African expansion covers] ten countries; our target is fourteen cities on the continent. We're currently just . . . in two cities because, how you operationalize something like this, it's a city-to-city conversation. . . . You want to be in a position to really help the storefront. You have to have a field sales team, a support team, an on-boarding team that goes to inspect things like business licenses and all of that. . . . We need a minimum of fifteen thousand businesses that will qualify to be part of our serviceable addressable markets, so Accra obviously qualifies. . . . What we need to sign up to break even, it's around six thousand businesses [per city]. (Small business ERP provider in West Africa)

For businesses that have not been able to generate significant revenue in home markets, funding an expansion is usually elusive, even from one city to another:

> For sure, Douala is the economic capital. But the reason we haven't yet moved to Douala is two things. First, the extra cost to have us get started there, and secondly, we're trying to master our product with the local content before really scaling. . . . We prefer to master . . . and we become like the experts. . . . Why? Because in Cameroon, for people to invest is almost impossible. . . . Banks don't invest in ideas—never, never. . . . You have to really work so hard and try to scale up gradually based on the savings you make. (Entrepreneur in Yaoundé)

An entrepreneur in Kigali is resigned to a scenario in which his enterprise would be sustainable and making money locally, making foreign expansion a bonus but not necessarily the most important goal for his growth:

Actually, you need to have, from day one, have a plan, to make money with your current options, rather than thinking "I'm going to learn how to ride this donkey, so that then I can ride an elephant later." Because, you know, maybe the donkey's the only chance you'll get.

Summary: The Lure of Scalability

The results in this chapter show that only those African digital enterprises that can rely on upfront investments, resources saved from domestic expansion, or trusted relationships with partners and customers are able to pursue opportunity at a distance successfully. Vast scaling economies like those of US digital platforms were unavailable for African digital enterprises. Marginal cost was only decreasing per added customer where markets were homogenous. Yet geographic barriers (correlating with social, cultural, and statutory boundaries) delimited homogeneity at a relatively small scale, mirroring the fragmentation and limited reach of markets for physical goods. Urban and national borders mattered especially: depending on the type of digital product, enterprises almost always reach customers located in their home city or country more easily, while reaching beyond requires major effort.

Exponential network-effect-based growth known from Silicon Valley digital platforms did not materialize here, because distance could only be bridged by maintaining individual customer relationships. In fact, the more distant the market, the more ad hoc and relationship-driven an enterprise's customer base seemed to be. The few African enterprises that tried tapping into existing global software and app markets were unsuccessful because these markets were occupied by superior competition from elsewhere in the world.

The findings in this chapter therefore suggest that the vast and self-sustaining growth paths of role model US digital platforms (see chapter 1) are inherently unavailable to most digital enterprises, in Africa and everywhere else. US role model platforms have been able to blend (1) the fast, cheap, generative scaling of software with (2) a platform business model that incorporates others' value creation into one's own value proposition, with (3) a lock-in strategy in which the firm's products become compulsory end user interfaces or digital building blocks that others depend on, with (4) occupying particular product categories as quasi-monopolists across international markets, and with (5) access to vast financial and human capital where their headquarters are. Through cost advantages, long-term investments, and good timing, cities and regions in East Asia, Southeast Asia, and South Asia have been able to become specialized world-leading production centers for some digital product categories, but the most scalable and ultimately most profitable markets have remained with US-American corporations that started their rise in the early 2000s (Srnicek 2016).

That is why, contrary to early hopes (Adepoju 2015; Tredger 2012), "the next Facebook" or "the next Google" is unlikely to come from Africa. Platform markets as we know them today have already been occupied: there was a particular window of opportunity in industrial evolution (Giachetti and Marchi 2017) that US American incumbents aggressively and astutely pursued. Digital enterprises from Africa and elsewhere in low-income countries will have to develop business models and process innovations (differentiation and localization) to survive in niches that global incumbents find too costly to address. This chapter therefore suggests that we should not expect digital enterprises to generate exponential growth and ultimately transform African economies because they are themselves constrained by local market conditions.

4   Viable Strategies

Chapter 2 highlighted that African digital enterprises focus mostly on domestic and regional markets. Chapter 3 showed how they become deeply entrenched into their local contexts through learning from customers and adapting to conditions, while global competition is overwhelming in digital markets where scaling depends less on physical assets and social relations. The key implication is that African digital enterprises need to use contextualized unique strategies to become sustainable and grow. By virtue of enterprises being located in African cities, these strategies will have to look different from those of Silicon Valley role models. African digital enterprises achieve sustainability not by pretending that the digital market playing field is geographically level, but by doing the opposite: turning their ostensible locational disadvantage into a unique value proposition and competitive advantage.

This chapter analyzes how exactly African digital enterprises do this: how they can become sustainable and grow. There are countless aspects that a given entrepreneur in a given city may learn over time about the complex, diverse, nascent, and uncertain African digital market environments around them. Yet our analysis suggests that most successful digital enterprises pursue one of four strategies: (1) scaling based on customer and partner relationships, (2) becoming local information platforms, (3) investing in local assets that have value for corporate customers in high-income countries, or (4) blending a digital platform backend with an analog structure to reach end users with limited digital infrastructure access (what we call *last-mile platforms*). This chapter dedicates one section to each strategy.

Overall, this chapter shows that the growth trajectory even of successful African digital enterprises very rarely resembles a hockey stick. Instead, almost all enterprises in our sample followed slower, linear scaling patterns, not dissimilar to analog enterprises. The ones that were able to exploit network effects and scale exponentially only did so up to the threshold that their market access allowed them to. In the end, African digital enterprises find ways to achieve sustainability and success, but this takes time, and they often face an upper threshold to growth that is set by proximate economic legacies.

This chapter's scholarly contribution is the development of a theory on competitive digital entrepreneurship strategies in resource-constrained environments and an explication of how analog value creation works in concert with digital infrastructure as an external enabler of entrepreneurial opportunity (Briel, Davidsson, and Recker 2018). The four strategy templates also provide a more concrete understanding of the "Goldilocks embeddedness" of digital enterprises (Quinones, Heeks, and Nicholson 2017) in local and global sociotechnical networks.

Scaling Based on Customer and Partner Relationships

The first strategy is also the oldest: enterprises develop software and scale based on good relationships with customers and partners. This strategy is usually preferred by software development and IT systems companies (like Pivot Access in Rwanda or Champier in Mozambique, as well as freelance software developers and microenterprises). In our sample, localized and often sector-specific enterprise resource planning systems (ERPs), supply chain and logistics management systems, full-service IT consultancies, and business analytics providers were dominant.

In this approach, digital enterprises interact directly with customers (through calls, meetings, conversations, emails, etc.) when selling software, code, and related services to them. Enterprises usually also engage with clients after sales, mostly to conduct maintenance and provide customization to meet evolving client needs. Growth happens when enterprises are able to deliver high technical quality at locally competitive prices because this usually triggers customer referrals or allows enterprises to integrate with larger partner networks. Given the high cost per user that comes with regular trust-based interactions, customer relationship scaling exists almost only as a business-to-business strategy.

We found that this strategy suited the capabilities and constraints of many African digital enterprises. Founders did not typically need large up-front investments: they made the first revenue through their own labor as software developers or worked in very small teams—for instance, using free and open-source software development kits and content management systems (like WordPress or Ruby on Rails) to set up customized websites or servers for local businesses. This strategy is also simple and brings sustainability more predictably for founders: digital enterprises make money immediately after launch, directly from clients instead of from third parties.

For many enterprises in our sample, the strategy was also advantageous because strong local relationships brought protection from global competition. Through customer interactions, digital enterprises learned how to customize products specifically to local customers' needs in ways that off-the-shelf solutions from globally operating providers could not. Moreover, international providers were typically too expensive and offered a level of technical sophistication or complexity that was too high for local demand. Foreign competitors' products were also sometimes unaligned to domestic regulations or other local conditions (e.g., cost-prohibitive/impossible international payment integration, not considering currency risks, no maintenance available in Africa). In most cities we visited, we found local ERP providers who could provide simpler, cheaper, and locally adapted versions of SAP (a global software provider with a focus on ERP software suites). A business analytics provider relates an apt metaphor for this type of differentiation:

> We were like, "Look, you guys are paying $2,000 for [the global incumbent's solution]. Here is almost the same: beautiful design, fantastic data. I'm going to charge you $300." Companies . . . were like: "But you don't have functionality of [the global incumbent]." I'd look at these guys, and I'm like, "Wait . . . you're willing to pay $2,000 for a Lamborghini to sit in Nairobi traffic?"

Finally, customer relationship scaling evolved easily from many entrepreneurs' personal and professional backgrounds. Many entrepreneurs started their own companies after first working at larger local software development firms, and initial customers and partners were often friends or colleagues. Similarly, some entrepreneurs used their unique positioning in local business networks as a foundation of their businesses. In one case in Accra, an entrepreneur had coordinated the financial technology community in the city by running events and an online community. Not only did this let him understand a key market need (fragmented credit information for rural and low-income customers), but he also saw administrative and regulatory pitfalls. Maybe most importantly, he established himself as a trustworthy partner for other financial firms. This founder's social positioning thus made him a trustworthy expert that firms agreed to exchange sensitive financial information with, which both was a prerequisite asset and served as protection from foreign competitors.

Like for this Ghanaian financial tech entrepreneur, large corporate customers often doubled as partners for African digital enterprises. Several entrepreneurs described how they built up trusted relationships in sometimes painstaking and time-intensive encounters with corporate decision-makers because this would pay off once representatives started to exchange internal information and began to solve problems together with entrepreneurs. With very large corporations, enterprises also were able to roll out their software through the corporation's structure (e.g., equipping different offices with the same software or supplying more extensive segments of a supply chain) and to improve both their reputation and experience:

> So, we got Nestlé, a big thing for us, credibility. . . . So there's nobody who is bigger, really. . . . They're renewing, and their account has increased—and we can handle [any other customer as a result]. Whoever you are, we can handle you . . . because we can work with enterprises and we've proven it. . . . Number two is, we understand even better what they need to hear because we know the KPIs, and we know the budgets. . . . It becomes a lot more seamless. (Founder of a food supply chain digital enterprise in West Africa)

The key scaling trade-off of relationship scalers' enterprises was to balance standardizing their digital products with customizing them to each individual client's requirements. At the outset, software development enterprises benefited from production-side scaling economies—namely, the ability to use freely available building blocks like open-source coding repositories, or the near-zero cost of producing additional copies of software. Yet copying and pasting code was rarely enough to gain a satisfied customer willing to pay, meaning that the marginal cost of the second copy tended to be almost as high as that of the first for most relationship scalers. The longer enterprises operated in local contexts, the better they were able to partially standardize their offerings. They learned which building blocks they could most easily repurpose for local customer groups:

So we've been trying building our products for the market but then you realize . . . clients always say, "I want that, but not that." . . . So we custom-build solutions, which is not very sustainable, I must admit. So right now, we're trying to kind of find that niche. . . . Now we are trying to productize some of our services." (Kenyan entrepreneur discussing the rollout of digital learning systems across different schools)

Practically the same trade-off applied to postsale maintenance and support, as a Kenyan small-business ERP provider explains:

The payroll module existed within [our old product]. So that was the same code, but now they're three different products. A lot of the code has been reused, but it's still different products that need to be managed differently . . . so we're very strained when it comes to human capacity and human resources. . . . There's different sets of customers, they're more or less in the same cluster. And then, because we've done this for so many years, it's very unlikely that we ever get questions that you've not had before . . . but with scalability, it will be trouble if we ever get to a point when we have thousands of customers! [*laughter*] At that point, we'd have grown the team and also automated a lot of the support. Already we're doing a lot of it: we've backed up a huge chunk of the systems with self-help videos [and we] will have a bit of user manuals in there that customers can access. But for some reason, people just want to call and ask. . . . It's normal human behavior.

Relationship scalers thus grow step by step, acquiring local customers one by one, with limited opportunities for standardization and scale-free rollout of their services. This means that most of these businesses become sustainable quickly while they mostly remain rather small (five to twenty full-time employees).

The exceptions to this rule were early-mover IT systems companies, usually starting to target local corporate sectors with the highest willingness to pay (like banks, utilities, insurance companies, hotels, or hospitals) from the late 1990s or early 2000s. It appeared that in every city we visited, there was at least one such early-mover local IT company that had grown quite large, with dozens and sometimes hundreds of employees. A founder of a large systems development company in East Africa claims that there is no secret to the enormous growth of his venture into one of the biggest employers in the local technology sector:

I think it just happened. There was no special initiative that I had, and really just, it was a natural growth. You try a few times, you fail, you try again, you fail. Among ten people, one of them would give you an opportunity. That's how

I think it all started. . . . It's purely recommendations from one customer to the other customer, banks in the beginning. . . . I had an IT manager next to my house, so he helped me to get into his bank. Then his bank helped me to get into the other banks and that's how it increased. . . . When [the] first customer came in, I was the only one. Then we made some money, then work came in, so I hired like two other guys. Then again work came in so we hired like another five. It was purely, I think, organic growth. There was nothing like, you know, a business plan [or] investments, it was just how it happened.

Local Information Platforms: Digitizing, Curating, and Mediating Local Content

The second strategy is to become a local information platform that offers relevant digital content to African users that is not otherwise available. Typically, this business model has worked in product categories in which users, advertisers, or other third parties are willing to pay to receive or distribute local information, like news and entertainment, classifieds sites, job boards, agricultural and health information providers, digital learning tools, and bulk SMS and ringtone intermediaries. Information is sometimes crowdsourced from users (e.g., traffic information or local news), but mostly, African digital enterprises engage professional third parties as information providers (bloggers, doctors, advertisers, teachers, etc.). Altogether, the value proposition of such an enterprise is to be a platform that digitizes, curates, and mediates locally relevant information.

Often, African local information platforms adopt similar strategies as their high-income-country counterparts (e.g., investing in brand recognition)—yet they typically make crucial tweaks in response to local conditions. Namely, enterprises typically adjust content and formats to local language and culture, and they make interactivity technologically simple. Laptop or desktop computer functionalities or broadband access are rarely if ever required, and smartphone apps are offered only as a complementary and never as an exclusive interface. For instance, these information portals use simple online forums, Facebook groups, and Twitter as crowdsourcing channels, or they integrate SMS and USSD codes.

While most local information platforms stay small, some first-movers are among the biggest digital enterprises in Africa. In fact, some of the transaction platforms identified in a 2014/2015 Center for Global Enterprise study (David-West and Evans 2015) belong in this category. The authors used desk research to compile data on African platform enterprises that had raised $1 million or more in investments. Among the forty-two identified platforms, long-standing portals with a Pan-African profile are featured, such as IROKOtv, OLX, Cheki, Jobberman, and BrighterMonday. These enterprises exploited windows of opportunity to pursue local market leader status in the early 2010s, later giving them the brand recognition and resources to expand across Africa or to merge with companies that had become domestic market leaders elsewhere (e.g., consolidating under the umbrella of the One Africa Media Group and later Ringier One Africa Media). A founder of a job portal describes an approach not dissimilar to the user base scaling strategy known from US transaction platforms (see chapter 1):

> This [was] before we got funding. . . . At that time, we had to do some growth hacking. . . . At that time [in 2011], even though internet was free on campus, not everybody could access it because you had to know either a lecturer or a friend that could give you some ID [and] internet was available in the town but it was quite expensive . . . At that time, Facebook was pretty much popular within the school community. . . . So what did we do? . . . We were going to invite them to [our page] on Facebook. So our strategy was, invite everybody together, start pushing the jobs through that page and they will click and it will grow from there. [I'd give] you twenty minutes worth of data [for Facebook] but after then, you give me your username and password. I'm not going to use it [other than] to invite people into [our] page. It's a job's page . . . because they really, really wanted to check their Facebook. . . . Before we knew what was happening we got five thousand members, seven thousand members and we started posting jobs into the Facebook page and all of a sudden our traffic started growing . . . and the whole of [our home city and nation] started knowing about [our portal]. . . . We were not really concerned about competition. We were really focused on the product itself, on the website. We wanted to have all the jobs. [We only] asked ourselves, "What are the things that we can do for these guys to use us more?"

While this focus on growing a user base as quickly as possible is similar to, say, Facebook's strategy, it is striking that no African companies have been successful at leading in those information platform markets in which content is entirely user generated. These digital product categories were always dominated by US platforms. For instance, we were unable to find African social network sites, social media, and messenger services (competing with Facebook, Twitter, Instagram, Pinterest, Gmail, or WhatsApp). The few travel portals we found (like Pan-African Jumia Travel [formerly Jovago], Hotels.ng in Nigeria, or GetRooms.co in Ghana) are competing with globally operating platforms like TripAdvisor, Booking.com, Airbnb, and the like, but on a closer look, they differentiate themselves via unique access to local information, typically sourced through extensive partner networks. Platforms that do not offer unique local information appear to have faltered soon after the arrival of broadband and smartphones—when US-based user-generated content platforms started to penetrate the African market and overwhelm local providers with combined national- and international-level network effects. For instance, South African social networking service Mxit, which was initially celebrated as an African role model digital enterprise, stopped operating despite its product design arguably being a better cultural and technological fit to local markets (Chigona and Chigona 2008; Thomas 2015). The local information platform strategy, as we identify it, thus involves a combination of localized procurement and curation of information to compete in the local attention economy of consumer-oriented digital services and applications (see Wu 2016).

Yet local information platforms are *asset-light* (Evans and Gawer 2016) in the sense that they do not build up analog operations to reach end users (e.g., drivers, kiosks, warehouses, agents). Information portals may set up small call centers or digitally facilitate and secure interactions between users, but they do not internalize analog interactions and transactions into their value proposition (e.g., the actual sale of a car is not handled by Cheki). We therefore do not categorize African e-commerce companies with extensive in-house logistics and analog customer outreach under the information portal category, instead discussing them as last-mile platforms ahead.

Although some relatively large African digital enterprises fall into the local information platform category, they have remained much smaller than comparable companies in high-income countries. Our analysis suggests that this is because network effects can only unfold to a smaller extent, given that user-driven interaction and content generation is more limited. As a result, neither user lock-in nor data-driven scaling economies typically materialize (see chapter 1), while returns from online advertising also remain low (see chapter 2). The job portal founder quoted earlier highlights how his company's strategy shifted when the user base scaling effect had been exhausted:

> The growth rate reduced, but at that time, one of the things we were looking at now is to consolidate, make money. . . . The goal is "How do you develop a fantastic revenue model from this [charging employers seeking to advertise

jobs]?" . . . Now one of the other things we did was to also turn off some of the marketing cost.

Distant Markets, Local Assets: Labor, Market, and Culture Brokers

Scaling into high-income countries involved competing internationally by using unique local assets. The most common type of enterprise employing this strategy is the *labor broker*. Unsurprisingly, software outsourcing firms were dominant in this category, including notables like Andela and Gebeya (see box 4.1). To effectively tap into international markets, software outsourcing companies typically conducted dedicated customer acquisition and relationship management, establishing a local office or placing a permanent representative in important target countries. This was typically a response to trust deficits and scale disadvantages toward Asian competitors in the commoditized global software outsourcing market (see Lehdonvirta et al. 2019; Mann and Graham 2016). These enterprises also depended on and actively nurtured local and offline assets (like physical training facilities, employee satisfaction, etc.), even if this can be costly and a financial risk:

> This had to make money. . . . If you're investing infrastructure, so for example, you pay for buildings a year in advance—and these are things that are required for the business to thrive. You pay for generators a year in advance, or two or three years in advance. There is not like a leasing option or anything. You have to buy assets. Computers had to be paid for in full! [*laughter*] So there is very high capex [capital expenditure] to do this very well. (Cofounder of an outsourcing firm)

The smaller outsourcing companies in our sample were typically unable to secure up-front investments. These businesses instead relied on immediate revenue generation, based on long-term trust-based relationships with select foreign customers, referrals, and competing on price:

> We'd develop it, roll it out in Europe, get iterative feedback, make whatever changes are necessary, even . . . compete based on price because . . . we could afford to develop [software] cheaper than our competitors in Europe. (Outsourcing company founder in Yaoundé)

Initial contacts with customers were typically established ad hoc—for instance, through referrals, at events, or from founders' previous stays abroad. In effect, these digital enterprises were customer relationship scalers, but the initial relationships were with customers in high-income countries:

Box 4.1
Andela and Gebeya: African Adaptations of Software Outsourcing

Unabating demand for programming in high-income countries has propelled software outsourcing sectors in the Asia-Pacific region to become major technology employers. African outsourcing has lagged early policy hopes (Mann, Graham, and Friederici 2014; Mann and Graham 2016), but two African digital enterprises, Andela and Gebeya, have recently rekindled optimism and investor interest. Each is offering a unique twist to traditional outsourcing.

Andela started with formal headquarters New York City and a campus in Nigeria, soon expanding across Africa by setting up sites in Nairobi and Rwanda. The word "campus" gives away Andela's ambition: to be more than a soulless software factory and instead offer a full-fledged educational program for young software engineers. Coders are trained over several months, up to a point at which they can conduct projects for customers with little supervision. To become particularly appealing to top graduates, the company heavily invests in a distinct organizational culture and brand. Andela stresses its mantra that "talent is global, but opportunities are not," uses multimedia storytelling about the career potentials of software developers, and emphasizes its high-profile investor network, including Mark Zuckerberg and Generation Investment Management, an investment firm cofounded by Al Gore. Andela's US American and Nigerian team of founders are well-connected, and they have quickly become media darlings, with numerous features in global tech media outlets like TechCrunch (e.g., Shieber 2019). Andela's New York headquarters serves as a legal liaison for its customers, who are mostly based in the US. Andela is a unique example of an ambitious American-African enterprise able to mobilize significant risk capital to build analog structures in African cities at an efficient scale.

The lesser-known but no less ambitious Gebeya attempts to create a marketplace for software developer talent. African coders are matched to suitable jobs from clients from around the world—so far, mostly from Europe. Although Gebeya offers quality control and offers trainings, its approach ultimately employs a lower degree of process control and seeks to leave a greater share of revenue with software developers than that of Andela. Gebeya uses its access to Ethiopia's vast number of technology graduates. Amadou Daffe, Gebeya's CEO and cofounder, also draws on his connections to software developer scenes across Africa, built up through his long-standing work with Coders4Africa. Gebeya recently established a London representation to interface with UK customers.

Last year, [there was] this big Japan-Africa conference, so, [we were] very much featured during that whole thing . . . [but] there are definitely some contracts that we will not even touch. I will not walk into Toyota, or even if they came to us, those are basically deals that will break you, and at this point I'd rather go slow, but we basically get to the finishing line. There is Japan, the people in France, they were talking to us because they saw what we were able to do for the Japanese market. . . . Right now, basically, small- to medium-sized companies are what you might call our niche market and also, startups . . . they can't afford a Japanese developer, then they start looking for outsourcing. (Outsourcing founder in Rwanda)

Beyond labor brokers, we found *market brokers* that directly targeted business customers in high-income countries. These digital enterprises turned local market knowledge into a product with value to organizations in high-income countries. For example, one digital enterprise in Ghana had long functioned as an agricultural information provider for local farmers when it realized that its years of experience and growing database on agricultural supply chains had become a unique asset with value to the global food production industry. The enterprise decided to place an account manager in Geneva, letting this person become a liaison between food corporations and the enterprise's local knowledge and network. At the time of our fieldwork, the enterprise was planning to add technologies like drones and further deepen its farmer network to improve the informational value that it could add to global supply chains. We found similar market brokerage underway from a business analytics provider in Accra, an accountability-oriented social enterprise in Lagos, and a men's fashion e-commerce provider in the Ivory Coast.

The third type of enterprise we found using particular local assets to target an audience in high-income countries is the *culture broker* (cf. Pijnaker and Spronk 2017). In our sample, there was only one example: the success story of Kiro'o Games (box 4.2), located in Yaoundé. It has acquired seventy-five thousand customers, most of them in the United States, by placing its role-playing game on the Steam platform.

Last-Mile Platforms: Asset-Heavy User Base Scaling with a Digital Backend

We're forging ahead into relatively uncharted territory; E-commerce in Africa is a massive market to conquer, but there are no hard and fast prototypes from which to follow; We cannot simply replicate Western models here; we have to build our

Box 4.2

Playing Games

As he opens the gate, the CEO explains that the innocuous façade of the building that houses the studio is purposeful. It's a form of security. Indeed, no one would suspect that inside there are about fifteen designers and programmers employed in the task of creating a web-based role-playing game.

The CEO discusses how he had wanted to design a game to his specifications since he was a teen. In 2013, in his early twenties, he and a partner set up the studio. Although the game play is in English, the app uses Swahili as the language of the game's world rather than one of Cameroon's 255 languages, in order to eliminate a sense of its particularity. This might be effective for a Central African audience, but its African lore, words, and avatars must seem very specific to its primary user base, located in the United States. The CEO hoped that the game could help to counter the negative image that many have of Africa. The game can be found on Steam (a gaming platform), and it has seventy-five thousand users.

Cameroonian developers, and those from many African nations, are not able to sell on the Google Play platform. This acts as a disincentive to the development of a mobile game and reduces the firm's ability to reach customers in Africa. The CEO says that a government official has tried to help by speaking to Google about the lockout, to no avail.

The company has struggled to sell games in Africa, mainly due to its inability to accept digital payments. Platforms like Google Play prevent it from accessing markets, while most locals do not have credit cards. The CEO has taken it upon himself to find a solution. "To be disruptive, I have to fix the problem." He intends to make it possible for people to pay using mobile money. Another problem with the local market is piracy. Apparently, the game costs less than a pirated game would ($4). He feels that piracy has become a habit.

The firm is revenue positive, but not because of the game. It consults for other "startuppers," teaching them how to raise funds, recruit, and manage projects. The company itself has not raised any venture capital, despite frequent international media coverage. Apparently, foreign investors do not believe that there is a business case for a game company in Africa. "I am trying to learn their language. They won't understand me. Their ideas will never work with our realities."

own blueprints from scratch, which takes significant investment, both in terms of time and money. (Hotels.ng founder Mark Essien, quoted in Nsehe 2015)

Last-mile platforms are the fourth and final local asset-driven strategy we identified. Of the three strategies targeting local and regional markets, it is the most interesting one because last-mile platforms combine the scaling potential of digital technologies with an explicit approach to tackling market limitations at scale.

Many African adaptations of e-commerce belong in this category, which includes some of Africa's biggest digital enterprises. Most e-commerce holdings of Africa Internet Group (AIG), Africa's widely celebrated first tech unicorn[1] (Knowledge@Wharton 2016), are last-mile platforms (see chapter 7 for a discussion of AIG's African identity). These holdings were mostly driven by Rocket Internet executing its venture builder approach (Baumann et al. 2018), rolling out e-commerce verticals (Carmudi for cars, Lamudi for real estate, Hellofood for food delivery, Easy Taxi for taxis, etc.) across African nations, and setting up customer-facing local operations (drivers, business development units, call centers, etc.) while centralizing organizational control and the technology stack in Paris and Berlin (Rocket Internet's headquarters). Later, many AIG verticals were consolidated under the Jumia brand. Similar nationally and regionally operating e-commerce providers include Takealot (South Africa), Konga.com (Nigeria), and Tonaton.com (Ghana).

We refer to African e-commerce providers as *last-mile platforms* to draw a distinction from asset-light information platforms and the digital platform business model known from US and Chinese corporations (see chapter 1; Evans and Gawer 2016; Parker, Van Alstyne, and Choudary 2016). We find that last-mile platforms actively address market barriers in the local analog world (see chapter 2). What they offer African end users is usually similar to what American digital platforms would offer their end users: for example, both Konga.com and Amazon allow users to have an electronics product delivered to their homes. But how customers are reached and which elements of the supply chain are internalized by those two platforms radically differs.

A last-mile platform compensates for incomplete internet access, digital infrastructures, and technological capacities by building up an *analog outreach structure* that complements its digital platform. These enterprises are asset-heavy: they actively create physical points of interaction for end users, as well as extensive physical supply chains. Analog outreach structures typically consist of a combination of the following approaches:

- *Human intermediary between customer and technology:* A person (agent, driver, etc.) equipped with a device (POS device, tablet, or smartphone), interacting face to face with the customer wherever convenient for them (farm, busy intersection, local marketplace, etc.) to conduct transactions (e.g., cash on delivery) or digitize the customer's information (e.g., recording a farmer's stock)

- *Customer and supply chain training and onboarding:* Extensive technology- and product-related workshops and seminars for customers and operational staff (agents, drivers, etc.)

- *Physical supply chain and logistics:* Warehouses, drivers, motorcycles, and so on as proprietary company assets rather than outsourced to third parties

- *Low-tech customer support:* Enabling SMS, USSD, and WhatsApp-based support; building up local call center capacity for quick callbacks

A Ghanaian e-commerce entrepreneur explains how market needs drove him to adopt these strategies, despite the higher cost:

> Ideally, we want the business to be run online. It would help us scale faster but we still have . . . a customer service person take his [the customer's] call because either he's not too comfortable browsing or they want the face behind the website. . . . We have that option because we can't stop people . . . so we help them through the process. . . . We get our . . . leads monthly, 45 percent [via] SMS, about 33 percent would be calls, and then rest emails.

While African e-commerce providers have been recognized to employ these strategies (David-West and Evans 2015; Kaplan 2018), the last-mile platforms in our sample cover other domains as well, such as payments (using kiosks and agents to allow customers to buy mobile credit), agriculture (stock management and aggregation for small-holder farmers), logistics (aggregating domestic shipping demand for small businesses), and connectivity (solar-powered internet kiosks aggregating local content and services). Star products like M-Pesa and M-Kopa Solar are also last-mile platforms per our definition: they are celebrated as digital enterprises, but their key innovations lie in how they blend digital scaling potential and physically reaching out to millions of end users (Joseph 2017).

These examples show that last-mile platforms can grow relatively large and benefit from network effects, provided they are able to establish a solid and widespread user-facing structure. Still, the growth that last-mile platforms can achieve is inherently slower than that of asset-light digital platforms from the United States. This is because asset-heavy last-mile platforms by definition face higher marginal costs per user, and they by definition lose out on some of the potential of digital technologies to let users cocreate value (see chapter 1). African platforms thus internalize a larger proportion of total value creation compared to known digital platforms from high-income countries. As a result, they have to achieve relatively higher margins in a context in which users and advertisers usually have a low willingness to pay (see chapter 2).

This insight may explain why, after an investor gold rush on African e-commerce in the early 2010s, ambitions have recently been tempered. Emerging findings call into question whether asset-heavy platforms can satisfy risk investors' expectations of vast, self-sustaining financial returns upon securing market leader positions. Significantly, media reports indicate that Rocket Internet has withdrawn as the lead investor of AIG (Akinloye 2018; Ekekwe 2015; Mutegi 2017). Disrupt Africa (2017a), using 2015–2017 data from 264 e-commerce providers active across twenty-three African nations, assesses that less than 30 percent of those providers were profitable.

The entrepreneurial challenge for African last-mile platforms is thus to accept that the build-up of analog outreach structures may be necessary while doing so in a cost-efficient way, drawing on more limited up-front investments. This means last-mile platforms have to be creative when it comes to scaling. They face difficult balancing acts: their market environment may signal that they should internalize and control value creation (top-notch software engineers; owning devices, kiosks, motorcycles; employing drivers, agents, etc.), but this comes at higher cost and higher risk, effectively running counter to the value orchestration idea of digital platforms (see chapter 1). Well-thought-out incentive schemes for field agents are often a must:

I saw you can actually be a vendor and a reseller of airtime . . . so we came up with a scheme of credit. We give [our agents in the field] twenty-four to forty-eight hours of microcredit on services that they can resell—that doubled our revenue! (Internet kiosk provider in East Africa)

Especially in Rwanda, where interviewees often cited their ambition to contribute to the nation's development agenda, founders were satisfied that, through outreach structures, they contributed to job creation for underprivileged populations:

> One thing that I get so grateful [about] is the external layers of [my product] because . . . now close to two hundred people are making commission money out of the system [by selling] airtime, electricity [vouchers]. That's a big number and I feel grateful about it. . . . This is an ecosystem that is always going to be dependent on [our product]. There's always people who are making money because we created the system. (Experienced entrepreneur in Kigali)

Most last-mile platform startups in our sample did not receive major up-front investments, or what they received was used up to build software engineering capacity. As a result, partnerships with well-resourced and well-known local corporations and institutions became an important alternative to improve a platform's branding or outreach structure. The entrepreneurs we interviewed explicitly framed their efforts as building *ecosystems* and *networks*:

> We're building a deeper financial ecosystem for the drivers. . . . We want to make a system that lets them to be able to automatically save money for children's school fees, build an additional credit score. . . . The exciting thing is linking those features in a digital wallet, so that, basically, we can gamify, or make carrots and sticks, for the driver . . . trying to create behavioral incentives, to nudge people towards the way we want to work. (Ride sharing enterprise in East Africa)

> Essentially, what you're asking is the dilemma you face in building a two or even a three-sided marketplace. In our case, the first side you always build is supply because if someone makes a request and then you can't fulfil it, then you've lost that customer and maybe a whole lot more. So it was important to first have capacity on the network, so we started out with three riders. . . . So the way we are scaling is not by considering to buy or finance motorcycles ourselves, not with investor funds, but rather working with top parties who will finance motorcycles, for a very small fee. For example, we've got a partnership with [the regional government] to finance about twenty motorcycles at about 5 percent interest rate per annum, which is much better than the 25–30 percent we'd get from the Nigerian banks. We're also working on a financial scheme to allow more drivers to come on board our network, even if they don't have their own motorcycles. . . . We look at our data, we look at how many deliveries we're doing, we look at all the factors that are influencing our performance. (Delivery provider in West Africa)

In sum, we find that last-mile platforms represent a promising digital enterprise strategy that is well suited to address sizeable African consumer or small-business markets, not because they copy the digital platform model that has been successful at a global scale (Parker, Van Alstyne, and Choudary 2016), but because they explicitly address infrastructural and capacity challenges that transnational competitors cannot address. Yet how exactly analog outreach structures can be blended with digital platform backends is not easily generalizable. Instead, last-mile platforms are currently engaging in intricate process and business model innovations, based on iterative managerial and entrepreneurial learning and intervention (see Athreye 2005; Kashyap and Bhatia 2018; see box 4.3).

Summary: Location-Based Strategies and Hyperlocalization

In this chapter, we presented four strategies that have allowed African digital enterprises to achieve sustainability, detailing our findings from the previous chapter that suggested African enterprises are localization experts. The businesses we analyzed make money and survive. Even self-sustaining user base scaling existed for some platform enterprises in some local and regional market niches (see table 4.1). However, their growth was inherently confined to be slower, and it was capped earlier than for transnational digital platform corporations. Notably, African digital enterprises' value creation and capture strategies almost never used artificial intelligence or other sophisticated data collection and processing techniques—a stark difference to the archetype of the data-driven platform business model (see Mayer-Schönberger and Ramge 2018; Srnicek 2016; Zuboff 2019). Large transnational digital corporations extract data wherever their users are while analyzing the data in specialized centers (Malecki and Moriset 2007; Singh 2017). African digital enterprises, however, may be able to neither target distant markets nor mine and process data at significant scale, which sets a low threshold for growth when local markets are small, as in most African countries.

The most promising digital enterprises blend digital and analog value creation. Such assemblies of locally specific knowledge, organization, finance, and so on are remarkable innovations in their own right (Rodrigues et al. 2018; Taura, Bolat, and Madichie 2019). They have significant scaling potential, but this potential is still not comparable to Silicon Valley business models. Notably, within coherent home markets, self-sustaining, network-effect-driven user base scaling was possible to an extent for some

Box 4.3

AgroCenta: Transforming Food Supply Chains through a Digital-Analog
Agricultural Platform

Francis Obirikorang and Michael Ocansey are about to leave the city, head-
ing toward Ghana's Northern Region, squeezing in our research interview at
the Airport Shell Mall Accra. They insist that digital entrepreneurs—especially
techies like they once were—ought to "get out into the field more" if they really
want to understand how digital products can conquer markets at the bottom
of the pyramid and address the needs of the rural poor, with all their complexities and challenges. The two founders had been coders for most of their
careers, creating well-designed and functional apps and software. They are still
proud of their developer skills, but their experience with launching AgroCenta
taught them that having a great app is a necessary but not a sufficient condition to build a great digital enterprise. After years of engaging with farmers in
the north of Ghana, they realized that the existing supply chain—offtakers
and other middlemen placing orders, shipping whatever produce was there,
and coming back days later to pay and place new orders—came with vast inef-
ficiencies. Goods were spoiled when they were not procured, and smallholder
farmers could not satisfy larger requests on short notice. Across the thousands
of farmers in the region, high-value produce was abundant and sometimes
went to waste, but there was no cost-effective way for offtakers or large corporate customers to understand stock levels.

The market opportunity was now clear: stock management and aggregation of demand and supply across smallholder farmers in the north of Ghana.
However, through their interactions, Francis and Michael knew that farmers
would not independently use digital technologies in the foreseeable future
and that farmers wanted to have cash in hand when selling their produce.
Only a combination of agents equipped with tablets and a digital platform
backend could work to effectively engage all stakeholders of the agricultural
supply chain (farmers, distributors, offtakers and traders, corporate clients).
AgroCenta decided to recruit trusted, locally based agents who regularly
engage with farmers. The enterprise also employed agents with smartphones
to sit on delivery trucks to make sure that less produce gets lost on the way.
For large corporate food producers like Guinness, AgroCenta was soon able to
deliver sufficient quantities of produce at a cost that producers could never
match if they tried to do the same with their own field agents. Over time,
AgroCenta integrated more apps in their product line—for instance, ones
allowing third parties like loan and insurance providers to interface with farmers. Ultimately, AgroCenta created a blended digital-analog regional agricultural platform, solving information, transaction, and allocation problems for
all sides involved.

Table 4.1
Four viable strategies for African digital enterprises

	Value creation	Market scope	Scaling pattern
Relationship scalers	Developing customized software for local business-to-business market	Local corporate sectors (banks, insurances, etc.)	Linear, one-by-one customer acquisition, standardization vs. customization
Local information platforms	Digitizing, curating, and mediating locally relevant information	Local consumers and businesses	Localized user base scaling (network effects) with limited revenue potential (limited online ad market)
Local assets, distant markets	Local assets (labor, market knowledge, culture) with value offered to high-income country clients	Corporate clients in high-income countries	Linear, ad hoc, based on relationships or customer acquisition
Last-mile platforms	Analog outreach structure with agents (drivers, kiosk owners, etc.) and devices (tablets, etc.); digital platform backend	Local consumers and microbusinesses	Localized user base scaling (network effects) at high marginal cost

local information and last-mile platforms. However, we did not find any instances of user base scaling for African digital enterprises targeting high-income countries.

The bottom line of our findings is that impressive individual success stories of digital enterprises exist, but we cannot find strong evidence that a significant number of ventures are attaining the scale that would be necessary for significant local economic development to result from this activity. Contrary to images of swift and easy growth on the back of "ubiquitous" digital technology, the enterprises in our sample almost always experienced slow and painstaking progress.

Contrary to what digital entrepreneurship discourses claim and what management theory implies (see chapter 1), for each strategy, the fact that digital enterprises were located in Africa mattered greatly for effective and

workable strategic choices. In each case, physical space and physical embodiments of digital enterprises (founders and their networks, employees, infrastructures, etc.) affected which market opportunities these enterprises were
able to exploit and how. In each case, the availability of digital technologies
was an external enabler of entrepreneurial opportunity (Briel, Davidsson,
and Recker 2018), but enterprises blended digital technologies with analog local contextual realities. The strategy templates thus provide a more
grounded and concrete sense of what specialization in localization consists
of. Similarly, the templates explain the "Goldilocks embeddedness" of digital enterprises in low- and middle-income countries (Quinones, Heeks, and
Nicholson 2017), highlighting exactly how they become embedded in both
global and local sociotechnical structures.

In the end, African digital enterprises are succeeding by doing the opposite of competing for vast, level, unbounded, global digital markets. The
most successful enterprises *hyperlocalize*, if in ways that still exploit some of
the scaling potential of digital technologies. One experienced investor we
interviewed in Ghana articulates how hyperlocalization may work at scale:

> My thesis is very simple. There are a lot of African businesses that are offline
> that make money. The strategy is that everybody has a phone so my fundamen-
> tal investment is "invest in businesses that are driving those businesses online."
> Simple, because in the innovation world, you are not going to change people with
> technology. You have to look at what people already do and say: "You can do it
> better with technology." . . . Separate companies, and they're mostly in urban
> centers. Then, I want to create a Pan-African delivery company but what I'm
> going to be doing is invest in these guys to become more hyperlocal. So I now
> start getting from Lagos to Abuja . . . it's hyperlocal. So you need to have guys
> who have a lens that is zooming further in—not zooming out. . . . Because really
> the biggest advantage you have is knowing how to deliver in Lagos, and I want
> you to take that and apply it to Abuja; I want you to apply that to Port Harcourt,
> because it will be much more harder for you to come from Nigeria and figure
> that out in Accra. If somebody is [already] doing it in Accra? Great: you become
> partners. He focuses on Ghana, becomes more hyperlocal in Ghana. You become
> more hyperlocal in Lagos and my promise to you is that I can get you DHL, so
> I get you big business. So I get you into the B2B play, which makes you money
> because individually you can't go talk to DHL, but because I create the hold-
> ing corp[oration], which will sit in London or Berlin or somewhere, I can go to
> DHL and say: I can do deliveries, seven countries. . . . DHL doesn't want to be
> hyperlocal—they're a global company.

5   Uneven Ecosystems

In their fittingly titled TechCrunch blog post "The Rise of Silicon Savannah and Africa's Tech Movement," US journalists Jake Bright and Aubrey Hruby (2015b) capture a period of hope and ambition for African digital entrepreneurship:

> Across [Africa,] new Silicon Savannahs are in the making and the components of a budding . . . tech culture and ecosystem emerge. . . . iHub-like innovation centers are becoming a mainstay of the continent's progressing ICT infrastructure. . . . These IT spaces are becoming central connect points for ideas, entrepreneurs, investment, and innovation across the continent.

As is evident in this quote, the setup of Nairobi-based iHub in 2010 and the moniker "Silicon Savannah" to refer to Kenya's technology landscape had turned into symbols for the continent as a whole (we will return to this in chapter 7). Innovation hubs and, with them, the ideas and excitement around digital entrepreneurship had diffused across Africa in a relatively short period of time (Friederici 2019). In the mid-2010s, policymakers and media conveyed that vibrant digital entrepreneurship ecosystems existed everywhere in Africa, with impressive maps visualizing hundreds of innovation hubs (Bayen and Giuliani 2018; Boucher 2016; Firestone and Kelly 2016). Bright and Hruby (2015a) went so far as to proclaim that "the Next Africa" had become "a global [economic] powerhouse."

Chapter 2 already called parts of this narrative into question, highlighting vast differences in digital entrepreneurship activity between African cities. In this chapter, we analyze how and why the observed differences have arisen. In the following section, we first briefly introduce entrepreneurship ecosystem theory. The next section further details unevenness among African digital entrepreneurship ecosystems. The final five sections review the most pressing bottlenecks in African ecosystems.

This chapter shows that ecosystems of digital entrepreneurship have indeed emerged across the eleven analyzed cities. However, the degree to which ecosystems support digital enterprises effectively is drastically different. We discern three tiers of African ecosystems: learning, incipient, and maturing. Worryingly, vicious cycles resulting from bottlenecks in ecosystem evolution can lead to lower-tier systems being stuck at relatively nascent levels.

Our theoretical contribution is to highlight that different types of entrepreneurial resources play different roles as ecosystems evolve (see Mack and Mayer 2016; Motoyama and Knowlton 2017). We also show that enterprises are embedded in ecosystems, but ecosystems are themselves embedded in wider structures. Entrepreneurial resources (e.g., market knowledge, investment capital) must be converted from nonentrepreneurial resources (e.g., markets, traditional capital). We show some of the mechanisms of interactive resource conversion (see Motoyama and Knowlton 2016; Spigel and Harrison 2018) and thus highlight how ecosystems are tied to the economic destinies of their nonentrepreneurial urban and national surroundings.

Entrepreneurial Ecosystems: Concepts and Theory

Practitioners and policymakers find the "entrepreneurial ecosystem" to be an extremely appealing concept (Malecki 2018; Spigel 2017; Stam and Spigel 2018). At the same time, it has caused a lot of confusion and critique (Alvedalen and Boschma 2017; Stam 2015). Therefore, we start this chapter with a short conceptual excursion, outlining what we mean when we talk about entrepreneurial ecosystems.

In Silicon Valley and most large cities in high-income countries, digital enterprises can access an array of support resources in their vicinity. It is easy for founders to talk face to face with experienced entrepreneurs who attempted similar business models. Coworking spaces and incubators are abundant, offering work space and access to partners and peers with related interests. Associations and informal groups of professionals organize regular networking events and share information. Universities provide technology transfer services and coordinate extensive alumni networks that reach into the technology industry. City and national governments give out startup grants with no or few strings attached. Venture capital and angel investors provide venture-suitable funding and organize pitching events and demo days. All these location-based "interdependent actors and factors, coordinated in such a way that they enable productive entrepreneurship within a particular territory" (Stam and Spigel 2018), are summarized in the entrepreneurial ecosystem concept.

The makeup of an entrepreneurial ecosystem has direct consequences for entrepreneurship. Ecosystems differ in *quality*, which is defined as the chance of success for the same growth-oriented enterprise in one ecosystem compared to another. Notably, Silicon Valley's technology industry has been able to simultaneously diversify and specialize (Saxenian 2006), as qualified and experienced entrepreneurs and professionals constantly network and develop new ideas, moving flexibly between positions or starting new ventures (Barley and Kunda 2004; Benner 2008). Ecosystems evolve over years and decades (Saxenian 1994; Storper et al. 2015), harboring complex but potentially generative interdependencies (Ferrary and Granovetter 2009; Spigel and Harrison 2018).

The current dominant understanding of ecosystems sees them as relational (ecosystem elements interdepend to determine ecosystem quality) and processual (ecosystem elements variously affect each other over time to determine the system's evolution in quality; Mack and Mayer 2016; Spigel 2017; Spigel and Harrison 2018). This theory was developed in response to a number of criticisms with regard to policy-driven component-based conceptions of ecosystems (like Babson's model or Startup Genome's ranking)— for instance, that they are static, tautological, and conceptually ambiguous (Alvedalen and Boschma 2017; Stam 2015).

A key concept that relational processual ecosystem theory uses is the notion of *entrepreneurial resources*, defined as "resources specific to the entrepreneurship process . . . rather than other types of industrial benefits found in clusters that accrue to firms of all sizes and ages" (Spigel 2017, 52). Entrepreneurial resources can be cultural (e.g., individuals' willingness to leave stable employment), social (e.g., risk capital from angel investors, talented startup employees, or mentorship), or material (e.g., incubators, physical infrastructure, and policy affecting the startup process) (Spigel 2017).

This entrepreneurship-specific notion of resources has implications for the kind of knowledge that matters for entrepreneurial ecosystem quality and evolution. Spigel and Harrison (2018, 156) note that market and technical knowledge are important, but that *entrepreneurial knowledge* (i.e., knowledge about the entrepreneurial process itself) is just as relevant.

Entrepreneurial knowledge includes "skills such as opportunity identification, business planning, and pitching for investment [as well as] cultural norms regarding how an entrepreneur should act and present themselves to others." Based on this understanding of resources, the theorists posit that entrepreneurial ecosystems are "ongoing processes of the development and flow of entrepreneurial resources. . . . The presence and circulation of these resources helps explain how ecosystems evolve and transform over time and allows us to distinguish between strong, well-functioning ecosystems and weaker, poorly-functioning ones" (Spigel and Harrison 2018, 152).

The key argument is that entrepreneurial ecosystems depend on resource endowments, but also on the system-internal configuration of those resources, which affects whether early-stage, growth-oriented entrepreneurs rather than incumbents, rent seekers, or non-growth-oriented businesses have access to them. Spigel and Harrison (2018, 164) note that it is difficult, if not impossible, to create entrepreneurial ecosystems from scratch. Instead, resources in an ecosystem are enriched over time through mutually beneficial exchanges (mentorship, investments, deals, etc.). Exchanges are based on interpersonal and interorganizational ties, which themselves are based on trust, norms, and contracts.

Ecosystem quality and development thus depend on a system's endowment of entrepreneurial resources, as well as on the interplay of resources. Well-functioning ecosystems are defined as those "with dense networks between entrepreneurs, investors, advisors, and other key actors . . . [which] support the flow of resources within the ecosystem, making it easier for entrepreneurs to access them" (Spigel and Harrison 2018, 161). The higher the quality of an ecosystem, the easier it is for enterprises and their supporters to effectively exchange and augment resources in an ongoing, location-specific process (Mack and Mayer 2016; Spigel and Harrison 2018). At the same time, because different resources depend on each other, the absence of a given resource can become a bottleneck for ecosystem advancement.

Unevenness of African Ecosystems: Discerning Three Tiers

In chapter 2, we introduced the extremely skewed distribution of digital entrepreneurship activity across Africa, with only four countries (South Africa, Nigeria, Egypt, and Kenya) making up 60 percent of Africa's total activity, the next eight covering 25 percent, and the last forty-two countries accounting for the remaining 15 percent. As mentioned, the six metrics used for these calculations have severe limitations and can only be seen as indicative. However, to understand the variation of ecosystem challenges across Africa in more depth, these indicators can usefully be divided into three categories: startups, angel investors, and hubs. When examining the distributions of these categories of digital entrepreneurship organizations separately (see figure 5.1), it becomes apparent that they differ in the degree of skewedness. Namely, the distribution of angel investors across Africa is skewed much more extremely than the distribution of hubs. For instance, in the Angel.co database, 35 percent of all angel investors in Africa are in South Africa, while none at all (0 percent) are located in the bottom thirty-six African countries. For hubs, the skewedness of the distribution is still drastic but less so than for angel investors: South Africa has 18 percent of all African hubs, exactly like the bottom thirty-five African countries combined. Even if we assume that the Angel.co database vastly underrepresents the actual number of angel investors in incipient ecosystems (e.g., because angel investors there do not register on an international database), these stark differences suggest that the degree of skewedness increases from the number of support organizations (like hubs), through the number of startups, to the number of angel investors in African countries.

This is also in line with our own and others' qualitative analysis (see Bramann 2017; Drouillard et al. 2014). We know from interviews that in cities like Kampala, Abidjan, and Kigali, a significant number of digital enterprises have emerged and two or three hubs have been established; yet venture financing like angel and venture capital investments is rare or completely missing. In comparison, digital enterprise numbers are much more limited in cities such as Maputo and Addis Ababa, even if they also boast two or three hubs. In other words, the distribution of digital enterprise activity seems to be more skewed than hub counts appear to suggest. We therefore question estimates of startup activity that extrapolate from the number of hubs, like Bright and Hruby (2015a) are attempting.

These observations lead us to discern *three tiers of African digital entrepreneurship ecosystems* (see table 5.1). These tiers should not be understood as precise or static delineations. For instance, Kigali's ecosystem unites the bottlenecks of tier 2 and 3, while Accra has elements common in tier 1.

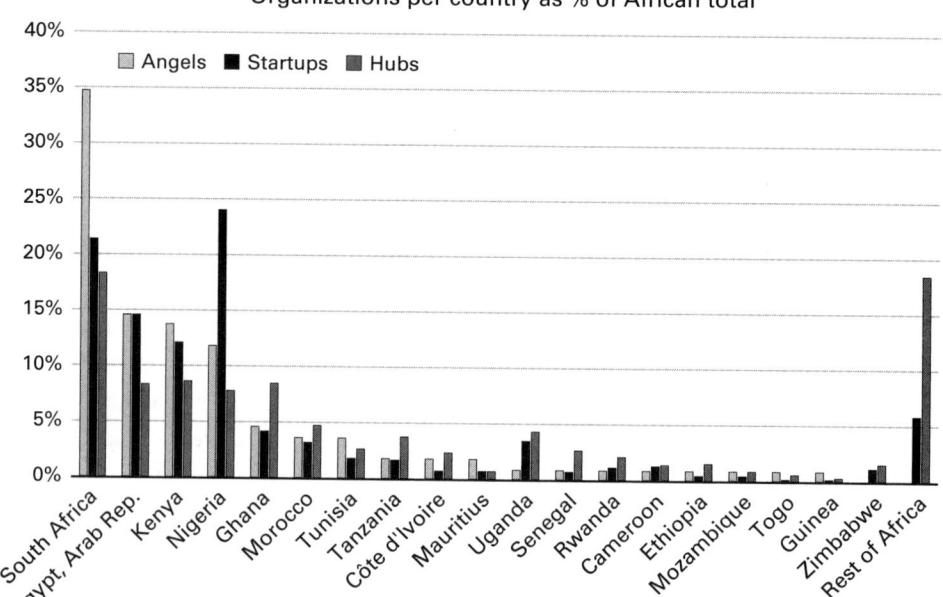

Figure 5.1

Distribution of three types of digital entrepreneurship organizations across Africa. *Note:* Data for fifty-four African countries was analyzed. The bars are percentage values indicating a country's value as a share of the continent-wide total in three categories: angel investors, startups, and hubs. Countries are in the order of highest to lowest value for the "Angels" value. Values for startups are averages of two indicators: F6S.com and Crunchbase.com. Values for angels are based on Angel.co. Values for hubs are averages of three indicators: BongoHive (2017), Firestone and Kelly (2016), and Boucher (2016). "Rest of Africa" includes, in the order of average values from highest to lowest: Zambia, Benin, Mali, Burkina Faso, Seychelles, Botswana, Malawi, Namibia, Angola, Democratic Republic of Congo, Liberia, Algeria, The Gambia, Madagascar, Sierra Leone, Rep. of Congo, Sudan, Burundi, Somalia, Niger, Mauritania, Gabon, Lesotho, Libya, Central African Republic, Swaziland, Djibouti, Sao Tome and Principe, South Sudan, Guinea-Bissau, Comoros, Chad, Cabo Verde, Equatorial Guinea, and Eritrea.

Table 5.1
Three tiers of African digital entrepreneurship ecosystems

Ecosystem tier (cities analyzed in this book)	Number of active innovation hubs[a]	Examples of leading digital enterprises[b] (estimated number of employees)	Ecosystem bottlenecks				
			Markets and infrastructures	Entrepreneurial knowledge and mentorship	Venture labor and talent	Hubs and support organizations	Funding
1—maturing (Lagos, Nairobi, Johannesburg/Pretoria)	Three to eight, including at least one with Pan-African recognition	Africa's Talking, Andela, Cellulant, Craft Silicon, IROKOtv, Interswitch, Paga (100–500)	Leading enterprises address Pan-African or cross-national B2C and B2B[b], make tens of millions of US dollars in annual revenues	Range of experienced entrepreneurs across diverse business models; mentorship exists, but fragmented and not specialized	Specialized and internationally competitive software engineers (algorithms, IoT, financial technology, etc.)	Disconnect between major enterprise success cases and hub scenes; scaling and coordination issues	Internationally competitive venture funding needed for scaling, ticket sizes of US$2–20 million
2—incipient (Accra, Kampala, Dakar, Abidjan, Yaoundé)	Two to four	Hubtel, Rancard, Wari, Taxijet (50–200)	Leading enterprises address national B2C and B2B, or B2B in proximate countries; make millions of US dollars in annual revenues	Several entrepreneurs have achieved product-market fit, including in B2C business models; few of them are mentoring	Engineers with product development and craft skills; "missing middle" affordable high-skilled	"Jack of all trades" syndrome; guiding small ventures to investability	Venture-suitable risk investments (esp. angels) of US$50 thousand to 2 million
3—learning (Kigali, Addis Ababa, Maputo)	One to three	Rwanda Online, Pivot Access, C-Net, Apposit, Emprego (20–150)	Leading enterprises target national B2B, make hundreds of thousands of US dollars in annual revenues	Most entrepreneurs with short experience; have not yet achieved product-market fit; almost no active mentors	Any full-stack software developers	Mobilizing active entrepreneurial community (beyond freelancers and graduates)	Funding of any kind; ticket/grant sizes of US$20 thousand to 1 million

[a]We use "active hubs" as a category here that is qualitatively assessed based on interviews and our own impressions when visiting hubs. We also exclude incubators and support programs that are not specifically targeted at digital entrepreneurship. This number is therefore significantly lower than numbers quoted in hub mappings (see Boucher 2016; Firestone and Kelly 2016).

[b]Excludes mobile operators, subsidiary offices of foreign technology companies, and digital enterprises with top management and software engineering teams mainly located outside of Africa (e.g., Jumia).

Instead of being firm demarcations, the three tiers serve to focus attention on *differences in ecosystem bottlenecks*. We conceive of bottlenecks as those factors that hamper an ecosystem to advance further. To some extent, these factors are idiosyncratic to any given ecosystem, but there may also be systematic patterns of certain bottlenecks prevalent at distinct stages of ecosystem evolution (see Mack and Mayer 2016).

In the remainder of this chapter, we discuss the most pressing bottlenecks for African digital entrepreneurship ecosystems in five areas, roughly in line with Isenberg's popular component model of ecosystems (Isenberg 2014): (1) markets and infrastructures, (2) entrepreneurial knowledge and mentorship, (3) venture labor and talent, (4) hubs and support organizations, and (5) access to funding. We use this categorization of entrepreneurial resources due to its popularity among policymakers and practitioners, but we do not assume that the categories are exhaustive, independent, or static (see Iacob, Friederici, and Lachenmayer 2019). We omit the oft-used "entrepreneurial culture" dimension because this ecosystem component is difficult to imagine and assess as a resource that reaches from poor to rich (see Spigel and Harrison 2018), making it impossible to meaningfully compare African cities (see appendix B for observations on each ecosystem).

Bottleneck #1: Markets and Infrastructures

Our analysis suggests that *access to sizeable markets* is the most important bottleneck for digital enterprise ecosystems across Africa. The previous chapters extensively discussed market and growth barriers from an enterprise perspective. They highlighted that the markets enterprises were able to access had a lot to do with where ventures were located. Only well-resourced enterprises were able to address urban and rural areas at the same time or cater to customers abroad at scale. Chapter 2 also documented that addressable local market sizes are determined by physical local infrastructures (both digital and analog infrastructures, like roads and power networks). In sum, these chapters demonstrated that the vast majority of African digital enterprises are confined to fragmented small local markets.

What remains in this chapter is to discuss the (eco)systemic nature of these market and infrastructure barriers and to analyze differences across Africa. Market and infrastructure challenges for enterprises become systemic bottlenecks by how they unfold their effects together in a similar fashion for all enterprises in a city. This system-level aggregation of addressable demand allows us to conceive of market access as a place-based resource for enterprises in a given location (Spigel and Harrison 2018).

When examining market access at the system level, it is striking how closely the ecosystem tiers outlined in the previous section correspond to proxy values for local digital market sizes (see table 5.2). When comparing tables 5.1 and 5.2, it is apparent that tier 1 ecosystems (Nairobi, Lagos, and Johannesburg) are all (a) large cities (b) that represent major economic and trade hubs (c) in populous African countries (d) with relatively high mobile and internet penetrations and (e) a GDP per capita that is around or above the African average. Tier 2 ecosystems (Accra through Kampala) lack some of these features, while tier 3 ecosystems (Kigali, Addis Ababa, and Maputo) lack most or all of them.

Our interview data substantiates that the diverse demand challenges mentioned in chapters 2, 3, and 4 apply across all African ecosystems, and that they exacerbate each other in bottom-tier ecosystems. Digital enterprises located in small poor countries with small capital cities in which consumers and small businesses have low disposable incomes do not have access to the kinds of digital mass markets that are needed to make products like e-commerce platforms or payment services viable. Because large businesses (banks, insurances, hospitals, etc.) are typically the only actors with high enough willingness to pay for digital products, they represent the customers that digital enterprises in those ecosystems focus on. Meanwhile, megacities like Lagos or Nairobi represent bigger and more homogenous digital markets than small African countries like Rwanda or Mozambique.

Ultimately, the overall analog economic legacy of a given location thus unfolds an important role for digital entrepreneurship, as it strongly determines the size of addressable digital product markets. Problematically for low-tier ecosystems, they are relatively *less able* to escape the confines of local markets than top-tier ones because only enterprises in leading ecosystems typically are able to generate enough revenue in domestic markets to fund costly international expansions (see chapter 3). Accordingly, African ecosystems in general and the most nascent ones in particular face a stubborn bottleneck in the form of limited market access. Access to affordable broadband internet is a necessary condition for digital enterprises to operate, whereas local infrastructures, willingness to pay, and capacity issues in local markets constitute early thresholds for enterprise growth.

Table 5.2
Broad indicators of domestic digital market ceilings

Country (case study)	Mobile subscriptions per 100 inhabitants	Number of internet users per 100 inhabitants	Population in largest city (millions)	Urban population (millions)	GDP per capita (current US$)	Income per capita per day (2011 purchasing power parity US$)
South Africa (Johannesburg)	164.5	51.9	9.40	35.65	5,718	–
Nigeria (Lagos)	82.2	47.4	13.12	87.05	2,672	–
Kenya (Nairobi)	80.7	45.6	3.91	11.80	1,377	–
Ghana (Accra)	129.7	23.5	2.60	14.81	1,370	6.6
Senegal (Dakar)	99.9	21.7	3.52	6.61	900	–
Côte d'Ivoire (Abidjan)	119.3	21.0	4.86	12.30	1,399	–
Cameroon (Yaoundé, Buea)	71.8	20.7	3.07	12.69	1,217	–
Uganda (Kampala)	50.4	19.2	1.94	6.28	705	3.2
Rwanda (Kigali)	70.5	18.0	1.26	3.34	697	2.6
Ethiopia (Addis Ababa)	42.8	11.6	3.24	19.35	619	3.6
Mozambique (Maputo)	74.2	9.0	1.19	9.01	529	2.7

Note: – indicates missing data. Income per capita includes mean consumption data based on 2014–2016 World Bank data. All other data is 2015 World Bank data. Cities are arranged in descending order for internet subscription figures. The largest city was also the case study examined, except for Cameroon.

Bottleneck #2: Entrepreneurial Knowledge, Mentorship, and Experience

A second key bottleneck across Africa is the *low local stock of entrepreneurial knowledge*. It is particularly pressing in tier 3 ecosystems, while it is narrower and more specific in tier 2 and tier 1 ecosystems.

Although academic and policy literatures often emphasize a "lack of skills" as a key constraint for African innovation and development (Blimpo et al. 2017; Carmody 2013; Venables 2009), they have rarely recognized entrepreneurial knowledge as a particular type of expertise that is essential for ecosystem evolution. *Entrepreneurial knowledge* is an understanding of how to operate and grow a venture and how to do so in a given local context (Spigel 2017). Such knowledge is largely tacit and contextual. It can thus barely be acquired from codified and standardized information (books, media, online courses, etc.). This is what makes entrepreneurial knowledge location-specific and space-bound: due to its tacit and situational nature, it cannot easily be transferred across distances. Instead, it builds mostly from entrepreneurs' direct experience with setting up a digital enterprise and from their face-to-face interactions with others who have this knowledge: experienced entrepreneurs who act as mentors or angel investors. This *recycling* of existing experiential and situational entrepreneurial knowledge by mentors interacting with newcomers has been identified as a key process in ecosystem evolution (Mack and Mayer 2016; Spigel and Harrison 2018).

Given how new digital entrepreneurship is to most African cities, almost all locally relevant entrepreneurial knowledge has only recently started to be built, mostly through painstaking acts of learning by doing. As chapter 3 highlighted, templates of how to run a digital enterprise from elsewhere can be used as a starting point, but they typically require major context-specific adaptations that are hard to predict upfront (see Rodrigues et al. 2018):

> These [learnings] are things that don't come just falling from the clouds. It's very much been an evolutionary process of understanding the market. . . . This is actually what I think it means to have a local awareness. (Entrepreneur in Kigali)

Experienced entrepreneurs in Lagos and Nairobi told us that although digital entrepreneurship may recently have entered a period of maturity in those cities, this has been the result of a lengthy and sometimes wasteful process of learning from past mistakes:

What [investors] were doing then [in the early 2010s] was really badly structured and shooting in the dark. It gave a lot of people opportunities to test out. . . . They were dishing money out left, right, and center. Somebody was like Oprah with the free cars: "You get 25K! You get a deal! You get a deal!" You could have ripped them off, and there were some people who took money and never showed up again—get 25K and then you change your number and you're done: you've got 2.5 million shillings. (Experienced entrepreneur in Nairobi)

The market corrected itself at some point. . . . A lot of people started setting up very, very funny businesses. Some people wanted to compete with Facebook; some people wanted to compete with Twitter. . . . They were burning a lot of cash. They were paying to acquire fake users and whatnot. It sounded like a good business model, but at some point, foreign capital met with local capital—remember the guys behind the local capital are traditional guys. . . . As a result, all the companies that were not focused on revenue started dying. So that corrected itself. Now, from day one, you have to show the revenue potential. (Experienced Nigerian entrepreneur)

Even where a number of experienced entrepreneurs exist, given the challenges of scaling within African markets (see chapter 3), they may be preoccupied with guiding their business to sustainability for long periods of time. Moreover, being a mentor and role model is not for everyone:

A lot of times, I'll walk into a place and people are like, "Oh my God, this is [interviewee's name]," and I keep thinking, "Okay, it's kind of awkward, I'm just a regular guy. I'm just somebody who is trying to figure out how to get this thing to work half the time." People are seeing what you've done, [while] you're seeing what's *not* yet done. You're always feeling inadequate, you're always feeling I could do better, we could go faster. (Experienced Kenyan entrepreneur)

This implies that several generations and a critical mass of entrepreneurs must have been active in a particular ecosystem for locally relevant entrepreneurial knowledge to develop into a collective resource that is shared and circulated (see Spigel and Harrison 2018). If there are only a handful of entrepreneurs with relevant experiential knowledge and if these entrepreneurs are not inclined to share their insights as mentors, a novice entrepreneur is forced to start her learning process from scratch, making all costly mistakes again:

There's nobody's footsteps we're following in. . . . You look at M-Pesa: it's an Israeli product bought by Vodafone and shoved into Safaricom. You look at Hellofood, and this is Rocket Internet. Who's done it yet? Rather than this being a pessimism thing, it's an optimism thing. I like the idea that we're the pioneers and that, if we're successful, we'll be the ones who are the case studies that lead the way for other people. It's also inherently frustrating because it means that every single lesson learned is really a tough lesson to learn. . . . The fact that nobody's done the first steps is a terrific opportunity, because it means you don't always have to have a crisis of realizing everything you dream about has been done a hundred times. That's also a real challenge because it's like building a house and realizing that you just want to go move in and put the furniture in, but you've got to start by clearing the trees from the lot. (Entrepreneur in Kigali)

In tier 1 ecosystems, entrepreneurs have accumulated knowledge on how to execute standard digital business models, but they have yet to acquire specialized and niche knowledge. Examples of specializations in entrepreneurial knowledge include, for instance, leading a digital enterprise to profitability within particular sectors (ERP systems for hospitals vs. insurance companies), monetizing different types of digital technologies (e.g., payment platforms as smartphone apps vs. blockchain-based), or applying strategies that deviate from Silicon Valley role models (see chapter 4):

> The entrepreneurs at that time were guys that were just fresh out of school; [they] had very little knowledge about business. Even if you look at IROKOtv, Jason [Njoku] was just, I don't know, maybe just new in town—there were no mentors. . . . At that time, there was no advice. You do it well or you flop, right? So you had to do all the learning yourself, you had to grow fast . . . and we're not making money and a lot of people did not understand your model because the traditional businesses could not fathom why you do a business without making money and posting losses on a monthly basis. (Founder of a local information platform in Nigeria)

A very consistent finding was that formal work experience served as a significant compensator for the scarcity of entrepreneurial knowledge and mentorship opportunities. We found work experience to have a fourfold virtuous effect (see Sørensen and Fassiotto 2011) in that formal employment

- was a source of startup capital;
- provided a professional alternative and backup for individuals needing to (temporarily) quit entrepreneurship;
- was an environment in which to learn skills and cultural knowledge; and
- allowed entrepreneurs to develop fruitful connections that could be turned into customers and business partners.

Unsurprisingly, employment at digital corporations came with particular opportunities. For instance, we interviewed four individuals in three cities who had formerly worked at national telecom operators and were able to leverage that experience to create new ventures. Some of them counted their former employers and their former employers' customers among their clients:

> I left the company that I was working for, which is SATCOM, and then I opened my own company. . . . One of our customers is an ISP [internet service provider] that we helped develop. So we designed the whole technical network and we still give them support. Because of my experience with SATCOM, we're involved other aspects in the roles of telecommunications. We work with a lot of banks . . . and we work with companies that want to implement internet solutions or want to implement telecommunications in general. (Entrepreneur in Maputo)

Many other (mostly younger) entrepreneurs we encountered had never been formally employed, and this affected their social capital and their business knowledge. One common and unsurprising reason were local constraints on employment opportunities. Another more unexpected pattern was found with techie entrepreneurs who developed coding skills at a young age and who wanted to remain independent, choosing to stay self-employed and work as freelancers. We also found evidence that the startup imaginary has gained ever-greater cultural influence, thus permeating livelihood and lifestyle decisions. The implication for these entrepreneurs' social networks was a negative side effect: they did not experience the benefits of formal employment (Sørensen and Fassiotto 2011).

Some participants had entered employment after trying their hands at entrepreneurship. They confirmed that employment had provided them with knowledge that would have been vital to their entrepreneurial endeavors:

> I think if I was to develop a solution right now, I would do a much better job. And actually, the whole team, I think it would be much better and would be much prepared to do it. But still I—what I noticed from trying to create all these products, because there was a time that I was crazy about creating products, but then trying them into the market, it was like, it was bad. I understood that it is better to improve myself. The strategy that I chose was to improve myself, to gain the skills that I needed to about product management, about knowing the market, about marketing, about financial management, about human resources management. All of those things, those are skills that I'm learning. I've been learning a lot actually that would help me to develop my own company. Actually, when I started working at [a big four consulting company], one of the things that I told my boss is that I'm here because I want to be able to create my own company in the future. (Former serial entrepreneur in Maputo)

Similarly, an entrepreneur in Johannesburg, who had gone into business after being employed in a big consulting company, pointed to a variety of entrepreneurial skills that she gained during her employment. These include dealing with administrative and operational tasks, as well as the ability to speak convincingly about business matters to potential supporters:

> Do not rush to become an entrepreneur. Every phase that you're in will prepare you for where you need to be. I went in and I knew nothing about business and I had worked in different departments in different industries. Different types of projects from your revenue projections to cost recovery, projects, operational improvement, people optimization, to culture. I think work experience is probably one of the biggest things you can have before you leave. It's knowing when you can leave. Because you're always taking a risk . . . but I think you're taking a bigger risk if you go naïve.

Last but not least, employment also benefits entrepreneurs by providing them with a financial base for their enterprise. An American entrepreneur in Nairobi spoke of using the entirety of their savings and credit lines, which left them in a position of great financial uncertainty:

> It's been the biggest struggle of my life for sure. I've put all the money I had saved from seven years of working, and I put $40,000 on credit cards that I came into this, never having a credit card balance in my life, and four years later I have like 99 percent of my credit space utilized. And whatever, I have like $107 of credit card space left.

Of course, for many African entrepreneurs, credit card debt is not an option in the first place because they simply do not have access to credit cards. Both the mentioned entrepreneurs' former employment and salary and their origin are thus important factors in determining a high level of credit. More broadly, any source of funding beyond personal and familial sources may depend on financiers' judgment of a person's credit, which is itself influenced by their assessment of how affluent the debtor is.

Bottleneck #3: Digital Venture Labor and Talent

Digital enterprises depend on highly skilled, creative knowledge workers, including software engineers, designers, product developers, project managers, data scientists, social media managers, and so on. African digital enterprises struggle to effectively attract and retain highly skilled and reliable labor. We identified a mismatch between local demand and supply for venture labor as a barrier across all African ecosystems, making it the third important ecosystem bottleneck. Similar to entrepreneurial knowledge, this bottleneck becomes more specific and narrower from tier 3 to tier 1 ecosystems. In turn, the mismatch seemed to be the most pronounced in tier 2 ecosystems, in which a number of enterprises had identified product-market fit and were eager to hire but were unable to find employees able to take on involved technical and managerial roles.

Africa's Technologist Workforce: A Wide Spectrum of Talent and Principals

The professional group we found to exist across all ecosystems was made of *technologists*: software developers and engineers, working either as freelancers for local and distant clients or as employees of local digital enterprises. Across Africa, interviewees in this group reported to us that they were motivated by "creating something," making "easy money," and by independence.

Initial coding skills were typically obtained from local universities and online courses. In all eleven cities, participants reported that most local universities and educational institutions did not prepare young people for the job market. Typical complaints were that these institutions only taught the theory but not the practice of computer science, that teachers' programming knowledge was outdated, and that learning methods did not encourage critical and creative thinking. Accordingly, a lot of learning happened by doing. Many coders started by developing simple websites (often with WordPress templates) for friends or family.

Especially talented technologists then came to realize that what is easy for them could generate significant income, leading them to complete further online courses. Many technologists alternate between part-time and short-term employment and freelance work, depending on the options they can find locally and online at any given point time. Those who stay freelancers and consultants enjoy being their own bosses. The technologists we interviewed were keenly aware of the concrete financial value of their skill. Often, freelancers established a local base of loyal customers and iteratively increased their portfolios through online freelancing. In a clear pattern, talented developers often get paid among the highest monthly incomes available to young urban professionals (e.g., about $500 in Addis Ababa or $2,000 in Accra).

Many freelancers preferred to work with clients from high-income countries, not only because of higher rates, but also because they claimed that such gigs pushed them to achieve higher quality standards and work toward deadlines in a disciplined fashion. A further advantage of online freelancing is that income opportunities are less affected by local economic issues, like currency fluctuations or economic downturns. Technologists we interviewed were skeptical of general digital labor platforms, such as Upwork, citing the risk that clients would not pay, the piecemeal nature of the work, and low hourly wages. Instead, they obtained international contracts either through personal contacts or specialized software developer platforms, such as Toptal or LinkedIn and Slack groups. For the most talented and experienced software developers, online freelancing provided much better job opportunities compared to regular employment at local corporations or startups. For instance, one Nigerian software developer reported that the rates he obtains through Toptal are ten times those he would attain locally.

A New Breed of Entrepreneurial Workers

We found more variation across ecosystems for the second professional group: *entrepreneurial workers*. Digital enterprises often have malleable organizational structures and engage in constant knowledge exchange, requiring workers to be flexible and engage in professional communities beyond the enterprise (Auschra et al. 2017; Benner 2008; Ibert 2004). Accordingly, managerial and soft skills are often valued just as highly as technical skills in digital entrepreneurship ecosystems. Ultimately, even employees who are not executives may be required to adopt an entrepreneurial approach, as they design products, share risks, get rewarded through company shares rather than salaries, and partake in strategic decisions (Neff 2012). In such a context, some workers can attain high incomes, but career paths are more uncertain and workloads can be overwhelming (Barley and Kunda 2004; Neff 2012).

We found a critical mass of such workers to exist in tier 1 ecosystems (Lagos, Nairobi, and Johannesburg) and to a lesser extent in tier 2 ecosystems (Accra and Abidjan). Kigali was an exceptional tier 3 ecosystem in which we found some entrepreneurial workers, potentially due to Rwanda's concerted push to institute entrepreneurial ideas across society (Root 2016).

Like entrepreneurs (see previous section), entrepreneurial workers acquired important skillsets over time and social networks played an important role for learning and identifying opportunities. In tier 3 and some tier 2 ecosystems, founders seeking to hire entrepreneurial workers reported that recent university graduates often were not independent and reliable enough, making workers who had been exposed to professional corporate environments the preferred candidates. They bemoaned the narrow range of options for graduates to learn about how to comport themselves:

> People who will work [are those] who are competent or they can train easily to get in the flow of your business. So, work ethic is different in Cameroon and maybe in Kenya, or in [the] US or Europe, because first of all, [here] there no student jobs. So, people don't get into professional work and learning work ethic until usually they finish university and they get into a new job. You have to train people [in] work ethic, getting to work on time, respecting deadlines, being conscious of their lines. Having the results-focused culture, not dropping the form, not building excuses that you don't care about. Wearing the professional face when they come to work. Don't pull your personal drama to work! I mean, all these things that will seem like common sense usually aren't very common. (Hub manager in Yaoundé)

Our findings confirm that this new professional class of confident, young, well-educated, and skilled workers is exploring career options rather freely and deliberately (see Avle 2014; Avle and Lindtner 2016). They usually seek to balance salaries with skill development and job quality, while placing lower emphasis on employment security. These professionals feel part of a wave of positive and long-overdue transformation in their home countries or in Africa as a whole:

> [It] is really important to drive products coming from Africa that are very tailored to this context in the coming future. . . . It's nice that [Google is] making products but you also want to produce an Uber, an Airbnb. There's a lot of digitizing. These [new] digital cultures are producing their own digital products. . . . Perhaps global cultural homogeneity is not the best thing. I think I feel very strongly about that. That's what informs this 'African solutions to African problems' type of thing. (Startup employee in Nairobi)

For entrepreneurial workers, digital enterprises are an environment in which they can hone and deepen managerial skills and build careers with a more long-term orientation. In particular, they feel that working for a digital enterprise lets them actively partake in building useful products and gain entrepreneurial experience without being entrepreneurs. Workers benefit in particular from being closely involved with business processes, reasoning that they learn essential skills for their own companies, which they are envisioning to start at a later point. They tend to like the flatter hierarchies and friendlier organizational cultures that many startups have compared to traditional and larger local corporations. Money definitely matters for entrepreneurial workers, but it is not everything, and they are often content so long as salaries cover their living standard. They often forego higher salaries attainable at corporations, at development organizations, or in the government:

> I didn't think too much about money. I just wanted to be in an IT company where I can practice what I did in school. . . . I wanted to be focused on one thing, because the IT, it's expanding. I wanted to find my place. . . . I have inside of me that entrepreneurship thing. I want to create something. Even if I'm not the CEO, to me, that's not the problem. I just want to know we achieved what we wanted together. (Startup employee in Kigali)

Competing for the Best, with Limited Resources

Although the number of software developers has mushroomed across Africa, digital enterprises especially in tier 2 ecosystems have suffered from a *missing middle of skill and talent* (cf. Grugulis and Stoyanova 2011). A central issue was that ventures often require not just software developers but software engineers, who are able to build compelling digital products, coshape a venture's strategy, and lead teams of junior developers. Self-taught developers with basic skills existed in relatively large numbers in most cities we visited, but they did not show the application and comprehensive skillset required for product development:

> We were with a Kenyan self-taught developer for two-and-a-half years, who is great for where he learned his skills, but now we've got this French guy who is just a super star! (Entrepreneur in Nairobi)

In turn, the few highly skilled and experienced engineers that exist command high prices for their labor, excluding most digital enterprises from accessing such outstanding workers. Participants noted that usually only software engineers from high-income countries or foreign-educated Africans were able to meet all the requirements of working independently in a fledgling enterprise:

> A lot of the people that we took here studied or worked abroad. I mean two of the people working on [our startup] worked in Ghana. Joel, that you can see over there worked in India. You have Janet who studied in Canada, we have Paula who studied in Morocco. You have me, who studied in England, Joseph who studied a little in the US as well. So yeah, we're really trying to take the best. . . . We can

find talent in Ivory Coast, but a lot of times, it's talent that we have to reshape. For instance, [an employee] has a lot of potential because he has energy, he has an extremely classic mind to begin with. But he was taught in the ways that will make him a good web designer. . . . He may even know how to do CSS and JavaScript, which are mainly used for websites. But here we're building strong software so you need "deeper," if you will. Languages such as Python or C++ and [talent that know] those languages are extremely hard to find in Ivory Coast. (Entrepreneur in Abidjan)

In addition, multinationals are often able to attract the best local talent:

A lot of people are just thinking: How can I get paid as much as possible, how can I work for blue chip companies and that's why startups have such a problem attracting talent sometimes because you're competing with Safaricom, which has name recognition and this is someone who is fresh out of school. In a few years, I'll be able to take a huge pay cut to join a startup or to build my own company because you've already got something set aside, but a lot of people who are young and just coming out of school don't have that luxury, you don't have the luxury of working at a small company when you could have started your career at a bigger company and moved a lot more. (Entrepreneur in Nairobi)

Ultimately, the required talent was often unaffordable or wholly unavailable for African digital enterprises:

When I began, the idea was like, "let's just have ten software devs and crack this code." Now, it's realizing that we're really looking at [our CTO as the only software engineer]. I think he's the best software developer in East Africa. Having spent so much time at MIT and CMU [Carnegie Mellon University], I think he knocks it out of the water in terms of how his brain thinks of these things. You can't get someone else like that . . . Our dear competitors, they've been trying to hire a CTO, and they've been having that post advertised for 5 percent equity of the company, for 75,000 dollars a year—they still haven't been able to fill it. You know, that's more than half our yearly budget! (Entrepreneur in Kigali)

In tier 1 ecosystems, skill gaps were more specific. Here, entrepreneurs bemoaned that local coders missed specialized technical skills beyond basic web and app development (server administration, niche programming languages, algorithmic computing), craft software engineering skills (writing clean, elegant, and efficient code; understanding the product development context of software development), and secondary skills (documenting code, collaborating with other software developers, time management and realistic scheduling, maintaining focus on a single project):

Things like web development, mobile, that's fairly low hanging fruit. But now when you want to start doing things like banking systems, serious integrations, robotics, AI—if you don't have a proper theoretical foundation, you're probably just going to be using Google libraries, and [we] will never get to the point where we're able to write those libraries ourselves (Startup employee in Nairobi)

However, enterprises in tier 1 ecosystems also had more means to compensate for shortages. Especially in Nairobi, immigrant venture laborers from the US and Europe were often willing to accept pay cuts:

So I spent quite a bit of time in Berlin. There's a good tech scene there . . . Cheap developers because all of Ukrainians and Eastern Europeans want to come to Berlin. Through our local networks, we stumbled upon [our lead developer]. He was bored to death in [his job there] and, when we asked him if he minded moving to Nairobi, he [agreed and came] here because it's the Wild West and it's exciting, right? (Foreign-born entrepreneur in Nairobi)

As a result, a number of digital enterprises across Africa outsource software development, mostly to India and sometimes to Europe. Entrepreneurs noted that despite coordination and communication issues, the quality-price ratio was better in particular for projects of medium complexity and size, for which teams of software developers need to be assembled for a few months:

Well, we tried to do it internally. We realized, it was so much—it was quite an issue trying to scale that. The market was not really willing to pay premium, and the talent was pretty much expensive to get the right sort of people. (Entrepreneur in Lagos)

Bottleneck #4: Innovation Hubs and Other Support Organizations

The fourth bottleneck concerns innovation hubs and other digital entrepreneurship support organizations. This challenge is most pressing in tier 2 ecosystems, in which significant numbers of enterprises exist that demand support, while organizations tend to struggle to streamline and scale their offerings in a way that effectively responds to demand. In tier 3 ecosystems, informal community-driven support organizations usually exist, while the narrow set of entrepreneurial experiences, small market access, and shortages of venture labor supply represent the most pressing bottlenecks. In tier 1 ecosystems, again, the bottleneck becomes more specific: several hubs and other organizations usually exist in those cities, while they suffer from coordination challenges and sometimes struggle with legitimacy among experienced entrepreneurs.

Innovation Hubs: What Does Their Ascendance Really Tell Us?

As alluded to earlier, the fast increase in the numbers of innovation hubs across Africa was aided by the symbolic role of iHub and an ideological match between current paradigms in development (e.g., participatory and community-driven development), digital technology (e.g., openness), and hub principles (e.g., grassroots entrepreneurship). In media reports and popular books, the sheer growth in numbers of hubs is often taken as evidence of a rise in digital entrepreneurship as a whole (Bayen and Giuliani 2018; Bright and Hruby 2015a; McGee 2017).

A growing body of empirical evidence (Friederici 2017a; Jiménez and Zheng 2018; Littlewood and Kiyumbu 2018; Marchant 2018; Rodrigues et al. 2018) suggests that such an understanding is problematic. The social realities of hubs are immensely complex, and hub managers and funders struggle to fully understand the strengths and weaknesses of the strategic options at their disposal. Ultimately, many hubs had to scale back their ambitions or move away from iHub's archetypical "hub" approach, in the sense of an open community-driven space with limited intervention by managers (Moraa 2012; Toivonen and Friederici 2015).

In the end, hubs' quick rise is merely evidence of their popularity among their funders (mostly development organizations, foundations, tech corporations, and local governments), not of their effectiveness (Friederici 2019, 2018). We will discuss their underlying ideology in more depth in chapter 7.

Lofty Goals and Mundane Purposes

Many hubs start out with high aspirations, often including some notion of "building ecosystems." Indeed, assembling entrepreneurial communities, which give members a sense of collective identity and meaning, has been found to be the most transformative outcome of hubs (Friederici 2017a; Marchant 2018). Hubs have also become the first points of contact for foreigners entering a given entrepreneurial ecosystem and they thus serve an important orientation function (Littlewood and Kiyumbu 2018). They can also be boundary organizations in which indigenous creative traditions are blended with foreign ideas and technologies (Eglash and Foster 2017).

Yet the social dynamics of community formation can be fickle (Bølling-toft 2012; Garrett, Spreitzer, and Bacevice 2017), and African hubs often have struggled to strike the right balances of inclusion and exclusion

(Friederici 2018; Jiménez and Zheng 2018). Hubs (like coworking spaces and incubators) have a basic function that resonates with African environs: they alleviate the overhead costs of running a small business and create opportunities for horizontal scaling, in which small firms rely on each other to provide competencies that are not available in-house, like market research and professional development (Hersman 2013). It is thus easy for hubs to be workspaces for students, consultants, software developers, free-lancers, and so on—but establishing communities (as purposeful social collectives) has proven to be more elusive. Accordingly, hubs have sometimes struggled to be "more than just a space" and to avoid being considered glorified internet cafes:

> But just sitting next to each other without a structure . . . I don't really [believe that works]. It depends on your company [but] we have very strong methodologies from the beginning. We started very strong in business [advice]. (Entrepreneur in Kampala)

Moreover, active entrepreneurial communities can be very valuable in many ways, but they are not in and of themselves a generator of growth-oriented or sustainable ventures. An expectation that hubs can "create startups" may therefore be misguided, even where hubs are extremely successful, because immediate startup creation is simply not an outcome that the organizational actions of hubs could ever achieve (Friederici 2017a). Especially in tier 3 ecosystems, hub managers may justifiably be inclined to neglect venture development for the sake of softer goals:

> Building something, a little bit, the ecosystem. We found a very lean way to build it . . . in the beginning [in 2012], just to say, "Hey, awareness creation." Because there was no other hub, nobody was talking about startups or entrepreneurship. . . . I think that was really how we also defined our mission, saying "Okay, let's find some cool people who got an idea, let's try to bring them to the next level, having a prototype, a business plan." But that was in a very unstructured way. . . . I think the main task was really making events, bringing entrepreneurs to the university to give speeches, having round tables, providing space for interest groups . . . just building a community and I think that's what we basically did for the first couple of years. . . . I think [it was about] creating the demand. (Hub managers in Addis Ababa)

Beyond the difficulties of community facilitation, hubs have struggled at the organizational level from lacking clarity concerning goals, best practices, target groups, and impact. Like incubators, accelerators, and technology transfer offices, innovation hubs are boundary organizations that mediate interests of funders (principals) and beneficiaries (agents) (Guston 2001; Hackett and Dilts 2004). These interests may be conflicting (e.g., governments wanting to create employment vs. startups wanting to employ few productive staff), and there may be substantial cognitive distance between the two groups (e.g., a foundation in Europe may fund hubs without its staff having set foot in an African hub or talked to local entrepreneurs). Compared to incubators, both funders and beneficiaries of hubs are typically more openly defined and rather unorganized groups of actors, which makes hubs' intermediary role even more complicated and their success more ambiguous (Friederici 2017a; Littlewood and Kiyumbu 2018). Especially in tier 2 and 3 ecosystems, hub managers often do not have an entrepreneurial background, inviting criticism:

> I think from the hub side, [the key to success] is picking the right idea, having a more stringent process for reeling it through your door, [and] mentors and the people leading the programs being entrepreneurs themselves and not teaching from a book. It's also very valuable because if you've never had your own business, or anything, how are you going to teach me how to get through these really tough times? (Entrepreneur in Johannesburg)

Similarly, in tier 2 and 3 ecosystems, hubs' struggle for effectiveness has been exacerbated by the number and magnitude of challenges for entrepreneurs, leading hubs to try to take on more problems than they can realistically handle given their usually modest budgets, short histories of operation, and limited organizational capabilities. Hub managers have been found to be "winging it" and suffer from "feature creep" (Rodrigues et al. 2018). As some hubs have attempted to satisfy too many principals and too many different kinds of entrepreneurial needs, they have become jacks of all trades, masters of none.

The Mutual Dependence of Support Organizations and Ecosystems

Finally, and maybe most importantly, African hubs had to relearn two old lessons from business incubation (Bøllingtoft and Ulhøi 2005; Hansen et al. 2000; Rice 2002): they depend on active contributions by entrepreneurs and on the already available resources in the local ecosystem. In African cities, both these contextual dependencies become pitfalls for hubs because their own effectiveness can be hampered by the very problems they are trying to address, especially the absence of entrepreneurial knowledge and of mentors. In tier 2 and 3 ecosystems, experienced digital entrepreneurs and mentors that can contribute to hub activities may simply not be available. In tier 1 and some tier 2 systems, we regularly found divergence both of mindsets and of networks between established digital entrepreneurs and the more grassroots novices frequenting hubs and networking events:

> [My co-founders and I] hardly go for events. . . . We believe that it's relevant for the ecosystem but we also feel that those hubs and those engagements don't give out the right message. We still pass the message that as long as you have an idea, that's great: you'll get investors. . . . But having been in the online business for a while . . . you can have the idea and you can grow at rocket speed. You'll probably do that for a year. Afterwards you have to understand that a sustainable business has to be sound from day one. That is not readily preached. . . . By the time you get to CcHub [Nigeria's best-known innovation hub], you need to ask yourself, How many businesses have actually been incubated and how many have been successful? . . . I think I've done about three or four speaking engagements . . . talking to startups, talking to internet companies. . . . But for example, if you ask me if I'm going for the Social Media Week next week, no. . . . I'll only go when my time [is] really requested . . . , or when I see that there is a lot of value to attract from it. . . . So we talk to a lot of people. There are different channels. We're in WhatsApp groups. . . . There is quite a lot of stuff to do. . . . We also invest in them. So we know what is happening, but we don't—permit me to use the word *jump around*—and [we don't] go for all the events because we believe that there is so much to do. (Experienced entrepreneur in Lagos)

But in tier 3 ecosystems, community- and event-oriented interventions often are more widely appreciated given the overall dearth of activity. An example of a particularly extensive and locally popular program is the Science, Technology and Innovation between Finland and Mozambique (STIFIMO) project. Aside from providing mechanisms for assisting Mozambique with its national science, technology, and innovation strategy, STIFIMO also provided funds for networking opportunities among digital entrepreneurs and funded entrepreneurs' trips to Slush, a major pitching competition and conference in Finland:

> So at my third year at my university, I attempted my first hackathon organized by Sciences and Technology minister with partnership with Finland. It was a project called—let me remember. It was a STIFIMO. So that was the first hackathon that I participated and unfortunately, I didn't win the first prize but we learnt a lot about how we can use hackathons to just expose ourselves and connect with good organizations that are willing to build solutions or tech solutions for local or global problems. (Founding member, developer community in Maputo)

Still, it is questionable whether such support initiatives are well-positioned to advance tier 3 ecosystems to compensate for other bottlenecks. For instance, it is hard for hub managers to teach entrepreneurial knowledge that would usually be established through direct entrepreneurial experience:

> So we've been evolving a little bit that way. We're dealing with like true seeds of ideas. Young guys who are like "I know code; I'm thinking about building these couple of projects as a product"—they have no business sense whatsoever. They're just thinking it's a good idea. So we don't discourage them but we say, "Take it too its logical conclusion. Work your idea through all of these steps: Viability? What kind of team do you need?" And not only that, but we try to train and focus people, right. Many think that they can have a great idea and tomorrow it becomes Facebook, but we have to sensitize them to the market realities. It's that your startup may continue to be a startup until it's the teenager, again, because the market is moving a lot slow. You can't expect to hit massive penetration when you only have 30 percent internet penetration and your country is 50 percent under fifteen. (Hub manager in Kampala)

This quote illustrates that market and entrepreneurial knowledge bottlenecks can make efforts like hubs futile, leaving exiting entrepreneurship as a more appealing option. We found a similar dynamic in many tier 2 and 3 ecosystems, including in Maputo (see box 5.1), where STIFIMO had provided valued support options. In such settings, a critical mass of sufficiently experienced grassroots entrepreneurs cannot be convened, thwarting peer-mentoring and other self-sustaining community dynamics that hubs have been praised for.

Accordingly, most of the more recent boom in funding for digital entrepreneurship support organizations has focused not on innovation hubs but on modern versions of incubators, such as structured mentorship programs and accelerators (see Pauwels et al. 2016 for a definition and review). Notables include Google's Lagos-based accelerator, giving $3 million in investments and in-kind support (Jackson 2018a); the World Bank's XL Africa program that connected twenty enterprises from all over the continent with investors at events in South Africa (Kapil, Andjelkovic, and Lu 2018); the GSMA Innovation Fund, giving mentorship and amounts of $1–$2.3 million million per enterprise, also sourced from the entire continent (Mulligan 2017); and the Make IT program by GIZ, which set up a large-scale and complex initiative to support several dozen startups, offering (among other services) access to hubs in Nairobi and Lagos.

Box 5.1

The Maputo Living Lab: Tilting at the Windmills of Structural Inequality

The Maputo Living Lab (MLL) was a program that was established to provide youth trained in computing with the skills to develop enterprises. The alumni we interviewed felt that their time in the incubation program equipped them with codified knowledge about professionalism that was expected to enable them to succeed as digital entrepreneurs. Yet they also reported that despite the intensive MLL program, they still did not have a good sense of what the market needed, and they did not obtain the skills to a run a company.

After the MLL program's demise, the alumni faced difficulties as entrepreneurs. The program had attempted to be inclusive: all candidates had been selected from a local public university rather than from the private schools where local elites send their children. Alas, none of the alumni now had the financial wherewithal that might have enabled them to learn by doing, fail up, or otherwise wait for startup success.

Many of the alumni were, however, able to find high-level corporate jobs. Their academic performance and experience with the program seemed to have made them ideal recruits for global companies. Many of them reported that they had a whole new outlook on the business world through work. Those who have plans to eventually leave employment to try entrepreneurship once more feel that they will be much better equipped.

Such organizations and initiatives have a much higher ratio of resources per supported venture compared to hubs. Yet they are typically only available to already relatively successful startups that have proven some product-market fit. Concerning their impact, similar questions present themselves as for incubators because "ideally, only those firms that are 'weak-but-promising' (weak due to a lack of resources, but promising in the sense that they have built a compelling business case) should be considered . . . candidates" (Hackett and Dilts 2004, 62). In reality, such a determination may be anywhere from difficult to impossible to make, especially for Pan-African programs. Implementers also have a strong incentive to pick ventures that are successful either way because rigorous impact evaluations that attribute a program's contribution to a venture in precise terms are almost never done (see McKenzie 2015 for the only exception we are aware of).

Here too, the prescriptions of frameworks for digital entrepreneurship do not completely apply in Africa. The expectation by donors and other organizational funders is that, over time, firms should cease relying heavily on support organizations. Ideally, incubators and accelerators should jettison firms that do not achieve their milestones at the target rate. Yet across Africa, there were numerous instances in which organizations did not actually follow this model. Detractors of entrepreneurship support organizations often framed this negatively as propping up failures, but we found it also to be true that if one eliminated all digital ventures in tier 2 and 3 ecosystems subsidized in some way, there would be very few firms left in those ecosystems:

> A lot of the incubators are terrible. All of them must have actually forgotten what it is that they're supposed to be doing. They did a blanket approach to enabling entrepreneur. Whether you're mid-stage, late-stage, early-stage, they teach you the same thing which is usually not that useful. Maybe incubators need to start talking amongst themselves and say, "Okay, so who are you incubating with? What are they giving you?" It's open and fair in a way to the other startups as well. (Entrepreneur in Johannesburg)

An interesting market access–oriented intervention is Alibaba founder Jack Ma's Electronic World Trade Platform (eWTP), the goal of which is to allow African traders to sell their goods in the Chinese market (Moloi 2018). Ma's goal of facilitating digital entrepreneurship in Africa is philanthropic, but also has the added benefit of connecting African and Chinese markets through platforms that Ma has developed. eWTP is complemented by an UNCTAD partnership. The program provides fellowships for training at Alibaba's business school in China. Rwanda has also been the first country to sign up.

In tier 1 and 2 ecosystems with high numbers of support organizations, an additional challenge becomes effective coordination across an ecosystem: connections with universities and established businesses in particular may be explored weakly, while links to tech corporations and mobile operators may come with long-term risks and conflicts of interest (Rodrigues et al. 2018). Accordingly, even when there is a great number of accelerators and innovation hubs, tight entrepreneurial communities may not always follow. In Johannesburg, despite the large number of organizations, entrepreneurs frequently lamented the lack of pulling together and community in the ecosystem:

> One thing we don't really do well is we don't really support each other, and so we need to that whole supporting structure. I mean if I have an opportunity, I should

be able to pull you in and say "Okay, here's an opportunity," but at the same time I should pull you in because of merit. Because yes, I know you're really good at this. . . . We should be able to pull in the right people. Those that are not skilled, and we pull them in to upscale them. I think once we get that right, we'll probably be in a better position. (Founder of a technology production and consulting startup in Johannesburg)

Bottleneck #5: Inadequate and Exclusive Funding

The fifth bottleneck concerns missing funding, especially when it comes to investments that are appropriate for digital ventures to achieve both growth and sustainability. The overall amount of investments matters for an ecosystem's evolution, but which firms have access to funds and which ones do not is just as important. Most resource exchanges in ecosystems are by nature exclusive to some entrepreneurs and not open to all. From an entrepreneur's perspective, his or her networks are important for acquiring financing, contracts, and advice, leading to an improvement in the performance of firms (Khayesi, George, and Antonakis 2014).

It is unsurprising, then, that entrepreneurs in our sample who were independently wealthy or who had relationships able to support their entrepreneurial efforts had better chances. The distribution of resources in any ecosystem is necessarily uneven. However, what determines an ecosystem's conduciveness to productive entrepreneurship is the degree to which those exchanges are enabled that benefit viable new enterprises rather than incumbents and rent seekers (Spigel and Harrison 2018; Stam and Spigel 2018). In this section, we thus also will examine in what ways social networks in African ecosystems are able to channel resources to entrepreneurs with high-potential digital products, irrespective of their preexisting status and socioeconomic position.

As with the previous four, the funding bottleneck also materializes in different ways across ecosystem tiers: in tier 3, fledgling startups tend to struggle to attain financing of any sort, especially enterprises helmed by underprivileged entrepreneurs; in tier 2, small pots of money are available from entrepreneurs' savings, innovation competitions, and kinship networks; and in tier 1, small VC funds, angel investor networks, and an abundance of innovation competitions are available, even if ticket sizes available to most ventures are still too small to take on foreign competition.

Traditional Channels, Traditional Challenges

A complaint across all ecosystems was that traditional channels of finance, such as bank loans and government grants, are unavailable or wholly inadequate to be accessed by digital enterprises. The vast majority of entrepreneurs' whose firms had reached financial sustainability had achieved this by reinvesting revenue (see chapters 2 and 4) while relying on no or very small amounts of external funds.

Traditional small and medium enterprise support programs set up by government agencies often require physical assets as collateral and for candidate firms to be at least three to five years old, excluding a large share of digital enterprises from eligibility. Many respondents (e.g., in Kampala, Maputo, Yaoundé, and Abidjan) perceived their governments as paying lip service to supporting them. These entrepreneurs pointed to evidence such as a lack of business grants or government procurement practices that privilege global corporations:

> Starting and running a business is a real uphill task for young entrepreneurs . . . with all the licenses, taxes, and lack of access to capital. (CEO of e-commerce site, Maputo)

The refrain among participants was that not enough accommodations are made for bootstrapping startups, wrongly treating startups like other businesses, despite their low revenues and young age. In some locales, these costs were heightened by the burden of expediting stalled bureaucratic processes:

> [It] is not easy to work with this government and the taxes are excruciatingly high. Yeah, and just the roadblock in administrative red tape [makes it] really hard to get things [done] quickly. Things are intentionally done so that they will be slow, so that you need to pay [an] "expedited fee" for it to go first. When you're not really comfortable with paying "expedited fees" that are unofficial, it puts you in a very embarrassing situation. (Hub manager in Yaoundé)

However, the strength of government support varied strongly across Africa. Enterprises in countries like South Africa and the Ivory Coast, where better-resourced governments gesture toward commitment to the digital economy, benefit from initiatives like targeted funding, favorable taxation regimes, and ease of registration and licensing.

Clearly, the "friends, family, and fools" category of financiers also tends to be more limited for African enterprises than for their high-income-country counterparts. The distress of entrepreneurs was palpable as some founders spoke of the need to sometimes "delude" themselves and to focus attention on small gains, while fielding the reality of imminent failure and the social scrutiny that seemed to come with engaging in mass-market digital entrepreneurship:

> The challenges are many, but people ask me, why do I stick in when the business is not making money. [The business] is not making money, but we've been able to meet our costs. We are at the initial break-even point. (Founder of an e-commerce site in Kampala)

Innovation Competitions: Problematic Incentives, but Often without Alternatives

In the absence of traditional financing, entering innovation competitions is the only widely available funding channel for most fledgling digital enterprises in tier 2 and 3 ecosystems. We define *innovation competitions* broadly and include any initiative where in-kind support or prize money is delivered to ventures or teams as part of a competitive and relatively short-lived process (one night to a few months), such as in business plan competitions, pitching and demo nights, hackathons, bootcamps, and the like.

While local governments sometimes back such competitions, development organizations of all stripes, as well as corporations, are their dominant funders. Many corporation-funded competitions are done as corporate social responsibility campaigns, thus following similar logics and aims as those of development organizations. Hubs are often the executing entities of innovation competitions because commissions and consulting fees represent an important revenue stream for them. Yet as a result, hubs are also under pressure to reproduce donor ideals when implementing competitions (Rodrigues et al. 2018).

Novice entrepreneurs often seek access to investors through such events, but soon realize that this is not the actual outcome. An interview respondent in Johannesburg, who was very successful in the competition circuit, expressed her disappointment at the fact that no investments had flowed from the spotlight. She had, however, managed to convert visibility and name recognition into a revenue stream by generating speakers' fees. She spoke of the challenge of maintaining a successful façade as she experienced the stressors of keeping the business going.

Many entrepreneurs also reported that they would prefer support from profit-oriented or risk investors (such as angel investors) but that development funders are much more easily accessible or sometimes the only funders, especially for business models with unclear market opportunities:

> In Cameroon, we don't have local [foundations]. . . . Most of them are international but with an office here. Just one internal office here in Cameroon, then others are religious [from] Europe, and don't have an office here. . . . [There are no local angel investors], just [an] incubation hub. (Entrepreneur in Yaoundé)

Yet the reward structures of prizes have also led to the emergence of competition entrepreneurs, or *compreneurs*. Participants in Kenya used this term to refer to mostly young and inexperienced entrepreneurs with a technological background who participate in innovation competitions to win prize money and recognition, but without showing any commitment to developing a digital venture:

> People actually plan and say, "Okay, when the year starts, I'll be entering A, B, C, D competition, because I know there is money." So they enter with one idea in different competitions. The idea is that the whole point is not to showcase the idea, but it's to say . . . "I want to take the money." That's how I think the entrepreneurs have started hacking the system. . . . People are [even] hopping into incubators. You find one startup is incubated by three, four, five different incubators . . . They go grab your money and then they get something else from someone . . . Now, the problem with that is, from what I'm thinking, is you're recycling the same people. (Entrepreneur in Johannesburg)
>
> It's the same with the competitions . . . where people run after money here and there, 10 thousand and maybe 20 thousand. It's a lot of money if you think about the short term . . . but what it does [is] it changes your priorities for your business. (Entrepreneur in Kampala)

Many performative practices are thus dedicated to the attraction of resources and status (we will discuss this in more detail in chapter 7). More often than not, a good idea and confident presenter trumps working prototypes with traction. Especially in more nascent ecosystems, only few engineering-focused competitions require the presentation of a material artifact rather than a five-minute slide presentation. Winning these higher profile events typically led to media coverage and celebrity within the community.

Angel Investors and Venture Capital: Chicken and Egg

It is undeniable that risk financing in digital enterprises is growing immensely across Africa. Year-on-year growth rates are in double- or triple-digit percentage points in most reports tracking such investments

(Collon 2017, 2018; Disrupt Africa 2016, 2017b, 2018; VC4Africa 2014, 2016, 2017, 2018; WeeTracker 2019).

Still, relative to startup cities in high-income countries, the reported amounts are rather small. For instance, in its most recent report, Wee-Tracker (2019) finds US$725.6 million to have been invested in 2018 across all of Africa (a continent with about 1.3 billion people and a GDP of roughly US$2.2 trillion). For comparison, startup investments in Berlin (a city of about three million people and US$0.18 billion GDP) alone were EUR 2.6 billion in that year—about four times more (Voss 2019). It seems that even in the oldest and resource-richest African ecosystems like Lagos and Nairobi, only the cream of the crop of ventures are attractive to risk investors. Hundreds and maybe thousands of ventures are operating in those cities, but only a few dozen or so attain significant risk investments each year (WeeTracker 2019).

It is challenging to understand whether risk investments in African cities rarely happen because startups are not investable or because there is simply not enough money to go around (Drouillard et al. 2014). On the one hand, both investors and entrepreneurs are inspired by the ostensibly vast market opportunities for fast-scaling consumer-oriented digital products (see chapters 1 and 3). On the other hand, enterprises struggle to attain hockey stick growth, and early financiers pursuing prerevenue investments to scale user bases quickly have been burnt.

It seems that those ventures are able to attract significant amounts of risk financing that fulfills either or both of two features. The first is proven product-market fit in a scalable market. Many participants told us that significant traction and substantial revenue are preconditions for risk investors to consider a startup investable:

> I talk to PE [private equity] guys a lot. I talk to VC guys a lot. It's extremely difficult finding very good businesses to put money in. They are out there but the businesses don't get the revenue fundamentals. (Experienced entrepreneur in Lagos)

Yet even proven revenue itself is not necessarily enough. Instead, revenue needs to be combined with (perceived) scalability, which is a challenging proposition in African markets (see chapter 3):

> I wouldn't say we don't like tech companies but it has to be a company that is solving a massive need, that is potentially using tech to solve that need. They're not there to say: "I've developed some fantastic software or an app and that's it,

my job is done." It's a different set of entrepreneurs I think, that are looking to address very large needs and then figuring out what [is] the best way to do it, and tech might be one of the ways to do it. I think it's a different mindset perhaps. (Investor in Nairobi)

From the entrepreneur's perspective, engagement with risk investors represented yet another experiential learning process, in which a specific and localized kind of entrepreneurial knowledge was formed. For instance, especially in tier 3 ecosystems, entrepreneurs mistook investors for their customers, and investments for personal income:

> The average entrepreneur would want to see a traction in revenue before he decides to take in money, and even when he takes in money, he wants to retain control. In the earlier days, control was not really so much of a problem, right? "Hey, I'm a loss-making business. You're telling me just to acquire all the guys on the streets? Oh, that's easy. Oh, okay." "So, we're going to give you a million. When you need money again, let me know. We'll send you another million." So, I come in, I get nice cars, I just get people on my platform and I get millions in dollars. (Entrepreneur in Lagos, Nigeria)

Somewhat paradoxically, the emphasis on early-stage financing rather than a single-minded focus on revenue was particularly conspicuous among novice entrepreneurs in nascent ecosystems—the group that is least likely to access such financing. Astute entrepreneurs came to understand the concept of market traction in digital entrepreneurship (Nicoll 2000), in which even unprofitable and nonpaying users may have value. A Maputo-based entrepreneur who had expanded into a neighboring country explained why it did not matter if they were financially successful in the new market:

> The realization that this market was not big enough for us to become a big company was sort of quick, and we understood that for us to be able to get to the level that we wanted, especially attract investors and whatnot, you would need to have presence in multiple countries. . . . We were just feeding the platform to increase our traction but that's it. I can't even say that we have business in Angola because we are not making money in Angola yet. . . . A lot of startups is all about raising the interest of the next investor. So we start up with a strong concept, a strong pitch—you know, you've got a two-paged business plan. And you get someone to put 200 to 300 thousand in your products that you've just launched, and you've got little traction and it's actually just a prototype. . . . So if you do that long enough to show some sort of stability, you might raise real funds and then you might be playing with a million or two. So where I'm trying to get here is: Angola gave us profile even if it wasn't generating money. If let's say that we are in five countries and we've got two countries that are making a lot of money. I come to

an investor and I say "Guys, our presence is in five markets and we're making this much money," all right, he's not going to care which market is doing what and I don't care about the other three.

Other entrepreneurs realized that coming up with good technology was not enough to attract funding where they were and that seeking funding may not be the right path for them:

I just look at myself. I think if I was in the Silicon Valley environment, I would also be one of the geeks who are raising money here and there. I also have like friends who would really do a better job than people in the Silicon Valley to raise money. . . . So for me it's always a learning process. If someone says "no" for some reason, then we go back, we realize what happened—I also check if they really have the money [*laughter*]. . . . The same energy I use to deliver this app is equivalent to the same energy that we used to run after this investor, getting rejected, and another investor. I feel like . . . we're [now] channeling this through a different model to something that maybe can work for us and for Rwanda. (Experienced Rwandan entrepreneur)

Detachment from Established Local Business

In the end, the financial resources to support digital ventures have to come from somewhere. Digital entrepreneurship ecosystems' newness and cultural distance from traditional business seemed often to prevent actors from gaining information, learning, and resources. Local investors prefer low-risk investments such as real estate (Hersman 2012). What we found in most cities was that digital entrepreneurs felt that they were too detached from well-established local business arenas:

I think also we don't have like mature companies here to work with big companies. Most of the clients are big companies. You must have like a big startup to work with them, and also you must just prove that you are worth it. (Former entrepreneur in Maputo)

Advantages thus accrued to entrepreneurs able to act as brokers between otherwise distant professional realms (Sapsed, Grantham, and DeFillippi 2007). For instance, a Kenyan participant left stable employment for entrepreneurship after realizing the value of her relationships:

I asked myself, why does the government want me, why does IBM want me, why does Google want me, why do all these people want me for consultations? Because, one, I have a good connection with the government because I've worked there for a while. Then two, they think I'm smart, and then three, I have good knowledge: I'm a software engineer and I work with data and data is becoming a thing right now. [A mentor told me], "You are possibly the most connected young person I know, whether you're connected to people who can give you money, or you're connected to people who can give you work, but you are that person—and your network is your net worth." I'm like, "Okay, I guess, if you say so!" (Entrepreneur in Nairobi)

Summary: Bottlenecks and Vicious Cycles Thwart Ecosystem Evolution

This chapter has shown differences across digital entrepreneurship ecosystems in Africa. Ecosystems are locally bounded social contexts and assemblies of resources that affect the success of digital enterprises from a given location. Digital enterprises all over Africa have gained improved access to basic resources like support organizations (hubs, innovation prizes, angel investor networks, tech parks, etc.), professional talent, mentors, and startup funding. Yet any ecosystem in Africa—whether it is Cape Town, Cairo, Nairobi, or Lagos—offers more limited access to entrepreneurial resources (knowledge, investments, etc.) than ecosystems like Silicon Valley, London, or Tokyo (see Rodrigues et al. 2018). Market-related bottlenecks were particularly concerning for Africa's ecosystem when compared to Silicon Valley: international mass scaling, beyond the threshold imposed by the size of the local economy, was a rare exception. Our interview data suggests that markets are the more important bottleneck for entrepreneurial ecosystems in Africa compared to various supply-side dimensions (such as social networks, organizational capacity, and institutional factors), which have been identified as success factors for the world's leading ecosystems (Spigel 2017; Storper et al. 2015).

Within Africa, tier 1 ecosystems have very different bottlenecks compared to tier 3 ones. This finding will be rather unsurprising for anyone studying evolutionary processes in ecosystems, or related concepts like regional innovation systems or business clusters (Audretsch, Kuratko, and Link 2016; Colombo and Delmastro 2001; Mack and Mayer 2016; Stam 2015): due to the complex interdependence of locational factors (tacit knowledge, infrastructure, etc.), positive (and negative) feedback loops and path dependencies reinforce initial (dis)advantages over time (Bathelt and Cohendet 2014; Spigel and Harrison 2018). But this chapter filled this broad theory with empirical detail about what distinguishes different African ecosystems—and what holds them back.

We discerned three tiers: learning, incipient, and maturing. Distinguishing tiers and the bottlenecks that are most likely to apply to a given tier can be a helpful framework for policymakers, investors, and other supporters of digital entrepreneurship when seeking to identify the most relevant interventions for a given context. Typical bottlenecks were found to differ drastically between ecosystems with rich versus narrow sets of resources. Broadly speaking, basic supply-side interventions like hubs and innovation prizes exist in all ecosystems, but they do not seem to be able to compensate for bottlenecks like market access or the incipient nature of entrepreneurial knowledge. As ecosystems advance, the most pressing bottlenecks shift. For instance, in higher-level ecosystems, venture labor is usually available, just not at critical mass (incipient ecosystems) or with the required technical specializations (maturing ecosystems). As a result, software development projects of medium complexity and size often have to be outsourced to India or to Europe.

It is likely that every African nation will develop a sustainable but small domestic digital enterprise sector, serving local niche markets. However, concerningly for nascent ecosystems, negative feedback loops may hamper any evolution beyond this state, making it hard to supersede ingrained economic legacies. Ecosystems evolve through the interplay and enrichment of entrepreneurial resources (Spigel and Harrison 2018). Especially where entrepreneurial knowledge and market access are lagging, support organizations and other resource infusions are likely to be insufficient to advance the ecosystem because these organizations themselves depend on minimum local capacity (Friederici 2017a). African ecosystems thus can be stuck with a slow pace of evolution.

We ultimately find that African digital entrepreneurship is anything but location independent. Instead, local economic histories and social contexts differ across cities, and they affect what is possible or not for the average enterprise in a given city.

6   Transitioning Identities

For me, Africa is the future. (Entrepreneur in Dakar)

Digital entrepreneurship is still mostly framed as a received and appropriated practice (Afele 2002; Baro and Endouware 2013; Davidson and Vaast 2010; Hildrum, Ernst, and Fagerberg 2010) rather than one that is developed in situ (Mavhunga 2017; Olivier de Sardan 2005). It is thus understood to consist of a decontextualized set of practices, identities, and ideas. Aspirations and identities in particular are shaped by Silicon Valley, as it continues to symbolize a mental model upon which enactments of digital entrepreneurship are judged and around which success is framed (Hill and Mudambi 2010; Katila, Laine, and Parkkari 2019; Wentland 2016). Likewise, in entrepreneurship and management studies, entrepreneurs often are characterized as a unique class made of individuals who share particular attributes such as tolerance to risk, extraversion, and other personality-based and cognitive traits (Spigel and Harrison 2018).

But whatever mindsets and skillsets might be constitutive of digital entrepreneurship, it is never enacted in the same way at two different locations or at two different points in time. This is because entrepreneurs, as its enactors, are embedded in specific social environments that consist of particular configurations of geography, history, and institutions (Autio et al. 2014; Welter 2011).

This chapter discusses what it means to be an African digital entrepreneur in Africa. "Africa" thus plays a twofold role for this analysis: once as a denominator of distinct entrepreneurial identities and once as a set of societal contexts. Identities express subjective collective understandings of "who we are" and "what we do" (Navis and Glynn 2011), where, in our case, "we" concerns African digital entrepreneurs as a group of people. In line with the two gospels outlined in chapter 1, we divide the nine identities we found into those relating to "digital" aspirations and those concerning what it means to be an "entrepreneur." Identities are by definition subjective, so we draw heavily on entrepreneurs' own reflections in interviews, letting readers vicariously experience their experiences and perspectives (Tracy 2010). We discuss societal contexts insofar as they influenced entrepreneurs' subjective experience of priorities and ambitions. This chapter focuses on identities conveyed to us by citizens of African nations. We leave out immigrants—first, because their individual journeys proved to be rather distinct, and second, because their identities played an important role for the tensions that are the subject of the next chapter.

We find that entrepreneurs are reconciling decontextualized ideals and norms of digital entrepreneurship with their careers and with the social worlds they are embedded in. In doing so, African digital entrepreneurs are breaking new ground, transitioning preexisting professional identities in African cities into a new professional and creative class. They employ the startup as a new organizational form, pursue dreams of technology-driven wealth and transformation, and are sometimes in direct (if reluctant) conflict with government. A worrying finding is that this cultural avant-garde is mostly an urban elite, which means that preexisting socioeconomic positionalities have changed in style but mostly been reproduced. Although digital entrepreneurship represents a departure from old boy networks in business and government, it still appears to be elitist and to exclude people from poor and rural backgrounds. Our contribution to theory is to confirm that a universal model underestimates the complexities that emerge from contextualizing it (Tracey, Dalpiaz, and Phillips 2018; Weiss and Weber 2016) while also pointing toward the possibilities of new cultures developing from the blending of a foreign model and preexisting local identities.

Digital: Technological Aspirations

Being located in Africa induces particular enactments and perceptions of digital entrepreneurship. This section explores how the fact that entrepreneurs seek opportunity specifically through digital technologies affects their trajectories.

Techies

Digital entrepreneurship requires a level of technical knowledge. Not all entrepreneurs who we encountered have a background in the science and technology of ICTs, but many do have the skillsets to create the products that they are introducing to the market. One unique attribute of the digital arena is that it is a form of scientific knowledge that does not usually require certification for the practitioner to convey legitimacy. One can claim to be a self-taught programmer without reputational damage.

A cadre of digital entrepreneurs we found to identify through their digital skills can be described as *techies*—that is, predominantly technically minded entrepreneurs with software developer backgrounds. They are drawn to digital entrepreneurship because it presents them with an opportunity to apply their skills and their passion for technology to create novel digital artifacts. In our research, we came across individuals with varied qualifications, ranging from high school graduates to PhD scientists. A graduate of Uganda's Makerere University described how his company's origins emerged from his undergraduate final year engineering project:

> I got very good marks for the project but to my surprise—Orange, there used to be a telecom called Orange. It was operating here and at the time it ran a competition. It wanted to reward basic innovators. Then I said, "Alright, I can just try my luck and put my project up." Surprisingly, I competed, I was short-listed, and I won. So that was showing me that there could be something in this. (Founder in Kampala)

Many techies were young freelancers. The more experienced entrepreneurs were, the less likely we found it to be that they would extol technology as the core of a viable business model. The more experienced entrepreneurs, even if they were technically minded in the beginning, began to realize that knowing how to code was a necessary but not a sufficient condition for running a viable digital startup. In the example of Li-Fi LED in Côte d'Ivoire (see box 6.1), an entrepreneur is a leader in a cutting-edge area of science but is disheartened that the award-wining product is currently unable to gain market traction or attract investment.

Scalers

Interviewer: Would you call yourself a "technology entrepreneur"? . . .

Respondent: I'm moving with the times, let me put it this way. I'm an entrepreneur. I've done all kinds of businesses . . . so it's not like I'm a technology entrepreneur. I just adopted technology so I can scale my business, really.

Like this participant, an entrepreneur in Kigali, many people we interviewed mentioned that they hope that digital technologies will help their enterprise scale quickly and widely. In chapter 1, we showed that this understanding is also widespread in popular and academic discourses about African digital entrepreneurship. Especially entrepreneurs with a low or medium level of success and experience believe that the digital-technology-specific patterns of scaling (see chapter 1) represent viable pathways to grow their enterprise. These *scalers* feel that their solutions can imitate the trajectories of Silicon Valley role model products, basically expanding to wherever there is internet connectivity:

> [Our founders were] like, "Okay, there's M-Pesa." . . . Just adoption of data usage is growing 6 percent per quarter, which is really significant growth. . . . It's not elusive: Facebook is zero-rated. . . . For me, it's a no-brainer. In Europe everyone is using their phones—I don't see how it would be different here. (Foreign-born entrepreneur in Kenya)

The techies among the scalers understood digital technologies to be structured in "stacks." In their view, a particular technology stack, once it has been developed, can be easily plugged into other stacks elsewhere:

> One of our companies here is . . . an Uber for [farming equipment]. It's a global company because there's no other person in the world who's doing that. . . . Sitting in Africa, they're envisioning a model which is basically as scalable as Uber, whether it is globally or whether it's for Africa, it doesn't really matter.

Box 6.1
Li-Fi LED in Abidjan

There has been no shortage of recognition for Li-Fi LED and its technology, which transmits data through beams of light. Over twenty plaques and awards are displayed on the walls of the founder's office, announcing its legitimacy. Furthermore, four hundred rural customers imply that it can gain traction. Yet Li-Fi LED has not drawn any attention from investors, even though its entrepreneur is one of the few people to deploy Li-Fi in the wild. He has also been drafted to adapt his technology for the French space program. The Li-Fi scientist attributes being off the investment radar to his location in Francophone Africa and his inability to speak fluent English. He asserts that he needs financing to expand operations to the critical mass at which the enterprise could become profitable.

It's a system and it stacks . . . and whether that tech stack can be duplicated in multiple markets, that's basically the question. (Incubator manager in West Africa)

Novice entrepreneurs with a software developer background feel that the stacking property of digital technologies can provide them with an easy business opportunity:

Maybe because we're all techies, we know what to do. If you only set up a version of [our product] in, let's say, Nigeria, because it's one of the biggest markets, in an hour you can just set up a whole new thing and it's ready to go, so it's pretty scalable. The cultures are very similar so you don't need to do too much tweaking: you only have to adapt by listening to what people are saying, making quick changes. . . . It's not like what it used to be in the past. . . . It's not so bogged down where you need to set up an office here. . . . We run this software from our bedroom. (Entrepreneur in Ghana)

More business-minded entrepreneurs also believe in the scaling opportunities of digital products, but they contextualized this opportunity differently. Some saw opportunity in replicating a locally developed technological innovation in another geographical context without setting up operations there:

So we're going to Uganda and Nigeria. . . . I've adopted what we call a master franchise business model. We're physically going to be in only two countries, as a company, and after that, we'll just start getting partners, 100 percent licensing the technology. (Entrepreneur in Kigali)

Those that create a business to have a positive socioeconomic impact often believe that digital technologies will allow them to do so more easily and on a grand scale:

We wanted to come up with a business idea that scales quickly to millions of people . . . We wanted to build kind of a self-sufficient engine of change. (Employment platform CEO in Nairobi)

If you look across the whole continent . . . we're looking at 1.1 billion people, thereabouts. All we're saying is that we want to connect at least 10 percent of these people to [sharing economy service providers], in real time. We don't think that is too ambitious . . . If you look at the demographics, it's very achievable. The continent is still growing. (Entrepreneur in Nigeria)

Grand ambitions often relied on the belief that once a digital product worked in a given local context, it would fit into other African and low-income contexts as well:

The whole point is to find like the . . . rightful model for here . . . and just go and implement it somewhere else. Like, I have great ties in Ivory Coast . . . and that's like probably one hundred times the Rwandan market. . . . So now, I see Rwanda more like a giant proof of concept . . . My plan is to actually to start looking at various African capitals. (E-commerce entrepreneur in Kigali)

I'm stereotyping a bit, but . . . it's more exemplary of the typical African business what you find in Kampala and in the surroundings than it would be in [Nairobi or Lagos]. So, I think it's a good starting point and it's also a very nice place to experiment on as you are less exposed to market pressures (Entrepreneur in Uganda)

Similarly, this entrepreneur felt that the underlying technological functionality of an initially localized product could be expanded to become relevant to new locales:

If you look at any startup that's coming out of Silicon Valley, they're solving a local problem, and it's influenced by the problem that they have locally and the culture locally. We would never have come across [our] idea . . . if it weren't for the challenges of Nairobi that forced us to think like that . . . [But] what we realized was that, the same way Amazon started as a bookseller and realized what they had built to sell books made them incredibly efficient to sell anything, we sort of built the same thing. We built this [technology] to serve up recommendations for our [customers], and then at some point realized that in fact trust is the much more important and much, much larger opportunity and problem globally, and that [our technology] can actually be used to recommend and provide trusted advice about any service that somebody might want to hire in any sector. (Entrepreneur in Nairobi)

We found that international scaling ambitions seemed to be induced by risk and impact investors, as they were much more prevalent among entrepreneurs who had already attracted such investments or were seeking to do so:

Our investors very much came on board first to replicate this across sub-Saharan Africa—it's not just a Kenya thing . . . they want us to build something scalable, that we can replicate, and as soon as we can nail [our new feature], we can replicate it in so many locations because that runs by itself. . . . Then the algorithm. . . . We can even have bots. . . . Then we could open in Tanzania, Uganda, Somalia tomorrow, at very low cost. (Entrepreneur in Nairobi)

So now the whole big issue is to democratize healthcare access in emerging markets and we decided to start with a particular [foundation]. [In one year from now], we are hoping to bring . . . content on Facebook [and] through SMS in one environment, a mobile phone application. . . . There are seven countries we prefer, but the key countries are Cameroon, Kenya, Nigeria, and Ghana. (Health information startup in Nigeria)

Infrastructure Builders

A small section of experienced and already successful entrepreneurs in our sample was motivated by building infrastructure for Africa's fledgling digital economy. One example is a Maputo-based entrepreneur who developed an app builder. The tool costs fifteen dollars and allows users to build functionalities using a drag and drop feature, thus reducing the need for personal computing knowledge or to hire developers. He is now able to channel the profits to support his more bleeding-edge technological efforts:

> They asked, "Can you help us to sort this problem." . . . I said, "Now I have to think on a solution to build that." That's when I started research and—I like to do things fast. I said, "If I'm going to do this from scratch, it would take too much time and I would be losing too much time on testing." And clients, at the end of the day, don't like to be the first users, they're the beta testers. I search everywhere; I find it in a piece of code that was already built. I gave a proposal for the owner of the code: "Don't you want to sell me your code?" Then I bought the code and started putting all my modifications; then adding all the needs that all the other companies will need. (Founder in Maputo)

Several entrepreneurs we interviewed in Lagos thought bigger. They wanted their digital products to become digital infrastructure that is used at the Pan-African or global scale (see also figure 6.1). For one interviewee, this was a smart and exciting business proposition that would have positive ripple effects for the rest of the economy:

> Based on the insight I had looking at other companies around the world that were very successful, like Alibaba and Amazon, if you really x-ray these companies, the core competence, the first set of capabilities they built were in fulfillment, not necessarily in building highly optimized websites. . . . If you build a really powerful, highly efficient local delivery network or logistics network, do you really realize that we can literally put anything we want on top of it? Some of the examples and inspiration that we have are people like Vanderbilt who built the rail lines in America and could essentially put anything on those rail cars. . . . Our insight was that once you own the infrastructure that enables everything else, you have a lot of leverage. (Entrepreneur in Lagos)

This Rwandan entrepreneur adds the sentiment that developing African digital infrastructure can be a means to counter the continent's technological dependence on high-income countries:

> If we don't build an African ecosystem, investors and access to capital besides banks, what's going to happen is we're going to still be consumers for foreign

ABAN ABAN Angels
@ABANAngels

Following ⌄

"We use Spotify, a platform built in Sweden, all across the world and in Africa. Why can't a Nigerian platform power #payments in Mexico or Guatemala?" @oviosu CEO @Paga at the 1st African panel on the main stage at TechCrunch #DisruptSF - via @AaronQFu

3:19 AM - 8 Sep 2018

17 Retweets 55 Likes

💬   🔁 17   ❤ 55   ✉   ⬇

Figure 6.1
Nigerian entrepreneur announces vision to build global digital infrastructure at Silicon Valley event. *Source:* ABAN Angels 2018.

solution . . . where there's only one or two African companies in that space, especially hardware. (Entrepreneur in Kigali)

In sum, in terms of their ambitions and perception of opportunity, African digital entrepreneurs of many stripes buy into the idea that digital technologies help surpass geographical barriers and open up vast markets. Yet barely any of the entrepreneurs we interviewed had actually achieved the type of international expansion they were aspiring to.

Entrepreneurs: Agents of Change

Startuppers

African entrepreneurship has traditionally been associated with *subsistence* and *necessity*. These terms imply that entrepreneurs become entrepreneurs to survive, and they also denote their socioeconomic background (Delacroix, Parguel, and Benoit-Moreau 2018; Kaplinsky et al. 2009; Viswanathan et al. 2014). The fact that entrepreneurship has come to have a similar stature to stable employment is a cultural shift. Entrepreneurship had previously been cast as precarious:

> I did a research study on the impact of African entrepreneurs that migrate or Africans that migrate to the States or the UK, and obviously looking at Kenya and Nigeria and South Africa being the largest groups that migrate to those places. It's funny because a lot of the first generation left their countries and went to the UK and the States at professional jobs, and the second-generation immigrants were kind of conditioned to follow the same footsteps and go study and get a professional job. A lot of them actually opted to take on entrepreneurship. (Hub manager in Johannesburg)

> So the current African entrepreneur: Now there is a need to separate it. There are entrepreneurs and there are entrepreneurs. There are entrepreneurs that are entrepreneurs as a result of life, as a result of the fact that they can't get a job, and there are entrepreneurs that decided to leave even their lucrative job to focus on the business and figure out how to grow it. (Seasoned Nigerian entrepreneur)

Educational attainment in one of the professions was typically cast as the best and fastest way out of precarity and into high income. Digital entrepreneurship, however, evokes a different imaginary from straightforward entrepreneurship. It is viewed as a respectable endeavor and an opportunity for young people to succeed economically, attain high social status, and partake in the mission to build a thriving local economy.

In most cities, but especially in Francophone Africa, these economic actors were seen not as traditional entrepreneurs but as *startuppers*: a new type of entrepreneur that establishes a small, nimble, formalized, and modern organization that is driven by technology and sells technology. The startup was popularized in particular by the lean startup methodology (Ries 2011) and its key tool: the business model canvas (Osterwalder and Pigneur 2013). The startup can certainly be considered an appropriate organizational form for African contexts (Mavhunga 2017). Startups are often small and nimble, and they make decisions as a reaction to scarcities in their environment (Hersman 2012; Mavhunga 2017; Srinivas and Sutz 2008).

Digital entrepreneurs told us about tensions, however, when it came to a startup's implied trajectory of growth. The early-stage startup is meant to be only the first stage of a big idea, transcending a local context incrementally but ultimately growing rapidly (Ries 2011). Tensions are particularly evident in Nairobi and Kigali, where we interviewed Kenyan and Rwandan entrepreneurs, as well as a number of entrepreneurs who had migrated there from high-income countries. Kenyan entrepreneurs often seemed to engage in hustling (Weiss and Weber 2016)—that is, making money in the short term from several parallel jobs and investments. They usually see enterprise survival and revenue generation as key success factors.

Westerners, on the other hand, basically follow the stereotypical vision of Silicon Valley startups more directly, looking for quick scale, attracting risk capital, and pursuing a big and global vision. Yet as previous chapters showed, hockey stick growth is elusive for all but a very small circle of African startups. Reckoning with this reality is a significant part of what it means to be an experienced digital entrepreneur in Africa:

> I do think that it just means that things have to be slower, and that's irritating. I want to make sure this doesn't get codified into my DNA of being CEO. But it just means that, unlike in the US, you couldn't make a FarmVille clone, or it had to be monetized very effectively. (Entrepreneur in Kigali)

The startup has also brought new performative practices, which entrepreneurs are compelled to master to convey legitimacy. For instance, participants valued a confident PowerPoint presentation and practiced their elevator pitches (Davidson and Vaast 2010; Katila, Laine, and Parkkari 2019). The elevator pitch tests the ability to interest a listener in your endeavor within thirty seconds. The notion of digital entrepreneurship that is performed here is optimism, urgency, and equanimity in the face of trial. In interviews, it often took a while before participants broke out of this mode of selling their ideas, which was indicative of the unique socialization that the startup realm had exerted upon them.

Economic Developers

Africa's digital entrepreneurs are navigating expectations not only about what performing digital entrepreneurship entails, but also what its outcomes should be for Africa. The digital entrepreneur mythos is that of entrepreneurs being transformational agents that "introduce major innovations, create many jobs, and disproportionally contribute to productivity growth" (Decker et al. 2016).

The entrepreneurs that we encountered generally believe in the ability of the digital economy to change the trajectory of society, and they want their startups to have a positive impact. Many reported having an ethos of social responsibility and an interest in community development:

> Only the resilient and the intelligent can see the third option of entrepreneurship as the future . . . I'm [also] getting into the [second option]: public service . . . I'm really pressed to become a judge, from my moral obligations. I will not abandon entrepreneurship, because it is not about the money, about the financial things. It's also about how I can save the community. That's why I'm still in for the third option despite the second option of public service. (Hub founder in Buea, Cameroon)

> Yeah, because I think when I returned, there was that hype and passion. I was twenty-one, and I just wanted to change so I can impact people. I didn't really think about the financial part. (Entrepreneur in Cameroon)

> I also want it to be a case study, an example, to show that companies, world-leading companies can be able to exist here. Especially ones that have a strong social impact. Let's show that you can make money in Africa doing things that maximize profit, but in a way that is because it's delivering a service that people take great value from. (Entrepreneur in Kigali)

A more specific expectation of digital entrepreneurship's role for society is that it could be an engine for employment. Several interviewed entrepreneurs indicated that they are particularly motivated to create jobs for youth in their home nations. One Ugandan entrepreneur describes how his personal goals interact with the experiences of his employees and his ability to retain them:

Towards the end of our final semester, I realized that I'm going to the marketplace that doesn't have jobs for all of us. I challenged myself to start up something that can be able to decently employ me, and even employ others who did not have a job. (Entrepreneur in Kampala)

Yet here as well, it is questionable whether digital entrepreneurship practice meets the demands of local problems, leading to tensions in entrepreneurs' aspirations. A hub manager reflects on the depth of unemployment among African youth, and finds that solutions would also have to consider institutional capacities and policies:

It's actually quite scary sometimes when you go into areas outside of urban areas. Even peri-urban is a sort of okay. But, if you go to a place where, for example, in the Northern Cape, where it's just small towns, not even a city available anywhere nearby. You see most of young people that are doing nothing. That's really scary, and you ask yourself, "Where is the future of this town going?" It's not like there aren't resources or there is no way of actually stimulating this economic development. Then again, you find political structures and you've got people that are in positions politically that aren't necessarily qualified to actually improve the status of those particular areas. You'll find that it's going to take quite a bit of time to fix the problems that we have in South Africa. (Hub manager in Johannesburg)

Providers

Limited access to traditional formal sources of finance (credit cards, loans, etc.) is a major reason that kinship networks play an increased role for African digital entrepreneurs. *Kinship* refers to extended family and community ties that emerge from cultural and ethnic origins (Verver and Koning 2018; Williams and Williams 2011). Scholars have observed that "in most societies kinship is the most important social institution that affects one's identity, livelihood, and career" (Verver and Koning 2018, 632).

Kinship networks are particularly relevant for determining entrepreneurial identities and mindsets in African settings, and our findings confirm several patterns discussed in the literature. One important issue is the low dependability of (formal) agreements with distant connections:

I returned from the US with that [expectation], you know, like if a company pledges, they will [deliver on their pledge], but then they let you down. So, like three days before the competition, you have to call your family, your parents, your uncle, to bail you out. That has happened twice. This guy, who is like family, also bailed me out. Then, I have to make sure that we didn't fall into trap of relying on sponsors, so we decided to organize a fundraising event. That also came with a share of troubles and disappointments and failures. (Hub manager in Yaoundé)

As alluded to in chapter 5, a second issue is the dearth of formal support structures, such as government-provided small business loan programs and social safety nets. African digital entrepreneurs may be able to operate on relatively low budgets, but they mostly require sustenance for several years before achieving product-market fit (see chapter 3). In these circumstances, the role of kin ties as important sources of entrepreneurial support is amplified, and entrepreneurs from underprivileged families and groups are less able to take risks. This is not only because they have fewer resources, but also because ripple effects on kin in case of failure can be consequential. Whenever a family depends on an individual to be the breadwinner, the pursuit of digital entrepreneurship creates a financial risk and an existential threat, particularly if other options for income generation are unavailable:

> The fact [is] that in Africa, for most people, if you're doing a job [and] you decide to do a startup, the risk of failure is higher. You can actually condemn your family to poverty pretty much if you're not careful. Most people will play it safe: they'll either seek employment whereas they're actually quite capable of doing business, or once they get in those startups, they'll make decisions that will either play it too safe or make it very risky. So, trying to make it big too fast or being very conservative in building businesses. (Entrepreneur in Lagos)

Our data confirms that entrepreneurs from underprivileged backgrounds feel increased pressure to abandon their ventures when they do not immediately produce income. The alumni of the MLL (see box 5.1) provide a useful illustration of how socioeconomic background can override potential in influencing entrepreneurial trajectories. Their recruitment into the MLL incubation program was contingent on their academic performance in computer science and engineering programs at the Universidade Eduardo Mondlane (UEM). UEM is a public university, and though it has a good reputation, well-off individuals attended private universities like ISTEC. After exiting the program, alumni reported that they had strong financial responsibility for others. They often felt duty-bound to contribute to providing for their families and communities that had supported them through their student years. One interviewee spoke of the conundrum faced by many university graduates:

> Imagine this situation. In your house probably between your brothers and everything—it's not my case but it's the case of many students that come from

the provinces—you're the only one that is, was able to enter in the [university]. And the remaining members of your family, they live with basic income, and they're expecting [that] after you finish you give some support. And then you've finished, you entered in the [Maputo Living Lab] and you're explaining them that you will do so in four to five years. But there is someone from the same village that is considered not as knowledgeable as you but has a better lifestyle. (Director of a bank in Maputo)

The interviewee also noted that other members of the MLL cohort who enrolled in the incubation program found it difficult to hold out for the indeterminate future gains of entrepreneurship. Ultimately, they could not reconcile their entrepreneurial ambitions when they saw former classmates who were not as academically adept as they had been surpassing them in terms of standard of living.

In contrast, a successful digital entrepreneur from the same city recalled his career struggles in an interview. Although he experienced changes in fortune, the resultant uncertainty did not affect his extended family:

I was a lousy student in college. I went to study in Cape Town, I did a BBA degree in marketing management. . . . I was hired by a big FMCG [Fast-moving consumer goods], and basically then, I was earning less than $200. I was a marketing coordinator and doing more of delivery boy work. . . . Then I was fortunate to join a joint venture from that group, and another where my career started really progressing and. . . . Well, at some point I was the country manager for LG electronics within maybe eight years of a career. (Entrepreneur in Maputo)

Despite what he regarded as an undistinguished academic career, he experienced an upward professional trajectory. This was rooted in a socioeconomic background that had facilitated his education at a well-regarded institution and family ties. Low socioeconomic status thus clearly not only represents a lack of immediate access to capital, but also means extended financial obligations (Daspit and Long 2014; Grimm et al. 2013; Khayesi, George, and Antonakis 2014). Entrepreneurs with means and/or from individualistic societies (like the US) are only required to be concerned about themselves and the risk to their own careers, while many African entrepreneurs are obliged to care for extended communities as a facet of both cultural and socioeconomic factors.

Kinship responsibility undoubtedly represents a mental strain for entrepreneurs, but does it also thwart enterprise and ecosystem success? Daspit and Long (2014) argue that localizing resources within kinship networks creates a moral hazard because it makes entrepreneurs beholden to family, community, and social circles rather than to business management principles. Indeed, we find such cases in our data:

> So basically, even if you want to be an impact investor, when you become wealthier, you're often restricted by family circumstances. Even if you want to become a social entrepreneur or just any mainstream entrepreneur, you're often restricted, not only because you don't have access to capital, but because your resources have to go in supporting family. So the risk becomes higher. If you fail, your entire family is affected by the failure of your venture. (Director of an incubator in Johannesburg)

However, "moral hazard" as a negative applies only to the perspective of an individual enterprise. We, like other authors (Grimm et al. 2013; Khayesi, George, and Antonakis 2014), find evidence for positive outcomes of kinship networks at the community level. Notably, kinship obligations are reciprocal. Therefore, they can obligate benefactors of entrepreneurs to channel more resources to them than they would do in the absence of the obligation. This dynamic can have an inclusive effect, particularly where kin extends beyond the nuclear and extended family. In those cases, resources of high-net-worth individuals can be allocated to high-potential but poor entrepreneurs:

> So what I have seen, and I have been in these networks, someone comes from a township, from the community and they become a high-net-worth individual. They came to give back, and they go to trusted individuals and go to trusted spaces—and I'm one of them. They ask me where to find the entrepreneurs or to host pitch nights. They do not make a song and dance about what they're doing. It's not explicit—it's not up for research because they haven't publicized that they're investing. A lot of impact investors in the mainstream, which is mostly white led, do market that they are investors or VCs. So people know how to find them, but it doesn't mean that they're the only ones investing. And in fact, when you work as an investor, an angel investor who's from the community, they understand the socioeconomic issues and they take high risk in making the investment. (Entrepreneurship incubator manager in Johannesburg)

African entrepreneurs' responsibility to community before their own enterprise is thus not necessarily detrimental to productive digital entrepreneurship. In the absence of public sector safety nets, family and communities provide an essential financial cushion (Foster 2000; Heymann and Kidman 2009; Khayesi, George, and Antonakis 2014; Mildred 2014; Rwezaura 1985). Especially with experience from abroad, these entrepreneurs thus become contributors of resources and knowledge as part of their social responsibility:

> [I] did [my] secondary here and then went back to the UK to do university. I did electrical and electronics engineering. After that I stayed an additional two years, I was working, and I was into the tech space. So, with the electrical and electronics engineering, I tried to combine it with software and interacting hardware or software. This is called IoT, internet of things. I went to a lot of hackathons and was developing many prototypes, different systems. And this is probably the thing that, let's say the passion, I had for developing the solutions. But then at some point I saw that there was a need for me to contribute back to Mozambique and that's the decision I had to come back and try to work here with the market. (Entrepreneur in Maputo)

Dreamers and Grown-Ups

Digital entrepreneurship is for the young—this popular sentiment in policy and tech media (see chapter 1) was also reflected in interviews:

> Last year we had a guy who had a lot of experience, he's thirty-seven, he's the oldest person on the leadership team, and even from that experience I'm not going to hire anybody over that thirty-seven-year age, no. I don't think that is where we want to be. We are looking for people, we try to hire potential and that potential is not just potential in the things that they can do. (Entrepreneur in Lagos, Nigeria)

Indeed, most entrepreneurs we interviewed were under thirty, even most of the experienced ones with three or more years of experience running a startup. Yet, as alluded to in previous sections and chapters, we found that age—or more precisely, experience—may be an important asset. We found young (approximately under twenty-five) and inexperienced entrepreneurs to be overly optimistic and sometimes naïve. In contrast to our findings about local and slow growth, young entrepreneurs often had simplistic ideas about how easy and how necessary it is to scale and to obtain risk investments. They directly subscribed to Silicon Valley ideas, which they absorbed from online courses, tech blogs, or trainings at local innovation hubs. They also believed in the viability of charging users directly or making money through advertisement revenues, and were generally convinced that their startups would grow quickly through the use of digital technology. The following excerpt of an interview with a young Ethiopian technologist illustrates all of these themes:

Respondent: So then I understand how iWeb [an Apple app builder] works, so I made my first sample website that I can show off to my friends. I was thinking, maybe the contents that I've been seeing and the YouTube links that I was seeing, if I can collect them altogether and if I put them on my page, maybe my classmates can share the benefit with me . . . I don't think anything is impossible, if you want to change it, you can change it. That's the kind of gift we have as being a human, choice . . . As long as I'm working on the website, there are some revenue streams . . . Maybe ads, maybe Google ads, views, but that's not the point. I come up with a very unique idea how to make money through my project and how to make it sustainable. How to pay back my investors.

Interviewer: So you have investors?

Respondent: Not right now, but I'm working on the MVP, minimum viable product. So after that, I'll pitch it to the investors.

Interviewer: Who are the investors? Who are you going to pitch it to?

Respondent: Essentially, the investors are going to come through xHub [an innovation hub in Addis Ababa]. The xHub members are going to bring the investors, and they have impact investors interested in the vision of social impact.

Experienced digital entrepreneurs, on the other hand, still believed in the ultimate potential of digital technologies, but they had markedly different notions about how big markets were, how soon enterprises would grow, and how easily success would be achieved. This is typical of startup entrepreneurship environments (Garud, Schildt, and Lant 2014; Roundy 2016). The struggle to arrive at product-market fit became a defining part of one Rwandan's entrepreneurial story:

Respondent: I thought I was going to make a dollar per charge, that's what I thought.

Interviewer: That's a lot.

Respondent: I spent too much time in the States! [*laughter*] So that's what I thought I was going to make. . . . This is the first business I actually did a little bit of research [for], by testing dozens of different models. I started charging a lease fee, a monthly fee—that didn't work out. Then I started asking them to pay me a percentage of their sale, that didn't work out because they were lying a lot. I worked on the prototype myself for three months. I was there every day, [from] 7:00 a.m. to 5:00 p.m. (Entrepreneur in Kigali)

We found that the longer actors were engaged in the practice of digital entrepreneurship, the more likely they were to display pragmatism about their business and distance themselves from a belief in Silicon Valley as an ideal model for how their business should behave. They shifted their efforts toward acquiring paying customers before looking for investors or stopped relying on investors entirely. A different Rwandan entrepreneur describes his experience that investments have not been necessary to advance his company, though he worries that novices may have different expectations toward him:

> From the ground up, I had to lower my expectations. [*laughter*] If someone comes to me and says, "I'll bring a 10 million investor tomorrow," well, I say, "Yes, please do," but that's not exactly what I'm waiting for in order to keep developing my company. . . . If so many people—especially the young entrepreneurs—know that I'm spearheading this, and they don't see me raising the necessary investments, somehow they're going to keep getting discouraged. (Entrepreneur in Kigali)

Experienced entrepreneurs also sometimes drop any romantic notions of having large-scale social impact when they realize that the segment of the market they are targeting does not have the financial wherewithal to make their businesses sustainable:

> I don't wake up in the morning to make a lot of money, although sometimes it's hard. I used to talk only about my startup in social impact terms, but the more I got into it and the more I got the serious money and the serious team, the more I'm now talking about the mechanics . . . and it becomes this scientific experiment, and you don't at all see how you might be changing lives. You just become absorbed in the machinery of it. I don't know, I'm also growing up. So maybe something is happening in my brain where you forget about idealism somewhere. But also if we don't look seriously at the mechanics and we have nothing, then it's a vanity project. (Entrepreneur in Nairobi)

An Indian-born Kenyan CEO emphasizes that patience and persistence are key:

> **Interviewer:** Why did you make it and maybe others didn't?
>
> **Respondent:** . . . But for us, I personally think that Kenyans are too impatient, so they try something and if it doesn't succeed in a year or two, then they just switch over to something else. For us, from day one, personally, if you ask me, we never had a plan B, so when you don't have a plan B, you just do whatever needs to be done for plan A.

In sum, we found a very clear pattern: digital entrepreneurs with three or more years of experience are more customer- and business-focused, maintaining a belief in the importance of their work and the transformative potential of digital technologies, while also being realistic about limitations.

Our analysis of these entrepreneurs' stories shows that they learned hard lessons through small and large failures whenever they tried uncritically to apply the Silicon Valley model to local contexts.

Bilateral Actors

African digital entrepreneurs who had been exposed to high-income countries were smaller in number than entrepreneurs who had stayed in their home country, and yet they dominated the ranks of role models and success stories. Returnees are often local elites—and if they were not when they left, they are when they return. Their skills were highly regarded:

> Maybe that is the African industry realization and capital building, let's say that this migration to Europe and then coming back is actually that way for building the competence base. (Immigrant entrepreneur, Nairobi, Kenya)

> The entrepreneurs who have succeeded, who are doing well, are entrepreneurs who are foreign trained. Who are returnees, who schooled in US, who schooled in the UK, who have the experience, who have got an internship in McKinsey. If you put that foreign founder right here and you put a home-grown entrepreneur right here, the skill gap is so high. (Entrepreneur in Lagos)

When asked to articulate how stays abroad facilitated returnees' performance, they typically pointed to the technical knowledge that they had obtained and the professional standards to which they had become accustomed. A Rwandan entrepreneur, who had spent his adult years in the United States and recently relocated to Kigali, went further:

> And another thing: if I didn't go to the States, I don't think I'd be the entrepreneur I am today. The states really taught me how to be an entrepreneur, I mean really. I would have been an entrepreneur, but I would have been a local entrepreneur: store, something small, basic. But the States taught me how to think big.

These entrepreneurs develop an important ability to function as bilateral actors. A good example was that of a CEO of a startup in Dakar that sells software for managing health records. He started a business in California with a local doctor and has since expanded his business to Africa:

> I was in LA [Los Angeles] and then being an IT consultant and . . . with one doctor who has his own practice. Then, he had some issues with the software. I started helping. Then from that came the idea to build a software. Basically, my partner, the doctor, he's the pocket man and I'm the developer. So, the first version we have, the whole programming I did myself. Then we started making sales and then from there we could survive. . . . So, basically what we did is, first, we

develop the software for my partner to use. So, which means that it wasn't like something that was just an idea. It was something that needed to work, so for his own practice, that's the first thing.

A similar case was that of an entrepreneur in Dakar, who spoke about how his postgraduate business education in Italy allowed him ultimately to be a broker between Asian IT companies and local markets:

> [I was] in China for two years. Then from China, I was working there as a finance advisor and after that I came back in Senegal. From here, I went to India where I worked for Airtel. So Airtel is one of the biggest mobile operators in Africa. . . . I came back to Senegal and I was still working for them. Then now, presently I have my company on the telecom field, and I'm doing also several other activities. But mainly what we do is we're a telecom intermediary company and IT business development consultants.

This enterprise essentially replicated his individual role during employment. He spoke about how his ability to code switch was one of his greatest assets. Code switching is switching between language styles and culturally specific performances via a "dual cultural personality" (Mercado 2010, 225). Details such as accents, email styles, and a familiarity with clients that might be deemed overly friendly in other settings were among the skills on which his technology consulting company was based. In fact, an awareness of the importance of sociocultural elements informed his expansion strategy: he expanded to other countries by identifying local partners who could navigate local arenas with ease.

It is important to note the performativity of the greater success that returnee entrepreneurs attain. When national, ethnic, and racial attributes are linked with values of authority, capability, and professionalism, the former can be assumed to convey the latter (Healy 2015; MacKenzie, Muniesa, and Siu 2007; Pollock and Williams 2016). Entrepreneurs that are steeped in Western norms are the most successful at navigating the promissory landscape of digital entrepreneurship and signal legitimacy within it, in large part because the landscape itself is configured according to Western norms. Attributions of status and success become self-fulfilling prophecies, as entrepreneurs are rewarded for displaying Western attributes. Incubators, events, and success stories play their role to create a sociomaterial environment that transmits the valuing of particular skillsets and to teach the "correct" performance of digital entrepreneurship. For example, the ability to speak and think "in MBA" is a vital component of being seen as credible

(Katila, Laine, and Parkkari 2019). The rewards arrive in the form of status but can also be monetary, as this excerpt from an interview with an investor in Nairobi illustrates:[1]

> We don't have any bias but I think we are still in the early stage where from an ecosystem perspective, where it is still the entrepreneurs that are coming from say the West that are saying: "I can do this," and they have the perspective of: "I want to exit"—because that's a big one. "I want to build a very big company and I don't mind having a very small share but of a very big company." That's slowly happening in terms of local entrepreneurs but that hasn't always been there. We're looking for people who are thinking like that and we don't want to have an issue later on. . . . I'm seeing that change, I'm seeing Kenyan entrepreneurs having seen that as well, even if they haven't lived and worked abroad, even if they've only lived in Kenya, seeing that that's a potential route for business rather than just, "I'll build a small business, very gradually," which is what all our parents have done. That's what the business mindset is here.

The more experienced digital entrepreneurs we interviewed in Nairobi, Accra, and Lagos especially were keenly aware of this dynamic, sometimes using it to their strategic advantage. For instance, African-born entrepreneurs used direct or indirect affiliations with elite Western educational institutions to convey legitimacy:

> Harvard Business School, Yale, McKinsey—I mean that's pedigree. So the thing is, we've come to understand how business works, we've come to understand some of the things that we need to do to prove [it]. (Enterprise cofounder in Nairobi)

One already successful Nigerian entrepreneur felt compelled to complete an executive MBA at the University of Oxford, giving him a feeling of status and responsibility that his successful business and many awards had not:

> I thought it was significant. I was surprised. I did an MBA, running a business of, at that time, probably sixty people. . . . I'm doing it in the top ten business school globally, according to the [*Financial Times*]. It's remarkable, but that also puts its own pressure because it's my alma mater now, I'm connected to the school forever and I have to keep up to those high expectations because they're very high expectations. It's not just collecting an award and slumping in your seat. It's about collecting that award, and even moving faster, marching faster, making sure you're delivering and doing the right things.

Activists

Although entrepreneurs are adversarial to policy in a number of locales, progressive activism as such seemed to be entwined with the digital entrepreneurship sectors in Uganda, Kenya, and Senegal. For instance, in Nairobi, the ecosystem as a whole has been associated with the development of Ushahidi, a tool developed during contentious elections. In Uganda, one interviewee expressed his assessment of an old guard being out of touch with the young population that understands digital technologies, an opinion which he also expressed on social media:[2]

> However, I don't see that turning over to being a lot more conducive for another ten years . . . all the people who are in the powerful positions are the very same ones. They are in the top three demographic percent above 58, which is our life expectancy for the country. And those are the postcolonial guys. They are now fighting for another time, a time they know they can't win. So for us guys down here, we're positive. We're like, "Yeah, ten years you are going to be out. We're not going to fight you, we're not going to go to the streets, we're just going to wait. It's cool we enjoy your postcolonial stories 'When we were in the bush.' Oh, come on guys, I wasn't even born when you were in the bush, I don't know what you mean" . . . We have those kinds of the people in power trying to describe to them what the technical innovation is like. (Founder in Kampala)

In Cameroon, we came across reluctant activists. The government's internet ban was aimed at reducing the spread of dissent and penalizing rebel strongholds in the west of the country. The effect was the disruption of digital companies located in Buea, also known as Silicon Mountain. An entrepreneur in Yaoundé explained that the government had acted in this way because it felt politically threatened:

> We have something very good in Cameroon [which] is, if you don't try to do something that will take the power, they will leave you in peace. (Entrepreneur in Yaoundé)

In the Anglophone areas of Cameroon, internet connectivity has emerged as an arena of contestation because of the political unrest that is emanating from a separatist element (see box 6.2). Intermittent disconnections from the internet have had a significant impact on the entrepreneurs of Buea:

> I'm sure many entrepreneurs have told you before what happened. No internet and a lot of entrepreneurs became what they call "internet refugees." All right, so you know what a coworking space is and internet is like a basic resource in a cowork space and without internet, if we could not provide a basic resource . . . will make entrepreneurs and subscribers look for internet elsewhere. That's how our difficulties in sustaining our business model when internet went off. We lost a lot of subscribers. Subscribers who had already paid, they had to go do Douala,

> **Box 6.2**
> Buea: Silicon Mountain in a Tense Political Climate
>
> The main town in Cameroon's Anglophone region, Buea, has acquired the nickname Silicon Mountain.[3] Yaoundé is the seat of government, and Douala is the economic capital and ostensibly the center of digital entrepreneurship activity. Buea, however, has been anointed with the Silicon Something moniker. This is because the visible digital firms in Cameroon are in Buea. Despite its much smaller size, the hubs that have sprung up in Douala have seen fit to also have a presence in Buea. Within Cameroon, Buea is recognized as having a student population that has the right attitude and skillset to succeed in technological career paths. As the political situation that pits the government against separatists from Western Cameroon becomes deadlier, it is clear that there is a darker subtext to this praise. Being Anglophone represents a difference in a way that is not innocuous.

Yaoundé, Baffousam, the French-speaking zones of Cameroon. When their suspensions ended and there was no internet, business was flat. (Hub founder in Buea)

Advocating on behalf of their businesses has transformed Cameroon's entrepreneurs into political activists even if it was not a particular interest of theirs to agitate against the government. The government does not facilitate a conducive environment for business at the best of times (Ngoasong 2018). However, the fact that their livelihoods are threatened by the limitation of their access to the internet provides these entrepreneurs with the incentive to protest their exclusion:

[When the government] don't do their job we can lose light [electric power], we cannot have water, but we are in a place where sun and water and everything is there. But it's really bad management. Even for the internet, you see we are trying three providers at the same time to decide where we go now, because for [some] illogical reason [even with] the actual provider we have, every day from 11:00 a.m. to 2:00 p.m., we don't have internet. (Entrepreneur in Yaoundé)

The situation in Anglophone Cameroon was the most extreme example of exclusion and negative gatekeeping that we observed. Nevertheless, it provides some perspective on the difference in outcomes between disinterested facilitators and those making an active attempt to limit the activities of entrepreneurs.

Summary: An African Avant-Garde?

The goal of this chapter was to identify the identities that the context "Africa" produces when individuals enact "digital entrepreneurship" as a received practice. We highlighted shared themes and entrepreneur attributes that are broadly observed at all sites. The cross-cutting threads were often the result of the adoption of the same Silicon Valley imaginary. The chapter revealed that exposure to a particular discourse on the commercialization of technologies is common to digital entrepreneurs in Africa.

However, it would be a mistake to see African identities and enactments purely as replication or mimicry. Local entrepreneurs appropriate, repurpose, and contextualize this discourse, to create and maintain new entrepreneurial identities. Our analysis was thus an exercise in finding common threads within a multifaceted mosaic. The only true universals are those that are able to become pluralities (Mbembe 2016; Tsing 2005).

African digital entrepreneurs break new ground compared to established professional identities in their local context. Paradoxically and interestingly, the emerging professional class at the same time mirrors old social inequalities' positionalities and sees itself as an avant-garde that does things differently. Young foreign-educated, affluent urbanites with connections often dominate the ranks of successful entrepreneurs, and yet their social image is one of newness, change, and sometimes rebellion against older foreign-educated, affluent urbanites with connections. Every single identity we found has something to do with driving change and transitions from an old analog world (which is slow, survival-oriented, corrupt, unfair, inefficient, and fragmented) to a brave new digital one (fast, transformation-oriented, fair, efficient, and seamless). Yet entrepreneurs were unable to shed ties to the old world, like careers enabled (or not) by their parents, kinship networks, professional experience, and humbling experiences with local markets, at least in the short term. In a very basic sense, it became clear that the pursuit of digital entrepreneurship can be a resource-intensive aspiration and is often economically not the safest and most rewarding alternative, limiting who can afford to participate. More broadly, we thus see social asymmetries in African nations and cities being reproduced, mirrored, and sometimes reinforced in the digital entrepreneurship arena.

7 Silicon Tensions

Whether it is talk of Africa as rising or hopeless, the continent's fortunes are set in contrast or comparison primarily to Western locales (Ascione 2016; Mosse 2005; Seth 2016). Such perspectives echo outmoded positions—namely, the goal of modernizing peripheries (Escobar 2011; Rostow 1960) and views of technologies as determinants of social history (MacKenzie and Wajcman 1999). However, despite evolutions in scholarly debates, these points of view continue to underpin how policymakers, the media, some academic disciplines, and global popular culture see Africa's best course of action: that it should modernize and Westernize.

Silicon Valley's influence in particular looms large over the global digital entrepreneurship imaginary (Avle, Lindtner, and Williams 2017; Carver 2010). For cities and regions, it has long been the global benchmark for innovativeness and growth (Bresnahan, Gambardella, and Saxenian 2001; Engel 2015; Steiber and Alänge 2016).

This is true also in Africa. Just as the United States was a universal standard for modernist understanding of economic development, Silicon Valley has defined the archetype of ideal behavior, language, norms, and symbols of digital entrepreneurship.

In each of the previous chapters, we presented evidence that African contexts are incomparable to Silicon Valley and that no African ecosystem will become like Silicon Valley at any point in the future. Although common patterns and issues are discernible, African contexts are on distinct development paths, and comparisons to Silicon Valley "best practice" are, at best, a distraction from efforts to do what works locally. We are not alone in pointing this out: entrepreneurs and commentators have begun to articulate that Africa is incomparable to Silicon Valley (Grin and Eloff 2018;

Ndiomewese 2017). Still, already the existence of such discussions signals that social constructions of African digital entrepreneurship are always in relation to Silicon Valley. Wikipedia's list of Silicon Somethings[1] enumerates countless cities and regions, stretching across every continent, including four in Africa: Silicon Cape (Cape Town), Silicon Lagoon (Lagos), Silicon Mountain (Buea), and the Silicon Savannah (Nairobi).

This chapter seeks to understand how Silicon Valley's ideals are transported to African contexts and how actors in Africa are dealing with them. We want to analyze how actors negotiate and circumvent what one may see as a foreign intrusion. The first section thus outlines how Silicon Valley ideals merged with those of international development and through which channels and actors the resultant blend of ideas spread and took root across Africa. The following two sections discuss what we identified as the most important clashes: the Silicon Valley model's unfitness for African market realities and its inbuilt racial bias. The final section identifies local actors' responses, including the now-infamous white fronting strategy.

This chapter shows that Silicon Valley and international development norms and aspirations have conspired to exert an omnipresent influence on African digital entrepreneurship. This has led to tensions when Africans' understandings of how to run a business in local conditions were dismissed and replaced or when Africans were crowded out from access to resources. Despite their indignation, local entrepreneurs reluctantly find pragmatic answers, sometimes mimicking developmentalist ideals to access resources and other times blending them with tried and true ways. In the end, digital entrepreneurs in Africa need to not only understand how to run a business organization but also wield mythologies and expectations of the global digital entrepreneurship agenda to attract attention and capital.

Silicon Somethings and the Digital Developmentalist Aspiration

Scholarship has extensively documented the heterogeneities and multiplicities of capitalism and innovation (Arora and Romijn 2009; Pavitt 2006). Yet Western ideas of modernization, perpetuated through discourses and media, have continued their hegemony over the global zeitgeist (Gikandi 2001; Hecht 2011; Ngũgĩ wa Thiong'o 1986; Zeleza 2009). Norms and modes of thought of high-income countries—and America in particular—are rendered as universal best practices, which others should subscribe to in order to improve their situation (Bourdieu and Wacquant 1999; Hecht 2011; Tsing 2005).

We find that a similar dynamic applies to the relationship between digital entrepreneurship practices and Silicon Valley. Although local instantiations of digital entrepreneurship in Africa are diverse (see chapters 2 and 5), Silicon Valley's fast-growth model is held up as the modern ideal that everyone everywhere should aspire to and is measured against (Avle, Lindtner, and Williams 2017), as an entrepreneur in Dakar confirmed:

> So, there is this stigma that identify technology intelligence to the Western world. So, if somebody who has the same first name as [mine] or a last name of your neighbor, and then say, "I master the technology," you know, people have doubts. But still, Africans are making great, I would say, technology.

Idols in the Media

Silicon Valley's symbolic role was a staple in the interviews we conducted. Entrepreneurs frequently referred to role model entrepreneurs and businesses from Silicon Valley. As interviewers, we tried our best to avoid introducing Silicon Valley into the conversation, and yet participants mentioned star entrepreneurs including Mark Zuckerberg (fifteen mentions), Bill Gates (ten), Steve Jobs (eight), Tim Draper (two), and Elon Musk (one). We soon found that for many, success stories transmitted through popular, news, and social media serve as inspiration and blueprints for how to perform as a digital entrepreneur:

> I got more interested and I continued reading about softwares on Google, and then I was so inspired by a guy who made the software for Yahoo!, which could combine the news. So that small guy made that application and they gave him about $10 million. So I was like, "This thing has money. I should also get into it." (Nineteen-year-old entrepreneur in Kigali)

Silicon Valley and high-income countries, in many Africans' minds, are where technological and social frontiers have pushed ahead, and they feel compelled to catch up with and become part of it:

> When you think about "potential," you think about "digital." That is, always moving, always changing. Today, it's Instagram; tomorrow, it's Snapchat; tomorrow, it's big data; next, it's analytics. They're moving fast and it's for people who have potential, who question the status quo, who are energetic, who think "innovation" all the time. Those are the people who can move with digital, with the trends in digital, always moving. (Entrepreneur in Lagos)

Accordingly, African entrepreneurs were often drawn to digital entrepreneurship because they hoped it would be a means through which they could circumvent old ways of doing business and powerful cliques:

> We don't want our business to be controlled by a few people: big business or government. I've done this for years, like eight years is in total. You have to go, sucking up to people and making them feel good and all that. Individual product is the best. I would rather go into the broader market where there are a million people, and nine hundred thousand [of them] like me. One hundred thousand may not like me . . . but I'd rather put my fate and my destiny in the hands of nine hundred thousand people than in ninety people. (Entrepreneur in Lagos)

We asked a manager of a coworking space in Abidjan why he thought it was that relating local companies to the Silicon Valley model was common. He implicated technology media:

> IT has a media coverage at a level that draws, that excites the imagination of people. It's like sports. There are so many other sports, but you only keep hearing about soccer and basketball. You think those are the only two sports that exist in the world. . . . The media, some NGOs, some hubs, and some incubators, coworking spaces—everybody starts becoming this, what do we call it? Evangelist, or the miracle tool, or miracle.

Likening Silicon Valley's capture of the global economic imagination to the popularity of major sports is an apt analogy because it reflects the dominance of Western culture in Africans' lives. Interestingly, novices, Westerners, and Westernized Africans bought most into the notion that digital technologies allow for Silicon Valley–style international expansion and that such expansion is the ultimate goal and sign of success:

> You can't claim success until you are doing it at a global stage. I think we're already doing it at global standards, and we've been recognized as such by some reputable institutions. An article about it came out in the *Financial Times* yesterday. I was super proud. . . . It's about financial inclusion, and how this whole thing that we are doing might bring change. Again, "might," but I think it's already changing, but you want to see it scale. (Entrepreneur in Maputo)

iHub and the Silicon Savannah

Media are definitely essential channels through which the idolization of Silicon Valley is nurtured and sustained. Yet understanding how the notion that Africa could be like Silicon Valley took hold requires looking to one particular ecosystem and one particular organization: Nairobi's Silicon

Savannah and its leading innovation hub, the iHub. From around 2010, both became essential symbols for other ecosystems across Africa (Friederici 2019; Graham 2015; Graham and Mann 2013; Marchant 2018; Ndemo and Weiss 2017a).

iHub is regarded by many as the focal organization of the Silicon Savannah (Marchant 2018; Ndemo and Weiss 2017a). It originally occupied several floors of the Bishop Magua building on Ng'ong Road, the epicenter of startup activity in Nairobi and the location of five hubs and incubators other than iHub (see box 7.1).

iHub's founders—most prominently Erik Hersman—proposed an explicit vision of how the hub would become a network infrastructure to support and interconnect far-flung actors with complementary competences (see Friederici 2019 for details). First, iHub asserted itself as a facilitator of the

---

Box 7.1
iHub and the KBW Network

iHub, established in 2010, is a product of a particular local community in Nairobi. The founders of iHub were the technologists and activists involved with Ushahidi, an information crowdsourcing tool that was used during Kenya's 2007–2008 postelection crisis. Their history goes further back than even before they were all present in Kenya. Namely, the iHub founders originated with the The Kenya Blog Web (KBW) Ring, a virtual community of bloggers with Kenya links. Belonging was not determined by citizenship: some of them were located in Kenya, but others were Kenyan emigres who lived and studied abroad. A core close-knit group of about ten individuals went on to establish the organizations that are most associated with Nairobi's Silicon Savannah: Ushahidi and iHub. The visibility of Ushahidi due to global media interest and its subsequent adoption in various humanitarian emergencies around the world led the team to register it as a charity and collect donations that helped fund iHub and other spin-off companies, such as BRCK and Savannah Fund. The popularity and success of iHub then led to the establishment of revenue-oriented simulacrums: for example, m:lab, a mobile technology business incubator, and Nailab provide seed funds, workspace, mentorship, and an introduction to venture firms like Savannah Fund or 88mph in return for equity. All the while, the network of ten grew tenfold with each new organization and with every individual who went to work in its coworking space. Firms such as eLimu, Kytabu, and many others remain tied together through their relationship with iHub.

local entrepreneurial ecosystem. Drawing on an understanding of ecosystems similar to the relational theory of ecosystems outlined in chapter 5, iHub was envisioned to enhance the quality and coherence of connections among actors in Nairobi:

> One grouping [within a tech ecosystem] is starups [*sic*], another is investors, another is large tech companies, and yet another is researchers. There are bloggers, digital creatives, visiting techies, SME [small and medium enterprise] leaders who've learned their lessons, and freelancers moonlighting from their day jobs. It's a big mixed bag and we all together form an ecosystem. . . . [A] healthy tech ecosystem is where the different parties are able to and want to work together. (Hersman 2015)

But iHub soon began to influence a far wider geographical expanse than Kenya's capital city. iHub's "connector" narrative resonated with contemporary trends of international development and broader aspirational discourses around digital entrepreneurship, which were emerging across Africa. iHub was new and hip, playing into a number of development paradigms such as community, participation, grassroots, and, of course, entrepreneurship and innovation (Brinks and Ibert 2015; Friederici 2019; Seo-Zindy and Heeks 2017). iHub's perceived success started to nurture a widely held belief that hubs can be transformative for entire nations and regions. For instance, the argument that iHub builds skills that are relevant for digital entrepreneurship together with assertions about its far-reaching influence were ultimately used to explicitly contend that iHub contributes to economic development in Kenya (Moraa 2012; Moraa and Mwangi 2012).

At its symbolic peak in the mid-2010s, Nairobi had become the perceived leader of all African entrepreneurial ecosystems (Henry 2015; Hersman 2013; Oluwafemi 2013).[2] The number of success stories widely celebrated in the media had now expanded beyond iHub, Ushahidi, and M-Pesa and come to include startups like M-Kopa Solar, Kopo Kopo, MFarm, BRCK, Eneza Education, and BitPesa. The visibility of these organizations ultimately went a long way toward inspiring the interest of youth in digital entrepreneurship, thus growing the network even further.

The core group of iHub-affiliated people also became gatekeepers; their public perception and positions within the network gave them power. They broker relationships and are the ones that media and funders gravitated toward time and again, whenever those external actors wanted to interact with the Silicon Savannah. When Barack Obama spoke at the 2015

Global Entrepreneurship Summit in Nairobi, he shared the stage not only with Kenya's President Uhuru Kenyatta but also with Judith Owigar (CNN 2015), founder of AkiraChix, a small iHub-affiliated grassroots organization supporting girls learning how to code and pursuing careers in technology. Another widely shared photo of Obama's visit shows him next to an M-Kopa Solar kiosk—displayed, for instance, in an African Business Central (2015) blog post, fittingly titled "The African Tech Startup Scene Has Been Transformed in Just Four Years."

Spreading the Gospel

It is impossible to say how big iHub's impact has been in economic terms, but clear evidence exists for iHub's symbolic role across the continent, sparking numerous imitations (see Friederici 2019 for a detailed review). People with a connection to or an interest in digital entrepreneurship heard about iHub or read about it via international mainstream media (BBC, *Forbes*, *Wired*) and African tech media (Disrupt Africa, VC4Africa, *African Tech Roundup*, etc.). A Pan-African community of hub managers also started to organize, notably through BongoHive's crowdsourced map and the founding of AfriLabs, a kind of hub association (BongoHive 2013; Hersman 2011). These participants in Ghana explicitly referred to iHub as a motivator for their efforts in interviews conducted in late 2014:

> So I feel like one thing Kenya has better than us is their brand. You know, everyone knows Kenya—it's sort of the tech Mecca! . . . When you think about technology, from the outside, you think about Kenya, you think about M-Pesa, you think about the Kenyan developers. So I know iHub has investors throwing money, and I thought it would be good [to have something similar here] because I think, there are really brilliant developers in Ghana, but we're not together, so there was really not a community per se. (Founder of a social enterprise)

> What we had seen in iHub and what it had spurred on in that economy gave us some ideas on what we could also do here. So I would say we didn't do this in isolation. A lot of this was done trying to look at what had happened in other parts of this continent. . . . At the time, the hype and stories around entrepreneurship—it was a community within Nairobi, and how iHub had played a big role in making that happen . . . So if you looked at Erik Hersman . . . all these people who have been a big part of the Kenyan iHub, and gave that serious credibility within the African market but they were moving out to bigger things. . . . And just the idea that an entity like a hub could actually be a catalyst in creating a whole new culture for entrepreneurship. (Hub manager in Accra)

Such grassroots ambitions productively overlapped with the merger of entrepreneurship, technology utopist, and development discourses (Avgerou 2003; Kaplinsky and Keynes 2011; Kaplinsky et al. 2009). Market-oriented practice benefitted from a change in development thinking that now started to understand innovation as a means to progress rather than simply evidence of it (Neveling 2017; Porter 1998; Shakya 2017; Srinivas and Sutz 2008). An ever-wider range of actors thus began to champion the idea that social development can and should be addressed by entrepreneurs commercializing digital products, with the market functioning as a selection environment for "sustainable" solutions. This is evident in how startup buzzwords have come to inhabit the lexicon of development practice (Akpan 2011; Shakya 2017).

Given their fit within this paradigm, innovation hubs became the primary channel through which development organizations, foundations, technology corporations, and other development funders tried to support digital entrepreneurship (Friederici 2019). These actors implicitly or explicitly subscribed to the developmentalist understanding of the Silicon Valley digital entrepreneurship imaginary, considering it "best practice" both for beneficiaries and for the intervention itself (Hart 2003; OECD 2003; Shakya 2017; Williams and Williams 2011). They provided resources for a distinct version of digital entrepreneurship to become widespread across Africa.

This became evident not only in the mindsets, language, and behavior of entrepreneurs but also in the sociomaterial landscapes that developed across Africa as in the rest of the world (Boxenbaum and Lounsbury 2013; Katila, Laine, and Parkkari 2019; Tracey, Dalpiaz, and Phillips 2018). One of the strongest through lines between sites thus was the iconography of Silicon Valley in physical spaces (Jasanoff and Kim 2016; Suchman 2011). We saw casually dressed young people focusing on laptop screens in coworking spaces and open plan offices in every city that we visited. Often, we met interviewees in the inevitable cafes colocated within shared workspaces or in coffee shops with good Wi-Fi around the city.

Although the formulaic similarities belie diversity in underlying local cultures, contingencies, and prospects, the ubiquity and similarity of iconographies is evidence of a shared understanding about the constitutive elements of digital entrepreneurship, which form the basis of how actors value and legitimize each other's efforts (Lee 2001; Tracey, Dalpiaz, and

Phillips 2018). As with traditional professions, individuals develop familiarity with the professional ecology of digital entrepreneurship (including its codes, languages, and sensibilities) through social learning (Adams, Wiebe, and Scherer 1989). The universalization of digital entrepreneurship has the effect of creating expectations about how entrepreneurs should behave, what mindset they should have, and what their level of ambition should be (Knight 2013; Spigel and Harrison 2018).

Frontierspeople

The diffusion of a universal digital archetype means that actors who are well-versed in it are standard bearers and are rewarded for holding this identity by powerful legitimating actors. Those actors include funders, media outlets, industry analysts and experts, regulators, and even customers—namely, any actors who are viewed as authoritative and from whose favorable assessment entrepreneurs can draw benefit and claim an accomplishment.

Given that the digital entrepreneurship archetype is foreign and Western, it often benefits foreign Westerners more than Africans. A kind of social indexing is at work in some of the cities that we studied (see Rodrigues et al. 2018), particularly in Nairobi, Johannesburg, Kigali, and to a lesser extent Lagos and Accra, which are sizeable economies, which offer high degrees of safety and comfort, and/or in which international development has an extensive presence.

Scholarship has demonstrated that returning diaspora and immigration are net positives for digital entrepreneurship ecosystems (Avle 2014; Kemeny and Cooke 2018; Saxenian 2006). Discussions on immigration are usually framed from the perspective of entrepreneurs seeking prosperity by moving from less to more affluent societies. Yet immigrant digital entrepreneurs in Africa are almost all from Europe or North America as opposed to Asia or South America.[3] These individuals have moved from more to less affluent contexts. African economies and societies are not usually preferred career destinations for Westerners. In fact, enterprises looking to attract technical expertise from abroad report that they have to financially compensate Westerners for their negative perceptions:

> Even if we're charging Silicon Valley prices, we really can't bring people here. People are scared of Africa, and it's been a really tough challenge. (Entrepreneur in Nairobi)

Instead, white immigrants in digital entrepreneurship scenes of Nairobi and other African cities are seeking something other than money: they can be described as *frontierspeople*. Africa has developed a reputation as the new frontier (Nyamnjoh 2013), where underdevelopment, hardship, and scarcity are reinterpreted as a worthy challenge, giving Westerners an opportunity to escape unfulfilled, boring lives and make their legacies:

> I was here [in Nairobi for my previous job in international development], meeting with movers and shakers from government, from private sector, from startups, from hubs, from you name it, seeing all this fascinating stuff happen. At the same time, I was very, very frustrated with the bureaucracy of development, and I liked the work, but the process was terrible, and I'd been doing it for about six and a half years. I was ready for a change. (Entrepreneur in Nairobi)

We found that these individuals tend to have received a good formal education, but they are not typically very experienced at their time of arrival in East Africa. Their expressed goals mostly revolve around some notion of having "impact":

> I want it to be a company that does save lives and even for all the business surrounding that, [this] still sincerely motivates me. . . . I want it to be a company that's scaling and very successful because that's the only way it can have impact. I want it to be a place mainly that can be my soapbox to stand on and give me the best life I can live. (CEO in East Africa)

Those looking to hire Westerners expressed that they could motivate candidates' sense of altruism and adventure:

> I spent quite a bit of time in Berlin, there's a good tech scene there, good talent, good, at least word in the street, cheap developers because all of Ukrainians and Eastern Europeans want to come to Berlin. So through our local networks here, we stumbled upon him, he was bored to death. When we asked him if he minded moving to Nairobi, he answered anything but [*inaudible*] would be an upgrade, and he was bored because his startup had already, it was at maturity, so no more product development. He's kind of earning money on the side from that and coming here because it's the Wild West, and it's exciting, right? (Immigrant entrepreneur in Nairobi)

Initial business ideas are typically drawn from inspiration from the settings of their origins, often wanting to bring African contexts up to the same level:

> Then I flew to Washington. I remember exactly when this was. . . . I took something like seven different types of transportation that were all powered by technology. I took an Uber, a car2go, a bikeshare, a metro train that I checked the

schedule [for] on an app, and then I coordinated that with the bus schedule on a different app, and so by the end of the day I was sitting at home and I thought: "Wow, I took seven different tech-powered transport things today, two years ago not one of them existed." Then I thought how fundamentally that had changed my relationship with the city as someone who didn't have a car, and then I thought back to Nairobi, where I'd just come from, where we have all these problems in transport. (Entrepreneur in Kenya)

One or two years after their arrival, many then face a period of reckoning, in which they realize that running a small business in settings that are foreign to them is taking a financial and mental toll. Savings and networks in their home countries sometimes help them secure enough capital to sustain their companies for a few years. It was interesting that none of the migrant founders we interviewed had initially planned on staying, and none were committing to staying, even those that had been in the country for many years and ran successful companies.

Clearly, white immigrants from high-income countries are virtually never moving to nor staying in African cities out of economic necessity. Perceiving African locales as adventure-filled opportunities is a choice and a luxury. Instead, their mobility and relocation are a reproduction of their privilege in that they, as globally more privileged actors, are able to freely travel and settle in new areas (Massey 1999):

To me, I didn't do the sacrifice by coming here. Actually, it was quite the opposite. When you're a white guy from the middle class in Paris, from Sciences Po, the risk is not really present here. If I fail, what do I do? I can just come back to my parents' home and look for a job and I'm probably going to find it. So, I don't really have a risk, and the money problem is obviously a problem, but because I could work as a freelance thanks to my former experiences, actually I never had any money problem. I started here very poor, but quickly I could just work left and right, find solutions, so I never had neither the money problem nor the risk problem. I never even ask money to my parents, I didn't need it because I could earn it. (Immigrant entrepreneur in Accra)

Such complete absence of existential risk and social responsibility is a stark contrast to the realities of most African digital entrepreneurs (see chapter 6). The reverse situation, in which, say, a Nairobian entrepreneur travels to Berlin to take up a post at a startup, would be much more difficult to facilitate. The global migration system places greater restrictions on Africans than on Westerners interested in taking on the international opportunities newly created by digital technologies.

Interestingly, the rationales we heard for why the presence of white immigrants also may be a net positive for locals were founded in the logics of global markets and competition:

> We're seeing a lot of new entrepreneurs—really good new entrepreneurs—coming in, and I think that's because this is Nairobi, part of the ecosystem. . . . There's some very smart people from all over the world who might, sort of, be tired of what they're doing somewhere else. Like, "I can use my intelligence and brain to do a lot, build something much bigger, or create a lot more impact if I do that here [in Nairobi] compared to doing it in the US." (Investor in Nairobi)

> Now, in terms of Rwanda for Rwandans, Africa for Africans, I just see it as a misguided protectionist mindset that isn't so different than Brexit or Trumpism. It's like the idea that the external is a threat. And "They're the problem, we're the solution," rather than realizing that as I just said, I think it is a hybrid that will make it the most powerful companies . . . The Tour Rwanda, it's like the Tour de France, you know, it's a big race and Rwanda loves bicycling. . . . The first year Rwandans all came in dead last. It was really controversial, "Who are these foreigners to come here and beat us?" But then, after three or four years, Rwandans started doing better and better and then they started winning. And you know what? If there was never a foreigner in it—and it doesn't have to be a white foreigner—somebody who isn't from this home, this room, they wouldn't be, they'd be competing against themselves. There's something to make you realize how competitive the world is, to realize that you better raise your standards. . . . I don't feel like that's controversial. I've been on the record for this stuff. I did an article in TechCrunch talking about this, some other guy did a counter article against me. Yelling at me being the problem. "All these guys coming here just thinking that they get to own the place." Well, but you know what? Sincerely, [*expletive*]. Show me where it's working and then tell me that I'm the problem. (Immigrant entrepreneur in Kigali)

Down to Earth: Local Markets, Local Models

With currently available evidence, it is impossible to say whether white Western immigration has an overall positive or negative economic effect on Africans in digital entrepreneurship ecosystems. Yet what is clear from our analysis is that a sense of injustice has been fueled among Africans observing white immigrants being able to move anywhere and setting up companies with ease, while they are only able to be successful at home.

Unsurprisingly, tensions arise in particular when foreigners enact the Silicon Valley archetype in contradiction with local knowledge, institutions, and histories (Ngoasong 2018). African small enterprises traditionally do not require or are not able to deliver speed, disruption, and scale. Understandably, local actors feel they are best placed to know how to operate in their locality and what their ambitions should be, while distant others are more likely to face a learning curve (Knight 2013). It is frustrating to them when assumptions about the ideal archetype and implicit bias override the pragmatic usefulness of local knowledge.

This clash of models was reflected in a foreign-run and foreign-funded accelerator in Nairobi, which assigned foreign mentors to firms they had funded and asked beneficiaries to increase user numbers at all cost. A Kenyan entrepreneur, who had been part of the acceleration program, critiques it thus:

> They had a lot of perspectives that I didn't agree with. They'd bring in entrepreneurs-in-residence from outside the country. I'm trying to cut deals with [a regional East African media company], you've brought in a guy who has never heard of [the company]. To be my entrepreneur in residence, to help me cut those deals, how is that going to work? . . . I kept thinking, if people are willing to pay me $5,000 every month, when I've [already] got twenty thousand eyeballs [or users], why would I focus so much on [getting more] eyeballs? I should focus on getting ten of those people to pay me $5,000 and I have $50,000 every month from my twenty thousand eyeballs—that's fantastic return!

Pre-revenue financing in particular represents a juncture from established ways:

> I think you're seeing the startups—especially the more successful ones—have international founders, international teams; they've raised international venture capital: very much the Silicon Valley model. But my parents ran businesses, and how people grew their businesses before, it was extremely expensive back in the day, so you had to grow your business organically before applying for a loan. Now startups raise money with two or three customers, and that's the model from the ground up. (Entrepreneur in Nairobi)

It is revealing that this entrepreneur speaks of "successful" companies while discussing enterprises with very few customers. This suggests that he has adopted exogenous Western standards of what is economically desirable (Katz 2004; Neveling 2017; Olivier de Sardan 2005; Shakya 2017; Zeleza 2009). When asked whether he knew of any successful firms in the Abidjan ecosystem, a coworking space manager in Abidjan was more discerning:

> I have seen companies grow. I have seen companies reach a stage that's better in terms of having more advanced products, better understanding of the market,

better understanding of the consumers, increase of the revenue. So, if successful as meaning "saves funds," [then yes, there are success stories]. But, if by success, we mean what we see in the media? Then, I haven't seen that. But at a smaller scale, you're able to settle, able to increase revenue, able to get better product. But then, because I think of the—I don't know—the ecosystem or whatever it is in [this] environment, they're not able to get that last push. So maybe it's coming. Maybe this year, or maybe it's next year.

The cultural conflict about what is a successful African digital enterprise was on full display when Jumia, the Rocket Internet–funded e-commerce company, was listed on the New York Stock Exchange (NYSE) in March 2019. Global technology and business media were quick to report that Jumia, "the Amazon of Africa," was "the first African startup" to trade on the NYSE, exactly mirroring the messaging that the company had displayed on a large banner on Wall Street in New York (BBC News 2019; Bright 2019; Pilling 2019). Respected figures like Rebecca Enonchong (@africatechie on Twitter) used social media to voice their discontent with Jumia's branding as African. Both before and after the listing, Jumia has consistently been criticized for extractive and potentially fraudulent business practices, as well as a degree of arrogance on the part of the German and French founders (Mpala 2019). Jumia was accused of not adapting its business model to local market realities, of making the most significant investments in locations outside of Africa where its managerial and technical staff is located, and of merely maximizing share price at initial public offering (IPO) to guarantee its original investors attractive financial exits. Some of these criticisms seem to have been confirmed soon after the IPO, as Jumia's share price plummeted from US$14.50 in March to under $US5 in November 2019, when it also closed its operations in Cameroon without warning (Reuters 2019). Ken Banks, a known activist and analyst of digital development, summarized: "So there's been a fair amount of scrutiny as to whether Jumia really is an 'African startup' after this news broke yesterday. Headquartered in Germany, French founders, senior management in Dubai, technology centre in Portugal. What constitutes 'African'?" (Banks 2019).

Across Francophone Africa, the cultural distance was sometimes perceived as particularly large and exacerbated by language barriers. In Abidjan, digital entrepreneurs were referred to as *startuppers*, signaling the newness and difference of the startup as an organizational form compared to existing ways of doing business. A Cameroonian entrepreneur perceives the focus on scaling and social impact to be foreign ideas:

There are a lot of Anglophone startups. I think there are a lot of French start-ups. [There is a] distinction between . . . startups that are using tech to scale . . . versus the traditional small business that exist all over Cameroon and that had been existing for years. . . . The startups that are using tech . . . the innovations to change social problems—those ones I think are using more English . . . because I think that model in itself is [an] Anglo-Saxon model. So even the Francophone that are using this model to create businesses, they know that if they need to go beyond Cameroon to scale, they need to use English. And we're seeing how the lack of English speaking limits people.

Likewise, the manager of a small impact investment fund in Uganda is wary of firms that claim high valuations without revenue. The fund he works for learned to steer clear of such enterprises:

[Our fund prefers to invest in businesses that need] either working capital or asset acquisition. . . . What we always look out for is a need of the entrepreneur, not randomly wanting money. You're producing your revenue, your revenue is good, you are earning well and everything—but what is the need? What do we need to finance? We are so specific and keen with that. We believe we need to grow these entrepreneurs, not just the feeling that they need money for probably anything, but we try to be specific with the needs, and the needs that are in line with the business.

More experienced entrepreneurs had reconciled with the fact that modes of digital entrepreneurship were very contextualized and that aspiration to an ideal needed to be tempered by knowledge of what was possible from place to place:

The reason is the challenges you face in the various tech hubs and various environments vary. For example, [in] Silicon Valley you don't have to deal with the problem of languages. In the US, I guarantee you at least 90 percent of them can speak the English language. Well, that's not true because they have immigrants and stuff, but the question of literacy and language is not a challenge they have to solve. In Africa, when you come here, actually it's language literacy. In Ghana we have 148 languages. That's a huge problem. (Entrepreneur in Accra)

Another entrepreneur felt a sense of vindication and emancipation compared to the times when seeking any sort of fortune involved going abroad. He prefers fulfilling his ambitions at home, not having to deal with the struggles of emigration and assimilation:

Growing up, I really want to leave Kenya, I want to do a high-flying career abroad, go to university, do amazing things, and then come back when I'm fifty with a shit ton of money. But now, you can do that sort of thing here, you can build here. You don't have to struggle for visas. It's just being back [after] having to be the international version of myself for two years and then coming back and really starting to adapt to this context. I think, it's an identity thing and it's something that's very important to me and it might not be important to other people . . . but for me I think it's important that you have examples of people that grew up just as you did, making balls out of plastic bags, kicking stuff, running around, speaking the language, and they're able to grow a business to this level. (Entrepreneur in Nairobi)

Similarly, this Rwandan entrepreneur discusses how imitating Silicon Valley ideals is only worth it if this brings in resources:

If you bring someone from Silicon Valley and they come here with no money at all, they will not know anything what to do, but because I grew up in this environment, I know what to do with this environment. But if I want Silicon Valley money, then I need to learn how they talk to the environment. . . . So the Silicon Valley way was going to be a lot more difficult but the Rwandan way worked for me. (Entrepreneur in Kigali)

These quotes also illustrate that entrepreneurs grapple with appropriating Silicon Valley norms and aspirations, but ultimately blend the foreign archetype with local business cultures to form new legitimacy systems (Weiss and Weber 2016). In our dataset, enterprises with a balance of longevity and growth (see chapter 4) were often run by entrepreneurs and teams able to match foreign archetypes to local conditions:

I think the best way to make a company is a hybrid between people with outer Rwanda experience and inner Rwanda experience. Something that I've learned as a leader is that actually, usually, the leader should talk the least and listen to everybody else. It really is fantastic that the different feedback and viewpoints you get. The Rwandans in the company—really, we do have a great team—and their feedback is usually hyper valid. They might not be able to be the person who imagines bringing some Western technology or Western business model here but they're the ones who are best situated at modifying that foreign business model to work in a Rwandan context. (Entrepreneur in Kigali)

Racial Bias

Impositions of the Silicon Valley archetype can also lead to more immediate discrimination and bias. Not only can entrepreneurs from the West migrate more easily, they also epitomize the preferred digital entrepreneur archetype, and thereby they do not have to code switch to the same extent (see chapter 6). In the end, the already privileged entrepreneurs (white immigrants and elite foreign-educated Africans) are better able to assimilate with the Silicon Valley archetype, which is also extolled by virtually all available funders and supporters: from international institutions to investors to local governments.

Conversations about racial bias and discrimination, particularly with respect to funding, frequently trend on social media. The 2018 TechCrunch Battlefield competition in Nairobi is an example of an event that stimulated debate. In Lagos, a back and forth on Twitter in 2014 between leading digital entrepreneurs Marek Zmysłowski and Jason Njoku concerning local entrepreneurs' ability to attract investment over foreigners was another flashpoint. In August 2018, an infographic of what are considered leading startups in Kenya, showing mostly white CEOs, made the rounds on Twitter, sparking a heated debate about whether legislative measures should be in place to ensure that native Kenyans do not get locked out of digital entrepreneurship opportunities.

Research by Village Capital, an impact investment nonprofit based in Washington, DC, supports these perceptions (Strachan Matranga, Bhattacharyya, and Baird 2017). Its report shows that of "90% of disclosed investments [in East Africa] over the past two years went to startups with one or more European or North American founders" (48). Unsurprisingly, this finding stimulated intense exchanges on social media and was referenced by entrepreneurs we interviewed in East Africa:

> Do you know that there is a lot of VC capital that has been coming into Africa? But recent research has shown what we've always known. Recent research showed that about 90 or 85 percent of that goes to African startups that have foreign founders. In fact, even in Uganda here, I can tell you, the startups that have raised the most money are Safe Boda. They've raised over, I think, a million dollars. There is another company—I forget what they are called—I think MIDA something: over half a million dollars. Our biggest hit? 200,000 that we raised over three, four, five years. (Entrepreneur in Kampala)

One white entrepreneur in Kampala felt that the rhetoric around funding bias was overblown, though it was clearly an issue that preoccupied him:

I would be interested to hear [from you whether] people talk about it. Because it's a recurrent topic—foreign funders. So, I feel like there is a notion, and I think it's partly true, that foreign founders have it easier. Did you hear of that? . . . Well, I think, actually education was more important. I think that makes the difference because you know how to communicate with people. (Immigrant entrepreneur in Kampala)

Like this participant, other respondents and debates on social media argue that whiteness and Western-ness are simply correlates or proxies for particular skills and expertise and that there is thus nothing unexpected or iniquitous about investors' decisions. Once locals acquire this knowledge, whiteness would no longer be considered a proxy for it. The proxies-for-performance argument is also made in Silicon Valley and other environments (Pager and Western 2012; Prasad and Qureshi 2017). Other venture capital legitimation criteria are known to consist of proxies like graduation from an Ivy League university, participation in a global top-ten master of business administration (MBA) program, and previous work experience at a startup, failed or otherwise (Mainela, Pernu, and Puhakka 2011; Roberts et al. 2017; Strachan Matranga, Bhattacharyya, and Baird 2017; Tech 2018). This so-called pattern matching is an outcome of investors developing filters for sorting through firms. For instance, the Village Capital report quotes a financier: "I'm a busy investor: so how does a Kenyan entrepreneur cut through the noise of other companies that are emailing me cold or through people in my network? I need a filter" (Strachan Matranga, Bhattacharyya, and Baird 2017, 9).

Pattern matching, however, embeds bias and reproduces privileges and exclusion in legitimation and valuation processes, as it generally selects for affluent white men (Katila, Laine, and Parkkari 2019; Knight 2013; Park and Pellow 2004; Phillips 2005; Prasad and Qureshi 2017; Shih 2006). For instance, white founders receive investment capital from accelerators more frequently than entrepreneurs from emerging markets with the same qualifications, suggesting that "cultural bias might be driving [investors'] perception of lower entrepreneurial skills" (Roberts et al. 2017, 17). When talent is defined according to the Western digital entrepreneurship archetype, local business experience may be overlooked and Africans are unlikely to measure up. A West African creator of an application allowing black women to share advice on hair and fashion products talks about her firsthand encounters in Silicon Valley:

The typical investors in Silicon Valley are like white males in their forties or late thirties. They care less about hair, let alone their wives' or girlfriends' hair, let alone black women's hair. So when I said to them, about hair, if I had a thirty-minutes meeting with an investor, maybe twenty to twenty-five minutes are spent explaining why women do our hair, [that] there's different types of hair. "Why don't you just cut your hair? Do you have to spend so much money on your hair?" You never get to talk about your business or what you've done. It was kind of annoying at some point.

Preference for white foreign actors extends to local support organizations as well. In most cities we visited, entrepreneurs complained about the procurement practices of African government institutions and other large local private sector actors, for whom foreign companies or local companies helmed by foreign executives are preferred partners.

Postcolonial ties represented particular problems. In Maputo, for instance, Mozambican entrepreneurs found that their main competitors for contracts were Portuguese firms. Many entities in Francophone Africa looked to France to fulfill technological contracts. In Anglophone African countries, the United Kingdom was often mentioned as a place where business partners and competitors were based, but also where rules and institutions were adopted from:

> Yeah, it's all over the place, it's an enslaved mentality of—and this is the legacy of colonialism. You spend that many years being told what to do, how to do it, and that you're a lesser than, and that the whites have all the solutions. This is the result of it. Even now our government, even for things as easy as—this sounds absurd, our parliament invited the Korean government to teach us how to be patriotic. [*Expletive*] Answer that for me! I mean how deep is our colonial mindset? That is totally insane. I mean, come on: we still wear wigs in court! (Entrepreneur in Kampala)

A Ugandan government official confirms part of this narrative, but indicates that agencies have learned from experience to distrust local firms:

> There has been a trend where a foreign investor or foreign companies, or companies owned by foreigners get tax holidays and tax incentives. . . . The locals are saying: "Why can't we get tax holidays as much as these folks are getting?" That has created some kind of perception that perhaps government prefers foreigners. But there is another side to this story because there are some local investors that have been given tax holidays, that have been given incentives in form of capital from government, and they have collapsed. (Official from Uganda's ICT agency)

Reluctant Responses

African digital entrepreneurs are forced to grapple with the in-built assumptions and biases of the Silicon Valley archetype when they seek funding and support. Firms and ecosystems themselves feel pressure to make themselves "investable" and to connect to (usually foreign) investors. In this context, entrepreneurs may be aware that digital entrepreneurship is heterogeneous and situated, yet they convey their entrepreneurial story using the language and models of Silicon Valley. This is less because this is the lingua franca of digital entrepreneurship and more because of hard incentives to do so. A range of external audiences may require them to "speak" Silicon Valley, to meet expectations of what digital entrepreneurship entails.

White Fronting

A more extreme and a most contested approach to dealing with bias is the so-called white fronting strategy. In response to pattern matching's bias toward white male entrepreneurs, local actors began partnering with or hiring white individuals as a means of gaining access to the perceived advantage of this identity (see box 7.2). A discussion of this practice can be found on the blog of Ugandan digital entrepreneurship advocate Teddy Ruge (2014):

> One trend that I see happening (even though I completely disagree the strategy) is this: African startups are getting wise to the law of startup money. In the venture capital/startup world, money flows from like to like. In other words, sometimes it is not always about your product or business, it is about the people behind the business. Serial entrepreneurs in Silicon Valley are more likely to get funding quickly than someone no one has ever heard of or can relate to. In some African markets, this is manifesting itself as the "white front" strategy. You are more likely to get funding (or get that meeting) as an African startup if you have a white cofounder on your staff. If you are smart, you put that white guy in your marketing videos, and/or you make him CEO. An all-black African startup CAN get funding, but it is a lot harder to do.

Financiers are not the only possible legitimators; customers, the media, and others that have the ability to lend authenticity to a firm's operations act in this capacity. White fronting therefore also is used with these actors when entrepreneurs believe that they see whiteness as a proxy for competency. A firm in Yaoundé indicated that at the beginning, it had hired a

---

Box 7.2

Perceptive Partners

The founder we interview in Cameroon talks about why Percival[4] joined the team. He says it is partly because he used to work at an investment bank. When asked what the other reasons are, the founder mentions research out of Emory University (Roberts et al. 2017) that revealed that the vast proportion of VC funds go to white founders and CEOs. He says that he had always known that this was the case and that Percival had been invited to become CFO because he was a white Briton.

Percival was happy to be recruited and leave his post for something new, which, according to the founder, demonstrates his faith in their device. Percival is pragmatic about the ways of the world: it was he who made the pitch to join the company, explicitly advertising both his corporate and racial identities as assets.

Percival takes the lead at investor meetings, while the founder supplies the technical information about the product when called upon. This has made all the difference. Since Percival's arrival, the enterprise has come close to securing a $1 million deal. It is not just that Percival is white and British, the founder argues: it is also that he is a former investment banker and twenty years his senior, which communicates gravitas.

---

white French person to act as its liaison with an essential French business partner:

> It was difficult for us to finalize the partnership with the France [partner]. You know French people, when they see, this is a Cameroonian: "He is going to open an account with France? Are they serious?" And all of that, you know. Really, really difficult for us. So what we had to do is that we had to recruit a woman who was French to come and be the manager. And when she came, we got everything. It was really easy for her. She was a French. She was white. They were more able to trust her than us. . . . No, she's no more there. Things are now okay, so she left. (Country manager in Yaoundé)

The interview respondent also spoke of deliberately giving representatives of the French business partner the impression that he was acting on behalf of the white French interlocutor after she had left. It is also worth noting that the enterprise was helmed by French nationals of Cameroonian extraction. Hence, race and not nationality was the factor that determined who was able to act as the liaison with French partners.

Social Entrepreneurship and Development Dollars

African locales are often marked by a strong presence and the influence of global development institutions. The influences of their perspectives and the incentives that they produce have an effect on how individual aspirations are narrated by Africa's digital entrepreneurs (Marchant 2018). Rhetoric around the knowledge economy, bridging digital divides, and leapfrogging (see chapter 1) has influenced the entrepreneurs we interviewed. An interviewee in Maputo spoke of being "converted" from a for-profit business background after witnessing the impact of his company's job search tool on the local labor market. He later came to realize that a body of knowledge and ecology of practice existed that generates resources for encouraging altruism in business and that focuses specifically on Africa:

> Our motivation was social, so we understood the weak dissemination of job opportunities is one of the causes for unemployment. . . . We realized that we had to be sustainable. By then I didn't know what ICT4D [information and communication technology for development] for was; I didn't know what social entrepreneurship was. I came from a background that was purely business-driven. but then this thing started really growing in me because I could see the impact that it was having and people were getting access to jobs. . . . I thought I had invented the Robin Hood business model. Now, looking back that was kind of ridiculous. . . . We could afford to offer free of charge service to candidates, small enterprises, public academic institutions, and charities, and there was our social business model.

Within our eleven city case studies, international development and digital entrepreneurs were particularly entangled in Nairobi, Kigali, Addis Ababa, and Maputo. In these cities, development organizations serve as early supporters and reliable clients (Hersman 2014; Gichuru 2014). Mozambique is described as a "development darling" (Sabaratnam 2017, 9), and in Maputo, several participants indicated that they had developed tools for, and at the behest of, organizations like the World Bank, Save the Children, and the philanthropic arms of various corporations such as Microsoft. As a result, founders familiarize themselves with the narratives and language of ICT4D. The CEO who discussed his conversion to the nonprofit sector described a steep learning curve that followed seeking to tap into development resources. He is now well-versed in securing grant funding and support from philanthropic sources.

Other entrepreneurs expressed misgivings about grant financing, preferring that the broader market sustain their social good aims. These participants suspected that grants foster a reliance on aid agencies in the long-term:

> I would say [we are a] social enterprise but the lines are really blurred, because I don't really want us to be in that whole nonprofit mode. Even though I feel like the nonprofit status is just because we're yet to figure out our business model . . . There is enough to cover all our operations without even taking any donor funding. . . . I feel like at the point we will have to exit and be on our own. I think maybe in the next three years. . . . Because for us, it's just about how we also want—how we perceive Africa. We should not only solely be dependent on grants. We should also be able to create a model that is sustainable. (Social entrepreneur in Lagos)

Yet given the contextual conditions, some more experienced entrepreneurs had abandoned the idea that it is possible to address the base of the pyramid while also generating significant revenues. They felt that donors, and Westerners more generally, have unrealistic expectations, putting them in an impossible situation in which they have to trade off depending on subsidies to serve the poor and making money to become sustainable:

> Basically, I've had a lot of philosophical conversations on impact. They say, "Oh you focus on Nairobi surroundings and the big cities. Oh, you're not going rural?" I am like, "Well, for rural, the cost structure is very different." That's like first and foremost. And then secondly . . . there is a notion that Nairobi is affluent. Yes, [where we are sitting now to conduct this interview] is an affluent place, but 75 percent of people living in Nairobi are below poverty line. The impact market does not look at that—unless you are in [the] Kibera [slum] . . . but to operate a business in Kibera, you have to live in Kibera. . . . It drags you down because you are not looking for efficient, you are looking for impact convenience. . . . It's difficult to scale out of Kibera: power, water, space, security, talent pool. Nobody who is serious would want to go take a job there. (Entrepreneur in Nairobi)

In Maputo and Nairobi, many extolled the early financial and institutional support from development agencies.[5] In Nairobi, however, the initial universal celebration of social enterprise has given way to contestation between those who still value its framings and goals and those who feel that a focus on social impact diminishes the commercial possibilities of the ecosystem. Those who prioritize profit over social good feel that development actors have not gone far enough in invoking Silicon Valley's market-liberal ideals. In fact, they view social enterprise imperatives as a hindrance to the ecosystem's overall capacity to generate for-profit companies. According to these entrepreneurs, only through the establishment of a for-profit industry can national and individual economic development be realized:

> Grant money is very dangerous, very dangerous. . . . It's restricted funding: a lot of the grantors want the resources to go to other beneficiaries instead of operations. You end up basically doing all that work and you can't convert it into operating capital. You can't. . . . It's very devastating for business. . . . Your up-front cost, which is staffing or overhead, taxes, legal fees—all of those, there is nobody covering. (Health sector entrepreneur in Nairobi)

Accordingly, much of the previously mentioned early excitement about the Silicon Savannah has given way to disillusionment and a more level-headed outlook (see Marchant 2018 for an in-depth ethnography of the iHub community around the time of this shift). More and more entrepreneurs in Nairobi started to be dissatisfied with the focus from international actors on iHub and its network. Two typical complaints we heard in interviews in 2017 were that iHub-affiliated enterprises were mostly successes in terms of publicity but not commercially, and that the biggest business successes of digital enterprises based in Nairobi (e.g., Cellulant, Craft Silicon, Africa's Talking) operated independently from iHub and other hubs, slowly building up large operations without seeking fame. A CEO of a large technology company founded in the late 1990s describes this process from his perspective:

> For us, it was business as usual. I personally think it was a lot of hype. Look at iHub. It's good, a good initiative, but all these years we have never seen a company that has really scaled up. Even the "Silicon Savannah"—and other people keep talking about that—but I personally think that it has not added to what possibly they intend to do.

In general, the interest in iHub seemed to have declined among entrepreneurs and others "on the ground" even while it remained strong among outsider stakeholders (media, academics, development organizations, etc.; see, for instance, Mallonee 2018). In interviews, several Nairobi-based participants had become inured to the hype, trying to leave the Silicon Savannah narrative behind them:

> **Respondent:** Nairobi has gotten a fair share of [the Africa rising narrative], and I think that's more important than the Silicon Savannah story. I think that was a little—like nah.
>
> **Interviewer:** "We're over that," you think?

Respondent: We're totally over that! We're totally over that. Especially because there have not been the sort of exits and returns that you might have expected to see by now. Which just goes to show that this is a harder market. It's a different market and it's not going to be like "I can develop this app and I'll make a lot of money out of it." You have to do a lot more than that. You have to really understand who your customer is, and that's not that easy. (Investor in Nairobi)

I think what [iHub's story] did for the industry is it created attention—as a collective. You know, suddenly it became almost like a tourist destination. People would come to just see M-Pesa and Ushahidi and what's going on here. So I think it created interest, seed funds came, and people started trying to see how they could be part of this Kenyan miracle, or Kenyan moment, which I still believe was more hype than substance—I'm sorry. But I think we benefitted from the hype, but I don't know how much of it was substance. (Experienced digital entrepreneur)

Consequently, a more level-headed perspective on the Silicon Savannah also started to emerge in other ecosystems. For instance, for participants in other East African nations, Kenya was seen as a more advanced digital entrepreneurship environment, but not necessarily a role model:

Well, I mean you [Kenyan] guys are the big brother, the big cousin next door with all the successes, but we are a tiny shadow in terms of where we need to be. But we can't build our ecosystem thinking we want to emulate Kenya. It has to be contextually relevant, culturally relevant and owned largely by Ugandans. . . . Nairobi has a big market in terms of raising [venture] capital. (Entrepreneur in Uganda)

In Nairobi . . . you are quickly exposed and quickly pressured by the market and by the people—investors, stakeholders, whatever. Here [in Kampala], basically you are by yourself. I mean, there are basically no investors here, and in Nairobi, everyone calls himself as an investor these days. . . . I think it's totally overhyped, everything. Especially in Nairobi, it's totally overhyped. But it's still much more than here, relatively. (Entrepreneur in Uganda)

Compreneurs and the Survival of the Hippest

During the years of digital entrepreneurship hype and hope (between 2012 and 2016), many digital entrepreneurs we met had become role models, collecting awards and gathering media attention locally and internationally. They often considered awards to be superficial constructs of success, albeit a necessary evil when trying to signal legitimacy:

I was meeting a couple of other people and they googled who I was, so the whole discussion is different because it's suddenly based on those social indicators. I seem to know what I'm doing and I can bluff my way, drop a few other names, and everybody thinks you know what you're doing. . . . Here's an imposter syndrome: you're always feeling, I'm not really sure this thing [the product] has reached where I'd like it to be for me to be talking about it in the press. The thing isn't properly done. So if we get press, people are going to pile on it, it's going to fail, and then we're just going to look like we've got egg on our face. (Enterprise cofounder in Nairobi)

This excerpt illustrates how outsiders can regard a superficial performance as authoritative. The interviewee, trying to focus on the quality of his product, is ambivalent about the performative aspects of digital entrepreneurship and the manner in which one signals authority. This speaks to the risk of quick stardom: that entrepreneurs get distracted from the core of their business. Seeking attention from audiences like potential investors, development organizations, and media can seem more urgent than securing customers:

I was pushing this founder to actually break into the Kenyan space, but he suffered the startup syndrome. He is alone. . . . He's the sole decision maker. Also, he has too much attention; the government is interested in his work. He's going to the conferences. The guys are really interested in that solution. So this guy is always moving around, but he's not deployed. So he is full up. There is too much attention. He is always on TV. So he's lost that focus to say, "No, what is actually going to making me money is to deploy the solution." All these things are just excitement. . . . He goes to the United States. Yeah, all of this is just distraction. These guys are going to invite you, but until you get to deploy your solution to that environment, you're not going to make a million dollars. They will give you a couple thousand dollars per week. For you to sustain this as a startup and grow it to a billion-dollar business, you're going to have to deploy it. You're going to get the Chinese manufacturers to make the devices. You're going to run the business. You're going to get the numbers. You're going to see that it's deployed in farms. So he suffered a bit of that syndrome. The singleness syndrome, you're overwhelmed, you know. (University lecturer and investor in Kampala)

Pitching events and innovation competitions played a particular role in inducing such conflicts. Most entrepreneurs we interviewed weighed the cost of attendance against the opportunities that networking might bring. Yet so-called compreneurs (see chapter 5) may enter simply for the prize money, without serious ambitions to continue product development postcompetition. Their existence further confirmed how much the digital entrepreneurship space consists of strategic performances.

Quite apparently, donor organizations are not deliberately supporting problematic or disingenuous behavior. Instead, compreneurs are often exploiting programmatic flaws in innovation competitions. Namely, competition organizers typically primarily seek recognition for supporting local entrepreneurship among their audiences, which is most easily achieved by following the Silicon Valley archetype of "pitch nights," irrespective of outcomes. Furthermore, small grant sizes typically do not justify costly due diligence or follow-ups with winners. Given the uncertainties and diversity of African digital markets, it is genuinely hard to reliably assess the realistic market potential of digital product prototypes (a typical deliverable for competitions) or business plans. This problem is exacerbated when organizers engage nonlocals and nonexperts as jurors. There are also typically large cultural, institutional, and also geographical distances between funders, jurors, and grantees: they are rarely part of the same crowd, in the same place. Finally, distinctions between social and commercial enterprise seem less clear in Africa, because most economic activity can be reframed as fostering development.

To be fair, some organizers of innovation competitions (especially in incipient and maturing ecosystems) have responded to these challenges—for instance, by attempting to do more rigorous follow-ups (Friederici 2013; Roadburg 2017). It is also important to acknowledge the key arguments in favor of maintaining innovation competitions in some form: that it is better to have one imperfect source of funding than none at all, and that it is quite normal and acceptable for very early stage businesses to rely on grants (Hersman 2014; Mugambi 2014).

It remains, however, that what is rewarded at many innovation competitions is what is socially desirable in the eyes of jurors (and, by extension, the funding party) rather than what is economically viable. Many entrepreneurs we interviewed were very conscious of "what donors want to hear," leading them to develop a pitch that fits into these perceived expectations. Entrepreneurs made pragmatic compromises, diverging from their original intentions as much as they felt they had to in order to obtain donor support. A participant we interviewed finds this a subtle but dangerous trend, explicitly blaming the Silicon Valley archetype of digital entrepreneurship:

> Competitions are all over, and it's known for free money or free exposure and free this and free that. You do it in English, but to sell, because—and that's the

thing—the challenge that a lot of startups have now here in Cameroon is that because they have been so concerned with competitions with the Silicon Valley model of "Oh, I'll get high value for my startup and then maybe I'll exit and I'll sell it." Whereas the market is not even a little bit ready for that. Or "I'll raise funds in the series A and series B [rounds] and make $1.2 million dollars." But the paperwork is not ready for that either. So because of that sometimes they forget that they have to cater to the local market, the guys who are actually the customers. Who will actually pay for the products? (Entrepreneur in Yaoundé)

Others went even further and attested a more widespread culture of dependence and pandering to the hype, with severe long-term risks. Participants who emotionally identified with entrepreneurship as a process of establishing a value-creating sustainable organization or with entrepreneurship as an inherently difficult personal challenge (see chapter 6) were particularly critical of what they perceived as the selfish short-sightedness of compreneurs:

> [Many entrepreneurs are delivering] good news stories rather than actually building companies. . . . Most successful businesses usually don't have much flash. It's just about coming to work. . . . Here, it's all startup competitions and conferences. The number of startup founders who just seem to be permanently *on tour!* [*Expletive*], some guy who I don't know if you know, the guy was actually on his . . . Northern European tour—what does that even mean, man? . . . His metrics, he's doing the same . . . as he did two years ago. It's abysmal. . . . Some of the startup culture is like being in a rock band in high school. People aren't thinking of this as being a challenge, they're thinking of this as a way to get laid. Or the dream is to have a big desk that says "CEO" in front of it, and have like five phones in your hand and a picture of the President behind you. But people don't care about what it is they build, they just want to be able to take that picture . . . LinkedIn "Conference speaker." As like one of your career titles! [*mocking laughter*]. . . . I think that there's the option of complacency in what the current tech bubble is. Not just in Rwanda, I think this is what's happening in a lot of these tech hubs and a lot of these markets. It's okay to be a zombie. . . . Be broke but look cool. (Entrepreneur in Rwanda)

Summary: The Future Mirrors the Past

Although ideas about the center and periphery and modernization are said to be passé, they persist in popular imagination, policy, and practice (Hecht 2011; Mavhunga 2017; Mosse 2005; Olivier de Sardan 2005; Suchman

2011). Viewing African locales through this lens then produces knowledge hierarchies that undervalue local expertise and institutional arrangements that assess risk and opportunity based on the expectations of distant foreigners with capital and power. It is difficult to envisage the success story that fully counteracts the persistent image of African places as wild and inherently risky (Nyamnjoh 2013). Actors adopt strategies like white fronting to counteract these dynamics.

The deeper lesson is that Africa's entrepreneurs have to build their companies with an eye toward their global positionality—and the ways in which it can constrain them. Relative to Western digital entrepreneurs, African entrepreneurs face myriad challenges both within their home environments and outside of them. The narrative about the greater inclusivity of digital versus analog economies is overblown (Dy 2017; Dy, Martin, and Marlow 2018). Our observation is that some actors have the ability to create self-fulfilling prophecies through the exercise of power, embodied in capital but also in mental models of what is best practice and in their positioning as experts (Pollock and Williams 2016).

Digital entrepreneurs across Africa are slowly beginning to develop their own norms and value systems, born out of their own situated experiences. They show, for instance, that digital technologies can produce new and improved ways of doing things while still being commercialized in a staid and traditional manner. In fact, expecting more can produce disappointment and incentivize entrepreneurs to misrepresent the opportunities that are available.

Many entrepreneurs are beginning to emancipate themselves from the notion that success is equivalent to scale and visibility. The fact that a business is small and stays small does not mean that it is not innovative. The same is true for companies that are not engaging in cutting-edge computer science. The workings of the digital sector mean that "success" can be framed in different ways: Who is to say that unprofitable companies with millions of users and billion-dollar valuations (Silicon Valley model) are more successful than profitable companies with a dozen users and thousand-dollar valuations? Identifying new ways of generating revenues in small economies is necessary business innovation for firms in Africa. A heterogeneous view of possible paths and measures of success will allow for the varieties of digital entrepreneurship that are required to address

African markets effectively. It appears that many experienced entrepreneurs (both foreigners and locals) become more pragmatic while gaining self-confidence as they prove their sticking power in a tough environment. It will be crucial for them to continue on this path and to develop counternarratives to Silicon Valley and development discourses, which will allow future generations to avoid chasing the ghosts of effortless and unbounded digital-technology-driven growth for everyone everywhere.

This book has shown that African digital enterprises are creatively and productively applying and adapting digital technologies to their local economic, social, and political contexts. They create value in new and unique ways, complementing and diverging from the approaches of their Silicon Valley counterparts. Digital enterprises thus appear to have many hoped-for positive economic effects, such as increasing efficiencies, improving service quality, and creating high-quality jobs in local economies. Homegrown digital products have already become an important complement to the offerings of US and Chinese digital behemoths, and their impact is likely to grow as Africa's digitization progresses and diversifies throughout the twenty-first century.

However, we see that positive local impacts have so far happened at neither the rate nor the scale that widespread narratives about African digital entrepreneurship had suggested. The average African digital enterprise does not grow exponentially, does not scale internationally, does not attract venture capital, and does not disrupt cumbersome analog supply chains. As a result, we see significant waste and misguided efforts in the entrepreneurship support landscape: many advocates and supporters are too removed from the realities of digital entrepreneurs to design helpful and effective interventions. They look for quick wins and silver bullets to break out of imbalanced local and global socioeconomic structures established over decades and centuries. They also impose ideals of digital entrepreneurship that declare Silicon Valley trends as best practice, when in fact many of its premises conflict with local market realities and identities.

Digital entrepreneurship is not a cure-all for Africa's structural economic issues as it is itself shaped and constrained by those issues. The digital world may in fact offer fewer opportunities for global leveling and catch-up than the analog one because winner-take-all dynamics, distance-bridging potentials, and postcolonial dependencies bolster rather than undermine the superior positions of enterprises and entrepreneurs from high-income countries.

This book may be sobering to some because it has cast aside aspirations and instead tried to capture digital entrepreneurship in Africa as a complex real-world phenomenon. We sought not to omit the many impressive success stories that now exist across the continent, but we also tried to capture African digital entrepreneurship in its breadth and depth. We documented how entrepreneurs learn hard lessons, engage in far from glamorous day-to-day struggles, and face unexpected pitfalls. We have chosen to focus on thorny issues such as digital entrepreneurship's intersection with identities and race, vicious cycles in development processes, and the slower than expected pace of change. By reviewing the ways that African entrepreneurs have so far harnessed digital tools and by contrasting the changes brought about with the transformative hopes shared by so many, this book has built a nuanced review of what the digital revolution realistically means to African cities and nations.

Whether or not the story of African digital entrepreneurship is one of failure or of success is ultimately a matter of perspective. We have used rich empirical data and contrasted it against popular, policy, and management scholarship discourses. Compared to the hopes and assumptions underlying these discourses—namely, that the enormous growth of Silicon Valley and Chinese digital enterprises is replicable within Africa—outcomes have been disappointing.

But the findings of our book also suggest that Silicon Valley was never a reasonable benchmark to begin with. Scholars of economic geography, economic history, science and technology studies, ICT4D, and evolutionary economics will hardly be surprised by our finding that legacies and contexts constrain economic activity, even if it is of the "digital" sort. For them, we hope that our book offers interesting nuance and empirical detail about *how* economic actors (entrepreneurs and enterprises), digital technologies, and economic contexts have interfaced in Africa in the early twenty-first century. Our book also points to new pathways for interdisciplinary inquiry into digital innovation (e.g., on business model innovations like the last-mile platform), which could be more emancipated from the US-centric perspective that is still so dominant in scholarship (in the management discipline in particular) and in popular narratives (in tech media in particular).

Chapter Summaries and Testing of Analytical Framework

Chapters 2–7 provided a grounded account, drawn from our qualitative empirical analysis, of the defining elements of digital entrepreneurship in Africa. Through this empirical grounding, we were able to put the analytical framework suggested in chapter 1 to the test. Each empirical chapter challenged and nuanced expectations set forth in discourses. We find that some expectations were met, but largely, both popular and academic discourses give inaccurate images of digital entrepreneurship in Africa. Table 8.1 summarizes our findings.

Chapter 2 introduced macro-level proxy data about digital entrepreneurship and showed what African digital enterprises do using interview data. It highlighted that the lion's share of activity on the continent happens in just four countries: South Africa, Kenya, Nigeria, and Egypt. Significant but much lower levels can be found in Ghana, Tanzania, Uganda, Tunisia, Morocco, Mauritius, and Rwanda, and relatively little is happening elsewhere on the continent. Compared to activity in the rest of the world, even the continent's leaders remain far behind, and seem to fall further behind. Already this straightforward look at available datasets called into question expectations that Africa may be leapfrogging or that a kind of global leveling may be underway.

Still in chapter 2, we examined our sample of African digital enterprises. We saw that even though the rise of digital entrepreneurship in Africa has been enabled by the global digital revolution, local contexts significantly shape market opportunities and realities. Consumers' spending power is low and digital infrastructures remain incomplete. This gives rise to an abundance of innovative solutions to local constraints, and technological adaptations are commonplace. A different kind of digital entrepreneurship emerges than the one we know from academic literature and tech media: few enterprises manage to reach distant markets, stimulate significant user-driven value creation, automate information processing, or develop their own digital infrastructure that becomes the foundation for generative innovation. The absence of integrated digital payment systems is a key

Table 8.1
Evidence in favor of and against expectations for digital entrepreneurship in Africa

Expectation	Popular discourses	Academic discourses	Chapters presenting evidence	Evidence in favor	Evidence against
Greater inclusiveness and acceleration of entrepreneurial activity	Cambrian moment; Silicon Savannah; youthful continent; lean startup; mobile-first generation	Democratization of entrepreneurship; less bounded entrepreneurial agency; "same" digital infrastructure as ubiquitous enabler	3, 5, 6, 7	Many sustainable enterprises; creative innovations adapting technology and business models to local conditions; investments and supports multiplied (initially low levels)	Entrepreneurial learning takes time; resources complementary to connectivity missing (specialized knowledge, investment capital); entrepreneurs from privileged backgrounds; products for urban populations; only a few ecosystems show signs of specializations and innovations
Fast-paced and transformative growth	Leapfrogging; Africa rising; digital entrepreneurship revolution; startup nation; M-Pesa and Andela	Growth on steroids; generativity; digital transformation; network effects and user-based growth; digital platform business models	2, 3, 4, 5	Some digital platforms scale fast (e.g., payments and ecommerce), often coupled with analog outreach structure (last-mile platforms)	Enterprise growth slow, linear, and/or locally confined; local markets small and fragmented; innovations consist of technological adaptations, not technological products and components; no big data analysis; no production of digital infrastructure; ecosystem evolution bottlenecks; dependency on local economies creates threshold for growth
Africa catching up due to global leveling of opportunities	Flat world; digital innovation knows no borders; leapfrogging	Democratization of entrepreneurship; less bounded entrepreneurial outcomes; reduced role of clusters; value capture at distance	2, 5, 7	Software outsourcing makes use of labor cost advantages; foreign-educated Africans act as bridges	In most scalable product categories and for international expansion, digital enterprises face competition from Silicon Valley; African actors structurally disadvantaged; postcolonial dependencies persist

barrier to digital enterprises' ability to charge users and develop low-margin business models. Rather than creating complex and scalable analytical technologies and techniques, African enterprises focus on short-term revenue and conduct the digitization of information in direct exchanges with local actors.

Chapter 3 asked why it is that African digital enterprises rarely scale. We highlighted that digital enterprises are always embodied: they are run by real people embedded in physical and social contexts. They necessarily exist in, are governed by, and are enabled and constrained by the economic, social, political, and environmental geographies around them. This means that African digital enterprises, just like their Silicon Valley counterparts, identify opportunities in their environments, which they pursue in an iterative experimental process until their resources run out or until they reach product-market fit. Yet African enterprises do not usually find large addressable homogenous markets in their vicinity, as both infrastructures and demand for digital products are limited. They also depend on immediate revenue generation and cannot invest unlimited funds for uncertain gains over many unprofitable years.

This is where the entrepreneurial journey continues on a very different path compared to what the Silicon Valley playbook would prescribe: not African digital enterprises' immediately accessible demand nor their own initial resources nor the resources in their environments allow them to expand internationally in anything but a slow and piecemeal fashion. Accordingly, we find that exponential user base growth that has inspired management scholars and commentators seems to be possible only for enterprises located in a region where a number of conditions are in place that are not given in African cities. Only in niches where market knowledge is a competitive advantage and difficult to imitate can African enterprises sustain competitive challenges from large digital platforms. Ultimately, the more digital (and thus layered and scalable) products are, the less likely they are to be created and controlled by digital enterprises founded in economic peripheries.

Chapter 4 analyzed how African digital enterprises can still sustain themselves and grow under these competitive conditions. From among the countless small innovations and business model adaptations that entrepreneurs reported to us in interviews, four common strategies emerged. The first was to scale using good relationships to customers and partners. This linear and local scaling strategy works mostly with business customers needing specific software. The second was to become a local information platform, which digitizes, curates, and mediates local content for local consumers. Network effects and user base growth were possible here; however, margins are tiny in this business model given the limited revenue potential of online advertisements to African consumers. Charging small commission fees to one side of a platform market interested in relaying information to the consumers of the other side was a more viable approach. The third strategy was to invest in local assets that have value for corporate customers in high-income countries, such as labor, market knowledge, or a unique cultural artifact (like an online game with African characters). Outsourcing companies were dominant in this category. Scaling happens at a distance but is relationship driven and thus linear and often ad hoc. The final and maybe most promising strategy was the last-mile platform. Here, enterprises blend a digital platform backend with an analog structure to reach end users with limited digital infrastructure access.

The growth of even successful African digital enterprises thus rarely resembles a hockey stick. Most enterprises in our sample grew instead according to slower, linear scaling patterns, not dissimilar to analog enterprises. Some exploited network effects and scaled exponentially, but only up to the threshold that the size of the local market allowed it.

Chapter 5 more closely examined the entrepreneurial ecosystems within which African digital entrepreneurs are operating. It showed that ecosystems of digital entrepreneurship have appeared in many major African cities. Yet ecosystems differed. We categorized them into three tiers: maturing (1), incipient (2), learning (3). The chapter then discussed five different types of entrepreneurial resources, highlighting typical bottlenecks for each ecosystem tier.

Vicious cycles due to bottlenecks were particularly pressing in tier 3 ecosystems like Maputo or Addis Ababa. Ecosystem evolution can lead to lower-tier systems being stuck at relatively nascent levels. Efforts of governments and international development organizations can be futile here, not only because they lead to unwanted side effects, but also because their interventions are powerless in the face of overwhelming bottlenecks like the slow pace of entrepreneurial learning or lacking access to large enough markets.

Chapter 6 focused on the entrepreneurs themselves—recounting some of the identities and aspirations that they conveyed. Although a number of diverse identities emerged, African digital entrepreneurs generally tended to be inspired by rationales of Silicon Valley, such as fast technology-driven growth and transformation. Silicon Valley norms and aspirations are rarely adopted wholesale; rather, they are merged with local ideals, goals, and realizations. The practice of digital entrepreneurship thus becomes much more than just economic activity; it also becomes a set of aspirations for changing old ways. Yet most who can afford to participate in this African avant-garde are themselves affluent elites. It remains an open question to what extent they can consider and embrace African identities and livelihoods that for now seem excluded from the digital entrepreneurship arena, like the majority of Africans who, living outside of cities, are still unable to use digital infrastructure in any form.

Finally, chapter 7 discussed the continuity between Africa's historical and current place in the world and how this global positioning might impact the continent's technological aspirations. We have shown that some of the most successful entrepreneurs and those best able to signal legitimacy are those steeped in Silicon Valley modalities, which are themselves biased toward Westerners. We point, for instance, to pattern matching, a heuristic process used by investors, reproducing their biases and expectations about startups and thus leading to white, male entrepreneurs securing financing at higher rates and valuations than their nonwhite, female counterparts. To compensate, local actors develop strategies like white fronting as a means of recouping their agency. Similarly, entrepreneurs adopt the language of social entrepreneurship and impact to access resources of international development organizations.

This is not to make the argument that these performances are not important. Just because there is a disconnect between winning awards and understanding a market, that does not mean that this sort of performativity is not always an important part of being a digital entrepreneur. Some successful entrepreneurs have been able to, for instance, talk the talk about the "bottom of the pyramid" while walking a more realistic walk. These actors harness a nuanced understanding of symbols and myths.

Still, the metanarrative of pervasive marginalization and a view of Africa as nonmodern impedes the allocation of capital to the highest potential companies, instead directing it to those able to mimic developmentalist archetypes. Silicon Valley is held up as an exemplar, and success for African entrepreneurs is often judged against that benchmark, despite ample evidence that African digital markets are simply not amenable to a pure version of Silicon Valley–style high-growth startups. If investors are more willing to adapt their expectations to African settings, rather than have Africa adapt to their expectations, they may find that there are investment-worthy enterprises on the continent that require much lower funding outlays than in other locales. Building mechanisms for trust in unfamiliar territories is a new area of learning for them.

Digital Expectations

This book has shown that although beliefs about the transformative potentials of digital entrepreneurship are widespread and are articulated everywhere from World Bank reports to ICT ministries to innovation hubs, realities are far more diverse and sobering. Why do we see such a disconnect? Why are enormous resources deployed to support such untested strategies, especially in a world of scarce resources?

One part of the answer is the persistence of the idea that because digital technologies allow many digital products and services to be reproduced and transmitted at close to zero cost, spatial barriers matter less than ever. For enterprises based in Africa, far from some of the world's largest markets, this fundamental change in positionalities, if true, would have enormous implications. The issue here rests on two competing visions of what the internet is and what it can do. In one vision, the internet brings into being virtual, ubiquitous, and aspatial counterforces to space-bound mechanisms such as agglomeration (see Autio et al. 2018). In the other vision, the internet does none of those things. It is simply a network of networks that allows information to be quickly transmitted from place to place and—despite our best efforts—is something more akin to the Victorian telegraph system than to a virtual reality world.

These discourses about digital transformations do not just *reflect* Africa, they also *transform* it. What we should therefore be focusing on is not just why expectations do not match reality, but rather what realities those expectations help to bring about. As misguided as Silicon Valley comparisons may be, people and enterprises across Africa are forced to engage with them.

The digital entrepreneurs we interviewed often framed their visions, expectations, and conduct through this lens. Harvey's (1989) concept of time-space compression predicts that places that are digitally connected grow in cultural proximity with one another. It is difficult to imagine an entrepreneur anywhere in the world, who is designing and building digital technologies, who would be unfamiliar with the startup and Silicon Valley imaginaries.

We have shown that an important part of the work of the digital entrepreneur is not just bringing a product to market and the operational side of running a business, it is also helping to reproduce a core set of narratives about what digital entrepreneurship is. These frames can often be useful, as is seen when entrepreneurs seek to attract investment from international development agencies. Entrepreneurs are able to straddle skillfully the contradictions between hyperbolic framings of potential and actual nuanced business strategy (Graham 2015). But they can also serve as a distraction and, at worst, can begin to undermine effective operational strategies and investment decisions.

On the one hand, there is likely still utility in moving discussion away from creating the next Google and building services for a global market so that the next generation of entrepreneurs has a more grounded and nuanced sense of what is possible and practical. On the other, it is that excitement about potentials, rather than sober assessments about actual possibilities, that got many digital entrepreneurs interested in their work, got governments to offer supportive environments, and got investors to support much of the activity going on today.[1]

Global Ambitions

A key part of those digital expectations has been a strong set of global ambitions. Yet as we have shown, African digital enterprises will not play a significant role in commodified global digital markets any time soon. Africans will continue to use apps, software, and devices designed and made in high-income countries, but the reverse will not be true—barring a few potential exceptions. Here it is important to remember that digital products are much more than just software. Digital solutions always sit on top of layers upon layers of analog infrastructures, as well as locally contingent social, economic, political, and even environmental preconditions, affordances, and constraints. Meanwhile, the world's digital giants quickly gobble up the few opportunities that have true transnational resonance and are exploitable in an asset-light fashion.

If we look away from desires to create the "next Google" or "next Amazon," there are endless local problems awaiting local solutions. The biggest opportunities for African digital entrepreneurs therefore lie in locally and regionally oriented business models, integrating digital and analog value creation. Such integration requires deep local knowledge and experiential skill: something that will give a lot of African digital entrepreneurs an important competitive advantage against foreign competitors.

Down a Notch: Contextualizing the United States' and China's Digital Success

We should thus refrain from transferring policy and strategy lessons from Silicon Valley or elsewhere from high-income countries to Africa (see Rodrigues et al. 2018). Instead, we have to historically and geographically contextualize Silicon Valley's success to correctly assess its symbolic and practical relevance for African digital entrepreneurship now and in the future.

The global digital economy has grown quickly and widely, creating wealth, access to information, and opportunities for innovation. It has been underpinned by the unprecedented growth of select American digital platforms (as well as Asian and European digital infrastructure providers). These organizations have not only become large corporations in their own right, they have also created facilitative infrastructures for digital entrepreneurs and innovators in practically any internet-connected location.

Our findings do not deny that US digital platforms have had an enabling effect for digital entrepreneurship in Africa. The global diffusion of the internet and digital infrastructure has indeed been an external enabler of entrepreneurial opportunity at a global scale, including in Africa (Aldrich 2014; Briel, Davidsson, and Recker 2018; Nambisan 2017). However, transnational digital platform corporations have strategically monopolized precisely the most scalable digital product categories, outcompeting upstarts from other locations based on financial advantages, multipronged scaling economies, and lock-in effects. In the early 2000s, at the time that the diffusion and increasing capacity of the internet began to open up global market opportunities, only the US West Coast boasted the entrepreneurial knowledge, the organizational networks, the human capital, and the financial resources required to take on a software platform market leader approach (Bresnahan, Gambardella, and Saxenian 2001; Saxenian 1994; Schiller 2000; Storper et al. 2015; Zook 2002). These corporations built on the legacy of computer firms from the same region and complemented their offerings, but they differed from hardware providers as they were light on physical assets and "scaled without mass" (OECD 2017, 218; see also Parker, Van Alstyne, and Choudary 2016).

Especially for digital products that depend on a large user base, like that of Facebook, it was also essential that the United States represented a large, homogenous, and keen domestic consumer market, making it easier to reach a self-sustaining critical mass and ultimately user numbers that eclipsed those of all similar competitors abroad. The same was true for many companies founded in the first decade of the century, like Airbnb, Netflix, Twitter, Pinterest, Instagram, WhatsApp, Uber, Priceline, Upwork (or oDesk/Elance), and many other end user-facing transaction platforms. Only Silicon Valley offered the access to human and financial capital necessary to conquer a user base quickly enough to reach self-sustaining market leader positions:

> If you see how Facebook started, Facebook also started as a very simple app. It grew, in my view because there's a lot more people with big pockets in Silicon Valley, in America, than here. . . . I think the money aspect is a big deal. I think, as much as we say, "the internet is an equalizer," the fact that an app that's a clever app will start here and then as soon as they've got enough money, they'll move to Silicon Valley to try. . . . With that money, you get the best developers, you get and all that complexity built-in, and all those value chains and the big expansion. (Entrepreneur in Johannesburg)

A different pattern with a similar result applies to leading innovation platforms and companies combining transaction and innovation platform products—so-called integrated platforms (Evans and Gawer 2016). The competitive strategies involved in building innovation ecosystems like those of Google, Microsoft, or Apple are highly complex and resource intensive. Key levers are competitive trade-offs of openness that need to be incorporated into application programming interfaces and decisions about whether to offer one's own products at the risk of cannibalizing the innovation ecosystem (Boudreau 2010; Gawer 2014; Teece 2018). Later, merger and acquisition strategies formed another key element in securing innovation platform leadership (Chen, Werle, and Moser 2018; Henningsson, Yetton, and Wynne 2018). Such strategies only become possible for well-financed corporations with control over "unavoidable" infrastructural products (like Google Search and Gmail, Microsoft Windows, or Apple's iOS; see Thun and Sturgeon 2017).

Note also that today's incumbent digital platform companies have rarely competed head-on. Mostly, they have complemented each other and benefited from each other's rise and the global diffusion and standardization of hardware digital infrastructure. They sometimes forayed into each other's markets (Google Plus for Facebook or Apple Maps for Google Maps), but they often had to abandon attempts at challenging market leadership positions and resorted to dividing up quasi-monopolist positions for different product categories.

This explains why Chinese companies have largely been the only ones able to keep up and catch up with US digital behemoths. China's "Great Firewall" gave rise to US-incumbent equivalents (Tencent's WeChat for WhatsApp, WeChat Pay and Alipay for PayPal, Baidu for various Google products, Alibaba for Amazon, etc.), thriving in a vast domestic market that demanded those same products with a few years delay (Huang et al. 2017; Thun and Sturgeon 2017). Yet China's technology industry had long built up significant innovation capabilities and momentum (Fan 2006; Meng and Li 2002; Mu and Lee 2005), suggesting that protectionism and the domestic market alone would not have resulted in the same growth. Recently, some Chinese companies (especially Alibaba and Tencent) have begun international expansion and acquired foreign technology companies, but the scale and scope of this endeavor remains small compared to their American counterparts (Chen, Werle, and Moser 2018; Jia, Kenney, and Zysman 2018).

Aside from US West Coast and Chinese platforms, other companies for which the global diffusion of digital technologies opened global markets have been mass producers of hardware (such as smartphones, chips and processors, and sensors) and code (such as outsourcing providers; Gregory, Nollen, and Tenev 2009; Malecki and Moriset 2007; Steinbock 2003). For hardware (especially processors and smartphones), infrastructure makers in East Asia (mainly China and Taiwan) exploited specialization economies, cheap labor, and physical mass production scaling economies (Chen 2004; Gregory, Nollen, and Tenev 2009; Zhou et al. 2011). Similarly, the outsourcing industries of India and some nations in Southeast Asia benefited from good timing and entrepreneurial learning, competitive advantages in the cost of human capital, and sometimes from favorable policy regimes (Arora et al. 2001; Athreye 2005; Gregory, Nollen, and Tenev 2009; Heeks 2006). Overall, Asian companies thus benefitted from some scaling economies, but not from the same network effect and big data–driven scaling economies and lock-in dynamics underlying user base scaling. They grew into billion-dollar industries, yet they continue to face rather different scaling thresholds and profit margins.

Local Realities

It is likely that every African nation will develop a sustainable but small domestic digital enterprise sector. Those local opportunities are necessarily more bounded than the expectations they arrive in the wake of. With local problems and local solutions come upper thresholds for enterprise size. In other words, the local market size at urban or national levels sets a limit on the scalability of solutions and thus necessarily limits the growth potential for enterprises in small cities or nations. This implies a key difference from digital enterprises in high-income nations: even if they are also unable to scale abroad, their domestic market opportunities of differentiation and localization are vastly bigger than those of their African counterparts. Ultimately, both the average African and the average European digital enterprise may be confined to local markets, but *local markets* means something rather different on the two continents. Because there are few sizable African markets for most of the solutions offered by digital entrepreneurs, we are unlikely to see a significant number of large African digital enterprises (many hundreds of employees, billion-dollar valuations, etc.) emerge any time soon.

However, in the goldilocks zone between globalized and local infrastructures and global and local solutions (Quinones, Heeks, and Nicholson 2017), it is likely that African digital enterprise ecosystems will sustain themselves by occupying market niches that are unattractive for global competitors and by innovating unique and new products. Unique local instantiations of digital entrepreneurship emerge out of attempts at both reproduction and emancipation from Silicon Valley. Our analysis suggests that ideally, such efforts will take advantage of an ability to scale regionally, focusing on problems and opportunities that are both common across Africa and foreign enough to the digital giants to prevent a barrier to entry. These likely clusters in South Africa, Kenya, Nigeria, and Ghana will still need years to develop, but as they grow they will progressively benefit from economies of scale and specialization.

The core point here is that the geography of digital economies remains double-edged (Malecki and Moriset 2007). Paradoxically, in the digital age, the potential of a given place to establish a local digital economy thus depends on its ability to nurture and retain what cannot be digitized and distributed. Digital entrepreneurship therefore is anything but footloose. Digital entrepreneurship is deeply embedded in local economies, which means that its success and development impact fundamentally depends on preexisting local conditions such as the availability of skilled labor, tacit knowledge exchange, collaboration and cospecialization, and trust-based networks. Crucially, such localized productive activities and resources interdepend, which leads to virtuous circles for the development of locales that are already successful and vicious circles for those that are not.

Uneven Development

What do the realities of digital entrepreneurship mean for economic development in Africa? We should be cautious about its potentials as a wide-reaching tool for development for two reasons. First, most of our findings show that successes are exceptional. Every chapter highlighted limitations and pitfalls, sometimes significant ones. Almost all startups and almost all support organizations realize quickly that progress is slow and painstaking, rather than swift and easily enabled by ubiquitous technology. Digital entrepreneurship therefore will not be transforming Africa any time soon. The average African digital enterprise is not a disruptor; it is not growing exponentially; it is not exporting internationally; and it is not able to attract risk capital. That is not to say that these enterprises are not making valuable contributions to local economies. They are. But the African digital enterprise is far from the disruptive and transformative organization many want, hope, and expect it to be. The selective perceptions offered, for instance, in works like *The Next Africa* (Bright and Hruby 2015a) tend to lead to misguided conclusions about overall trends.

The preceding discussion has shown that digital entrepreneurship is far from footloose. We therefore cannot simply expect digital-entrepreneurship-led development to happen just anywhere. Digital entrepreneurship is a fundamentally skills- and knowledge-based economic activity. Entrepreneurs require access to both specialized technical knowledge and the sort of entrepreneurial knowledge that involves running and scaling a digital startup under local conditions. This is not knowledge that can simply be imported, and it is hard to codify (it would be hard to teach much of it in a class, for instance). Rather, it is learned over time through iterative and tacit processes. In every one of the African centers of activity, there were cases of pioneer entrepreneurs who started many years ago. Over the first two to four years of their journeys, entrepreneurs mature and get a fundamentally different outlook; while doing so, they shift the trajectory of the entire ecosystem.

This, in tandem with the other centrifugal clustering forces mentioned earlier, leads to the conclusion that digital entrepreneurship is unlikely to fundamentally unsettle already existing economic cores and peripheries (see Birtchnell 2011). Large cities that have traditionally been hubs of transport, trade, mobility, culture, and education are also at the forefront of the digital economy. The importance of legacy economic structures and local markets therefore cannot be overstated. Digital entrepreneurship, in other words, does not represent an unexplored new industry that can be tapped into in order to foster economic development. It may, in fact, do little to address uneven development if the myriad infrastructures and the human, social, and economic capital that shapes and nurtures digital economies are not also present.

The digital revolution seems to have enabled the emergence of African digital entrepreneurship, but meanwhile it has benefited Silicon Valley and other locations where digital infrastructure is produced to a much greater extent. Today, the US West Coast, Asian technology clusters, and select urban hot spots in high-income countries have established thriving local digital economies. Africa has seen a drastic increase in the consumption and usage of digital products, while productive activity has remained limited when compared to other world regions.

Expectations that Africa's development progress should be reflected in its convergence with Western structures and practices is likely to lead to further disappointment for everyone. Attempts to enact a specific model of digital entrepreneurship in different African cities have resulted in challenges. It appears that neither African markets nor funding environments are designed to cater to the Silicon Valley model of high-growth startups.

Although foreign investors and foreign entrepreneurs have the funds and independence to persist in enacting this particular form of digital entrepreneurship, African-born entrepreneurs often distance themselves from it.

The question of markets is a particularly dark shadow that hangs over African digital entrepreneurs' ambitions. Many are inspired by pursuing opportunities that have been touted in tech and development discourses, such as supposed riches at the base of the pyramid or Africa's growing middle class, but entrepreneurs regularly experience disappointment when realizing that markets are actually smaller and harder to penetrate (see chapters 2 and 3).

Also, the demographic makeup of the digital entrepreneurship sector may mean that digital inequality is increased rather than decreased through it. The culture and immediate geographical environment that most digital entrepreneurs are steeped in is urban (Strachan Matranga, Bhattacharyya, and Baird 2017), which means that the rural customer is often not well understood or entirely neglected (Wyche and Steinfield 2016). In turn, if urban entrepreneurs exclusively use their localized knowledge and cater to urban segments, this necessarily further reinforces digital divides. Entrepreneurs might also do this inadvertently because of their lack of knowledge of the affordances of users who are distant from them (see chapters 2, 3, and 6). Whenever we found effective products for rural customers, they had been designed by exceptional entrepreneurs who had both extensively familiarized themselves with those contexts and were able to mobilize the significant resources necessary to achieve critical mass.

Local entrepreneurship may thus compound existing imbalances of digitization and availabilities of digital infrastructure. Infrastructure development is a primary means through which governments have tried to widen the opportunity for digital entrepreneurship geographically (Ngoasong 2018). Our findings show that extending digital infrastructures to rural areas is not enough, as infrastructure needs to be supplemented by resources, competencies, and knowledge for digital products to emerge that are better suited to rural contexts. This was one of the lessons of Kenya's Digital Villages project. Dr. Bitange Ndemo, the former permanent secretary of the country's Ministry for ICT, reflected on the outcomes of the project:

> We should have given proper consideration to, and sought to gain, an adequate understanding of the prevailing cultural orientation towards business processes in the rural areas. Many years of handouts (grants) had eroded any understanding

of other forms of financing, such as loans, in this case to the extent that majority of recipients had no intention of repaying the loan. With such intentions, some recruits diverted the loan into other uses depleting their operational expenditure. Unfortunately, these were areas where the business would have been sustainable if they had had financial discipline. However, this did not deter the team from pushing other projects that they felt could help the country succeed in becoming the regional ICT hub. There was still promise because many youths who could code were now moving to Nairobi to try their luck. (Ndemo 2015)

This is not to say that Silicon Valley's learnings are completely inconsistent with the needs of African locales. In fact, our analysis shows that some Silicon Valley principles, in particular the lean startup (Ries 2011), resonate in situations in which resources are scarce. Then again, it requires an entity with institutional heft and capacities to provide services to low-income customers and surmount infrastructural deficiencies.

A Long-Term, International Game

Together these findings reveal that though there are impressive individual success stories of digital entrepreneurship across Africa, we do not know yet how important for Africa's economic development it will be because it builds momentum only at the regional scale and only through long-term processes. There is no short-term fix or shortcut that will allow the next Silicon Savannah, Silicon Cape, Silicon Lagoon, or Silicon Mountain to emerge in Africa and to emulate Silicon Valley.

Developing African clusters of digital entrepreneurship will take time because experiential, localized, and interactive learning and adaptation have only just begun. It is noteworthy that most digital entrepreneurs themselves—and their investors—recognize this long-term trajectory.

This does *not* mean that the situation is futile for entrepreneurs, governments, and anyone else concerned with economic development. It is worth looking to Rwanda and Kenya as countries that are building entire supporting ecosystems for their country's entrepreneurs. When compared to peers in terms of GDP per capita or the Human Development Index, the momentum of digital entrepreneurship is indeed impressive in those countries. This book has described why there will be upper thresholds for entrepreneurial opportunities and why the next Google probably will not come from Kigali, but that does not have to stop Kigali from investing in its digital economy. And as clusters in places like Kigali mature, it is possible that some of them will begin to evolve specialization economies—perhaps last-mile platforms (see chapter 4) around smallholder agriculture, bottom of the pyramid services, entertainment, local government services, or transport.

Digital tools and technologies do have space-bridging, scale-free, and zero-marginal-cost properties, but that does not mean that they can allow anyone to transcend underlying and surrounding economic, social, and political geographies. Those properties can necessarily only be brought into being by select actors in certain places at specific times. Yes, a file can be instantly transmitted to the other side of the planet for little cost—but no, that does not mean that the many other individual and structural advantages and disadvantages that shape economic development can be circumvented.

In turn, these observations point to where African digital entrepreneurship is currently having its most significant impacts and where it could be even more impactful. As shown in this book, African digital enterprises have excelled at adapting digital technologies to economic structures and processes that they find in the world around them. They have built *new sociotechnological infrastructures for others' economic activity*, usually blending analog and digital technologies in new ways that make sense in local contexts. This is a domain of entrepreneurship to which international competitors make no claim, as they have neither a financial interest nor the innovative capabilities to do so.

The catch, so far, has been that such localized infrastructures are hard to scale beyond the context for which they were designed in the first place. Furthermore, combinatorial innovation is not as easy for analog-digital blends as it is for software (see chapter 1).

Therefore, we argue that African digital entrepreneurship can only supersede the economic legacies and market thresholds of its environments if it embraces either or both of two strategies. First, African digital enterprises ought to find ways to develop and disseminate unique products that Silicon Valley is unable to offer but that are useful and widely applicable in contexts outside of enterprises' home contexts, especially in other low- and middle-income countries. Second, African digital entrepreneurship needs regionally specific but integrated digital infrastructures to accelerate the potential of combinatorial innovation. African digital innovations in areas like digital payments, hacks to deal with mobile operator APIs, low-bandwidth apps and software, offline functionalities, blockchain, and others are abundant, but also scattered. They need a common open forum, allowing innovators to build on what others have done before them. The absence of African innovation platforms and Africa's dependence on Chinese and US platforms (like Android, Alibaba, etc.; Evans and Gawer 2016) is testament to this book's finding that African digital entrepreneurship is in large part unable to reverse the power imbalance of the global digital economy because it is always using but almost never creating digital infrastructures. It could begin by creating digital infrastructure for its own unique purposes and conditions (especially for digital payments), potentially unlocking some of the generative potential of digital innovation and becoming exporters rather than consumers of digital products. Both of these strategies require continent-wide and multistakeholder collaboration and openness.

Implications for Policy and Practice

After conducting fieldwork in eleven African cities and speaking to entrepreneurs, governments, development agencies, workers, and researchers, we have encountered an enormous breadth of plans, projects, businesses, and ideas. The innovations being designed and built from Dakar to Dar es Salaam are all shaped by the places that they are made in. These are not solutions that could have come from San Francisco or London. And they will play a role in turn in fundamentally shaping sectors as diverse as transport, retail, agriculture, and education in their home locales. Digital entrepreneurship thus undoubtedly is shaping and being shaped by the African cities that it takes root in.

Digital entrepreneurship in Africa thus is anything but a failed project. It is, however, a project that has failed to live up to the aspirations that many have tacked onto it. We hope that this book has given an account of not just successes and failures, but also the typical activities of Africa's digital entrepreneurs. In doing so, we hope to have moved beyond naïve hope and hype and instead helped focus attention on possible and probable futures for African digital economies.

In closing this book, we therefore wish to bring together the implications of a grounded, nuanced study of African digital entrepreneurship—implications that are sober but hopeful, realistic but wide-reaching. In the following section, we begin with a set of broad implications and from there move to discussing specific implications for entrepreneurs, hub and incubator managers, investors, local governments, donors, and researchers.

Cross-Cutting Implications

Silicon Valley cannot, and should not, be copied. Quite the opposite. African digital entrepreneurs need to focus on their unique offerings (in part to not have to compete with Silicon Valley firms). Local resources can be created and nurtured in ways that are in tune with local conditions.

Those local specializations should allow entrepreneurs to create digital products and product component modules that are widely needed, including outside of their locales. This requires regional or city-level coordination. Associations (or similar groups) can be used to coordinate within ecosystems and across to other ecosystems, in Africa and beyond.

Any investments of money, effort, and time need to be converted into entrepreneurial resources that are *locally sticky*. This means that the resource predominantly and sustainably benefits local entrepreneurs. Tacit, experience-based, and locally specific entrepreneurial knowledge may be the most important locally sticky entrepreneurial resource. It cannot be imported. The lean startup and other strategies may be useful templates, but entrepreneurs need to conduct deep and sophisticated local adaptations.

According to Storper et al. (2015), locally sticky entrepreneurial resources include lead and networking organizations, institutionalized organizational practices, and both dense and wide cospecialized networks. It should be noted that infrastructures of connectivity, such as affordable broadband, and physical infrastructure (roads, hub buildings, offices, tech parks, etc.) are only necessary preconditions for these resources to exist; they do not themselves represent the resource for the entrepreneur. Infrastructure only generates value when it is in (collective) use, which itself depends on entrepreneurial actions. It is also noteworthy that resources that are more locally sticky are also more intangible and long-term oriented. None of the resources mentioned is easy to generate, and none of them is commodified or easily commodifiable. In other words, resources/inputs are inimitable and ultimately provide local competitive advantage.

For scaling at distance, what have been called *smart specialization* strategies may offer clues. Digital entrepreneurs should not enter already commodified and already competitive sectors. If they do, they should be prepared for cost pressure and again small scale growth. The key questions are: What can be locally produced (a) that cannot or can only hardly be replicated elsewhere, (b) that will be needed elsewhere, and (c) that can be transported or duplicated there at relatively low cost? The answers to these questions could result in a specialization that can be locally nurtured. This does not have to be a product. It could be a product component, a business, a value-creation model, a cultural practice, or even a particular sector of the digital economy (e.g., marketing). Significant local competitive advantage and economic development may thus come from giving entrepreneurs resources, but they have to be invested with care and strategic discernment, and entrepreneurs cannot be expected to turn these into economic development over a short time frame.

Implications for Entrepreneurs

Be realistic, be prepared, be patient. The odds are stacked against you. Some of your challenges are surmountable, but some simply are not. Learning and adaptation will be time-consuming and sometimes frustrating. Depending on your location, your sector, and your network, you may have to revenue-fund for a long time and accept slow growth.

Know the possibilities and limitations of digital technology value creation in African markets. Identify niches and try to find opportunities to tap into generativity. You want to become the platform that others build on, while simultaneously you need to build a strong value-capture (monetization) mechanism into your business model.

Evaluate the trade-offs between perfecting your product for a local market versus scaling opportunities. Alternatively, look into work-arounds. Investigate cross-country partnerships, franchise models, and mergers and acquisitions strategies to combine local adaptation and international scaling.

Implications for Hub and Incubator Managers

Be ambitious, but also be clear to yourself and to others about who your stakeholders are and where the boundaries of your operations are. In doing so, it is worth paying attention to the parts of the ecosystem that don't care for you or are skeptical about what you're doing. Your role should be to be creative and to do things that are difficult to measure (e.g., community building). But that does not mean that you don't need to develop some form of measurement or accountability mechanism.

Implications for Investors

Be prepared for a long-term game. Most digital business models enter unchartered territory, so you will have to learn together with your entrepreneurs. The problem is that good data is hard to come by. Smartphone and internet penetration rates are not reliable indicators, and most widely available statistics are unsuitable to make realistic assessments of market size.

For foreign investors, be aware that entrepreneurs may not match your expectations and standards in terms of polish and experience. However, they often know local market conditions much better than you ever will. Listen to them and keep lines of conversation open.

Implications for Local Governments

Many of your officials will not understand much about how digital entrepreneurship works. There is much to be gained from listening to people in the sector and thinking carefully about how gaps in knowledge can be filled in.

It rarely makes sense to pour resources into physical infrastructure, such as incubators and tech parks. Such infrastructure is usually useless if it is not complemented by a number of soft factors, especially participation by key entrepreneurs. Government-run interventions will be seen skeptically by entrepreneurs in almost any country, so you cannot take participation for granted. If you build it, they will not come.

Avoid simple gap or needs analyses and surveys, as well as pillar- or component-based ecosystem or innovation system assessments. Entrepreneurship is not a box-ticking exercise. You cannot just "fill gaps"; instead, you will need to understand the dynamic and complex nature of digital entrepreneurship to design effective interventions, or limit yourself to "enabling environment" work.

Although the local job market cannot accommodate everyone, not everyone can, or should, be an entrepreneur. Moreover, importantly, the gains from digital entrepreneurship concentrate in just a few hands. Extreme care thus needs to be taken in allocating the scarce resources entrusted to government.

Implications for Donors

Resist the temptation to fund photo opportunities. African technology is appealing from a development PR standpoint—but, as noted, digital entrepreneurship is not an activity that spreads its gains widely. From a development perspective, resources are likely much better spent on lasting and sustainable investments in communities and infrastructures. And, finally, ensure that you invest in monitoring and evaluation. We still do not know enough about what works and what does not.

Future Directions

Ultimately, Africa needs to mix and match business models from elsewhere, developing its own unique adaptations. Successful strategies will be about compiling and combining local and international elements of value creation and local economic development. What we end up seeing may appear to be neither radically new nor different at face value, while significant change may be underway underneath the surface. Last-mile platforms (see chapter 4) are an example of a genuine digital business model innovation that is worth exploring more for researchers and practitioners alike.

This book has shown that the key to operating in a globalized digital economy is to establish or occupy strategic points of value extraction. It is an open and exciting question where these may be for African enterprises. Local economic development will happen if models are able to both create and capture value locally or when they allow cocreation of value abroad and capture value locally (like Silicon Valley platforms are doing).

We set out on our multiyear research project to better understand how digitization at a planetary scale affects economic opportunities in some of the world's most economically marginal places, and to ask whether digital entrepreneurship might be a promising new pathway for Africa's economic development. This book has shown that contrary to many hopes and aspirations for the sector, digital entrepreneurship is unlikely to foster broad-based economic development across Africa.

Businesses by their nature funnel profit upward rather than outward and benefit capital at the expense of labor. However, that integral feature of capitalism is often overlooked as it is deployed in the service of development because of the creative destruction that it can bring about. People in the world of international development recognize that capitalism concentrates wealth and resources at the top, but many accept that trade-off because the other side of the trade involves positive change: new jobs, new value chains, new industries, new services, and new ways of living.

Our research showed that African digital entrepreneurship has few broad impacts, and it is relatively exclusionary. We also showed that this is not just a feature of the *entrepreneurship* part of digital entrepreneurship, but also the *digital* part. Economic networks that are mediated by digital tools and technologies democratize access and participation, while creating bottlenecks that are captured, controlled, and managed by those with the resources and capabilities to do so.

It is important for African countries that as much as possible of the created value is *captured locally* as well. It is about not just building businesses, but also coming up with local solutions to local problems, and this book has shown myriad examples of the creative ways in which Africa's entrepreneurs are doing that. Africa's digital entrepreneurs are ultimately shaping lives, societies, and economies across the continent. They are not creating the next Google or Facebook, but they are hard at work ensuring that the communities that they work in are not subject to the next round of foreign digital extractivism made possible by ever-more connectivity and ever-more digital legibility of key social and economic activities. In an increasingly unequal global digital economy, this endeavor alone may make digital entrepreneurship a key part of Africa's twenty-first-century journey toward greater independence and economic empowerment.

Appendix A: Methodology

This appendix provides a window into the methodology and data underlying the findings of this book. For interested and skeptical readers, we thus seek to make the analytical process underlying our empirical project more transparent, highlight choices we made as involved investigators, and convey that we adhered to high standards of social scientific rigor (Miles and Huberman 1994; Tracy 2010). Although we cannot provide a detailed protocol for the research process from start to finish, we will report details insofar as they speak to whether our research adhered to commonly accepted quality criteria for qualitative research (Tong, Sainsbury, and Craig 2007; Tracy 2010).

We view entrepreneurship as a process that is triggered by both contextual and individual factors, leading to outcomes such as ventures or product innovations (Autio et al. 2014; Block, Fisch, and Praag 2017; Davidsson 2005; Santos and Eisenhardt 2009). Entrepreneurship studies have traditionally focused on evaluating the actions and drivers of individuals, but they have only just begun to investigate mutually shaping interactions between actor and context (Autio et al. 2014, 1099; Garud, Schildt, and Lant 2014). Gaining proximal knowledge and documenting the interplay of individual factors, enterprise-level processes, and entrepreneurial environments—all within an understudied empirical setting—could not be done from a distance. Semistructured interviews conducted during city visits were thus the primary data collection strategy of choice.

Our research was designed at a moment of radically changing connectivity throughout Africa. With this rapid expansion in digital access came myriad expectations from businesses, policymakers, and aid agencies that new friction-free prospects for globalized digital entrepreneurship in Africa could be brought into being. We sought out entrepreneurs and other stake-holders in order to investigate these presumptions and understand their perspectives as those who are "on the ground," living and implementing digital entrepreneurship. We thus sought to elicit entrepreneurs' own interpretive frameworks. For instance, we left the interview questions as open-ended as possible and avoided introducing development and entrepreneurship jargon.

Research Questions

Underlying our research was the motivation to understand whether and how digital entrepreneurship could contribute significantly to Africa's economic development. We did not expect to be able to measure economic development directly, and instead we investigated the growth and sustainability of enterprises (firm level) and whether digital entrepreneurship offered a significant departure from previous livelihood opportunities (individual level). Although the research design process was iterative and ongoing, we used four core questions to guide our inquiry throughout the life of our project: (1) Who are Africa's digital entrepreneurs (i.e., their backgrounds, motivations and mindsets)? (2) How are they and their enterprises pursuing market opportunities through digital technologies? (3) What markets (nature, size, scope) are they able to address? (4) How do their ecosystems support them (or not)?

Selection of City Cases

"Africa" as a scope mandated a multisited data collection effort at a minimum. To generalize and contrast, we used standard replication and comparative analysis (Yin 1994). Expectations about the potential of digital entrepreneurship were derived based on several informal and formal discourse analyses (see chapter 1; Friederici 2019; Friederici, Ojanperä, and Graham 2017). City selection aimed to facilitate close and distant comparison to these discourses and among cases.

We set the study boundary in line with that of the Geonet project (http://geonet.oii.ox.ac.uk). Geonet sought to investigate sub-Saharan Africa because countries within sub-Sarahan Africa were the last to be connected to the global fiber-optic undersea cabling system (Graham, Andersen, and

Mann 2015). Between January 2017 and February 2018, we went, in the following order, on field visits to Kigali (Rwanda), Nairobi (Kenya), Lagos (Nigeria), Kampala (Uganda), Accra (Ghana), Maputo (Mozambique), Johannesburg (South Africa), Addis Ababa (Ethiopia), Yaoundé (Cameroon), Abidjan (Ivory Coast), and Dakar (Senegal).

These cases represented cities in different geographic regions and also represented cities in Anglophone, Francophone, and Lusophone Africa. The countries in which they were located had varied levels of economic development and different sociopolitical environments. The cities were selected with a view toward capturing the geographic and sociocultural diversity of African states and with an eye toward analyzing the environmental factors that support digital entrepreneurship. These cases thus amount to a "least similar" selection logic: if patterns can be identified that apply across all or most of these diverse cases, it is likely that they also hold true in other cases that were not part of the sampling (i.e., other major African cities).

Across the eleven comparative city cases, we were able to develop robust themes supported by extensive source material. The first round of data collection involved fieldwork in *theory-development case study sites*, with the goal to develop theoretical frameworks that could answer our research questions (including the development of concepts, causal mechanisms, and thematic areas). The second round of fieldwork covered the remaining eight case studies, focusing on replication (verifying and refining the initial theory) and on understanding local idiosyncrasies that arise from Africa's immense economic and cultural diversity. A balance needed to be struck between producing thick descriptions and being able to develop themes that were relevant across the cities. This analysis is this study's strength and main contribution.

Kigali, Nairobi, and Lagos were investigated first to develop a preliminary theory on digital entrepreneurship in Africa, which could then be tested for its applicability to other African cities. These three cities were selected because they had developed a distinct profile in digital economy circles. Aside from media presence, we considered factors like the number of hubs, events and competitions, GitHub commits, and other indicators of an active digital economy.

We wanted to include cities along the spectrum of activity, but preferred to exclude places that appeared to have virtually no activity—for example, Liberia and Sierra Leone. We intended to discuss what factors enabled and constrained digital entrepreneurship, but we also needed a pool of interview subjects in order to base our analysis on empirics rather than speculation. We also needed to start in places with a longer history of digital entrepreneurship to begin to understand processes of learning and adaptation. We thus wanted to begin with at least two cases of top-tier cities in terms of activity (extent and diversity). We expected the top-tier countries to include South Africa, Kenya, and Nigeria; the middle tier to consist of Ghana, Egypt, Senegal, and Cameroon; and the lower tier of Rwanda, Tanzania, Uganda, the Ivory Coast, Mozambique, Botswana, and a few others (see chapters 2 and 5).

Lagos (Nigeria) and Nairobi (Kenya) exhibited similar attributes—namely, similarly high levels of digital entrepreneurship activity in absolute terms, an established entrepreneurial culture, large and well-connected cities, and large domestic markets. Close comparison between these two cities would allow us to establish a large array of digital enterprises and examine other variables in more depth—for instance, the level of NGO/development involvement, M-Pesa as a foundational or platform technology for the domestic market, and so on. Kigali, Rwanda, facilitated distant comparison but allowed us to ask what small countries with great infrastructure, government backing, and lots of ambition achieve, or not, compared to large ones.

The *replication-oriented case studies* (Accra, Dakar, Kampala, Yaoundé, Abidjan, Maputo, and Johannesburg) were opportunities to test emergent findings and to introduce greater variation into the theoretical framework. We sought to include countries with primary languages that were not English and which were operating in different geopolitical and socioeconomic orbits, as determined by their colonial pasts. Francophone countries, for example, use a currency that is pegged to the euro because of their ongoing relationship with France.

We excluded Cape Town as a theory development case study because of its exceptional situatedness and makeup, making it unlikely that we would find enterprise strategies and founder biographies there that would be generalizable to Africa. Not only was South Africa connected to fiber-optic cables much earlier than other regions of sub-Saharan Africa, but Cape Town also is usually seen as untypical of other ecosystems in Africa, given its strong connections to Silicon Valley. We considered including it in the replication-oriented case studies but decided on Johannesburg due to its closer ties to other cities across Southern Africa and for pragmatic research reasons, as we had better field access there.

Interviews

When it came to selecting the actors that we were going to interview, we were guided by the application of a broad definition of *digital economy*. The digital economy is a section of the quaternary sector of the economy (in which knowledge is a product rather than just a tool), IT-enabled services (taken from the main body of Malecki and Moriset's [2007, 6] description of the digital economy), and informal processes and practices of IT-mediated information production that tend to get left out of more formal models. Thus, a *digital enterprise* is an organization set up to deliver these products and services on a commercial basis. The digital entrepreneurship ecosystem is the social, organizational, and institutional environment that exists to support this activity (see chapter 5). We sought out entrepreneurs who fit within this categorization and the actors that helmed institutions that supported them, including incubator and hub managers and relevant investors and policymakers.

The process of identifying interview respondents was purposive and strategic. We used theoretical sampling and category development techniques. This entails selecting a diverse range of actors to cover the phenomenon as comprehensively as possible. One of the sampling strategy goals was to ensure variety within the sample. This sampling strategy means that the study cohort is not representative of a population (Bryman 2008). We included entrepreneurs, hub managers (the second most prominent cohort), users, government officials, academics and financiers. Table A.1 displays the enterprises that are within the cohort according to their core business or product offering. We selected entrepreneurs at different maturity stages (years of experience, age of startup), operating in different sectors (e.g., e-commerce vs. transport vs. education), using different organizational models (e.g., freelancers vs. CEOs of larger companies), and implementing different business models (e.g., B2C, B2B, B2Gov, social enterprise). We focused on incubators, hubs, and coworking spaces due to their proximity to entrepreneurs. The ecosystem also includes financiers, public sector organizations such as ministries of ICT, and other government agencies.

The process of identifying interview subjects began with internet research that entailed identifying local champions and leaders in the digital economy. Media articles on the digital economy in a particular city often yielded information about actors actively involved in the local digital economy. These articles provided some background to activities at the field sites but tended to be sensationalist in their tone, so we did not regard them as primary data sources. The websites of pitching competitions like Seedstars, Demo Africa, and others generated lists of past participants.

Founders/CEOs were often contacted via email prior to the trip to the field site to ensure that interviews were scheduled in advance of the trip. For the most part, access was not an issue: most respondents were happy to spare time for interviews. That said, there were differences from city to city. Cities that had stronger community attributes and digital entrepreneurship communities that had an international profile tended to be home to interviewees that were relatively open to being interviewed for research. In ecosystems with a strong community, snowball sampling in fact often occurred without our prompting. In ecosystems where professional sociality was less common, clearly, actors who were strangers to each other could not facilitate introductions. Aside from giving us some insight into the closeness of ties in the community, snowball sampling and the willingness of interviewees to introduce us to their counterparts further facilitated access (compared to cold calling). A clear limitation of our approach is that we were likely to exclude some firms that "fly under the radar" and are not connected to the core digital economy ecosystem. For instance, companies that serve institutional customers in particular sectors may be well-known in that particular industry while remaining invisible to digital economy actors.

City case studies were divided among the primary analysts. Friederici conducted fieldwork in Kigali, Rwanda (January 3–22, 2017); Nairobi, Kenya (January 22–February 12, 2017; Lagos, Nigeria (February 12–March 3, 2017); Accra, Ghana (October 15–November 3, 2017); and Addis Ababa, Ethiopia January 3–20, 2018), and Wahome visited Kampala, Uganda (October 4–22, 2017); Maputo, Mozambique (October 22–November 15, 2017); Johannesburg, South Africa (November 15–December 19, 2017); Yaoundé/Buea, Cameroon (January 4–25, 2018); Abidjan, CIV (January 25–February 12, 2018; and Dakar, Senegal (February 12–24, 2018). Field visits were between two and four weeks long. The project's principal

Table A.1
Sampled digital enterprises by sector and city case study

	Abidjan	Accra	Addis	Dakar	Joburg	Kampala	Kigali	Lagos	Maputo	Nairobi	Yaoundé*	Total
Agricultural supply chain	1	4				1						6
Artificial intelligence			1									1
Bulk SMS		1							1			2
Custom software development	1	1	1		3	2	4	1	5	1		19
Data and analytics		1						2		3		6
Digital marketing	1	1						1	1			4
E-commerce	1	3				1	1		2	1		9
Education	1	1								1	1	4
ERP systems		4	3	1			1	1	1	1	1	13
Financial technology		2	2			7	1	4	3	1	1	21
Gaming			1								1	2
Health		1		1		1		1		1	1	6
IoT, tracking							1	1	1			3
Job search	1		1			1	1	1	2	2	3	12
Last-mile online access	1						1					2
Logistics and supply chain (excluding agriculture)	1			1	1		1	2	1			7
Music streaming										1		1
News, content, and public information		2			1	1		1		2		7
Ride sharing							1	1		3		5
Technology consulting		1	1	2		1						5
Total	8	22	10	5	5	15	12	16	17	17	8	135

*Yaoundé includes two cases of job search enterprises located in Buea.

investigator (Graham) contributed to fieldwork in Accra, Addis Ababa, and Maputo. Semistructured interviews were planned in advance and primarily organized through email. They were captured on audio-recording devices for later transcription. Aside from business premises, coffee shops were a common location for interviews, as they are a popular workspace for nomadic digital entrepreneurs and many others. Several interviews were conducted remotely, often as a follow-up to an initial interview.

In all cases, we solicited information about ICT use, value chain position, change, failure, remaining barriers, and manager perceptions on the effects of faster, more reliable communications on labor costs and services sold. The semistructured interview allowed us to guide the direction of the interview (Bryman 2008) and to follow-up with questions that emerged from responses, thus maintaining the thematic direction of the conversations while allowing room for flexibility.

Most interviews were conducted by a single researcher. Because there were two analysts conducting interviews across multiple case studies, a semistructured approach to interviewing allowed us to gather consistent information and facilitated cross-case comparability while also allowing the lived experiences and perspectives of respondents to come through.

Field Notes

The primary researchers kept field diaries to supplement interviews and record impressions that would not be evident from an interview recording. Field diaries were the means of capturing impromptu, unforeseen informal interviews. We produced a total of 298 pages of field diary notes. Field notes were also particularly useful for recording encounters that could not be captured by recording devices, such as observations at events and other encounters. Our research was not designed as an ethnography, so the primary purpose of the notes was to keep track of interactions, thoughts, and ideas that emerged during interviews or that were observed in the milieu in order to remember to follow-up on them.

Field notes also served as a means of keeping each other apprised of emerging findings. The analysts exchanged and reviewed each other's notes during the data-collection process to jointly discover conflicting findings and new analytical pathways. By recording our vivid impressions as they happened, we were able to share our perspectives and enable other interviewers to comment on the qualitative data-gathering process from a distance.

Participant Observation and Desk Research

To develop an understanding of the social aspects of the ecosystems, we attended events and gatherings of actors in the digital entrepreneurship arena. The fieldwork travel calendar took into account when these events would be taking place in order to facilitate attendance. These events include a entrepreneur-investor matchmaking event in Kampala, Innovation Africa 2017, and the interministerial meeting for education and ICT held in Maputo, among others. Aside from enhancing our understanding of the sociomaterial environment that constitutes digital entrepreneurship ecosystems, these occasions yield opportunities for informal, unstructured conversations that also deepened our understandings of the local context and how actors benefit from regional and global entanglement. Because we are not able to cite these interactions or observations, we sought to verify and validate them in the interviews that followed.

Finally, we gathered publicly available information about the ecosystems we were travelling to as preparation for fieldwork and also retained the information that we verified firsthand for use as a secondary source of information. This information was located on media dedicated to the digital economy; therefore it was not particularly critical. The media has tended to highlight success stories and report on ecosystems uncritically. Social media, on the other hand, provided a mix of information and was a good source of secondary data. A different study could well rely on data-mining tools to determine the prevalence of particular sentiments or networks among African Twitter users (see Park and Martins 2017). In our case, such data is only supplemental to interviews.

Analysis

The analysis of fieldwork data was a tiered, ongoing process that began in the field. The first round of fieldwork was the first opportunity to test the expectations derived from the discourse analysis, and the rounds of field work that followed refined emergent findings in turn. The data-collection process yielded a large volume of data in the form of interview transcripts, field notes, and documentary evidence. All interviews were transcribed as quickly as possible, and transcripts saved in a single NVivo file for joint analysis by the two primary researchers (Friederici and Wahome). The data was coded beginning with the themes of the research questions and the discourse analysis.

The two primary researchers took turns coding, which meant that the data remained within the same file. We also kept a coding log, in which we shared notes about the coding process, indicated which files had been coded, and noted what insights had emerged from the coding and if it had led to changes in nodal categories. The thoroughness of the process translates into confidence in our findings.

Coding Based on Research Questions

The most significant limitation of interview data is that it is nonrepresentative and not standardized at the city or country level. This means that cross-country comparisons and generalizations can only be made based on careful, iterative interpretive analysis (Yin 1994). We used an open coding strategy to categorize the interviews along several thematic lines emerging from the research questions.

Entrepreneurs' Mindsets and Experiences

This category aimed to capture entrepreneur's backgrounds, attitudes, goals, and motivations. We were not necessarily concerned with whether there was such a thing as a typical African entrepreneur. The aim was to characterize the entrepreneurs' multifaceted goals and varying backgrounds and how these affect entrepreneurs' trajectories.

Enterprise Market Opportunity Pursuit (Strategy and Scaling)

Economic relations are seldom restricted to local, national, or even regional scales of analysis. By focusing on markets, networks, processes, and the trajectory of individual enterprises and products we were able to ascertain the effects of digital enterprises on spaces and relations.

Entrepreneurial Ecosystems

We sought to understand the contexts around digital entrepreneurs using the entrepreneurial ecosystem concept (see chapter 5), especially the forces that created entrepreneurial communities in these cities. We also wanted to know whether clustering reduced the costs and uncertainties of firms attempting to develop innovations (Maskell and Malmberg 1999) as had been observed in other ecosystems and whether we continued to witness the stickiness of tacit knowledge to the detriment of sub-Saharan Africa's emerging knowledge economy. However, as we see the beginning of a transformation of sub-Saharan Africa's knowledge economy, we can begin to ask, To what extent is proximity and clustering still necessary for innovation and economic development?

New Themes

A variety of subthemes emerged over the course of our interviews and were categorized under the themes noted previously for analysis. The result was a growing number of nodes within each thematic area. For instance, we discovered complementarities for certain modes of value creation (see Amit and Zott 2001), leading us to also code secondary modes. Over time, we refined the coding plan so that it was comprehensive but not unwieldy. From these categories, we developed concepts and explanations about the practice of digital entrepreneurship. We also hit on entirely new themes, which led us to a wider focus on the "So what?" of our original research questions.

Globalization, Distance, and Development

ICTs have the potential to lessen the importance of physical distance. However, frictions of distance and accessibility continue to influence and shape the ways in which we communicate and interact economically (e.g., Massey 2005; Sheppard 2002). Debates about globalization and development are highly relevant for sub-Saharan African value chains—especially as ICTs are increasingly being employed as tools to foster economic connections with the outside world. We wanted to understand whether firms in sub-Saharan Africa are able to set up productive operations away from the world's cores.

Digital Inequality

The question of who benefits from the establishment of digital infrastructures and technologies emerged as a theme. We observed that the entrepreneurs that we spoke to often were of an elite status group and that the products that they developed, while being open, also had the potential to exclude by virtue of the digital literacy and other affordances required to use them. We sought responses that addressed the extent to which the digital economy reduced or enhanced preexisting social asymmetries.

Validity and Reliability

Qualitative methods enabled us to develop thick descriptive and explanatory analyses using categorical coding of enterprises to condense information from a large sample in a manner that is easily digestible and validating. Although we did not explicitly use counting or frequency methods to quantify responses, coding using NVivo allowed us to be aware of the number of excerpts that were attributable to particular nodes and themes. Thus, every quote that is used in the text is representative of a number of similar sentiments expressed at different field sites. This is an outcome and benefit of using a semistructured interview strategy in which respondents are expected to develop answers to a consistent set of questions. Even when tangents emerged, they were related to a question and thematic area. The ability to have each sentiment validated by a number of respondents is also an outcome of having a large pool of interview subjects. Thus, though each notion might not represent all entrepreneurs, when we present a quote, it represents a significant number of individuals. The research design rests the validity of these insights on having a large number of interviews and on reaching a saturation of the explanations provided in this book.

Different sources of information—interviews, documentary sources, and observation—allowed us to triangulate our findings and also validate them. Archived documents such as news media and policy reports also supplemented our efforts to make note of important continuities and discontinuities that impacted various milieu. For instance, the rationales of South Africa's transformation program are rooted in its history, and the way the policy and its selection criteria are structured is reflective of this. The goal was to support Black Economic Empowerment (BEE) entrepreneurs but also to try to ensure that only the most deserving and capable entrepreneurs received funding. Such a risk-avoidant approach to funding technological entrepreneurship is not typical of other ecosystems, but it makes sense in the context of South Africa's experience. This kind of analysis required being able to validate entrepreneurs' reports with historical background.

The iterative nature of our research design ensured that we were undertaking a continuous process of validation. The fact that there were three of us served as a check on the interpretation of the data. We continuously shared information on our progress in the field and discussed our analyses to achieve a level of congruence among us.

Ethical Considerations

The research design passed the rigorous ethical review of the Oxford Internet Institute's Departmental Research Ethics Committee, a subcommittee of the University of Oxford's Central University Research Ethics Committee, and the screening requirements identified in the ethics screening were integrated into the project design at the moment of the grant agreement.

Appendix B: Case Study Notes and Market Data

Abidjan, Ivory Coast

Abidjan is the capital city of the Ivory Coast, and the economic center both for the country and for the entirety of Francophone West Africa. Abidjan is in competition with Dakar as the locus of Afro-Francophone geopolitical activity and influence. The fact that the politics of the Ivory Coast have been marked by armed conflict in the not-too-distant past is hardly evident in Abidjan. The UN peacekeeping mission that had separated Northern and Southern factions in the conflict departed as recently as June of 2017. Between 2003 and 2007, the Ivory Coast was split, with rebels holding the north and the government running the south. Ivorians rarely refer to this conflict and its aftermath unless probed.

The fact that the global digital entrepreneurship ecosystem is inherently Anglophone becomes evident once one enters this non-Anglophone society. The Anglicized term used to refer to the Francophone digital entrepreneurship ecosystem is Frenchtech (as opposed to TechFrançais or some other moniker). Participants are referred to as startuppers. That said, the continued influence of France is evident not least in the country's currency, the CFA, which is pegged to the euro. The language barrier translates into digital barriers; for instance, for a city of Abidjan's size, it is surprising to find that Google Maps is unreliable. Google Maps has become a digital infrastructure, and its absence creates an additional pain point for local firms—one that firms in other geographies take for granted not having to deal with.

Nevertheless, there are benefits to being located in Abidjan. The Ivory Coast's policy of encouraging foreign investment means that tech entrepreneurs who receive capital from outside the country receive multiyear tax breaks. The fact that the global tech world is primarily Anglophone might slow down the arrival of American multinational corporations, thus allowing local companies to establish their niches.

The availability of taxi-hailing apps became an unofficial indicator for the viability of the local digital economy. They suggested a populace that was willing and able to utilize digital applications and that platform infrastructures like Google Maps for logistics were reliable—though they were not reliable everywhere. Google Maps in Abidjan did not capture every road, and landmarks and premises were not always where they were indicated. As discussed in the main book text, this intimated something about the level of investment that digital conglomerates were willing to make in certain areas. Anglophone cities tended to have a strong presence of digital multinational corporations; Francophone and Lusophone Africa much less so. There were, however, two locally owned taxi-hailing firms, suggesting demand and perhaps indicating the presence of the oft-touted African middle class. One of the taxi companies is owned by Congolese investors, an outcome of the aforementioned Ivorian tax breaks for foreign investment.

Table B.1

Data Relevant to Digital Markets	
Total population	25.22 million (51 percent urbanization)
Mobile phone subscriptions	32.38 million (128 percent)
Internet users	11.06 million (44 percent)
Mobile internet users	10.15 million (40 percent)
Social media users	4.9 million (19 percent)
Mobile social media users	4.5 million (18 percent)
Annual Digital Growth (January 2018–January 2019)	
Total population	2.5 percent
Mobile phone subscriptions	3.4 percent
Internet users	69 percent
Social media users	14 percent
Mobile social media users	18 percent

Table B.1 (continued)

Population and Economic Data	
Female population	49.4 percent
Male population	50.6 percent
Annual change in population size	2.5 percent
Median age	18.7
GDP per capita (current international $)	3,953
Overall literacy (adults aged 15+)	44 percent
Female literacy (adults aged 15+)	37 percent
Male literacy (adults aged 15+)	51 percent

Mobile Connectivity Index (out of a possible score of 100)	
Overall country index score	45.73
Mobile network infrastructure	41.01
Affordability of devices and services	67.92
Consumer readiness	41.12
Availability of relevant content and services	38.19

E-commerce Data	
Has an account with a financial institution	42 percent
Has a credit card	1.3 percent
Has a mobile money account	34 percent
Makes online purchase and/or pays bills online	7.1 percent
Percentage of women with a credit card	1 percent
Percentage of men with a credit card	1.7 percent
Percentage of women making online transactions	5.3 percent
Percentage of men making online transactions	8.7 percent

Source: We Are Social 2019

Accra, Ghana

Ghana is the poster child for Africa's development and has a good reputation across the West African region. It is an English-speaking nation that has enjoyed relative peace and prosperity. It is increasingly becoming the destination for global ICT companies seeking to develop entrepreneurship talent in the region (see Avle 2014; Friederici 2017a). It has historic universities and a reverence for technology and technologists. There is a sense among participants, however, that most "techies" or engineers lack business acumen and are unable to make a technology product work as a business. Some entrepreneurs criticize technology-focused companies, arguing that Ghanaian and African market realities require customer focus and keeping technology simple and pragmatic. Some technically minded entrepreneurs describe feeling taken advantage of by shrewd, more business-oriented entrepreneurs.

There are a number of experienced, astute entrepreneurs, who tend to have set up at or before the beginning of the digital entrepreneurship hype cycle (i.e., around 2010–2012). Successful entrepreneurs tend to be well-educated, often abroad (mainly in the United Kingdom), and/or at one of Ghana's top universities, especially KNUST (engineering) and Ashesi (business). There are facets of elitism: often entrepreneurs come from well-off, upper- or middle-class backgrounds and have gone to the same handful of elite high schools. Some have international business backgrounds or have worked for international NGOs.

The domestic market for digital technologies is described as small. According to participants, this is partly an infrastructural and partly a human capacity issue: bandwidth and reliability have improved in cities, but not everywhere in the country, and digital literacy remains low. Ghanaian participants feel that government is an important actor and needs to be involved, despite its perceived incompetence and lack of understanding of the sector.

One organization, MEST, is somewhat of a media darling, maybe because it fits into conceived Silicon Valley wisdom about technology startups. Several early MEST incubatees and entrepreneurs have an explicit global focus. More recently, emphasis appears to have been shifted toward Pan-African or low- and middle-income markets. There are a few white immigrant founders and one from Kenya in our sample.

Table B.2

Data Relevant to Digital Markets	
Total population	29.78 million (56 percent urbanization)
Mobile phone subscriptions	38.78 million (130 percent)
Internet users	10.32 million (35 percent)
Mobile internet users	9.37 million (31 percent)
Social media users	5.8 million (19 percent)
Mobile social media users	5.4 million (18 percent)

Table B.2 (continued)

Annual Growth (January 2018–January 2019)	
Total population	2.2 percent
Mobile phone subscriptions	11 percent
Internet users	2.1 percent
Social media users	3.6 percent
Mobile social media users	10 percent

Population and Economic Data	
Female population	50.1 percent
Male population	49.9 percent
Median age	21.1
GDP per capita (current international $)	4,641
Overall literacy (adults aged 15+)	71 percent
Female literacy (adults aged 15+)	65 percent
Male literacy (adults aged 15+)	78 percent

Mobile Connectivity Index (out of a possible score of 100)	
Overall country index score	52.73
Mobile network infrastructure	43.56
Affordability of devices and services	56.53
Consumer readiness	59.80
Availability of relevant content and services	52.50

E-commerce Data	
Has an account with a financial institution	58%
Has a credit card	5.8%
Has a mobile money account	39%
Makes online purchase and/or pays bills online	7.8%
Percentage of women with a credit card	4.4%
Percentage of men with a credit card	7.2%
Percentage of women making online transactions	4.9%
Percentage of men making online transactions	11%

Source: We Are Social 2019

Addis Ababa, Ethiopia

Ethiopia has a centralized (and what is considered by some as an authoritarian) government. The state has an acknowledged interest in computing technologies for development, but it is less open to their connectivity attributes (Gagliardone 2016). This particular political economy allowed us to reflect on the role of the state in digital entrepreneurship ecosystems.

The opinion that Ethiopia's digital entrepreneurship feels like that of other African countries five to ten years back is expressed over and over again. This refers to internet penetration rates, revenue figures, number of startups, investment deals, and so on, but, more subtly, it also refers to entrepreneurial skill and experience. Because there have been very few startups that have been actually operational for a number of years, there are also very few entrepreneurs who have any sort of sense of business models, monetization, and localization/adaptation. Kenyans, for instance, appear to be way ahead and extending their advantage more and more—and this cannot be accounted for by the size of the domestic market/size of the local economy because Ethiopia's absolute GDP and GDP growth has clearly outpaced Kenya's in recent years. In contrast, some of our participants have argued that we are currently at a kind of tipping point or moment of change in Ethiopia, with small changes beginning to have bigger impacts.

Although Ethiopia's culture (as it translates to entrepreneurship) is also unique, this is, as usual, more difficult to capture or describe succinctly. It appears that entrepreneurs are not big visionaries and not focused on building empires or making a lot of money. Engineers are considered the best entrepreneurs, which is something that is considered foolish in other African countries. Business modeling and ways to make money are rarely discussed. Vast domestic market potentials are discussed in abstract terms, but few seem to actually tap into them.

One dynamic particular to Ethiopia is that entrepreneurs find workarounds or make use of regulatory constraints. Ethiopia's complicated licensing regime is mostly a burden, but it also shields exceptional enterprises that have identified this strategic opportunity.

Overall, the size of the digital technology sector is very small given the country's size. Similarly, the hub landscape appears small. Positive signs for ecosystem evolution are increasing legitimacy and normality of entrepreneurship among youth, and the government's careful and piecemeal opening toward this agenda.

Table B.3

Data Relevant to Digital Markets

Total population	108.8 million (21 percent urbanization)
Mobile phone subscriptions	68.34 million (63 percent)
Internet users	17.87 million (16 percent)
Mobile internet users	16.41 million (15 percent)
Social media users	6.1 million (5.6 percent)
Mobile social media users	5.6 million (5.1 percent)

Annual Growth (January 2018–January 2019)

Total population	2.4 percent
Mobile phone subscriptions	9.2 percent
Internet users	9.2 percent
Social media users	61 percent
Mobile social media users	56 percent

Population and Economic Data

Female population	50.1 percent
Male population	49.9 percent
Median age	19.8
GDP per capita (current international $)	1,899
Overall literacy (adults aged 15+)	39 percent
Female literacy (adults aged 15+)	29 percent
Male literacy (adults aged 15+)	49 percent

Mobile Connectivity Index (out of a possible score of 100)

Overall country index score	37.68
Mobile network infrastructure	34.86
Affordability of devices and services	43.51
Consumer readiness	35.18
Availability of relevant content and services	37.76

E-commerce Data

Has an account with a financial institution	35 percent
Has a credit card	0.3 percent
Has a mobile money account	0.3 percent
Makes online purchase and/or pays bills online	0.6 percent
Percentage of women with a credit card	0.2 percent
Percentage of men with a credit card	0.3 percent
Percentage of women making online transactions	0.4 percent
Percentage of men making online transactions	0.8 percent

Source: We Are Social 2019

Dakar, Senegal

Dakar is the capital of Senegal and is unique in the region because, though formerly colonized by the French, most Senegalese speak Wolof rather than French. This invited inquiry into the localization and appropriation of digital technology and the effect of this on entrepreneurship. It also had a locally owned M-Pesa equivalent, Wari, which allowed for comparison into how these platforms did or did not facilitate the development of local ecosystems.

The digital entrepreneurship space in Dakar is dominated by the success narratives of Wari and Jokkolabs, an incubator that has opened outposts across the region. Wari's regional scale has allowed it to purchase the Senegalese operations of mobile telecommunications operator Tigo in order to expand its already considerable reach. Jokkolabs is a coworking space and incubator that epitomizes the startup culture and ethos and provides a space for entrepreneurs to try their hands at the digital economy. Jokkolabs itself has been able to spread to other countries, including France, and a few of the companies housed within it have been able to become visible in their own right. Despite the outsized success of individual organizations, however, the ecosystem is not as cohesive or as variegated as others on the continent.

Applying our unofficial taxi-hailing application index, the lack of any taxi-hailing firm suggests that the local market for digital services is not well-developed. Société Générale, a bank with a regional footprint, has nevertheless established its innovation lab in Dakar (after considering Abidjan), indicating a growing sense of Dakar as a regional economic hub. Evidence of this sense of promise is the number of Senegalese that have returned from the diaspora to try their hand at digital entrepreneurship. As noted, the prevalent language in Senegal is Wolof, which is likely to complicate the appropriation of digital economy structures and practices.

Table B.4

Data Relevant to Digital Markets

Total population	16.52 million (47 percent urbanization)
Mobile phone subscriptions	16.69 million (101 percent)
Internet users	9.75 million (59 percent)
Mobile internet users	8.91million (54 percent)
Social media users	3.5 million (21 percent)
Mobile social media users	3.2 million (19 percent)

Annual Digital Growth (January 2018–January 2019)

Total population	2.8 percent
Mobile phone subscriptions	5.9 percent
Internet users	0.1 percent
Social media users	13 percent
Mobile social media users	10 percent

Population and Economic Data

Female population	50.8 percent
Male population	49.2 percent
Annual change in population size	2.8 percent
Median age	18.7
GDP per capita (current international $)	2,712
Overall literacy (adults aged 15+)	52 percent
Female literacy (adults aged 15+)	40 percent
Male literacy (adults aged 15+)	65 percent

Mobile Connectivity Index (out of a possible score of 100)

Overall country index score	37.30
Mobile network infrastructure	28.95
Affordability of devices and services	39.53
Consumer readiness	39.53
Availability of relevant content and services	29.65

E-commerce Data

Has an account with a financial institution	42 percent
Has a credit card	2.8 percent
Has a mobile money account	32 percent
Makes online purchase and/or pays bills online	10 percent
Percentage of women with a credit card	3 percent
Percentage of men with a credit card	2.7 percent
Percentage of women making online transactions	7.8 percent
Percentage of men making online transactions	13 percent

Source: We Are Social 2019

Johannesburg, South Africa

Johannesburg is an industrial hub of South Africa. The country has a number of major cities: Johannesburg is its economic heart, but Cape Town is the locus of the digital economy. Why this is the case was an interesting question to consider given that one consistent observation was that digital hubs developed where economic activity was the highest. The question of inequality was also particularly relevant here because the South African economy is much bigger than that of many of the other countries in Africa. The facts that money had been set aside by the government for entrepreneurship and that material infrastructure for connectivity was robust made it an ideal site to consider ecosystem determinants other than capital.

As Johannesburg is a top-tier city, one expects to find a robust digital ecosystem there. There are indeed many hubs and other support organizations that provide a variety of services for entrepreneurs. With respect to the taxi app index, Uber is present, and so is Taxify/Bolt, a firm of Estonian provenance that operates in Africa. The taxi apps operate in fraught, direct confrontation with the preexisting analog taxi economy. This is representative of a sense that one comes away with about the entire digital economy: digital entrepreneurship is a class-based activity. The narrative heard in less economically generative cities about the difficulty of attracting capital is echoed in Johannesburg, a place whose other name, Egoli, translates into English as *place of gold*. Johannesburg is an opportunity to understand that finance capital is heterogeneous. The kind of capital that is invested in extractive industries does not necessarily flow in other directions.

South Africa has a dedicated government program to reduce postapartheid economic disparity, which has channeled resources toward the digital entrepreneurship arena. The issue then becomes determining criteria for measuring who should receive these funds and considering whether these criteria are compatible with high-growth digital entrepreneurship. We have challenged the assumption that this conception of digital entrepreneurship has relevance for Africa, but until a new model emerges, this is likely the direction that many entrepreneurs and ecosystems will continue to pursue.

Table B.5

Data Relevant to Digital Markets

Total population	57.73 million (67 percent urbanization)
Mobile phone subscriptions	98.05 million (170 percent)
Internet users	31.18 million (54 percent)
Mobile internet users	28.99 million (50 percent)
Social media users	23 million (40 percent)
Mobile social media users	22 million (38 percent)

Annual Growth (January 2018–January 2019)

Total population	1.2 percent
Mobile phone subscriptions	9.8 percent
Internet users	1.2 percent
Social media users	28 percent
Mobile social media users	38 percent

Population and Economic Data

Female population	50.9 percent
Male population	49.1 percent
Median age	27.3
GDP per capita (current international $)	13,498
Overall literacy (adults aged 15+)	94 percent
Female literacy (adults aged 15+)	93 percent
Male literacy (adults aged 15+)	95 percent

Mobile Connectivity Index (out of a possible score of 100)

Overall country index score	59.89
Mobile network infrastructure	53.67
Affordability of devices and services	60.79
Consumer readiness	74.92
Availability of relevant content and services	52.64

E-commerce Data

Has an account with a financial institution	69 percent
Has a credit card	8.9 percent
Has a mobile money account	19 percent
Makes online purchase and/or pays bills online	14 percent
Percentage of women with a credit card	8.1 percent
Percentage of men with a credit card	9.7 percent
Percentage of women making online transactions	12 percent
Percentage of men making online transactions	17 percent

Source: We Are Social 2019

Kampala, Uganda

Kampala is the capital city and economic center of Uganda. Uganda shares a number of attributes with Rwanda: it is landlocked, it experienced a civil war in its recent history, and its rebel leader became a long-serving president. However, while the Rwandese state frames ICTs as an integral part of its national development plan, the Ugandan government has much less to say about the same topic. Kampala is also relatively close to Nairobi, which led us to consider whether geographic proximity to another digital entrepreneurship hub is an impediment or a boon.

Uganda has been touted as the most entrepreneurial country in the world by the Global Entrepreneurship Monitor. Much of this economic activity, however, can be classified as self-employment and lifestyle entrepreneurship, as opposed to high-growth entrepreneurship, which indicates a willingness in global policy institutions to adopt a more expansive definition of entrepreneurship. Ugandans' tend to supplement their incomes with a mélange of activities. Indeed, a large number of the digital entrepreneurs that we encountered were also in employment or worked as consultants.

Digital entrepreneurs are generally well-educated; a good number had attended the historic Makerere University. A number of them are returnees, and there were a few immigrant entrepreneurs.

Uganda is a primarily agricultural economy, and some digital entrepreneurs who had found success had done so by introducing digital solutions to the agricultural sector. Uber was available, suggesting that there was a market for digital goods. However, it appeared that B2B business models were more likely to meet with greater success than B2C ideas. The mass domestic digital market is described as small and was likely to shrink because the government had instituted a social media tax. Social media platforms are often platform infrastructures that foster economic activity. Uganda's very youthful population is governed by an old guard who, having quelled a civil war, are content with what they view as a peaceful status quo. It appears that younger Ugandans are biding their time until they can determine the trajectory of their country and make it somewhat more dynamic and progressive.

Table B.6

Data Relevant to Digital Markets

Total population	44.99 million (24 percent urbanization)
Mobile phone subscriptions	24.89 million (55 percent)
Internet users	19 million (42 percent)
Mobile internet users	17.48 million (39 percent)
Social media users	2.5 million (5.6 percent)
Mobile social media users	2.3 million (5.1 percent)

Annual Growth (January 2018–January 2019)

Total population	3.3 percent
Mobile phone subscriptions	2.7 percent
Internet users	0 percent
Social media users	-11 percent
Mobile social media users	-12 percent

Population and Economic Data

Female population	50.2 percent
Male population	49.8 percent
Median age	16.4
GDP per capita (current international $)	1,864
Overall literacy (adults aged 15+)	70 percent
Female literacy (adults aged 15+)	62 percent
Male literacy (adults aged 15+)	79 percent

Mobile Connectivity Index (out of a possible score of 100)

Overall country index score	36.49
Mobile network infrastructure	23.50
Affordability of devices and services	41.75
Consumer readiness	51.04
Availability of relevant content and services	35.38

E-commerce Data

Has an account with a financial institution	59 percent
Has a credit card	2.3 percent
Has a mobile money account	51 percent
Makes online purchase and/or pays bills online	9.5 percent
Percentage of women with a credit card	1.8 percent
Percentage of men with a credit card	2.8 percent
Percentage of women making online transactions	5.8 percent
Percentage of men making online transactions	13 percent

Source: We Are Social 2019

Kigali, Rwanda

Kigali is the capital city of Rwanda. Rwanda represents a vastly different context compared to our other theory-development cases, Nairobi and Lagos. It is a landlocked city with a small population (less than one million). It is an intriguing analytical puzzle to consider to what extent digital connectivity can help small and landlocked nations overcome market barriers from traditional sectors (e.g., small local markets, low bargaining power in international trade negotiations, etc.). Rwanda's state championing of the digital economy offered a different set of considerations than Lagos's market-driven environment or Nairobi's, which also has an international development influence.

Rwandan digital entrepreneurs indicated that they were not particularly motivated by money. Many would have better earning opportunities doing something else, and they do not expect this to change. Almost all digital entrepreneurship that is happening is targeted at the Rwandan market. At the same time, local markets also are limited in scale. Rwanda is small, with an even smaller middle class and few businesses that (think they) require software solutions, and so it is not the case that many huge technology businesses could thrive based on this demand. User inertia is a very prevalent theme. One might say that "old habits die hard," and digital entrepreneurs complain that a lot of "educating the user" is needed both for businesses and consumers. This has led to what entrepreneurs perceive as delays. Yet the narrative that Rwanda is ideal for piloting software solutions that can then be scaled across East Africa and Africa is extremely strong, although there do not seem to be existing companies that have done this.

There is a strong belief in technology's transformative power, beyond or separately from its economic potential, and a sense of "entrepreneurship by fiat" that external observers have pointed to (Strauss 2014). Most local entrepreneurs do not seem to actively seek media attention but get it because there are few local success stories and the government and media jump on cases that ostensibly fit into the narrative of the rising ICT nation. Rwanda is also viewed as a leading ICT destination by participants in other nations (especially Ghana). Yet as with most of the places we visited, the larger-scale (platform, infrastructural) technologies are imported or implemented by large companies or the government.

Table B.7

Data Relevant to Digital Markets	
Total population	12.65 million (17 percent urbanization)
Mobile phone subscriptions	9.73 million (77 percent)
Internet users	5.6 million (44 percent)
Mobile internet users	5.24 million (41 percent)
Social media users	0.62 million (4.9 percent)
Mobile social media users	0.58 million (4.6 percent)

Annual Growth (January 2018–January 2019)	
Total population	2.4 percent
Mobile phone subscriptions	14 percent
Internet users	50 percent
Social media users	19 percent
Mobile social media users	23 percent

Population and Economic Data	
Female population	51 percent
Male population	49 percent
Median age	20.3
GDP per capita (current international $)	2,036
Overall literacy (adults aged 15+)	71 percent
Female literacy (adults aged 15+)	66 percent
Male literacy (adults aged 15+)	76 percent

Mobile Connectivity Index (out of a possible score of 100)	
Overall country index score	40.01
Mobile network infrastructure	43.64
Affordability of devices and services	46.91
Consumer readiness	55.47
Availability of relevant content and services	22.58

E-commerce Data	
Has an account with a financial institution	50 percent
Has a credit card	0.7 percent
Has a mobile money account	31 percent
Makes online purchase and/or pays bills online	4.6 percent
Percentage of women with a credit card	0.2 percent
Percentage of men with a credit card	1.3 percent
Percentage of women making online transactions	3.4 percent
Percentage of men making online transactions	5.9 percent

Source: We Are Social 2019

Lagos, Nigeria

With eight million inhabitants, Lagos is Nigeria's largest city, even though Abuja is the capital. Abuja is the seat of government, but Lagos is the country's economic powerhouse. Nigeria's huge population (it is the most populous country in Africa) means that the possibilities for the development of a local market appear significant. We wanted to consider whether this changed the global versus local outlook of digital entrepreneurs.

Like in Nairobi, where there are some established, profitable technology companies with a long history, they similarly are not exactly integrated with the rest of the ecosystem. Nigeria has more of a gold rush and money-focused mentality (for fintech), as opposed to Nairobi's copresence of social impact orientation and business-mindedness. First and foremost, companies are trying to make money and be the first to capture the large Nigerian market. Revenue is king here, although significant funding rounds have gotten a lot of international exposure as well. There is also a greater amount of VC funds than elsewhere in Africa. Like in Nairobi, however, there might be investment money available, but it only goes to a few digital companies.

The government was interested in creating a narrative about putting ICTs and entrepreneurship on the agenda and showing that something interesting and important was happening in this space, and it has therefore invested in hubs and incubators. There appears to be geographic fragmentation: Yaba, the cluster where CcHub, IDEA, and several businesses are located, is detached from Victoria and Lagos Island, and these are again detached from Lekki, and neither of these is connected with Ikeja in the north (an older business district where the state government is). More so than in Nairobi and Kigali, it appears to be tough for startups to afford office space.

In terms of entrepreneurial culture, there appears to be more of a fend-for-yourself attitude here. This includes less rhetoric about social impact in a narrow sense, but, more importantly, there is not as much of a product and design focus, and also no talk of being passionate about building software, about recognition, or of legacy building as there is in Nairobi. Like in Nairobi, participants argue that there are differences in the approach to entrepreneurship between the Silicon Valley model for tech startups and what works locally and what locals would do. Also as in Nairobi, entrepreneurs appear to have a media/PR persona and a business persona, with latter being much more pragmatic and shrewd.

Table B.8

Data Relevant to Digital Markets

Total population	198.4 million (51 percent urbanization)
Mobile phone subscriptions	149.4 million (75 percent)
Internet users	98.39 million (50 percent)
Mobile internet users	90.91 million (46 percent)
Social media users	24 million (12 percent)
Mobile social media users	23 million (12 percent)

Annual Growth (January 2018–January 2019)

Total population	2.6 percent
Mobile phone subscriptions	7.4 percent
Internet users	3.8 percent
Social media users	26 percent
Mobile social media users	35 percent

Population and Economic Data

Female population	49.3 percent
Male population	50.7 percent
Median age	18.1
GDP per capita (current international $)	5,861
Overall literacy (adults aged 15+)	51 percent
Female literacy (adults aged 15+)	41 percent
Male literacy (adults aged 15+)	61 percent

Mobile Connectivity Index (out of a possible score of 100)

Overall country index score	45.91
Mobile network infrastructure	35.86
Affordability of devices and services	64.11
Consumer readiness	44.15
Availability of relevant content and services	43.75

E-commerce Data

Has an account with a financial institution	40 percent
Has a credit card	2.6 percent
Has a mobile money account	5.6 percent
Makes online purchase and/or pays bills online	6.3 percent
Percentage of women with a credit card	1.7 percent
Percentage of men with a credit card	3.4 percent
Percentage of women making online transactions	2.9 percent
Percentage of men making online transactions	9.4 percent

Source: We Are Social 2019

Maputo, Mozambique

Maputo is the capital and the center of all economic activity in Mozambique. It was one of the cities that we saw as representing low activity because of the economic dire straits that it had experienced in recent years. Maputo was an ideal site to investigate the opportunities that digital connectivity represented for individuals to make a sustainable living and see to whom those opportunities accrued. Mozambique is also a Lusophone country, which enabled an analysis of how language affects ecosystem development and market reach.

Mozambique underwent an economic crisis when the IMF discovered secret government debts that were pegged to Mozambique's future earnings from oil reserves, which led to a devaluing of the country's currency. It goes without saying that this had a dampening effect on any economic activity, including the digital economy. However, even (or maybe especially) in such conditions, small-scale and informal economic activity takes place, as people who might otherwise be employed become entrepreneurial to make ends meet. Digital platforms have the ability to facilitate this small-scale business activity. In fact, social media sites like Facebook did indeed allow traders to advertise their goods and contact information. In an underdeveloped economy, infrastructure projects represent a major portion of the economy. Young people with access and backing had the opportunity to establish telecommunications firms that could serve infrastructural functions.

In the middle of this high- and low-intensity economic activity was a small, close-knit group of individuals running startup firms. It is evident that participants in this ecosystem have a socioeconomic status that is higher than the country's average. A clue is that they are at ease speaking English. Mozambique is multilingual, and while it is considered Lusophone, much of the rural population does not speak Portuguese. In the city, Portuguese is widely spoken and English is prevalent in affluent circles. The primary sources of resources for startup firms are development agencies and philanthropy. Organizations like the World Bank, the Finnish government, Save the Children, Microsoft, and others provide small grants and commission services from the firms in the ecosystem. A group of enthusiastic technologists have benefited from this support. Software development teams are quickly assembled to resolve problems for these organizations.

Table B.9

Data Relevant to Digital Markets

Total population	30.97 million (36 percent urbanization)
Mobile subscriptions	14.26 million (46 percent)
Internet users	5.43 million (18 percent)
Mobile internet users	4.77 million (15 percent)
Social media users	2.5 million (87.1 percent)
Mobile social media users	2.2 million (7.1 percent)

Annual Growth (January 2018–January 2019)

Total population	2.9 percent
Mobile phone subscriptions	3.0 percent
Internet users	2.9 percent
Social media users	25 percent
Mobile social media users	22 percent

Population and Economic Data

Female population	51.1 percent
Male population	48.9 percent
Median age	17.7
GDP per capita (current international $)	1,247
Overall literacy (adults aged 15+)	56 percent
Female literacy (adults aged 15+)	43 percent
Male literacy (adults aged 15+)	71 percent

Mobile Connectivity Index (out of a possible score of 100)

Overall country index score	31.03
Mobile network infrastructure	18.69
Affordability of devices and services	42.49
Consumer readiness	39.84
Availability of relevant content and services	29.30

E-commerce Data

Has an account with a financial institution	42 percent
Has a credit card	8.9 percent
Has a mobile money account	22 percent
Makes online purchase and/or pays bills online	9.5 percent
Percentage of women with a credit card	7.5 percent
Percentage of men with a credit card	10 percent
Percentage of women making online transactions	8.1 percent
Percentage of men making online transactions	11 percent

Source: We Are Social 2019

Nairobi, Kenya

Nairobi, a city of over three million people (not counting peri-urban surroundings) that is the capital city of Kenya, has become known as the Silicon Savannah, yielding noted success stories in the realm of social digital entrepreneurship and inclusive innovation. The presence of regional and global offices of various international institutions makes Nairobi a global city in the eyes of many business and political leaders. This is reflected in the large population of diplomatic expats and economic migrants from around the world. We wanted to reflect on what effect, if any, this global status had on the trajectory of Silicon Savannah.

There is an interesting tendency for entrepreneurs in Nairobi to say that things are just getting started. However, there is a league of very experienced, very senior entrepreneurs who started their businesses in the late 1990s or early 2000s, grew their businesses organically, and operated largely unrecognized, long before iHub and Silicon Savannah. They are widely respected and venerated, but they are also reclusive and sometimes dismissive of anything Silicon Savannah related. Even if these entrepreneurs and companies are not actively visible in the ecosystem, they play an important role as role models and as builders of talent and professional communities: they have created a labor market and small pockets of networking and learning for software developers (and related jobs) that have now been in place for almost twenty years. More generally, clear social hierarchies and statuses are attached to whoever was there at the Silicon Savannah's famed beginnings or before. There is an inner circle, or several inner circles, centered on the very first generation of entrepreneurs who started businesses in the late 1990s or early 2000s, and then on a few of the Silicon Savannah veterans, who became active around 2010.

There is clear indication of evolutionary processes of human capital and social network development. There is a trend toward professionalization, such as hiring nonfounder CEOs or finding it important to institute an organizational culture in startups. A high number of people with five to fifteen years of relevant, high-level experience can be hired. Nairobi's long-standing role as a hub for East Africa and all of Africa is reflected in the significant presence of immigrant founders.

Businesses often appear to be serving the Kenyan market, but really only have customers in Nairobi. Nairobi is such a huge city that it appears to be a large enough starting market for many digital businesses. Entrepreneurs in the trenches feel that they have spent recent years figuring things out, learning/failing, iterating, working toward product-market fit, and so on, and that only now will growth begin for most businesses. There is still a buzz, even if it is not entirely clear how many businesses are ultimately economically viable. The plateauing in the last two to three years has had the positive effect of leading to a greater number of realistic, viable business developments and incremental innovations, advanced by not a huge but a decent-sized group of astute digital entrepreneurs who have outlasted the many not so serious wannabes.

Table B.10

Data Relevant to Digital Markets	
Total population	51.58 million (27 percent urbanization)
Mobile phone subscriptions	46.94 million (97 percent)
Internet users	43.33 million (84 percent)
Mobile internet users	39.86 million (77 percent)
Social media users	8.20 million (16 percent)
Mobile social media users	7.7 million (15 percent)
Annual Growth (January 2018–January 2019)	
Total population	2.5 percent
Mobile phone subscriptions	15 percent
Internet users	0 percent
Social media users	6.5 percent
Mobile social media users	10 percent
Population and Economic Data	
Female population	50.3 percent
Male population	49.7 percent
Median age	20
GDP per capita (current international $)	3,286
Overall literacy (adults aged 15+)	79 percent
Female literacy (adults aged 15+)	74 percent
Male literacy (adults aged 15+)	84 percent

Table B.10 (continued)

Mobile Connectivity Index (out of a possible score of 100)	
Overall country index score	50.95
Mobile network infrastructure	39.62
Affordability of devices and services	63.06
Consumer readiness	62.52
Availability of relevant content and services	43.15

E-commerce Data	
Has an account with a financial institution	82 percent
Has a credit card	5.7 percent
Has a mobile money account	73 percent
Makes online purchase and/or pays bills online	26 percent
Percentage of women with a credit card	3.5 percent
Percentage of men with a credit card	8.1 percent
Percentage of women making online transactions	20 percent
Percentage of men making online transactions	33 percent

Source: We Are Social 2019

Yaoundé, Cameroon

We classified Cameroon as mid-tier because of Douala, which is its economic and digital economy hub. Like Lagos, Douala is a noncapital primary city, so we decided to focus on Yaoundé, the capital of Cameroon. Yaoundé, a centrally located city and the government seat, represented an opportunity to understand why particular cities became digital entrepreneurship hubs. Douala has traditionally been the center for commerce, and it seems that this was the impetus for it taking the lead in terms of the establishment of yet another economic sector. Yaoundé does not have the buzz of Douala or of Buea (a city in Cameroon's Anglophone region that has been nicknamed Silicon Mountain).

But Yaoundé does have digital entrepreneurs, and we wanted to hear from them about why it was that other urban centers had a higher profile and why they remained in Yaoundé. The digital entrepreneurs there said that they did not feel cut off from the benefits of being located in the more visible ecosystems in the country. In fact, they associated being located in

Yaoundé with legitimacy. As in many other places, visibility was also seen as connected with hype, as opposed to authentic entrepreneurship. Some of the companies we spoke to did have well-funded products, but it remains to be seen whether the Cameroonian economy is strong enough to support an entire ecosystem of digital products.

The sociopolitical climate in Cameroon meant that it was also a site for investigating the role of the state and its impact on digital entrepreneurship. The fact that Cameroon is divided into French-speaking and English-speaking regions lead into conversations about language and cultural aspects of digital entrepreneurship. Entrepreneurs from Buea were thus also interviewed during the trip to Cameroon. Buea is home to some of Cameroon's most profiled entrepreneurs. Most recently, Buea and the rest of Anglophone Western Cameroon has been in the media because of a government-mandated internet shutdown. Entrepreneurs articulated the deleterious effect that the shutdown had on their internet-dependent businesses. Some sought to relocate to Douala, which is a few hours' drive away. Even if firms can scale globally and become independent of a reliance on Cameroonian customers, they still require institutional supports or, at the very least, not to be hamstrung by structural factors. None of these towns have taxi-hailing applications. Old yellow taxis swarm Yaoundé's thoroughfares, and they seem to be indicative of an economy that is stuck in the past.

Table B.11

Data Relevant to Digital Markets	
Total population	25 million (57 percent urbanization)
Mobile phone subscriptions	19 million (76 percent)
Internet users	6.13 million (25 percent)
Mobile internet users	5.79 million (23 percent)
Social users	3.6 million (14 percent)
Mobile social media users	3.4 million (14 percent)
Annual Growth (January 2018–January 2019)	
Total population	2.6 percent
Mobile phone subscriptions	5.4 percent
Internet users	0 percent
Social media users	24 percent
Mobile social media users	26 percent

Table B.11 (continued)

Population and Economic Data

Female population	49.9 percent
Male population	50.1 percent
Median age	18.8
GDP per capita (current international $)	3,694
Overall literacy (adults aged 15+)	71 percent
Female literacy (adults aged 15+)	65 percent
Male literacy (adults aged 15+)	78 percent

Mobile Connectivity Index (out of a possible score of 100)

Overall country index score	42.76
Mobile network infrastructure	25.69
Affordability of devices and services	58.64
Consumer readiness	54.90
Availability of relevant content and services	40.42

E-commerce Data

Has an account with a financial institution	35 percent
Has a credit card	3 percent
Has a mobile money account	15 percent
Makes online purchase and/or pays bills online	5.6 percent
Percentage of women with a credit card	2.2 percent
Percentage of men with a credit card	3.9 percent
Percentage of women making online transactions	4.7 percent
Percentage of men making online transactions	6.5 percent

Source: We Are Social 2019

Notes

1 Hopes and Potentials

1. We are aware of criticism that the discursive and administrative division of Africa in North Africa and sub-Saharan Africa can be understood as a postcolonial and racist social construct (Gikandi 2001; Mbembe 2001; and Zeleza 2009). Throughout the book, we refer to *Africa* because we do not want to perpetuate and invoke this problematic division and because we are confident that many of our findings apply to the entire continent (see appendix A). Here, we exceptionally use the term *sub-Saharan Africa*, and only in a strictly geographical sense, referring to nations that are situated south of the Sahara Desert, as this world region has been connected last to the global fiber-optic system.

2. *Imaginaries* represent sets of values, expectations, symbols, and materials that are used to produce visions of societies and social groups.

3. We define *digital entrepreneurship* as the novel creation of market- and opportunity-driven initiatives that is enabled or deeply impacted by digital technologies (Nambisan 2017), including the internet, mobile applications, social media, cloud computing, and artificial intelligence.

4. *Incubators* typically offer a clearly defined set of hands-on support services (e.g., work space, mentorship, networking), while *innovation hubs* provide only lightweight support and mostly help entrepreneurs form communities (see Friederici 2017a).

5. The GSMA Innovation Fund also illustrates how the agendas—and funds—of development organizations and technology corporations are comingled in the support of African digital entrepreneurship: the fund is administered by GSMA but financially supported by UK Aid and Australian Aid, which contributed undisclosed amounts.

6. Strictly speaking, affordances are not objective properties of technologies that predetermine organizational or individual action—instead, affordances are

actualized by actors in a partially indeterminate strategic process (Tan, Tan, and Pan 2016; Volkoff and Strong 2013). For simplicity, we use the more commonplace and intuitive notion of the term.

7. Admittedly, this limits the generalizability of our findings to this scope. Although we are confident that our findings apply in significant parts also to North Africa, as well as other low- and middle-income countries (see Quinones, Heeks, and Nicholson 2017; Ravishankar 2018; and Wentrup, Ström, and Nakamura 2016), any such translation has to be conducted with care. We opt for using the term *Africa* throughout the book because we do not want to perpetuate what may be construed as a racist and postcolonial division of North and sub-Saharan Africa (see previous note). We find that this approach balances requirements of sensitive language use and analytical precision, and results in only a negligible overgeneralization of our findings.

8. We should note that our perception is biased heavily toward the English-speaking world. However, our cursory review of francophone African technology media and interactions with multilateral development organizations and scholars of Latin America and Asia make us confident that there is a rather coherent popular macro discourse at global scale.

2   Taking Stock

1. Indeed, many participants felt that our main role as academic researchers was to document their firsthand experiences and collate relevant market information.

2. Academics based in high-income countries can of course suffer from similar biases, but groups with more direct (e.g., financial or activist) influence are emphasized here.

3. Participants in Addis Ababa explained that mobile broadband became widely available later there than in most African countries, meaning that Ethiopian users had not yet been locked into WhatsApp when Telegram emerged as a messaging service that offered superior functionalities. Indeed, we noticed that participants without an international contact network rarely had a WhatsApp account. Ethiopia is thus a good illustration for the importance of national-level network effects and timing in determining digital product adoption.

3   Bounded Opportunities

1. The mobile phone is an example of a device that has been integrated into societies around the world in distinct ways.

4   Viable Strategies

1. A *unicorn* is a private company with a market valuation of $1 billion or more.

6 Transitioning Identities

1. Investors preferring Westerner-run enterprises and startups' strategic response of "white fronting" also has a racial and postcolonial dimension. We will return to this issue in more depth in chapter 7.

2. Since the interview quoted here, Uganda has gone on to legislate measures to curb access to social media. In African cities, WhatsApp, Facebook, and Twitter are often bundled in deals offered by mobile operators in which these services are exempt from data charges. The move to charge users for access was seen as a method of reducing agitations against the end of the tenure of long-serving President Yoweri Museveni.

3. The former German-held colony of Cameroon was divided between the British and French after World War II. The result is francophone and anglophone Cameroon, the strained relationship of which is reflected in the development of a separatist movement in the western, anglophone region of Cameroon.

7 Silicon Tensions

1. See "List of Technology Centers" (2019), Wikipedia, https://en.wikipedia.org/wiki/List_of_technology_centers#Places_with_%22Silicon%22_names.

2. Both in media reports and research interviews, South African cities are often ignored in such implicit ranked comparisons. Participants often told us that Johannesburg and Cape Town are considered outliers, more comparable to cities in high-income countries but not to other cities in Africa.

3. This is in contrast to the larger economy, in which, depending on which country one is in, South Asian, Chinese, Lebanese, and other communities have become part of the mosaic.

4. Names have been changed.

5. In Maputo, the Cooperation in Science, Technology and Innovation between Finland and Mozambique (STIFIMO), established by the Finnish Embassy in 2010, was fundamental to the establishment of the local ecosystem (see chapter 5). The World Bank was identified as a significant actor in both Maputo and Nairobi.

8 Ways Forward

1. And, indeed, it is likely that excitement that got most readers to pick up this book.

References

ABAN Angels. 2018. "'We use Spotify, a platform built in Sweden, all across the world and in Africa. Why can't a Nigerian platform power #payments in Mexico or Guatemala?' @oviosu . . ." Twitter, September 8, 2018, 12:19 a.m. https://twitter.com/ABANAngels/status/1038325947710271488.

Acemoglu, Daron, and James A. Robinson. 2013. *Why Nations Fail: The Origins of Power, Prosperity and Poverty.* London: Profile Books.

Adams, Janet S., Frank A. Wiebe, and Robert F. Scherer. 1989. "Developing Entrepreneurial Behaviours: A Social Learning Theory Perspective." *Journal of Organizational Change Management* 2 (3): 16–27. https://doi.org/10.1108/EUM0000000001186.

Adepoju, Paul. 2015. "Q&A: What Africa Needs to Build the Next Facebook." *Ventureburn* (blog). August 31, 2015. http://ventureburn.com/2015/08/qa-what-africa-needs-to-do-to-build-the-next-facebook/.

Adesida, Olugbenga, and Geci Karuri-Sebina, eds. 2016. *Innovation Africa: Emerging Hubs of Entrepreneurship.* United Kingdom: Emerald.

Afele, John Senyo. 2002. *Digital Bridges: Developing Countries in the Knowledge Economy.* Hershey, PA: Idea Group Publishing.

African Business Central. 2015. "The African Tech Startup Scene Has Been Transformed in Just Four Years." *African Business Central* (blog). October 25, 2015. https://www.africanbusinesscentral.com/2015/10/25/the-african-tech-startup-scene-has-been-transformed-in-just-four-years/.

African Union Commission and OECD. 2018. *Africa's Development Dynamics 2018: Growth, Jobs and Inequalities.* Paris: OECD Publishing. https://doi.org/10.1787/9789264302501-en.

"Africa Rising." 2011. *Economist,* December 3, 2011. http://www.economist.com/node/21541015.

Ahmed, S. Amer, Marcio Cruz, Delfin S. Go, Maryla Maliszewska, and Israel Osorio-Rodarte. 2016. "How Significant Is Sub-Saharan Africa's Demographic Dividend for Its Future Growth and Poverty Reduction?" *Review of Development Economics* 20 (4): 762–793. https://doi.org/10.1111/rode.12227.

Akinloye, Dimeji. 2018. "Jumia's Major Investor Reportedly Planning to Withdraw." Pulse NG, March 17, 2018. https://www.pulse.ng/news/business/jumias-major-investor-reportedly-planning-to-withdraw-id8128909.html.

Akpan, Wilson. 2011. "'Local' Knowledge, 'Global' Knowledge, 'Development' Knowledge: Finding a New Balance in the Knowledge Power Play." *South African Review of Sociology* 42 (3): 116–127. https://doi.org/10.1080/21528586.2011.621244.

Al Jazeera English. 2014. "Innovate Africa." Al Jazeera English, December 3. https://www.aljazeera.com/programmes/innovate-africa/2014/11/technology-pays-20141117152113644911.html.

Aldrich, Howard E. 2014. "The Democratization of Entrepreneurship? Hackers, Makerspaces, and Crowdfunding." *Academy of Management Proceedings* 2014 (1). https://doi.org/10.5465/AMBPP.2014.10622symposium.

Allen, David. 1988. "New Telecommunications Services: Network Externalities and Critical Mass." *Telecommunications Policy* 12 (3): 257–271. https://doi.org/10.1016/0308-5961(88)90024-9.

Alvarez, Sharon A., and Jay B. Barney. 2005. "How Do Entrepreneurs Organize Firms Under Conditions of Uncertainty?" *Journal of Management* 31 (5): 776–793. https://doi.org/10.1177/0149206305279486.

Alvarez, Sharon A., Jay B. Barney, and Philip Anderson. 2012. "Forming and Exploiting Opportunities: The Implications of Discovery and Creation Processes for Entrepreneurial and Organizational Research." *Organization Science* 24 (1): 301–317. https://doi.org/10.1287/orsc.1110.0727.

Alvedalen, Janna, and Ron Boschma. 2017. "A Critical Review of Entrepreneurial Ecosystems Research: Towards a Future Research Agenda." *European Planning Studies* 25 (6): 887–903. https://doi.org/10.1080/09654313.2017.1299694.

Alvesson, Mats, and Dan Kärreman. 2000. "Varieties of Discourse: On the Study of Organizations through Discourse Analysis." *Human Relations* 53 (9): 1125–1149. https://doi.org/10.1177/0018726700539002.

Amit, Raphael, and Xu Han. 2017. "Value Creation through Novel Resource Configurations in a Digitally Enabled World." *Strategic Entrepreneurship Journal* 11 (3): 228–242. https://doi.org/10.1002/sej.1256.

Amit, Raphael, and Christoph Zott. 2001. "Value Creation in E-Business." *Strategic Management Journal* 22 (6–7): 493–520. https://doi.org/10.1002/smj.187.

Amit, Raphael, and Christoph Zott. 2015. "Crafting Business Architecture: The Antecedents of Business Model Design." *Strategic Entrepreneurship Journal* 9 (4): 331–350. https://doi.org/10.1002/sej.1200.

Arakji, Reina Y., and Karl R. Lang. 2007. "Digital Consumer Networks and Producer-Consumer Collaboration: Innovation and Product Development in the Video Game Industry." *Journal of Management Information Systems* 24 (2): 195–219. https://doi.org/10.2753/MIS0742-1222240208.

Aral, Sinan, Chrysanthos Dellarocas, and David Godes. 2013. "Introduction to the Special Issue—Social Media and Business Transformation: A Framework for Research." *Information Systems Research* 24 (1): 3–13. https://doi.org/10.1287/isre.1120.0470.

Arora, Ashish, V. S. Arunachalam, Jai Asundi, and Ronald Fernandes. 2001. "The Indian Software Services Industry." *Research Policy* 30 (8): 1267–1287. https://doi.org/10.1016/S0048-7333(00)00148-7.

Arora, S., and H. A. Romijn. 2009. "Innovation for the Base of the Pyramid: Critical Perspectives from Development Studies on Heterogeneity and Participation." Working Paper Series 2009-036. Maastricht, the Netherlands: UNU-MERIT.

Ascione, Gennaro. 2016. "Decolonizing the 'Global': The Coloniality of Method and the Problem of the Unit of Analysis." *Cultural Sociology* 10 (3): 317–334. https://doi.org/10.1177/1749975516644843.

Asemota, Victor. 2018. "Are African Technology Innovation Spaces Creating Growth?" *Guardian* (Nigeria), March 7, 2018. https://guardian.ng/technology/are-african-technology-innovation-spaces-creating-growth/.

Athreye, Suma S. 2005. "The Indian Software Industry and Its Evolving Service Capability." *Industrial and Corporate Change* 14 (3): 393–418. https://doi.org/10.1093/icc/dth056.

Audretsch, David B., Donald F. Kuratko, and Albert N. Link. 2016. "Dynamic Entrepreneurship and Technology-Based Innovation." *Journal of Evolutionary Economics* 26 (3): 603–620. https://doi.org/10.1007/s00191-016-0458-4.

Auerswald, Philip E. 2012. *The Coming Prosperity: How Entrepreneurs Are Transforming the Global Economy*. New York: Oxford University Press.

Auschra, Carolin, Timo Braun, Thomas Schmidt, and Jörg Sydow. 2017. "Patterns of Project-Based Organizing in New Venture Creation: Projectification of an Entrepreneurial Ecosystem." *International Journal of Managing Projects in Business* 12 (1): 48–70. https://doi.org/10.1108/IJMPB-01-2018-0007.

Autio, Erkko, Martin Kenney, Philippe Mustar, Don Siegel, and Mike Wright. 2014. "Entrepreneurial Innovation: The Importance of Context." *Research Policy* 43 (7): 1097–1108. https://doi.org/10.1016/j.respol.2014.01.015.

Autio, Erkko, Satish Nambisan, Llewellyn D. W. Thomas, and Mike Wright. 2018. "Digital Affordances, Spatial Affordances, and the Genesis of Entrepreneurial Ecosystems." *Strategic Entrepreneurship Journal* 12 (1): 72–95. https://doi.org/10.1002/sej.1266.

Avgerou, Chrisanthi. 2003. "The Link between ICT and Economic Growth in the Discourse of Development." In *Organizational Information Systems in the Context of Globalization*, edited by Mikko Korpela, Ramiro Montealegre, and Angeliki Poulymenakou, 373–386. New York: Springer Science+Business Media. https://doi.org/10.1007/978-0-387-35695-2_23.

Avle, Seyram. 2014. "Articulating and Enacting Development: Skilled Returnees in Ghana's ICT Industry." *Information Technologies & International Development* 10 (4): 1–13.

Avle, Seyram, and Silvia Lindtner. 2016. "Design(ing) 'Here' and 'There': Tech Entrepreneurs, Global Markets, and Reflexivity in Design Processes." In *Proceedings of the 2016 CHI Conference on Human Factors in Computing Systems*, 2233–2245. New York: ACM. https://doi.org/10.1145/2858036.2858509.

Avle, Seyram, Silvia Lindtner, and Kaiton Williams. 2017. "How Methods Make Designers." In *Proceedings of the 2017 CHI Conference on Human Factors in Computing Systems*, 472–483. New York: ACM. https://doi.org/10.1145/3025453.3025864.

Baldwin, Carliss, and Eric von Hippel. 2011. "Modeling a Paradigm Shift: From Producer Innovation to User and Open Collaborative Innovation." *Organization Science* 22 (6): 1399–1417. https://doi.org/10.1287/orsc.1100.0618.

Banks, Ken. 2019. "Jumia—What constitutes 'African'?" Twitter, March 14, 2019, 6:19 a.m. https://twitter.com/kiwanja/status/1106182969369214978.

Barley, Stephen R., and Gideon Kunda. 2004. *Gurus, Hired Guns, and Warm Bodies: Itinerant Experts in a Knowledge Economy*. Princeton, NJ: Princeton University Press.

Barnard, Helena, Alvaro Cuervo-Cazurra, and Stephan Manning. 2017. "Africa Business Research as a Laboratory for Theory-Building: Extreme Conditions, New Phenomena, and Alternative Paradigms of Social Relationships." *Management and Organization Review* 13 (3): 467–495. https://doi.org/10.1017/mor.2017.34.

Baro, Ebikabowei Emmanuel, and Benake-ebide Christy Endouware. 2013. "The Effects of Mobile Phone on the Socio-economic Life of the Rural Dwellers in the Niger Delta Region of Nigeria." *Information Technology for Development* 19 (3): 249–263. https://doi.org/10.1080/02681102.2012.755895.

Bathelt, Harald, and Patrick Cohendet. 2014. "The Creation of Knowledge: Local Building, Global Accessing and Economic Development—toward an Agenda." *Journal of Economic Geography* 14 (5): 869–882. https://doi.org/10.1093/jeg/lbu027.

Baumann, Oliver, Carsten Bergenholtz, Lars Frederiksen, Robert M. Grant, Rebecca Köhler, David L. Preston, and Scott Shane. 2018. "Rocket Internet: Organizing a Startup Factory." *Journal of Organization Design* 7 (1): 13. https://doi.org/10.1186/s41469-018-0037-2.

Bayen, Maxime, and Dario Giuliani. 2018. "1000 Tech Hubs Are Powering Ecosystems in Asia Pacific and Africa." *GSMA Mobile for Development* (blog). March 20, 2018. https://www.gsma.com/mobilefordevelopment/programme/ecosystem-accelerator/1000-tech-hubs-are-powering-ecosystems-in-asia-pacific-and-africa.

BBC News. 2019. "Jumia to Be First African Start-Up on NYSE." *BBC News*, March 13, 2019, sec. Technology. https://www.bbc.com/news/technology-47553656.

Benkler, Yochai. 2006. *The Wealth of Networks: How Social Production Transforms Markets and Freedom*. New Haven, CT: Yale University Press.

Benner, Chris. 2008. *Work in the New Economy: Flexible Labor Markets in Silicon Valley*. New York: John Wiley & Sons.

Birtchnell, Thomas. 2011. "Jugaad as Systemic Risk and Disruptive Innovation in India." *Contemporary South Asia* 19 (4): 357–372. https://doi.org/10.1080/09584935.2011.569702.

Blimpo, Moussa P., and Malcolm Cosgrove-Davies. *Electricity Access in Sub-Saharan Africa: Uptake, Reliability, and Complementary Factors for Economic Impact*. Paris and Washington, DC: Agence française de développement (AFD) and the World Bank.

Blimpo, Moussa Pouguinimpo, Michael Minges, Wilfried A. Kouamé, Theophile Thomas Azomahou, Emmanuel Kwasi Koranteng Lartey, Christelle Meniago, Mapi M. Buitano, and Albert G. Zeufack. 2017. "Leapfrogging: The Key to Africa's Development—from Constraints to Investment Opportunities." Working Paper 119849, World Bank, Washington, DC. http://documents.worldbank.org/curated/en/121581505973379739/Leapfrogging-the-key-to-Africas-development-from-constraints-to-investment-opportunities.

Block, Joern H., Christian O. Fisch, and Mirjam van Praag. 2017. "The Schumpeterian Entrepreneur: A Review of the Empirical Evidence on the Antecedents, Behaviour and Consequences of Innovative Entrepreneurship." *Industry and Innovation* 24 (1): 61–95. https://doi.org/10.1080/13662716.2016.1216397.

Bøllingtoft, Anne. 2012. "The Bottom-up Business Incubator: Leverage to Networking and Cooperation Practices in a Self-Generated, Entrepreneurial-Enabled Environment." *Technovation* 32 (5): 304–315. https://doi.org/10.1016/j.technovation.2011.11.005.

Bøllingtoft, Anne, and John P. Ulhøi. 2005. "The Networked Business Incubator—Leveraging Entrepreneurial Agency?" *Journal of Business Venturing* 20 (2): 265–290. https://doi.org/10.1016/j.jbusvent.2003.12.005.

BongoHive. 2013. *Hubs in Africa.* https://africahubs.crowdmap.com/reports/view/99.

BongoHive. 2017. "Public List of African Innovation Spaces." https://docs.google .com/spreadsheets/u/1/d/1DvXVB2ikFzUxi78lznojlZyDcR_Gn43i7m-Y3mkTrCQ/ edit?usp=embed_facebook.

Boucher, Victor du. 2016. "A Few Things We Learned about Tech Hubs in Africa and Asia." *GSMA Mobile for Development* (blog), August 5, 2016. http://www .gsma.com/mobilefordevelopment/programme/ecosystem-accelerator/ things-learned-tech-hubs-africa-asia.

Boudreau, Kevin. 2010. "Open Platform Strategies and Innovation: Granting Access vs. Devolving Control." *Management Science* 56 (10): 1849–1872. https:// doi.org/10.1287/mnsc.1100.1215.

Bourdieu, Pierre, and Loic Wacquant. 1999. "On the Cunning of Imperialist Reason." *Theory, Culture & Society* 16 (1): 41–58. https://doi.org/10.1177/026327699016001003.

Boxenbaum, Eva, and Michael Lounsbury. 2013. *Institutional Logics in Action.* Bingley, UK: Emerald Publishing Limited. http://ebookcentral.proquest.com/lib/ed/ detail.action?docID=1325125.

Braesemann, Fabian, Niklas Stoehr, and Mark Graham. 2019. "Global Networks in Collaborative Programming." *Regional Studies, Regional Science* 6 (1): 371–373. https://doi.org/10.1080/21681376.2019.1588155.

Bramann, Johannes Ulrich. 2017. "Building ICT Entrepreneurship Ecosystems in Resource-Scarce Contexts: Learnings from Kenya's 'Silicon Savannah.'" In *Digital Kenya*, 227–64. London: Palgrave Macmillan. https://doi.org/10.1057/978-1-13 7-57878-5_8.

Bratton, Benjamin H. 2015. *The Stack: On Software and Sovereignty.* Cambridge, MA: MIT Press.

Bresnahan, Timothy, Alfonso Gambardella, and Annalee Saxenian. 2001. "'Old Economy' Inputs for 'New Economy' Outcomes: Cluster Formation in the New Silicon Valleys." *Industrial and Corporate Change* 10 (4): 835–860. https:// doi.org/10.1093/icc/10.4.835.

Briel, Frederik von, Per Davidsson, and Jan Recker. 2018. "Digital Technologies as External Enablers of New Venture Creation in the IT Hardware Sector." *Entrepreneurship Theory and Practice* 42 (1): 47–69. https://doi.org/10.1177/1042258717732779.

Bright, Jake. 2019. "African E-Commerce Startup Jumia's Shares Open at $14.50 in NYSE IPO." *TechCrunch* (blog), April 12, 2019. http://social.techcrunch.com/ 2019/04/12/african-e-commerce-startup-jumias-shares-open-at-14-50-in-nyse-ipo/.

Bright, Jake, and Aubrey Hruby. 2015a. *The Next Africa: An Emerging Continent Becomes a Global Powerhouse.* New York: Thomas Dunne Books.

Bright, Jake, and Aubrey Hruby. 2015b. "The Rise of Silicon Savannah and Africa's Tech Movement." *TechCrunch* (blog), July 23, 2015. http://social.techcrunch. com/2015/07/23/the-rise-of-silicon-savannah-and-africas-tech-movement/.

Brinks, Verena, and Oliver Ibert. 2015. "Mushrooming Entrepreneurship: The Dynamic Geography of Enthusiast-Driven Innovation." *Geoforum* 65 (October): 363–373. https://doi.org/10.1016/j.geoforum.2015.01.007.

Brusoni, Stefano, Andrea Prencipe, and Keith Pavitt. 2001. "Knowledge Specialization, Organizational Coupling, and the Boundaries of the Firm: Why Do Firms Know More than They Make?" *Administrative Science Quarterly* 46 (4): 597–621. https://doi.org/10.2307/3094825.

Bryman, Alan. 2008. *Social Research Methods*. Oxford: Oxford University Press.

Brynjolfsson, Erik, Lorin Hitt, and Heekyung Kim. 2011. "Strength in Numbers: How Does Data-Driven Decision-Making Affect Firm Performance?" *ICIS 2011 Proceedings*. 13. https://aisel.aisnet.org/icis2011/proceedings/economicvalueIS/13.

Brynjolfsson, Erik, Yu (Jeffrey) Hu, and Duncan Simester. 2011. "Goodbye Pareto Principle, Hello Long Tail: The Effect of Search Costs on the Concentration of Product Sales." *Management Science* 57 (8): 1373–1386. https://doi.org/10.1287/mnsc.1110.1371.

Brynjolfsson, Erik, and Andrew McAfee. 2011. *Race against the Machine: How the Digital Revolution Is Accelerating Innovation, Driving Productivity, and Irreversibly Transforming Employment and the Economy*. Lexington, MA: Digital Frontier Press.

Burrell, Jenna, and Elisa Oreglia. 2015. "The Myth of Market Price Information: Mobile Phones and the Application of Economic Knowledge in ICTD." *Economy and Society* 44 (2): 271–92. https://doi.org/10.1080/03085147.2015.1013742.

Campbell-Kelly, Martin, William Aspray, Nathan Ensmenger, and Jeffrey R. Yost. 2013. *Computer: A History of the Information Machine*. 3rd ed. Boulder, CO: Westview Press.

Caribou Digital. 2016. *Winners and Losers in the Global App Economy*. Farnham, Surrey, UK: Caribou Digital Publishing. http://cariboudigital.net/winners -and-losers-in-the-global-app-economy/.

Carmody, Pádraig. 2013. "A Knowledge Economy or an Information Society in Africa? Thintegration and the Mobile Phone Revolution." *Information Technology for Development* 19 (1): 24–39. https://doi.org/10.1080/02681102.2012.719859.

Carver, Terrell. 2010. "Materializing the Metaphors of Global Cities: Singapore and Silicon Valley." *Globalizations* 7 (3): 383–393. https://doi.org/10.1080/14747731003669768.

Chair, Chenai. 2018. "After Access Highlights: Using Evidence from the Global South to Reshape Our Digital Future." *Research ICT Africa* (blog), January 15, 2018. https://researchictafrica.net/2018/01/15/after-access-highlights-using-evidence-from-the-global-south-to-reshape-our-digital-future/.

Chang, Ha-Joon. 2015. "Poverty, Entrepreneurship, and Development." *UNU-WIDER* (blog), August 18, 2015. https://www.wider.unu.edu/publication/poverty-entrepreneurship-and-development.

Chavula, Hopestone Kayiska. 2013. "Telecommunications Development and Economic Growth in Africa." *Information Technology for Development* 19 (1): 5–23. https://doi.org/10.1080/02681102.2012.694794.

Cheeseman, Nic, and Diane de Gramont. 2017. "Managing a Mega-City: Learning the Lessons from Lagos." *Oxford Review of Economic Policy* 33 (3): 457–477. https://doi.org/10.1093/oxrep/grx033.

Chen, Ava, Nick Feamster, and Enrico Calandro. 2017. "Exploring the Walled Garden Theory: An Empirical Framework to Assess Pricing Effects on Mobile Data Usage." In "ICT Developments in Africa—Infrastructures, Applications and Policies," edited by Ezer Osei Yeboah-Boateng, Alexander Osei-Owusu, and Anders Henten. Special issue, *Telecommunications Policy* 41 (7): 587–599. https://doi.org/10.1016/j.telpol.2017.07.002.

Chen, Shin-Horng. 2004. "Taiwanese IT Firms' Offshore R&D in China and the Connection with the Global Innovation Network." *Research Policy* 33 (2): 337–349. https://doi.org/10.1016/j.respol.2003.09.003.

Chen, Yu, Herbert Werle, and Roger Moser. 2018. "Critical Success Factors in Chinese Cross-Border Mergers and Acquisitions: A Study of Two Chinese Cases in Germany." *Nankai Business Review International* 9 (4): 457–471. https://doi.org/10.1108/NBRI-03-2017-0012.

Chigona, Agnes, and Wallace Chigona. 2008. "MXit It up in the Media: Media Discourse Analysis on a Mobile Instant Messaging System." *African Journal of Information and Communication* 2008 (9): 42–57.

CNN. 2015. "Obama Visits Kenya and Ethiopia." CNN, July 28, 2015. https://www.cnn.com/2015/07/25/world/gallery/obama-kenya-ethiopia/index.html.

Collon, Cyril. 2017. "VC Funding Raised by African Tech Startups Totals Record Breaking US$ 366.8 Million in 2016." *LinkedIn* (blog), February 28, 2017. https://www.linkedin.com/pulse/vc-funding-raised-african-tech-startups-totals-record-cyril-collon/?lipi=urn%3Ali%3Apage%3Ad_flagship3_pulse_read%3BgHRr%2FlRUSYGhfX2%2BrACaAQ%3D%3D&licu=urn%3Ali%3Acontrol%3Ad_flagship3_pulse_read-related.

Collon, Cyril. 2018. "In Another Record-Breaking Year, African Tech Start-Ups Raised US$ 560 Million in VC Funding in 2017, a 53% YoY Growth." *LinkedIn* (blog), February 20, 2018. https://www.linkedin.com/pulse/another-record-breaking-year -african-tech-start-ups-raised-collon/?trackingId=6ncsYxVeIpYLqWvU8n6CNg% 3D%3D.

Colombo, Massimo G., and Marco Delmastro. 2001. "Technology-Based Entrepreneurs: Does Internet Make a Difference?" *Small Business Economics* 16 (3): 177–190. https://doi.org/10.1023/A:1011127205758.

Danquah, Michael, and Joseph Amankwah-Amoah. 2017. "Assessing the Relationships between Human Capital, Innovation and Technology Adoption: Evidence from Sub-Saharan Africa." *Technological Forecasting and Social Change* 122 (September): 24–33. https://doi.org/10.1016/j.techfore.2017.04.021.

Daspit, Joshua J., and Rebecca G. Long. 2014. "Mitigating Moral Hazard in Entrepreneurial Networks: Examining Structural and Relational Social Capital in East Africa." *Entrepreneurship Theory and Practice* 38 (6): 1343–1350. https://doi.org/10.1111/ etap.12128.

Davidson, Elizabeth, and Emmanuelle Vaast. 2010. "Digital Entrepreneurship and Its Sociomaterial Enactment." In *Proceedings of the 2010 43rd Hawaii International Conference on System Sciences*, 1–10. Washington, DC: IEEE Computer Society. https://doi.org/10.1109/HICSS.2010.150.

Davidsson, Per. 2005. *Researching Entrepreneurship*. New York: Springer.

David-West, Olayinka, and Peter Evans. 2015. *The Rise of African Platforms: A Regional Survey*. New York: Centre for Global Enterprise (CGE). https://doi.org/10.13140/ RG.2.2.23965.72165.

Decker, Ryan, John Haltiwanger, Ron Jarmin, and Javier Miranda. 2016. "The Decline of High-Growth Entrepreneurship." *VoxEU.Org* (blog), March 19, 2016. https://voxeu.org/article/decline-high-growth-entrepreneurship.

Deichmann, Uwe, and Deepak Mishra. 2016. "World Development Report 2016: Digital Dividends." Washington, DC: World Bank. http://www.worldbank.org/en/ publication/wdr2016.

Delacroix, Eva, Béatrice Parguel, and Florence Benoit-Moreau. 2018. "Digital Subsistence Entrepreneurs on Facebook." *Technological Forecasting & Social Change* 146 (September): 887–899. https://doi.org/10.1016/j.techfore.2018.06.018.

Deloitte and GSMA. 2012. *Sub-Saharan Africa Mobile Observatory 2012*. http:// www.gsma.com/publicpolicy/wp-content/uploads/2012/03/SSA_FullReport_v6.1_ clean.pdf.

Disrupt Africa. 2016. *Disrupt Africa African Tech Startups Funding Report 2015*. https://gumroad.com/l/egbOX.

Disrupt Africa. 2017a. *Afri-Shopping 2017*. http://disrupt-africa.com/afri-shopping-2017/.

Disrupt Africa. 2017b. *Disrupt Africa African Tech Startups Funding Report 2016*. https://gumroad.com/l/AHAPM.

Disrupt Africa. 2018. *Funding Report 2017*. http://disrupt-africa.com/funding-report/.

Dolan, Catherine, and Dinah Rajak. 2016. "Remaking Africa's Informal Economies: Youth, Entrepreneurship and the Promise of Inclusion at the Bottom of the Pyramid." *Journal of Development Studies* 52 (4): 514–529. https://doi.org/10.1080/00220388.2015.1126249.

Donner, Jonathan. 2015. *After Access: Inclusion, Development, and a More Mobile Internet*. Cambridge, MA: MIT Press.

Draper, Robert. 2017. "How Africa's Tech Generation Is Changing the Continent." *National Geographic*, November 14, 2017. https://www.nationalgeographic.com/magazine/2017/12/africa-technology-revolution/.

Drouillard, Marissa. 2017. "Addressing Voids: How Digital Start-Ups in Kenya Create Market Infrastructure." In *Digital Kenya*, 97–131. London: Palgrave Macmillan. https://doi.org/10.1057/978-1-137-57878-5_4.

Drouillard, Marissa, David Taverner, Chris Williamson, and Martin Harris. 2014. *Digital Entrepreneurship in Kenya 2014*. London: GSMA.

Dy, Angela Martinez. 2017. "At the Interfaces of Digital Entrepreneurship: Beyond Discourse, towards a Realist Conceptualisation." *Academy of Management Proceedings* 2017 (1). https://doi.org/10.5465/ambpp.2017.11848abstract.

Dy, Angela Martinez, Susan Marlow, and Lee Martin. 2017. "A Web of Opportunity or the Same Old Story? Women Digital Entrepreneurs and Intersectionality Theory." *Human Relations* 70 (3): 286–311. https://doi.org/10.1177/0018726716650730.

Dy, Angela Martinez, Lee Martin, and Susan Marlow. 2018. "Emancipation through Digital Entrepreneurship? A Critical Realist Analysis." *Organization* 25 (5): 585–608. https://doi.org/10.1177/1350508418777891.

Easterly, William. 2001. "The Lost Decades: Developing Countries' Stagnation in Spite of Policy Reform 1980–1998." *Journal of Economic Growth* 6 (2): 135–157. https://doi.org/10.1023/A:1011378507540.

Eglash, Ron, and Ellen K. Foster. 2017. "On the Politics of Generative Justice: African Traditions and Maker Communities." In *What Do Science, Technology, and Innovation*

Mean from Africa?, edited by Clapperton Chakanetsa Mavhunga, 117–135. Cambridge, MA: MIT Press.

Eisenmann, Thomas. R., Geoffrey Parker, and Marshall W. Van Alstyne. 2006. "Strategies for Two-Sided Markets." *Harvard Business Review* 84 (10). https://hbr.org/2006/10/strategies-for-two-sided-market.

Ekekwe, Ndubuisi. 2015. "The Challenges Facing E-commerce Start-Ups in Africa." *Harvard Business Review* (blog), March 12, 2015. https://hbr.org/2015/03/the-challenges-facing-e-commerce-start-ups-in-africa.

Enders, Albrecht, Harald Hungenberg, Hans-Peter Denker, and Sebastian Mauch. 2008. "The Long Tail of Social Networking: Revenue Models of Social Networking Sites." *European Management Journal* 26 (3): 199–211. https://doi.org/10.1016/j.emj.2008.02.002.

Engel, Jerome S. 2015. "Global Clusters of Innovation: Lessons from Silicon Valley." *California Management Review* 57 (2): 36–65. https://doi.org/10.1525/cmr.2015.57.2.36.

"Entrepreneurial Ecosystem Snapshots." 2019. Aspen Network of Development Entrepreneurs. November 19, 2019. https://ecosystems.andeglobal.org/snapshots/.

Escobar, Arturo. 2011. *Encountering Development: The Making and Unmaking of the Third World*. Princeton, NJ: Princeton University Press.

Essien, Mark. 2015. "Startup Incubators in Africa and Why They Don't Work." *Venture Capital for Africa* (blog), April 21, 2015. https://vc4africa.biz/blog/2015/04/21/startup-incubators-in-africa-and-why-they-dont-work/.

Etzo, Sebastiana, and Guy Collender. 2010. "The Mobile Phone 'Revolution' in Africa: Rhetoric or Reality?" *African Affairs* 109 (437): 659–668. https://doi.org/10.1093/afraf/adq045.

Evans, Peter, and Annabelle Gawer. 2016. *The Rise of the Platform Enterprise: A Global Survey*. New York: Centre for Global Enterprise (CGE). https://www.thecge.net/app/uploads/2016/01/PDF-WEB-Platform-Survey_01_12.pdf.

Fan, Peilei. 2006. "Catching up through Developing Innovation Capability: Evidence from China's Telecom-Equipment Industry." *Technovation* 26 (3): 359–368. https://doi.org/10.1016/j.technovation.2004.10.004.

Farny, Steffen, Signe Hedeboe Frederiksen, Martin Hannibal, and Sally Jones. 2016. "A CULTure of Entrepreneurship Education." *Entrepreneurship & Regional Development* 28 (7–8): 514–535. https://doi.org/10.1080/08985626.2016.1221228.

Feld, Brad. 2012. *Startup Communities: Building an Entrepreneurial Ecosystem in Your City*. Hoboken, NJ: John Wiley & Sons.

Ferguson, James. 1990. *The Anti-Politics Machine: "Development," Depoliticization and Bureaucratic Power in Lesotho.* Cambridge: Cambridge University Press.

Ferrary, Michel, and Mark Granovetter. 2009. "The Role of Venture Capital Firms in Silicon Valley's Complex Innovation Network." *Economy and Society* 38 (2): 326–359. https://doi.org/10.1080/03085140902786827.

Firestone, Rachel, and Tim Kelly. 2016. "The Importance of Mapping Tech Hubs in Africa, and Beyond." *Information and Communications for Development* (blog), August 24, 2016. http://blogs.worldbank.org/ic4d/importance-mapping-tech-hubs-africa-and-beyond.

Foster, G. 2000. "The Capacity of the Extended Family Safety Net for Orphans in Africa." *Psychology, Health & Medicine* 5 (1): 55–62. https://doi.org/10.1080/135485000106007.

Friederici, Nicolas. 2013. "The Evolution of Startup Competitions: The Case of Pivot East." *Private Sector Development Blog*, August 26, 2013. http://blogs.worldbank.org/psd/evolution-startup-competitions-case-pivot-east.

Friederici, Nicolas. 2017a. "Innovation Hubs in Africa: Assemblers of Technology Entrepreneurs." Dissertation, Oxford Internet Institute, University of Oxford. https://ora.ox.ac.uk/objects/uuid:2e5c9248-15b4-450a-958a-0ce87cf6e263.

Friederici, Nicolas. 2017b. "Africa's Digital Revolution: A Researcher's Perspective." *Afridigest* (blog), July 25, 2017. http://afridigest.com/africas-digital-revolution-researchers-perspective/.

Friederici, Nicolas. 2018. "Grounding the Dream of African Innovation Hubs: Two Cases in Kigali." *Journal of Developmental Entrepreneurship* 23 (2): 1850012. https://doi.org/10.1142/S1084946718500127.

Friederici, Nicolas. 2019. "Hope and Hype in Africa's Digital Economy: The Rise of Innovation Hubs." In *Digital Economies at Global Margins*, edited by Mark Graham, 193–222. Cambridge, MA/Ottawa: MIT Press/International Development Research Centre.

Friederici, Nicolas, and Mark Graham. 2018. *The Bounded Opportunities of Digital Enterprises in Global Economic Peripheries.* SSRN Scholarly Paper ID 3249499. Rochester, NY: Social Science Research Network. https://papers.ssrn.com/abstract=3249499.

Friederici, Nicolas, Sanna Ojanperä, and Mark Graham. 2017. "The Impact of Connectivity in Africa: Grand Visions and the Mirage of Inclusive Digital Development." *Electronic Journal of Information Systems in Developing Countries* 79 (2): 1–20.

Gagliardone, Iginio. 2016. *The Politics of Technology in Africa: Communication, Development, and Nation-Building in Ethiopia.* Cambridge: Cambridge University Press.

Gao, Lucia Silva, and Bala Iyer. 2006. "Analyzing Complementarities Using Software Stacks for Software Industry Acquisitions." *Journal of Management Information Systems* 23 (2): 119–147. https://doi.org/10.2753/MIS0742-1222230206.

Garrett, Lyndon E., Gretchen M. Spreitzer, and Peter A. Bacevice. 2017. "Co-constructing a Sense of Community at Work: The Emergence of Community in Coworking Spaces." *Organization Studies* 38 (6): 821–842. https://doi.org/10.1177/0170840616685354.

Garud, Raghu, Henri Schildt, and Theresa K. Lant. 2014. *Entrepreneurial Storytelling, Future Expectations, and the Paradox of Legitimacy.* SSRN Scholarly Paper ID 2471304. Rochester, NY: Social Science Research Network. https://papers.ssrn.com/abstract=2471304.

Gawer, Annabelle. 2011. *Platforms, Markets and Innovation.* Cheltenham, UK: Edward Elgar.

Gawer, Annabelle. 2014. "Bridging Differing Perspectives on Technological Platforms: Toward an Integrative Framework." *Research Policy* 43 (7): 1239–1249. https://doi.org/10.1016/j.respol.2014.03.006.

Gawer, Annabelle, and Michael A. Cusumano. 2014. "Industry Platforms and Ecosystem Innovation." *Journal of Product Innovation Management* 31 (3): 417–433. https://doi.org/10.1111/jpim.12105.

George, Gerard, Christopher Corbishley, Jane N. O. Khayesi, Martine R. Haas, and Laszlo Tihanyi. 2016. "Bringing Africa In: Promising Directions for Management Research." *Academy of Management Journal* 59 (2): 377–393. https://doi.org/10.5465/amj.2016.4002.

Giachetti, Claudio, and Gianluca Marchi. 2017. "Successive Changes in Leadership in the Worldwide Mobile Phone Industry: The Role of Windows of Opportunity and Firms' Competitive Action." *Research Policy* 46 (2): 352–364. https://doi.org/10.1016/j.respol.2016.09.003.

Gichuru, Sam. 2014. "Before Anybody Convinces You That NGOs Are Messing Up the Tech Ecosystem." *Sam Gichuru* (blog), June 2014. http://www.samgichuru.com/before-anybody-convinces-you-that-ngos-are-messing-up-the-tech-ecosystem/.

Gikandi, Simon. 2001. "Globalization and the Claims of Postcoloniality." *South Atlantic Quarterly* 100 (3): 627–658.

Giles, Chris. 2018. "African Smart Cities: A Leap into the Future?" *CNN* (blog), January 16, 2018. https://www.cnn.com/2017/12/12/africa/africa-new-smart-cities/index.html.

Gillwald, Alison. 2017. *Beyond Access: Addressing Digital Inequality in Africa.* Centre for International Governance Innovation, GCIG Paper No. 48, March 10, 2017. https://www.cigionline.org/publications/beyond-access-addressing-digital-inequality-africa.

Gillwald, Alison. 2019. "South Africa Is Caught in the Global Hype of the Fourth Industrial Revolution." *The Conversation* (blog), August 20, 2019. http://theconversation.com/south-africa-is-caught-in-the-global-hype-of-the-fourth-industrial-revolution-121189.

Goldberg, Pinelopi. 2019. "Moonshot Africa and Jobs." *World Bank Blogs, Let's Talk Development*, March 28, 2019. https://blogs.worldbank.org/developmenttalk/moonshot-africa-and-jobs.

Government of Kenya. 2018. "Technology Will Be Major Driver for Big Four Plan, President Kenyatta Says." Official Website of the President, February 27, 2018. http://www.president.go.ke/2018/02/27/technology-will-be-major-driver-for-big-four-plan-president-kenyatta-says/.

Graham, Mark. 2015. "Contradictory Connectivity: Spatial Imaginaries and Techno-mediated Positionalities in Kenya's Outsourcing Sector." *Environment and Planning A* 47 (4): 867–883. https://doi.org/10.1068/a140275p.

Graham, Mark, ed. 2019. *Digital Economies at Global Margins*. Cambridge, MA: MIT Press.

Graham, Mark, Casper Andersen, and Laura Mann. 2015. "Geographies of Connectivity in East Africa: Trains, Telecommunications, and Technological Teleologies." *Transactions of the Institute of British Geographers* 40 (3): 334–349.

Graham, Mark, and Laura Mann. 2013. "Imagining a Silicon Savannah? Technological and Conceptual Connectivity in Kenya's BPO and Software Development Sectors." *Electronic Journal of Information Systems in Developing Countries* 56 (April).

Greengard, Samuel. 2010. "Cloud Computing and Developing Nations." *Communications of the ACM* 53 (5): 18–20. https://doi.org/10.1145/1735223.1735232.

Gregory, Neil F., Stanley D. Nollen, and Stoyan Tenev. 2009. *New Industries from New Places: The Emergence of the Software and Hardware Industries in China and India*. Stanford, CA/Washington, DC: Stanford Economics and Finance, Stanford University Press/World Bank. https://elibrary.worldbank.org/doi/abs/10.1596/978-0-8213-6478-9.

Grimm, Michael, Flore Gubert, Ousman Koriko, Jann Lay, and Christophe J. Nordman. 2013. "Kinship Ties and Entrepreneurship in Western Africa." *Journal of Small Business & Entrepreneurship* 26 (2): 125–150. https://doi.org/10.1080/08276331.2013.771854.

Grin, Steven, and Rob Eloff. 2018. "5 Ways the Silicon Savannah Differs from Silicon Valley." Pulse NG, February 9, 2018. https://www.pulse.ng/bi/tech/5-ways-the-silicon-savannah-differs-from-silicon-valley-id7954528.html.

Grugulis, Irena, and Dimitrinka Stoyanova. 2011. "The Missing Middle: Communities of Practice in a Freelance Labour Market." *Work, Employment & Society* 25 (2): 342–351. https://doi.org/10.1177/0950017011398891.

GSMA. 2017. *The Mobile Economy: Sub-Saharan Africa 2017*. London: GSMA. https://www.gsma.com/mobileeconomy/sub-saharan-africa-2017/.

Guston, David H. 2001. "Boundary Organizations in Environmental Policy and Science: An Introduction." *Science, Technology, & Human Values* 26 (4): 399–408.

Hackett, Sean M., and David M. Dilts. 2004. "A Systematic Review of Business Incubation Research." *Journal of Technology Transfer* 29 (1): 55–82. https://doi.org/10.1023/B:JOTT.0000011181.11952.0f.

Hansen, Morten T., Henry William Chesbrough, Nitin Nohria, and Donald N. Sull. 2000. "Networked Incubators: Hothouses of the New Economy." *Harvard Business Review* 78 (5): 74–84, 199.

Hargittai, Eszter. 2002. "Second-Level Digital Divide: Differences in People's Online Skills." *First Monday* 7 (4). http://www.eszter.com/research/pubs/hargittai-secondleveldd.pdf.

Hart, David M. 2003. *The Emergence of Entrepreneurship Policy: Governance, Start-Ups, and Growth in the U.S. Knowledge Economy*. Cambridge: Cambridge University Press.

Harvey, David. 1989. *The Condition of Postmodernity: An Enquiry into the Origins of Cultural Change*. Oxford: Basil Blackwell.

Healy, Kieran. 2015. "The Performativity of Networks." 56 (2): 175–205. https://doi.org/10.1017/S0003975615000107.

Hecht, Gabrielle. 2011. *Entangled Geographies Empire and Technopolitics in the Global Cold War*. Cambridge, MA: MIT Press.

Heeks, Richard. 2006. "Using Competitive Advantage Theory to Analyze IT Sectors in Developing Countries: A Software Industry Case Analysis." *Information Technologies & International Development* 3 (3): 5–34.

Henfridsson, Ola, and Bendik Bygstad. 2013. "The Generative Mechanisms of Digital Infrastructure Evolution." *Management Information Systems Quarterly* 37 (3): 896–931.

Henningsson, Stefan, Philip W. Yetton, and Peter J. Wynne. 2018. "A Review of Information System Integration in Mergers and Acquisitions." *Journal of Information Technology* 33 (4): 255–303. https://doi.org/10.1057/s41265-017-0051-9.

Henry, Zoe. 2015. "Nairobi Used to Be a Terrible Place to Do Business. How Did It Transform into a Tech Hub?" *Slate*, August 18, 2015. https://www.slate.com/blogs/moneybox/2015/08/18/nairobi_as_silicon_savannah_how_the_kenyan_capitol_grew_into_a_hub_for_digital.html.

Hersman, Erik. 2011. "Afrilabs Provide a Model for African Innovation, Collaboration." *Memeburn* (blog), February 8, 2011. http://memeburn.com/2011/02/afrilabs-provide-a-model-for-african-innovation-collaboration/.

Hersman, Erik. 2012. "Mobilizing Tech Entrepreneurs in Africa (Innovations Case Narrative: iHub)." *Innovations: Technology, Governance, Globalization* 7 (4): 59–67. https://doi.org/10.1162/INOV_a_00152.

Hersman, Erik. 2013. "3.5 Years Later, What Has the iHub Done?" *WhiteAfrican* (blog), October 15, 2013. http://whiteafrican.com/2013/10/15/3-5-years-later-what-the-ihub-has-done/.

Hersman, Erik. 2014. "Builders and Talkers: The Fallacy of the Grant vs Investment Debate." *WhiteAfrican* (blog), June 18, 2014. http://whiteafrican.com/2014/06/18/builders-vs-talkers-the-fallacy-of-the-grant-vs-investment-debate/.

Hersman, Erik. 2015. "The Cross Section of a Tech Ecosystem." *WhiteAfrican* (blog), August 5, 2015. http://whiteafrican.com/2015/08/05/the-cross-section-of-a-tech-ecosystem/.

Heymann, Jody, and Rachel Kidman. 2009. "HIV/AIDS, Declining Family Resources and the Community Safety Net." *AIDS Care* 21:34–42. https://doi.org/10.1080/09540120902927593.

Hildrum, J., D. Ernst, and J. Fagerberg. 2010. "The Complex Interaction between Global Production Networks, Digital Information Systems and International Knowledge Transfers." International Centre for Economic Research Working Paper Series, Working Paper No. 7/2010. http://citeseerx.ist.psu.edu/viewdoc/download?doi=10.1.1.614.5605&rep=rep1&type=pdf.

Hill, T. L., and Ram Mudambi. 2010. "Far from Silicon Valley: How Emerging Economies Are Re-shaping Our Understanding of Global Entrepreneurship." *Journal of International Management* 16 (4): 321–327. https://doi.org/10.1016/j.intman.2010.09.003.

Honig, Benson. 2017. "Compensatory Entrepreneurship: Avoiding the Pitfalls of Global Isomorphic Entrepreneurship Research and Activities." *REGEPE— Revista de Empreendedorismo e Gestão de Pequenas Empresas* 6 (3): 452–465. https://doi.org/10.14211/regepe.v6i3.723.

Huang, Jimmy, Ola Henfridsson, Martin Liu, and Sue Newell. 2017. "Growing on Steroids: Rapidly Scaling the User Base of Digital Ventures through Digital Innovation." *Management Information Systems Quarterly* 41 (1): 301–314.

Iacob, Nadina, Nicolas Friederici, and Jan Lachenmayer. 2019. "Operationalising Relational Theory of Entrepreneurial Ecosystems at City-Level in Africa, Asia and the Middle East." *Zeitschrift für Wirtschaftsgeographie* 63 (2): 79–102.

Ibert, Oliver. 2004. "Projects and Firms as Discordant Complements: Organisational Learning in the Munich Software Ecology." *Research Policy* 33 (10): 1529–1546. https://doi.org/10.1016/j.respol.2004.08.010.

IDC. 2017. "Smartphone Sales Slow in Africa while Feature Phones Remain Resilient." International Data Corporation, March 16, 2017. https://thebftonline.com/2018/world/africa/africas-mobile-market-remains-flat-as-smartphone-shipments-decline-for-second-successive-quarter/.

IDC. 2018. "Africa's Mobile Market Remains Flat as Smartphone Shipments Decline for Second Successive Quarter." International Data Corporation, June 7, 2018. https://www.idc.com/getdoc.jsp?containerId=prCEMA43969018.

IMF. 2018. "Balance of Payments Statistics." IMF DataMapper, September 4, 2018. http://www.imf.org/external/datamapper/datasets/BOP.

infoDev. 2013. "Mobile Usage at the Base of the Pyramid." Washington, DC: World Bank. http://www.infodev.org/mbopsummary.

"Innovation Maps." 2019. Briter. November 19, 2019. https://briterbridges.com/innovation-maps.

Isenberg, Daniel J. 2014. "What an Entrepreneurship Ecosystem Actually Is." *Harvard Business Review*, May 12, 2014. https://hbr.org/2014/05/what-an-entrepreneurial-ecosystem-actually-is.

ITU. 2017. "ICT Facts and Figures 2005, 2010, 2017." Telecommunication Development Bureau,International Telecommunication Union (ITU). http://www.itu.int/en/ITU-D/Statistics/Pages/facts/default.aspx.

Jackson, Tom. 2018a. "12 Startups Selected for First African Google Launchpad Accelerator." *Disrupt Africa* (blog), March 19, 2018. http://disrupt-africa.com/2018/03/12-startups-selected-for-first-african-google-launchpad-accelerator/.

Jackson, Tom. 2018b. "Why Africa's Youth Should Be Encouraged to Launch Tech Startups." *Disrupt Africa* (blog), August 14, 2018. http://disrupt-africa.com/2018/08/why-africas-youth-should-be-encouraged-to-launch-tech-startups/.

Jasanoff, Sheila, and Sang-Hyun Kim. 2016. *Dreamscapes of Modernity: Sociotechnical Imaginaries and the Fabrication of Power.* Chicago: University of Chicago Press.

Jerven, Morten. 2016. "Research Note: Africa by Numbers: Reviewing the Database Approach to Studying African Economies." *African Affairs* 115 (459): 342–358. https://doi.org/10.1093/afraf/adw006.

Jia, Kai, Martin Kenney, and John Zysman. 2018. "Global Competitors? Mapping the Internationalization Strategies of Chinese Digital Platform Firms." In *International Business in the Information and Digital Age,* edited by Rob van Tulder, Alain Verbeke, and Lucia Piscitello, 187–216. Bingley, UK: Emerald Publishing Limited. https://doi.org/10.1108/S1745-886220180000013009.

Jiménez, Andrea, and Yingqin Zheng. 2018. "Tech Hubs, Innovation and Development." *Information Technology for Development* 24 (1): 95–118. https://doi.org/10.108 0/02681102.2017.1335282.

Joseph, Michael. 2017. "M-Pesa: The Story of How the World's Leading Mobile Money Service Was Created in Kenya." Vodafone, March 6, 2017. https://www.vodafone.com/content/index/what/technology-blog/m-pesa-created.html.

Kallinikos, Jannis, Aleksi Aaltonen, and Attila Marton. 2010. "A Theory of Digital Objects." *First Monday* 15 (6). https://doi.org/10.5210/fm.v15i6.3033.

Kanza, Elsie S. 2016. "Africa's Digital Revolution: A Look at the Technologies, Trends and People Driving It." World Economic Forum, May 4, 2016. https://www.weforum.org/agenda/2016/05/africa-s-digital-revolution-a-look-at-the-technologies-trends-and-people-driving-it/.

Kapil, Natasha, Maja Andjelkovic, and Zoe Lu. 2018. "Is Acceleration the Panacea for Scaling Growth Entrepreneurs? Reflections from XL Africa." *World Bank Blogs, Private Sector Development*, February 2, 2018. https://blogs.worldbank.org/psd/acceleration-panacea-scaling-growth-entrepreneurs-reflections-xl-africa.

Kaplan, Marcia. 2018. "Africa: An Emerging Ecommerce Market with Many Challenges." *Practical Ecommerce* (blog), June 13, 2018. https://www.practicalecommerce.com/africa-emerging-ecommerce-market-many-challenges.

Kaplinsky, R., and M. Keynes. 2011. "'Bottom of the Pyramid Innovation' and Pro-Poor Growth." IKD Working Paper 62, Open University, Milton Keynes, UK.

Kaplinsky, Raphael, Jo Chataway, Rebecca Hanlin, Norman Clark, Dinar Kale, Lois Muraguri, Theo Papaioannou, Peter Robbins, and Watu Wamae. 2009. "Below the Radar: What Does Innovation in Emerging Economies Have to Offer Other Low-Income Economies?" *International Journal of Technology Management and Sustainable Development* 8:177–197.

Karanja, Harry. 2010. "Safaricom: King of Innovation." *Startup Kenya* (blog), May 5, 2010. https://startupkenya.blogspot.com/2010/05/safaricom-king-of-innovation.html.

Kashyap, Rina, and Anjali Bhatia. 2018. "Taxi Drivers and Taxidars: A Case Study of Uber and Ola in Delhi." *Journal of Developing Societies* 34 (2): 169–194. https://doi.org/10.1177/0169796X18757144.

Kässi, Otto, and Vili Lehdonvirta. 2018. "Online Labour Index: Measuring the Online Gig Economy for Policy and Research." *Technological Forecasting and Social Change* 137 (December): 241–248. https://doi.org/10.1016/j.techfore.2018.07.056.

Katila, Saija, Pikka-Maaria Laine, and Piritta Parkkari. 2019. "Sociomateriality and Affect in Institutional Work: Constructing the Identity of Start-Up Entrepreneurs." *Journal of Management Inquiry* 28 (3): 381–394. https://doi.org/10.1177/1056492617743591.

Katz, C. 2004. *Growing up Global: Economic Restructuring and Children's Everyday Lives.* Minneapolis: University of Minnesota Press.

Katz, Michael L., and Carl Shapiro. 1985. "Network Externalities, Competition, and Compatibility." *American Economic Review* 75 (3): 424–440.

Kemeny, Thomas, and Abigail Cooke. 2018. "Spillovers from Immigrant Diversity in Cities." *Journal of Economic Geography* 18 (1): 213–245. https://doi.org/10.1093/jeg/lbx012.

Khayesi, Jane N. O., Gerard George, and John Antonakis. 2014. "Kinship in Entrepreneur Networks: Performance Effects of Resource Assembly in Africa." *Entrepreneurship Theory and Practice* 38 (6): 1323–1342. https://doi.org/10.1111/etap.12127.

Knight, Melanie. 2013. "'New Markets Must Be Conquered': Race, Gender, and the Embodiment of Entrepreneurship within Texts." *Canadian Geographer/Le Géographe canadien* 57 (3): 345–353. https://doi.org/10.1111/cag.12019.

Knowledge@Wharton. 2016. "Meet Africa's First Tech 'Unicorn'—Are More to Come?" *Knowledge@Wharton* (blog), April 5, 2016. http://knowledge.wharton.upenn.edu/article/meet-africas-first-tech-unicorn-are-more-to-come/.

Kuo, Lily. 2015. "Video: Ory Okolloh Explains Why Africa Can't Entrepreneur Itself out of Its Basic Problems." Quartz Africa, September 15, 2015. https://qz.com/africa/502149/video-ory-okolloh-explains-why-africa-cant-entrepreneur-itself-out-of-its-basic-problems/.

Latour, Bruno. 1986. "Visualization and Cognition: Thinking with Eyes and Hands." In *Knowledge and Society: Studies in the Sociology of Culture Past and Present*, edited by Elizabeth Long and Henrika Kuklick, 1–40. Greenwich, CT: JAI Press.

Leamer, Edward E., and Michael Storper. 2001. "The Economic Geography of the Internet Age." *Journal of International Business Studies* 32 (4): 641–665.

Lee, Benny P. H. 2001. "Mutual Knowledge, Background Knowledge and Shared Beliefs: Their Roles in Establishing Common Ground." *Journal of Pragmatics* 33 (1): 21–44. https://doi.org/10.1016/S0378-2166(99)00128-9.

Lehdonvirta, Vili, Otto Kässi, Isis Hjorth, Helena Barnard, and Mark Graham. 2019. "The Global Platform Economy: A New Offshoring Institution Enabling Emerging-Economy Microproviders:" *Journal of Management* 45 (2): 567–599. https://doi.org/10.1177/0149206318786781.

Li, Haiyang, Yan Zhang, Yu Li, Li-An Zhou, and Weiying Zhang. 2012. "Returnees versus Locals: Who Perform Better in China's Technology Entrepreneurship?" *Strategic Entrepreneurship Journal* 6 (3): 257–272. https://doi.org/10.1002/sej.1139.

Littlewood, David C., and Wilkister L. Kiyumbu. 2018. "'Hub' Organisations in Kenya: What Are They? What Do They Do? And What Is Their Potential?" *Technological Forecasting and Social Change* 131 (June): 276–285. https://doi.org/10.1016/j.techfore.2017.09.031.

Mack, Elizabeth, and Heike Mayer. 2016. "The Evolutionary Dynamics of Entrepreneurial Ecosystems." *Urban Studies* 53 (10): 2118–2133. https://doi.org/10.1177/0042098015586547.

MacKenzie, Donald A., Fabian Muniesa, and Lucia Siu. 2007. *Do Economists Make Markets? On the Performativity of Economics.* Princeton, NJ: Princeton University Press.

MacKenzie, Donald A., and Judy Wajcman. 1999. *The Social Shaping of Technology.* Buckingham: Open University Press.

Mainela, Tuija, Elina Pernu, and Vesa Puhakka. 2011. "The Development of a High-Tech International New Venture as a Process of Acting: A Study of the Lifespan of a Venture in Software Business." *Journal of Small Business and Enterprise Development* 18 (3): 430–456. https://doi.org/10.1108/14626001111155655.

Malecki, Edward J. 2018. "Entrepreneurship and Entrepreneurial Ecosystems." *Geography Compass*, March 12, 2018. https://doi.org/10.1111/gec3.12359.

Malecki, Edward J., and Bruno Moriset. 2007. *The Digital Economy: Business Organization, Production Processes and Regional Developments.* London: Routledge.

Mallonee, Laura. 2018. "The Techies Turning Kenya into a Silicon Savannah." *Wired*, August 12, 2018. https://www.wired.com/story/kenya-silicon-savannah-photo-gallery/.

Mann, Laura, and Mark Graham. 2016. "The Domestic Turn: Business Process Outsourcing and the Growing Automation of Kenyan Organisations." *Journal of Development Studies* 52 (4): 530–548. https://doi.org/10.1080/00220388.2015.1126251.

Mann, Laura, Mark Graham, and Nicolas Friederici. 2014. *The Internet and Business Process Outsourcing in East Africa: Value Chains and Networks of Connectivity-Based Enterprises in Kenya and Rwanda.* Oxford: Oxford Internet Institute, University of Oxford. https://www.oii.ox.ac.uk/archive/downloads/publications/The_Internet_and_Business_Process_Outsourcing_in_East_Africa.pdf.

Manyika, James, Armando Cabral, Lohini Moodley, Suraj Moraje, Safroadu Yeboah-Amankwah, Michael Chui, and Jerry Anthonyrajah. 2013. "Lions Go Digital: The Internet's Transformative Potential in Africa." McKinsey &

Company, November. http://www.mckinsey.com/industries/high-tech/our-insights/lions-go-digital-the-internets-transformative-potential-in-africa.

Maskell, P., and A. Malmberg. 1999. "The Competitiveness of Firms and Regions: 'Ubiquitification' and the Importance of Localized Learning." *European Urban and Regional Studies* 6 (1): 9–25. https://doi.org/10.1177/096977649900600102.

Marchant, Eleanor. 2018. "Anyone Anywhere: Narrating African Innovation in a Global Community of Practice." Dissertation, University of Pennsylvania. https://repository.upenn.edu/edissertations/2746.

Markus, M. Lynne. 1987. "Toward a 'Critical Mass' Theory of Interactive Media: Universal Access, Interdependence and Diffusion." *Communication Research* 14 (5): 491–511. https://doi.org/10.1177/009365087014005003.

Massey, Doreen. 1999. "Imagining Globalization: Power-Geometries of Time-Space." In *Global Futures: Migration, Environment and Globalization*, edited by Avtar Brah, Mary J. Hickman, and Máirtín Mac an Ghaill, 27–44. London: Palgrave Macmillan. https://doi.org/10.1057/9780230378537_2.

Massey, Doreen. 2005. *For Space*. London: SAGE.

Mavhunga, Clapperton Chakanetsa, ed. 2017. *What Do Science, Technology, and Innovation Mean from Africa?* Cambridge, MA: MIT Press.

Mayer-Schönberger, Viktor, and Thomas Ramge. 2018. *Reinventing Capitalism in the Age of Big Data*. London: John Murray.

Mbembe, Achille. 2001. *On the Postcolony*. Berkeley: University of California Press.

Mbembe, Achille. 2016. "Decolonizing the University: New Directions." *Arts and Humanities in Higher Education* 15 (1): 29–45. https://doi.org/10.1177/1474022215618513.

Mbiti, Isaac, and David N. Weil. 2011. "Mobile Banking: The Impact of M-Pesa in Kenya." NBER Working Paper Series, Working Paper 17129, National Bureau of Economic Research, Cambridge, MA. https://doi.org/10.3386/w17129.

McCann, Philip, and Zoltan J. Acs. 2011. "Globalization: Countries, Cities and Multinationals." *Regional Studies* 45 (1): 17–32. https://doi.org/10.1080/00343404.2010.505915.

McGee, Chantel. 2017. "Jeremy Johnson Andela CEO: Future of Tech Is Africa." CNBC, June 18, 2017. https://www.cnbc.com/2017/06/16/jeremy-johnson-andela-ceo-future-of-tech-is-africa.html.

McKenzie, David J. 2015. "Identifying and Spurring High-Growth Entrepreneurship: Experimental Evidence from a Business Plan Competition." World Bank

Policy Research Working Paper No. 7391, Rochester, NY. http://papers.ssrn.com/abstract=2643193.

Meng, Qingxuan, and Mingzhi Li. 2002. "New Economy and ICT Development in China." In "The New Economy," edited by Matti Pohjola. Special issue, *Information Economics and Policy* 14 (2): 275–295. https://doi.org/10.1016/S0167-6245(01)00070-1.

Mercado, Jose. 2010. "Code Switching." In *Encyclopedia of Cross-Cultural School Psychology*, edited by Caroline S. Clauss-Ehlers, 225–226. Boston: Springer US. https://doi.org/10.1007/978-0-387-71799-9_74.

Mildred, T. Mushunje. 2014. "Interrogating the Relevance of the Extended Family as a Social Safety Net for Vulnerable Children in Zimbabwe." *African Journal of Social Work* 4 (2): 78–110.

Miles, Matthew B., and Michael A. Huberman. 1994. *Qualitative Data Analysis: An Expanded Sourcebook*. 2nd ed. Vol. xiv. Thousand Oaks, CA: SAGE Publications.

Moloi, Sello. 2018. "Jack Ma Opens a New Digital Startups Hub in Rwanda." iAfrikan, November 5, 2018. https://www.iafrikan.com/2018/11/05/alibaba-rwanda-startups-economic-development/.

Moraa, Hilda. 2012. "*iHub_ Model: Understanding the Key Factors of the iHub Model." Nairobi: iHub Research. http://research.ihub.co.ke/downloads/*iHub_Model_Report_Final.pdf.

Moraa, Hilda, and Wangechi Mwangi. 2012. "The Impact of ICT Hubs on African Entrepreneurs: A Case Study of iHub (Nairobi)." Nairobi: iHub Research. http://ihub.co.ke/downloads/ihub_entrepreneurs_report.pdf.

Morawczynski, Olga. 2009. "Exploring the Usage and Impact of 'Transformational' Mobile Financial Services: The Case of M-PESA in Kenya." *Journal of Eastern African Studies* 3 (3): 509–525. https://doi.org/10.1080/17531050903273768.

Mosse, David. 2005. *Cultivating Development: An Ethnography of Aid Policy and Practice*. London: Pluto Press.

Motoyama, Yasuyuki, and Karren Knowlton. 2016. "From Resource Munificence to Ecosystem Integration: The Case of Government Sponsorship in St. Louis." *Entrepreneurship & Regional Development* 28 (5–6): 448–470. https://doi.org/10.1080/08985626.2016.1186749.

Motoyama, Yasuyuki, and Karren Knowlton. 2017. "Examining the Connections within the Startup Ecosystem: A Case Study of St. Louis." *Entrepreneurship Research Journal* 7 (1): 3–23. http://dx.doi.org/10.1515/erj-2016-0011.

Mpala, Daniel. 2019. "Loss Making African Ecommerce Giant Jumia Files for NYSE IPO." *Ventureburn* (blog), March 14, 2019. https://ventureburn.com/2019/03/jumia-files-for-new-york-stock-exchange-ipo/.

Moyo, Dambisa. 2009. *Dead Aid: Why Aid Is Not Working and How There Is a Better Way for Africa*. New York: Farrar, Straus and Giroux.

Mu, Qing, and Keun Lee. 2005. "Knowledge Diffusion, Market Segmentation and Technological Catch-up: The Case of the Telecommunication Industry in China." *Research Policy* 34 (6): 759–783. https://doi.org/10.1016/j.respol.2005.02.007.

Mugambi, Josiah. 2014. "'NGO' Money: Really?" *IHUB* (blog), June 18, 2014. https://ihub.co.ke/blogs/19274/ngo-money-really.

Mulligan, Gabriella. 2017. "Africa Dominates GSMA Innovation Fund Grant Winners." *Disrupt Africa* (blog), April 28, 2017. http://disrupt-africa.com/2017/04/africa-dominates-gsma-innovation-fund-grant-winners/.

Murphy, James T., and Pádraig Carmody. 2015. *Africa's Information Revolution: Technical Regimes and Production Networks in South Africa and Tanzania*. Oxford, UK: John Wiley & Sons.

Musua, Zipporah. 2018. "Africa Grapples with Huge Disparities in Education." *Africa Renewal* (December 2018–March 2019). https://www.un.org/africarenewal/magazine/december-2017-march-2018/africa-grapples-huge-disparities-education.

Mutegi, Mugambi. 2017. "Jumia in Devastating Sh12.4 Bn Loss as Customers, Sales Drop." *Business Daily*, April 26, 2017. https://www.businessdailyafrica.com/corporate/tech/Jumia-loss-Sh12-4-billion-sales-drop/4258474-3904432-eqjrhgz/index.html.

Nambisan, Satish. 2017. "Digital Entrepreneurship: Toward a Digital Technology Perspective of Entrepreneurship." *Entrepreneurship Theory and Practice* 41 (6): 1029–1055. https://doi.org/10.1111/etap.12254.

Nambisan, Satish, Kalle Lyytinen, Ann Majchrzak, and Michael Song. 2017. "Digital Innovation Management: Reinventing Innovation Management Research in a Digital World." *MIS Quarterly* 41 (1): 223–238.

Navis, Chad, and Mary Ann Glynn. 2011. "Legitimate Distinctiveness and the Entrepreneurial Identity: Influence on Investor Judgments of New Venture Plausibility." *Academy of Management Review* 36 (3): 479–499. https://doi.org/10.5465/amr.2008.0361.

Ndemo, Bitange, and Tim Weiss, eds. 2017a. *Digital Kenya: An Entrepreneurial Revolution in the Making*. London: Palgrave Macmillan.

Ndemo, Bitange, and Tim Weiss. 2017b. "Making Sense of Africa's Emerging Digital Transformation and Its Many Futures." *Africa Journal of Management* 3 (3–4): 328–347. https://doi.org/10.1080/23322373.2017.1400260.

Ndemo, Elijah. 2015. "Political Entrepreneurialism: Reflections of a Civil Servant on the Role of Political Institutions in Technology Innovation and Diffusion in Kenya."

Stability: International Journal of Security and Development 4 (1): art. 15. https://doi.org/10.5334/sta.fd.

Ndiomewese, Ifeanyi. 2017. "Why the Silicon Valley Model Does Not Work for Nigerian Tech Startups." Techpoint.Africa. October 3, 2017. https://techpoint.africa/2017/10/03/breaking-silicon-valley-mentality-africa/.

Neff, Gina. 2012. *Venture Labor: Work and the Burden of Risk in Innovative Industries.* Cambridge, MA: MIT Press.

Neveling, Patrick. 2017. "The Political Economy Machinery: Toward a Critical Anthropology of Development as a Contested Capitalist Practice." *Dialectical Anthropology* 41 (2): 163–183. https://doi.org/10.1007/s10624-017-9450-0.

Ngoasong, Michael Zisuh. 2018. "Digital Entrepreneurship in a Resource-Scarce Context." *Journal of Small Business and Enterprise Development* 25 (3): 483–500. https://doi.org/10.1108/JSBED-01-2017-0014.

Ngũgĩ wa Thiong'o. 1986. *Decolonising the Mind: The Politics of Language in African Literature.* London: James Currey/Heinemann.

Nicoll, Derek William. 2000. "Users as Currency: Technology and Marketing Trials as Naturalistic Environments." *Information Society* 16 (4): 303–310. https://doi.org/10.1080/019722400457261.

Nkomo, Stella M. 2017. "Time to Look in the Mirror: Producing Management Theory and Knowledge for Africa." *Africa Journal of Management* 3 (1): 7–16. https://doi.org/10.1080/23322373.2017.1304629.

Noorloos, Femke van, and Marjan Kloosterboer. 2018. "Africa's New Cities: The Contested Future of Urbanisation." *Urban Studies* 55 (6): 1223–1241. https://doi.org/10.1177/0042098017700574.

Nothias, Toussaint. 2014. "'Rising,' 'Hopeful,' 'New': Visualizing Africa in the Age of Globalization." *Visual Communication* 13 (3): 323–339. https://doi.org/10.1177/1470357214530063.

Nsehe, Mfonobong. 2015. "Nigeria's Hotels.Ng Raises $1.2 Million." *Forbes*, May 26, 2015. https://www.forbes.com/sites/mfonobongnsehe/2015/05/26/nigerias-hotels-ng-raises-1-2-million/.

Null, Linda, and Julia Lobur. 2006. *The Essentials of Computer Organization and Architecture.* Sudbury, MA: Jones & Bartlett Learning.

Nyamnjoh, Francis B. 2013. "Africa, the Village Belle: From Crisis to Opportunity." *Ecquid Novi: African Journalism Studies* 34 (3): 125–140. https://doi.org/10.1080/02560054.2013.852786.

Odumosu, Toluwalogo. 2009. "Interrogating Mobiles: A Story of Nigerian Appropriation of the Mobile Phone." Dissertation, Rensselaer Polytechnic Institute. http://search.proquest.com/docview/304986497/?pq-origsite=primo.

Odumosu, Toluwalogo. 2017. "Making Mobiles African." In *What Do Science, Technology, and Innovation Mean from Africa?*, edited by Clapperton Chakanetsa Mavhunga, 137–150. Cambridge, MA: MIT Press.

OECD (Organisation for Economic Co-operation and Development). 2003. *Entrepreneurship and Local Economic Development: Programme and Policy Recommendations.* Paris: OECD Publishing.

OECD (Organisation Organisation for Economic Co-operation and Development). 2017. *OECD Digital Economy Outlook 2017.* Paris: OECD Publishing. https://doi.org/10.1787/9789264276284-en.

Ojanperä, Sanna. "Mapping Broadband Affordability in 2016." Geonet. October 30, 2018. https://geonet.oii.ox.ac.uk/blog/mapping-broadband-affordability-in-2016/.

Ojanperä, Sanna, Mark Graham, Ralph Straumann, Stefano De Sabbata, and Matthew Zook. 2017. "Engagement in the Knowledge Economy: Regional Patterns of Content Creation with a Focus on Sub-Saharan Africa." *Information Technologies & International Development* 13:33–51.

Olivier de Sardan, Jean-Pierre. 2005. *Anthropology and Development: Understanding Contemporary Social Change.* London: Zed Books.

Olopade, Dayo. 2014. *The Bright Continent: Breaking Rules and Making Change in Modern Africa.* Boston: Houghton Mifflin Harcourt.

Olupot, Nathan Ernest. 2018. "French President Emmanuel Macron Launches a USD$76M Africa Startup Fund." *PC Tech Magazine*, May 28, 2018. http://411ug.com/2018/05/french-president-emmanuel-macron-launches-a-usd76m-africa-startup-fund.html.

Oluwafemi, Bankole. 2013. "Why the iHub Is Cooler Than the CcHub | TechCabal." *TechCabal* (blog), October 17, 2013. http://techcabal.com/2013/10/17/why-the-ihub-is-cooler-than-the-cchub/.

Omwansa, Tonny K., and Nicholas P. Sullivan. 2012. *Money, Real Quick: The Story of M-PESA.* London: Guardian Books.

Onsongo, Elsie. 2017. "Institutional Entrepreneurship and Social Innovation at the Base of the Pyramid: The Case of M-Pesa in Kenya." *Industry and Innovation* 26 (4): 369–390. https://doi.org/10.1080/13662716.2017.1409104.

Osterwalder, Alexander, and Yves Pigneur. 2013. *Business Model Generation: A Handbook for Visionaries, Game Changers, and Challengers.* Hoboken, NJ: John Wiley & Sons.

Pager, Devah, and Bruce Western. 2012. "Identifying Discrimination at Work: The Use of Field Experiments." *Journal of Social Issues* 68 (2): 221–237. https://doi.org/10.1111/j.1540-4560.2012.01746.x.

Pansera, Mario, and Fabien Martinez. 2017. "Innovation for Development and Poverty Reduction: An Integrative Literature Review." *Journal of Management Development* 36 (1): 2–13.

Pansera, Mario, and Richard Owen. 2018. "Framing Inclusive Innovation within the Discourse of Development: Insights from Case Studies in India." *Research Policy* 47 (1): 23–34. https://doi.org/10.1016/j.respol.2017.09.007.

Park, Emma, and Kevin Donovan. 2016. "Is Your Mobile Phone Company Seeing like a State?" *Africa Is a Country* (blog), November 29, 2016. https://africasacountry.com/2016/11/is-your-mobile-phone-company-seeing-like-a-state/.

Park, Eunkyung, and Raphael Mateus Martins. 2017. "Entrepreneurial Ecosystem for Technology Start-Ups in Nairobi: Empirical Analysis of Twitter Networks of Start-Ups and Support Organizations." Paper presented at DRUID, New York. https://vbn.aau.dk/ws/files/267663437/Entrepreneurial_ecosystem_VBN_2017.pdf.

Park, Lisa Sun-Hee, and David N. Pellow. 2004. "Racial Formation, Environmental Racism, and the Emergence of Silicon Valley." *Ethnicities* 4 (3): 403–424. https://doi.org/10.1177/1468796804045241.

Parker, Geoffrey G., Marshall W. Van Alstyne, and Sangeet Paul Choudary. 2016. *Platform Revolution: How Networked Markets Are Transforming the Economy—and How to Make Them Work for You.* New York: W. W. Norton & Company.

Pauwels, Charlotte, Bart Clarysse, Mike Wright, and Jonas Van Hove. 2016. "Understanding a New Generation Incubation Model: The Accelerator." In "Technology Business Incubation," edited by Sarfraz Mian, Wadid Lamine, and Alain Fayolle. Special issue, *Technovation* 50–51 (April): 13–24. https://doi.org/10.1016/j.technovation.2015.09.003.

Pavitt, Keith. 2006. "Innovation Processes." In *The Oxford Handbook of Innovation*, edited by Jan Fagerberg, David C. Mowery, and Richard R. Nelson, 86–114. Oxford: Oxford University Press.

Phillips, Alexandra. 2014. "African Urbanization: Slum Growth and the Rise of the Fringe City." *Harvard International Review* 35 (3): 29–31.

Phillips, Damon. 2005. "Organizational Genealogies and the Persistence of Gender Inequality: The Case of Silicon Valley Law Firms." *Administrative Science Quarterly* 50 (3): 440–472. https://doi.org/10.2189/asqu.2005.50.3.440.

Pijnaker, Tessa, and Rachel Spronk. 2017. "Africa's Legends: Digital Technologies, Aesthetics and Middle-Class Aspirations in Ghanaian Games and Comics." *Critical African Studies* 9 (3): 327–349. https://doi.org/10.1080/21681392.2017.1371617.

Pilling, David. 2019. "Jumia Becomes First African Start-Up to List in New York." *Financial Times*, April 12, 2019. https://www.ft.com/content/8b5024e0-5d1d-11e9-9dde-7aedca0a081a.

Pollock, Neil, and Robin Williams. 2016. *How Industry Analysts Shape the Digital Future*. Oxford: Oxford University Press.

Porter, Michael E. 1998. "Clusters and the New Economics of Competition." *Harvard Business Review* (November–December): 77–90.

Prahalad, C. K. 2009. *The Fortune at the Bottom of the Pyramid: Eradicating Poverty through Profits*. 5th anniversary ed. Philadelphia, PA: Wharton School Publishing.

Prasad, Ajnesh, and Tanvir Qureshi. 2017. "Race and Racism in an Elite Postcolonial Context: Reflections from Investment Banking." *Work, Employment and Society* 31 (2): 352–362. https://doi.org/10.1177/0950017016661269.

Quinones, Gerardo, Richard Heeks, and Brian Nicholson. 2017. "Digital Start-Ups in the Global South: Embeddedness, Digitality and Peripherality in Latin America." Development Informatics Working Paper Series, Paper No. 67. Manchester, UK: Centre for Development Informatics. http://hummedia.manchester.ac.uk/institutes/gdi/publications/workingpapers/di/di_wp67.pdf.

Ramírez, Rafael. 1999. "Value Co-production: Intellectual Origins and Implications for Practice and Research." *Strategic Management Journal* 20 (1): 49–65. https://doi.org/10.1002/(SICI)1097-0266(199901)20:1<49::AID-SMJ20>3.0.CO;2-2.

Ravishankar, M. N. 2018. "Digital Social Entrepreneurship in India." *Development Implications of Digital Economies (DIODE) Strategic Research Network* (blog), March 31, 2018. https://diode.network/2018/03/31/digital-social-entrepreneurship-in-india/.

Reuters. 2019. "Africa Retailer Jumia Suspends E-Commerce in Cameroon." *Reuters*, November 18, 2019. https://www.reuters.com/article/us-jumia-tech-cameroon-idUSKBN1XS1YK.

RIA. 2017a. "Disentangling the Broadband Divide in Rwanda: Supply-Side vs Demand-Side." *Research ICT Africa* (blog), May 11, 2017. https://researchictafrica.net/2017/05/11/disentangling-the-broadband-divide-in-rwanda-supply-side-vs-demand-side/.

RIA. 2017b. "Cost of Smartphones Continues the Digital Divide in Tanzania." *Research ICT Africa* (blog), August 16, 2017. https://researchictafrica.net/2017/08/16/cost-of-smartphones-continues-the-digital-divide-in-tanzania/.

Rice, Mark P. 2002. "Co-production of Business Assistance in Business Incubators: An Exploratory Study." *Journal of Business Venturing* 17 (2): 163–187. https://doi.org/10.1016/S0883-9026(00)00055-0.

Ries, Eric. 2011. *The Lean Startup: How Today's Entrepreneurs Use Continuous Innovation to Create Radically Successful Businesses*. New York: Currency.

Roadburg, Alison. 2017. "The Journey Continues: Negawatt Accra Boot Camp." *AfriLabs* (blog), February 15, 2017. http://www.afrilabs.com/the-journey-continues-negawatt-accra-boot-camp/.

Roberts, Peter W., Abigayle Davidson, Edward Thomas, Cindy Chao, Kerri Heidkamp, and Jo-Hannah Yeo. 2017. *Accelerating Startups in Emerging Markets: Insights from 43 Programs*. Global Accelerator Learning Initiative (GALI). https://www.galidata.org/assets/report/pdf/Accelerating%20Startups%20in%20Emerging%20Markets.pdf.

Rodrigues, Gemma, Christopher Csíkszentmihályi, Daniel Mwesigwa, Jude Mukundane, and Michelle Kasprzak. 2018. *Social Tech Ecosystems in Sub-Saharan Africa*. Funchal, Portugal: Madeira Interactive Technologies Institute (M-ITI). https://doi.org/10.5281/zenodo.1244086.

Root, Tik. 2016. "Start-Ups for the State." *Foreign Policy* (blog), June 26, 2016. https://foreignpolicy.com/2016/06/26/start-ups-for-the-state-rwanda-entrepreneurship/.

Rose, Gillian. 2012. *Visual Methodologies: An Introduction to Researching with Visual Materials*. 3rd ed. London: SAGE Publications.

Rostow, W. W. 1960. *The Stages of Economic Growth: A Non-Communist Manifesto*. Cambridge: Cambridge University Press.

Roundy, Philip T. 2016. "Start-Up Community Narratives: The Discursive Construction of Entrepreneurial Ecosystems." *Journal of Entrepreneurship* 25 (2): 232–248. https://doi.org/10.1177/0971355716650373.

Ruge, Teddy. 2014. "Why Venture Capital Hasn't Taken off in Africa." *TMS Ruge* (blog), February 25, 2014. http://tmsruge.com/2014/02/25/why-venture-capital-hasnt-taken-off-in-africa/.

Rwezaura, Barthazar A. 1985. *The Changing Role of the Extended Family in Providing Economic Support for an Individual in Africa*. Warwick Law Working Papers, Vol. 7, No. 4. Coventry: University of Warwick, Legal Research Institute of the School of Law.

Sabaratnam, Meera. 2017. *Decolonising Intervention: International Statebuilding in Mozambique*. London: Rowman & Littlefield International.

Santos, Filipe M., and Kathleen M. Eisenhardt. 2009. "Constructing Markets and Shaping Boundaries: Entrepreneurial Power in Nascent Fields." *Academy of Management Journal* 52 (4): 643–671. https://doi.org/10.5465/AMJ.2009.43669892.

Sapsed, Jonathan, Andrew Grantham, and Robert DeFillippi. 2007. "A Bridge over Troubled Waters: Bridging Organisations and Entrepreneurial Opportunities in Emerging Sectors." *Research Policy* 36 (9): 1314–1334. https://doi.org/10.1016/j.respol.2007.05.003.

Saxenian, AnnaLee. 1994. *Regional Advantage: Culture and Competition in Silicon Valley and Route 128*. Cambridge, MA: Harvard University Press.

Saxenian, AnnaLee. 2006. *The New Argonauts: Regional Advantage in a Global Economy*. Cambridge, MA: Harvard University Press.

Schiller, Dan. 2000. *Digital Capitalism: Networking the Global Market System*. Cambridge, MA: MIT Press.

Schradie, Jen. 2011. "The Digital Production Gap: The Digital Divide and Web 2.0 Collide." *Poetics* 39 (2): 145–168. https://doi.org/10.1016/j.poetic.2011.02.003.

Seo-Zindy, Ryoung, and Richard Heeks. 2017. "Researching the Emergence of 3D Printing, Makerspaces, Hackerspaces and FabLabs in the Global South: A Scoping Review and Research Agenda on Digital Innovation and Fabrication Networks." *Electronic Journal of Information Systems in Developing Countries* 80 (1): 1–24. https://onlinelibrary.wiley.com/doi/abs/10.1002/j.1681-4835.2017.tb00589.x.

Seth, Sanjay. 2016. "Is Thinking with 'Modernity' Eurocentric?" *Cultural Sociology* 10 (3): 385–398. https://doi.org/10.1177/1749975516637203.

Shakya, Mallika. 2017. "An Anthropological Reading of the Policies of International Development: Export Competitiveness as a Conjunctural Case Study." *Dialectical Anthropology* 41 (2): 113–128. https://doi.org/10.1007/s10624-017-9451-z.

Shapiro, Carl, and Hal R. Varian. 1998. *Information Rules: A Strategic Guide to the Network Economy*. Cambridge, MA: Harvard Business Press.

Shapshak, Toby. 2016. "Africa Will Build the Future Says Zuckerberg, Visits Kenya on First African Trip." *Forbes*, September 1, 2016. http://www.forbes.com/sites/tobyshapshak/2016/09/01/africa-will-build-the-future-says-zuckerberg-visits-kenya-on-first-african-trip/.

Sheppard, Eric. 2002. "The Spaces and Times of Globalization: Place, Scale, Networks, and Positionality." *Economic Geography* 78 (3): 307–330. https://doi.org/10.2307/4140812.

Shieber, Jonathan. 2019. "Connecting African Software Developers with Top Tech Companies Nets Andela $100 Million." *TechCrunch* (blog), January 23, 2019. http://social.techcrunch.com/2019/01/23/connecting-african-software-developers-with-top-tech-companies-nets-andela-100-million/.

Shih, Johanna. 2006. "Circumventing Discrimination: Gender and Ethnic Strategies in Silicon Valley." *Gender & Society* 20 (2): 177–206. https://doi.org/10.1177/0891243205285474.

Siegele, Ludwig. 2014. "A Cambrian Moment." *Economist*, January 18, 2014. http://www.economist.com/news/special-report/21593580-cheap-and-ubiquitous-building-blocks-digital-products-and-services-have-caused.

Signé, Landry. 2018. "Why Africa Is Turning the Heads of Investors." *World Economic Forum* (blog), March 19, 2018. https://www.weforum.org/agenda/2018/03/capturing-africa-s-high-returns/.

Singh, Parminder Jeet. 2017. "Report on Developing Countries in the Emerging Global Digital Order." Bangalore: IT for Change. https://itforchange.net/sites/default/files/Developing-Countries-in-the-Emerging-Global-Digital-Order.pdf.

Smith, Adrian, Juan Mariano Fressoli, Dinesh Abrol, Elisa Arond, and Adrian Ely. 2017. *Grassroots Innovation Movements*. Abingdon, UK: Routledge.

Sørensen, Jesper B., and Magali A. Fassiotto. 2011. "Organizations as Fonts of Entrepreneurship." *Organization Science* 22 (5): 1322–1331. https://doi.org/10.1287/orsc.1100.0622.

Sotunde, Oluwa Busayo. 2013. "Kenya Techies to Launch 'Internet Back Up Generator.'" *Ventures Africa* (blog), June 20, 2013. http://venturesafrica.com/kenya-techies-to-launch-internet-back-up-generator-brck/.

Spigel, Ben. 2017. "The Relational Organization of Entrepreneurial Ecosystems." *Entrepreneurship Theory and Practice* 41 (1): 49–72. https://doi.org/10.1111/etap.12167.

Spigel, Ben, and Richard Harrison. 2018. "Toward a Process Theory of Entrepreneurial Ecosystems." *Strategic Entrepreneurship Journal* 12 (1): 151–68. https://doi.org/10.1002/sej.1268.

Srinivas, Smita, and Judith Sutz. 2008. "Developing Countries and Innovation: Searching for a New Analytical Approach." *Technology in Society* 30 (2): 129–140. https://doi.org/10.1016/j.techsoc.2007.12.003.

Srnicek, Nick. 2016. *Platform Capitalism*. Cambridge, MA: Polity Press.

Stam, Erik. 2015. "Entrepreneurial Ecosystems and Regional Policy: A Sympathetic Critique." *European Planning Studies* 23 (9): 1759–1769. https://doi.org/10.1080/09654313.2015.1061484.

Stam, Erik, and Ben Spigel. 2018. "Entrepreneurial Ecosystems." In *The SAGE Handbook for Entrepreneurship and Small Business*, edited by Robert Blackburn, Dirk De Clercq, and Jarna Heinonen, 407–422. Thousand Oaks, CA: SAGE Publications.

Steiber, Annika, and Sverker Alänge. 2016. *The Silicon Valley Model: Management for Entrepreneurship*. Cham: Springer International Publishing.

Steinbock, Dan. 2003. "Globalization of Wireless Value System: From Geographic to Strategic Advantages." *Telecommunications Policy* 27 (3): 207–235. https://doi.org/10.1016/S0308-5961(02)00106-4.

Stork, Christoph, Steve Esselaar, and Chenai Chair. 2017. "OTT—Threat or Opportunity for African Telcos?" In "ICT developments in Africa—Infrastructures, Applications and Policies," edited by Ezer Osei Yeboah-Boateng, Alexander Osei-Owusu, and Anders Henten. Special issue, *Telecommunications Policy* 41 (7): 600–616. https://doi.org/10.1016/j.telpol.2017.05.007.

Storper, Michael, Thomas Kemeny, Naji Philip Makarem, and Taner Osman. 2015. *The Rise and Fall of Urban Economies: Lessons from San Francisco and Los Angeles*. Stanford, CA: Stanford Business Books.

Strachan Matranga, Heather, Bidisha Bhattacharyya, and Ross Baird. 2017. *Breaking the Pattern: Getting Digital Financial Services Entrepreneurs to Scale in India and East Africa*. Washington, DC: Village Capital. https://vilcap.com/wp-content/uploads/2017/06/VC_Breaking_the_Pattern.pdf.

Strauss, Karsten. 2014. "Let's Build A Tech Startup in . . . Rwanda?" *Forbes*, April 1, 2014. http://www.forbes.com/sites/karstenstrauss/2014/04/01/lets-build-a-tech-startup-in-rwanda/.

Suchman, Lucy. 2011. "Anthropological Relocations and the Limits of Design." *Annual Review of Anthropology* 40 (1): 1–18. https://doi.org/10.1146/annurev.anthro.041608.105640.

Suri, Tavneet, and William Jack. 2016. "The Long-Run Poverty and Gender Impacts of Mobile Money." *Science* 354 (6317): 1288–1292. https://doi.org/10.1126/science.aah5309.

Sussan, Fiona, and Zoltan J. Acs. 2017. "The Digital Entrepreneurial Ecosystem." *Small Business Economics* 49 (1): 55–73. https://doi.org/10.1007/s11187-017-9867-5.

Tan, Felix, Barney Tan, and Shan Pan. 2016. "Developing a Leading Digital Multi-sided Platform: Examining IT Affordances and Competitive Actions in Alibaba.com." *Communications of the Association for Information Systems* 38 (1). https://doi.org/10.17705/1CAIS.03836.

Taura, Nasiru D, Elvira Bolat, and Nnamdi O Madichie. 2019. *Digital Entrepreneurship in Sub-Saharan Africa: Challenges, Opportunities and Prospects*. Cham: Palgrave Macmillan.

Tech, Robin P. G. 2018. *Financing High-Tech Startups Using Productive Signaling to Efficiently Overcome the Liability of Complexity*. Cham: Springer International Publishing.

Teece, David J. 2018. "Profiting from Innovation in the Digital Economy: Enabling Technologies, Standards, and Licensing Models in the Wireless World." *Research Policy* 47 (8): 1367–1387. https://doi.org/10.1016/j.respol.2017.01.015.

Thomas, Stuart. 2015. "Mxit: The Rise and Collapse of 'Africa's Largest Social Network.'" *Memeburn* (blog), February 27, 2015. https://memeburn.com/2015/02/mxit-the-rise-and-collapse-of-africas-largest-social-network/.

Thun, Eric, and Timothy Sturgeon. 2017. "When Global Technology Meets Local Standards: Reassessing the China's Mobile Telecom Policy in the Age of Platform Innovation." Working Paper 17-001. Cambridge, MA: MIT Industrial Performance Center. https://pdfs.semanticscholar.org/4895/5cfe17edd0f67e6bad7e877dcf45af56e9f5.pdf.

Tilson, David, Kalle Lyytinen, and Carsten Sørensen. 2010. "Research Commentary—Digital Infrastructures: The Missing IS Research Agenda." *Information Systems Research* 21 (4): 748–759. https://doi.org/10.1287/isre.1100.0318.

Toivonen, Tuukka, and Nicolas Friederici. 2015. "Time to Define What a 'Hub' Really Is." *Stanford Social Innovation Review*, April 7, 2015. http://www.ssireview.org/blog/entry/time_to_define_what_a_hub_really_is.

Tong, Allison, Peter Sainsbury, and Jonathan Craig. 2007. "Consolidated Criteria for Reporting Qualitative Research (COREQ): A 32-Item Checklist for Interviews and Focus Groups." *International Journal for Quality in Health Care* 19 (6): 349–357. https://doi.org/10.1093/intqhc/mzm042.

Tracey, Paul, Elena Dalpiaz, and Nelson Phillips. 2018. "Fish out of Water: Translation, Legitimation, and New Venture Creation." *Academy of Management Journal* 61 (5). https://doi.org/10.5465/amj.2015.0264.

Tracy, Sarah J. 2010. "Qualitative Quality: Eight 'Big-Tent' Criteria for Excellent Qualitative Research." *Qualitative Inquiry* 16 (10): 837–851. https://doi.org/10.1177/1077800410383121.

Tredger, Chris. 2012. "Could Africa Launch the Next Facebook?" *IT News Africa* (blog), June 8, 2012. http://www.itnewsafrica.com/2012/06/could-africa-launch-the-next-facebook/.

Tsing, Anna Lowenhaupt. 2005. *Friction: An Ethnography of Global Connection.* Princeton, NJ: Princeton University Press.

Tumwebaze, Peterson. 2014. "Digital Innovation a Vehicle for Transformation—Kagame." *New Times* (Rwanda), October 4, 2014. http://www.newtimes.co.rw/section/read/181601.

UNCTAD. 2019. *Digital Economy Report 2019: Value Creation and Capture: Implications for Developing Countries.* https://unctad.org/en/pages/PublicationWebflyer.aspx?publicationid=2466.

UNESCO. 2015. "Adult Literacy Rate, Population 15+ Years (Both Sexes, Female, Male)." UIS Data Centre. August 2015. http://data.uis.unesco.org/Index.aspx?DataSetCode=EDULIT_DS&popupcustomise=true&lang=en#.

VC4Africa. 2014. *VC4Africa 2015 Venture Finance in Africa.* VC4A. http://www.aspeninstitute.org/sites/default/files/content/docs/resources/Summary%20VC4Africa%202015%20Report%20-%20Venture%20Finance%20in%20Africa.pdf.

VC4Africa. 2016. *VC4Africa 2016 Venture Finance in Africa.* https://vc4a.com/blog/2016/05/18/new-data-shows-growing-investor-appetite-in-african-early-stage-startups/.

VC4Africa. 2017. *VC4Africa 2017 Venture Finance in Africa.* https://vc4africa.africa-newsroom.com/press/vc4a-research-proves-founder-teams-are-key-to-startup-success-in-africa.

VC4Africa. 2018. *VC4Africa 2018 Venture Finance in Africa.* VC4A. https://vc4a.com/research/.

Venables, Anthony J. 2009. "Rethinking Economic Growth in a Globalizing World: An Economic Geography Lens." *African Development Review* 21 (2): 331–351. https://doi.org/10.1111/j.1467-8268.2009.00212.x.

Verver, Michiel, and Juliette Koning. 2018. "Toward a Kinship Perspective on Entrepreneurship." *Entrepreneurship Theory and Practice* 42 (4): 631–666. https://doi.org/10.1177/1042258718783431.

Viswanathan, Madhu, Raj Echambadi, Srinivas Venugopal, and Srinivas Sridharan. 2014. "Subsistence Entrepreneurship, Value Creation, and Community Exchange Systems: A Social Capital Explanation." *Journal of Macromarketing* 34 (2): 213–226. https://doi.org/10.1177/0276146714521635.

Volkoff, Olga, and Diane M. Strong. 2013. "Critical Realism and Affordances: Theorizing IT-Associated Organizational Change Processes." *MIS Quarterly* 37 (3): 819–834. https://doi.org/10.25300/MISQ/2013/37.3.07.

Voss, Oliver. 2019. "Paris könnte Berlin bald überholen." *Tagesspiegel Online*, March 19, 2019. https://www.tagesspiegel.de/wirtschaft/start-up-barometer-paris-koennte-berlin-bald-ueberholen/24117016.html.

Wakoba, Sam. 2014. "You Are the Hope of Africa |Ban Ki-Moon Tells iHub." *TechMoran* (blog), October 31, 2014. http://techmoran.com/hope-africa-ban-ki-moon-tells-ihub/.

Walsh, J. P. 2015. "Organization and Management Scholarship in and for Africa . . . and the World." *Academy of Management Perspectives* 29 (1): 1–6. https://doi.org/10.5465/amp.2015.0019.

Watson, V. 2015. "The Allure of 'Smart City' Rhetoric: India and Africa." *Dialogues in Human Geography* 5 (1): 36–39. https://doi.org/10.1177/2043820614565868.

We Are Social. 2019. "Global Digital Report 2019." We Are Social. https://wearesocial.com/global-digital-report-2019.

WeeTracker. 2019. "African Venture Capital 2018 Report—USD 725.6 Mn Invested in 458 Deals." *WeeTracker* (blog), January 4, 2019. https://weetracker.com/2019/01/04/what-a-year-the-state-of-venture-capital-in-africa-2018/.

Weiss, Tim, and Klaus Weber. 2016. "Globalization in Action: Templates, Tensions and Strategies of Action in Kenyan Entrepreneurship." *Academy of Management Proceedings* 2016 (1). https://doi.org/10.5465/ambpp.2016.205.

Welter, Friederike. 2011. "Contextualizing Entrepreneurship—Conceptual Challenges and Ways Forward." *Entrepreneurship Theory and Practice* 35 (1): 165–184. https://doi.org/10.1111/j.1540-6520.2010.00427.x.

Wentland, Alexander. 2016. "Imagining and Enacting the Future of the German Energy Transition: Electric Vehicles as Grid Infrastructure." *Innovation: The European Journal of Social Science Research* 29 (3): 285–302. https://doi.org/10.1080/13511610.2016.1159946.

Wentrup, Robert, Patrik Ström, and H. Richard Nakamura. 2016. "Digital Oases and Digital Deserts in Sub-Saharan Africa." *Journal of Science and Technology Policy Management* 7 (1): 77–100. https://doi.org/10.1108/JSTPM-03-2015-0013.

Williams, Logan D. A., and Thomas S. Woodson. 2012. "The Future of Innovation Studies in Less Economically Developed Countries." *Minerva* 50 (2): 221–237. https://doi.org/10.1007/s11024-012-9200-z.

Williams, Nick, and Colin C. Williams. 2011. "Tackling Barriers to Entrepreneurship in a Deprived Urban Neighbourhood." *Local Economy: The Journal of the Local Economy Policy Unit* 26 (1): 30–42. https://doi.org/10.1177/0269094210391166.

World Bank. 2012. *Information and Communications for Development 2012: Maximizing Mobile.* Edited by Tim Kelly. Washington DC: World Bank. http://elibrary.worldbank.org/content/book/9780821389911.

World Bank. 2018. "ICT Service Exports (BoP, Current US$)." https://data.worldbank.org/indicator/BX.GSR.CCIS.CD.

World Bank. 2019. "Individuals Using the Internet (% of Population)." March 2, 2019. https://data.worldbank.org/indicator/IT.NET.USER.ZS.

World Wide Web Foundation. 2014. *Web Index Report 2014/2015: The Web & Growing Inequality.* Washington, DC: World Wide Web Foundation. http://thewebindex.org/wp-content/uploads/2014/12/Web_Index_24pp_November2014.pdf.

Wu, Tim. 2016. *The Attention Merchants: The Epic Scramble to Get Inside Our Heads.* New York: Penguin Random House.

Wyche, Susan P., and Laura L. Murphy. 2012. "Dead China-Make Phones off the Grid: Investigating and Designing for Mobile Phone Use in Rural Africa." In *Proceedings of the Designing Interactive Systems Conference*, 186–195. New York: ACM. http://dl.acm.org/citation.cfm?id=2317985.

Wyche, Susan, and Charles Steinfield. 2016. "Why Don't Farmers Use Cell Phones to Access Market Prices? Technology Affordances and Barriers to Market Information Services Adoption in Rural Kenya." *Information Technology for Development* 22 (2): 320–333. https://doi.org/10.1080/02681102.2015.1048184.

Yin, Robert K. 1994. *Case Study Research: Design and Methods.* Thousand Oaks, CA: SAGE Publications.

Yoo, Youngjin, Richard J. Boland, Kalle Lyytinen, and Ann Majchrzak. 2012. "Organizing for Innovation in the Digitized World." *Organization Science* 23 (5): 1398–1408. https://doi.org/10.1287/orsc.1120.0771.

Yoo, Youngjin, Ola Henfridsson, and Kalle Lyytinen. 2010. "Research Commentary—the New Organizing Logic of Digital Innovation: An Agenda for Information Systems Research." *Information Systems Research* 21 (4): 724–735. https://doi.org/10.1287/isre.1100.0322.

Zeleza, Paul Tiyambe. 2009. "What Happened to the African Renaissance? The Challenges of Development in the Twenty-First Century." *Comparative Studies of South Asia, Africa and the Middle East* 29 (2): 155–170. https://doi.org/10.1215/1089201X-2009-001.

Zhou, Yu, Yifei Sun, Y. H. Dennis Wei, and George C. S. Lin. 2011. "De-centering 'Spatial Fix'—Patterns of Territorialization and Regional Technological Dynamism of ICT Hubs in China." *Journal of Economic Geography* 11 (1): 119–150. https://doi.org/10.1093/jeg/lbp065.

Zittrain, Jonathan. 2009. *The Future of the Internet: And How to Stop It.* London: Penguin.

Zoogah, David B., and Mike W. Peng. 2019. "Behind the Emergence of Management Scholarly Communities in Asia and Africa." *Africa Journal of Management* 5 (1): 1–23. https://doi.org/10.1080/23322373.2018.1563466.

Zook, Matthew A. 2002. "Grounded Capital: Venture Financing and the Geography of the Internet Industry, 1994–2000." *Journal of Economic Geography* 2 (2): 151–77. https://doi.org/10.1093/jeg/2.2.151.

Zook, Matthew A. 2005. *The Geography of the Internet Industry.* Oxford, UK: Blackwell Publishing.

Zook, Matthew A. 2009. "Internet, Economic Geography." In *International Encyclopedia of Human Geography*, vol. 5, ed. R. Kitchin and N. Thrift, 555–561. Oxford: Elsevier.

Zook, Matthew A., and Michael H. Grote. 2017. "The Microgeographies of Global Finance: High-Frequency Trading and the Construction of Information Inequality." *Environment and Planning A: Economy and Space* 49 (1): 121–140. https://doi.org/10.1177/0308518X16667298.

Zott, Christoph, Raphael Amit, and Lorenzo Massa. 2011. "The Business Model: Recent Developments and Future Research." *Journal of Management* 37 (4): 1019–1042. https://doi.org/10.1177/0149206311406265.

Zuboff, Shoshana. 2019. *The Age of Surveillance Capitalism: The Fight for a Human Future at the New Frontier of Power.* New York: PublicAffairs.

Index

Page numbers followed by b refer to boxes; page numbers followed by f refer to figures; and page numbers followed by t refer to tables.